Applied Policy Rese:

Where many textbooks on policy research focus on methodological and statistical theories, leaving students to wonder how they will apply those theories to future policy positions, this innovative textbook takes theories of policy research and puts them into practice, demystifying the subject by translating it into real-world situations in which students can actively engage. Beginning with an orientation and overview of policy research, outlining the processes of policy analysis and evaluation from start to finish, *Applied Policy Research, Second Edition* then walks students through an examination of case studies to demonstrate how these theories play out in real policy situations. New to this edition:

- A rewritten Part I that includes new chapters incorporating the latest developments in applicable policy research design, implementation, and products, to provide a framework for conducting policy research.
- A matrix at the start of Part II to easily identify how each of the fifteen case-study chapters correspond with concepts and topics presented in Part I, showing the reader where to look for a specific real-life example of a given topic or concept. Each case is drawn from real instances of policy research to provide students with an opportunity to consider and learn how to grapple with the challenges posed by the needs of public programs and agencies. Cases include local, state, and nonprofit agencies as well as federal-state-local intergovernmental "hybrids."
- Each chapter is presented in a uniform format: (1) a detailed description of a policy research problem; (2) a discussion of the unique challenges posed by the problem; (3) a description of the policy research techniques used; (4) a summary of the outcomes or conclusions associated with the research as it was conducted; and (5) conclusions about the implications or lessons for policy research.

Illustrative figures help students understand the stages of policy research, and end-of-chapter tools such as discussion questions, assignments and activities, and case studies "at a glance" help students master not only the particulars of each case but the broader skills needed in future research. *Applied Policy Research, Second Edition* will be essential reading in all policy research courses with a focus on practical outcomes and student preparation for public service.

J. Fred Springer is Professor Emeritus of Political Science and Public Policy at the University of Missouri–St. Louis, Missouri, USA.

Peter J. Haas serves as Professor at the School of Global Innovation and Leadership, part of the Lucas School and College of Business at San Jose State University, where he also serves as Education Director at the Mineta Transportation Institute, California, USA.

Allan Porowski is a Principal Associate in the Social and Economic Policy Division at Abt Associates, Bethesda, Maryland, USA.

"*Applied Policy Research* draws on the authors' extensive and rich policy evaluation experience to convey fully its components and complexity. The text brims with wise insights and helpful tips."

—**E. Terrence Jones**, *University of Missouri–St. Louis, USA*

Applied Policy Research
Concepts and Cases

Second Edition

J. Fred Springer, Peter J. Haas,
and Allan Porowski

Routledge
Taylor & Francis Group

NEW YORK AND LONDON

Second edition published 2017
by Routledge
711 Third Avenue, New York, NY 10017

and by Routledge
2 Park Square, Milton Park, Abingdon, Oxon OX14 4RN

*Routledge is an imprint of the Taylor & Francis Group, an
informa business*

© 2017 Taylor & Francis

The right of J. Fred Springer, Peter J. Haas, and Allan Porowski
to be identified as authors of this work has been asserted by them
in accordance with sections 77 and 78 of the Copyright, Designs
and Patents Act 1988.

First edition published by Routledge 1998

Library of Congress Cataloging-in-Publication Data
A catalog record for this book has been requested.

ISBN: 978-0-415-80507-0 (hbk)
ISBN: 978-0-415-80508-7 (pbk)
ISBN: 978-0-203-87349-6 (ebk)

Typeset in Sabon
by Apex CoVantage, LLC

To Sydney, Liam, Molly, Nathan, Locke, Kia, Luka, Nyla, Sami, Jack, Kensi, and Greta . . . who make the morning welcome and bright

—J. Fred Springer

To my teachers and students

—Peter J. Haas

To Angela, Walter, Cynthia, David, and Linda . . . to family

—Allan Porowski

Contents

About the Authors

J. Fred Springer, PhD, is Professor Emeritus of Political Science and Public Policy at the University of Missouri–St. Louis, where he was first Director of UMSL's PhD in Policy Analysis program, and taught for eighteen years. Throughout his career, Fred has balanced academic research and publication with applied policy research. He was Research Director for EMT Associates, Inc., from 1986 to 2014, leading more than 100 national, state, and local studies. Major contributions to policy research include the internationally used Individual Protective Factors Index (IPFI) measure of adolescent resiliency and the ground-breaking national High Risk Youth study that received the 2000 American Evaluation Association study of the year award, as well as more than sixty-five journal articles, numerous book chapters, and five books. His current work, with Allan Porowski, focuses on natural variation research designs. Fred received his BA, MA, and PhD degrees in political science at the University of California, Davis.

Peter J. Haas, PhD, is currently Education Director at the Mineta Transportation Institute at San Jose State University. In that role, he administers a statewide program that prepares transportation professionals for upper-level management and executive positions throughout the transportation industry. He is also a member of the faculty of School of Global Innovation and Leadership in the Lucas College of Business at SJSU and has previously served as the Director of the Master of Public Administration program. Haas earned his doctorate from the Department of Political Science at the University of North Carolina at Chapel Hill in 1985. In 2003, Haas was awarded a Senior Specialist Grant from the Fulbright Foundation to teach and study in Latvia. In 2010, Haas received the Warburton Award as outstanding scholar in the College of Social Sciences at SJSU. For the past thirty years, he has also served as a consultant on applied policy research projects for local, state, and federal government agencies, as well as nonprofit organizations.

Allan Porowski, MPA, is a Principal Associate in the Social and Economic Policy Division at Abt Associates. He currently serves as the colead methodologist on the literacy reviews and lead methodologist for the postsecondary reviews for the U.S. Department of Education's What Works Clearinghouse, as a member of the Analysis and Reporting team for the Investing in Innovation (i3) evaluation, and as the principal investigator of the Experience Corps evaluation for the AARP Foundation and a Pay for Success evaluation for the Corporation for National and Community Service. Prior to joining Abt, Mr. Porowski was a Fellow at ICF International and served as principal investigator or lead methodologist on several high-profile evaluations, including the Drug-Free Communities, Communities In Schools, Social Innovation Fund, and Accelerating Connections to Employment national evaluations. Mr. Porowski holds an MPA from American University and a Bachelor's degree in policy analysis from Cornell University.

Contributors

Robert D. Blagg, PhD, is the Director of Evaluation for the University Consortium for Children & Families (UCCF), University of California, Los Angeles. He has more than ten years of experience as an evaluator and applied researcher and has conducted research on education, social, and health programs and policies. Dr. Blagg currently directs evaluation of the central training program for the social workers of the Los Angeles Department of Children and Family Services.

Christina Christie, PhD, is Professor of Education and Division Head of Social Research Methodology at the University of California, Los Angeles. Her scholarship examines evaluation practice and the conceptual frameworks used in evaluation. She has extensive experience conducting applied research and evaluation studies on education, social, and behavior programs targeting at-risk and underrepresented populations.

Heather Clawson, PhD, is the Executive Vice President of Research, Learning & Accreditation at Communities In Schools, where she seeks to expand the capacity of the network to use data to drive effective practice, to continue to strengthen the agency's evidence base, and to help identify and demonstrate innovation and best practices from within the network. Heather previously worked as a research consultant for fifteen years for ICF International managing and conducting research and program evaluations in the areas of education, juvenile justice, victim services, and child welfare. Her expertise and passion center around integrated student services and supports for the most vulnerable populations. For five years, Heather served as the principal investigator for the National Evaluation of Communities In Schools. She has a PhD in social psychology from the University of Nevada–Reno.

Todd Franke, PhD, is an educational psychologist with extensive experience in applied statistics and psychometrics who currently serves as Chair of the Department of Social Welfare at the University of California, Los Angeles. He has developed and led evaluations for multiple agencies that serve thousands of families representing unique geographic and cultural communities in California, particularly southern California counties. He conducts cross-sectional and longitudinal research and evaluation in the fields of education, child welfare, adolescent violence, particularly with gang-involved youth, and mental health. He earned his PhD at the University of Wisconsin in educational psychology.

Charles Herrick, PhD, is Vice President with Abt Associates. He is also adjunct faculty with the NYU School of Environmental Studies. He has more than twenty-five years of experience in applied environmental policy analysis, environmental program evaluation, and science/policy assessment in an environmental context. He has designed program and project theories of change, logic models, and real-time evaluation frameworks to elucidate and characterize a wide variety of program delivery mechanisms, process outputs, outcomes, and impacts for major foundations, government agencies, and various nonprofit organizations. He earned a PhD in public policy from the American University in Washington, DC, and has published in a wide variety of relevant journals.

Heather Hosterman, MEM, is a Senior Analyst with Abt Associates. She has more than eight years of experience in policy and economic analysis, with a focus on climate change impacts and adaptation, as well as ecosystem service valuation and natural resource damage assessments and restoration. She has experience designing, implementing, and analyzing results from several economic and policy studies, including studies aimed at improving knowledge and guiding public policy on climate change adaptation. Ms. Hosterman has a Masters of Environmental Management in environmental economics and policy from Duke University's Nicholas School of the Environment.

Jill Norton, EdM, is a principal associate at Abt Associates and specializes in education policy, research partnerships, and project management to bridge the education research, policy, and practice worlds. Ms. Norton has guided applied research initiatives in the public and private sectors, including as a senior policy adviser for the Massachusetts Executive Office of Education and as executive director of the Rennie Center for Education Research and Policy. She has collaborated with district leaders across New England to provide educators with customized professional development and support. Ms. Norton has authored and produced applied policy research on a range of topics, including teacher preparation, state assessments and accountability systems, and promising practices for reducing high school dropout rates. She holds a Master's of Education from Harvard Graduate School of Education.

Joël L. Phillips is the founder of EMT Associates, Inc. and has been an important innovator in applied policy research for nearly four decades. Though EMT has had important impacts on evaluation at local, state, and national levels, Joël kept the firm small to foster a creative, fulfilling work team environment. As owner and director of the firm, he always remained a colleague and work team member. EMT pioneered development of formative evaluation, cross-site evaluation methods, training, and dissemination of useful policy research products (including the EMT On-line University that developed practical applied courses on evaluation and evidence-based practices).

Elizabeth Sale, PhD, is the director of evaluation and a research associate professor at the Missouri Institute of Mental Health at the University of Missouri–St. Louis. She has more than twenty-five years of experience in the field of survey and evaluation research, with specific expertise in the evaluation of child and adolescent mental health and prevention programs. She has evaluated many nationally recognized evidence-based prevention programs and has extensive experience in the management and analysis of national longitudinal multisite evaluations. Dr. Sale is also an adjunct research associate professor at the University of Missouri–Columbia in the School of Public Health. She has published in a number of related peer-reviewed journals.

Victoria Stuart-Cassel, MPPA, has twenty-five years of public-sector experience conducting evaluation and policy studies and providing technical assistance to the education and behavioral health fields. Her areas of content expertise include behavioral health, school safety and violence prevention, and youth engagement. She is currently on staff with the U.S. Department of Education's National Center for Safe and Supportive Learning Environments (NCSSLE). Ms. Stuart-Cassel served as the coauthor of a national study involving a review of state antibullying legislation and case studies of legislative and policy implementation in schools, which she presented at the Federal Partners in Bullying Prevention Summit. She currently serves as a lead evaluator for the Tennessee Departments of Education and Mental Health and Substance Abuse Services. Ms. Stuart-Cassel is a graduate of the University of California, Davis, and holds a Master's Degree in public policy and administration.

Jason Vogel, PhD, has worked in consulting as a public policy analyst for more than years, most recently for Abt Associates. He was trained as a physical scientist, earning an MS in astrophysical, planetary, and atmospheric sciences before turning his attention to public policy, earning a PhD in environmental studies. Dr. Vogel has consulted with a range of clients on climate change adaptation issues, from water utilities and municipal governments to the U.S. EPA to international development agencies such as USAID. He has experience in policy analysis, climate change impact and adaptation assessment, project and program evaluation, decision analysis, vulnerability and risk assessment, capacity-building support, translating climate science for decision-making audiences, and qualitative and quantitative methods of information elicitation.

Robert W. Wassmer, PhD, is a professor in the Department of Public Policy and Administration at California State University, Sacramento, where he directs the Master's program in urban land development. His teaching and research interests are in microeconomics and public policy, urban policy, benefit/cost analysis, regression analysis, and state–local public finance. He earned his PhD in economics from Michigan State University in 1989. In 2011, he received Sacramento State's Outstanding Scholarly Achievement Award. His research has appeared in a variety of scholarly journals, and he serves as an associate editor of the journal *Economic Development Quarterly*.

Preface

Between the authors, this text is the product of more than a century of experience studying, teaching, and conducting policy research. A good part of that experience has accumulated since Taylor & Francis's *Applied Policy Research: Concepts and Cases* was first published in 1998. In the preface to that edition, we stated our purpose as giving students insight and experience in conducting and consuming policy research. We went on to argue that texts in the field at that time introduced readers primarily to theoretical and conceptual aspects of research—the way things *should be done*. They lacked reference to "real-life" situations and applications. Many texts instilled the impression that the way things *were actually done* was possibly necessary, but straying from the ideal produced inferior results. We countered this belief by asserting that policy research was not a flawed application of rigorous social science; it is a quite separate endeavor. Policy researchers use many of the tools of science, as needed, to "apply systematic information collection and analysis to organizational decision making" (Putt and Springer, 1989, p. xii). It takes place in the real-world environment and addresses problems that arise from and are influenced by human intention. It requires its own purposes, methods, and criteria for quality and success.

To focus more on the realities of actual policy research, our first edition provided real-life, richly detailed case studies intended to draw the student into as real a research situation as possible in a variety of contexts. Apparently we succeeded to some extent, because users of the text asked for an updated edition with more cases across a broader spectrum of policy areas.

In sum, our experience at that time led us to perceive a gap between policy research as practiced and policy research theory expounded in textbooks. This gap was not merely the conventional gulf between "theory" and "practice"; it represented a failing of prevailing theory about how policy research should be conducted. We argued that, as a rule, the demand for information useful to decision makers, the criteria for successful design and implementation of studies appropriate to the user context, and the recommendations for what tools would provide the best answers to user needs in public programs were quite different in practice from those prescribed by prevailing theoretical texts. As a result, we felt that students might finish a course in research but lack any confidence in their ability to really do policy research in a public agency context. More troubling, we felt that the prevailing approach to teaching and practicing policy research at that time reinforced this unproductive gap between researchers and practitioners—those charged with producing more accurate understanding of policy problems and those charged with using it. We set our sights on helping to bridge this gap, hopefully contributing to more relevant and usable research that results in more informed and successful policy.

As we embarked on this second edition, bolstered by a new colleague and almost two decades of additional experience, we realized that it had to be much more than a tweak if we were to stay true to our intention. We are even more convinced of the value of our original perception of the need for more practice-oriented education in policy research. However, there has been a lot of movement in policy research and related fields that we needed to acknowledge and incorporate into this edition. This helped us address weaknesses in the first edition that we ourselves had realized.

The first edition's Part I, the introduction to what policy research is and how to do it, lacked a well-developed conceptual framework for actually doing policy research that would be more useful in the problem and user contexts presented in the real-world case studies. The first-edition preface noted that the first four chapters of the text set out a practical approach to tackling policy research problems that does not force frequently idealistic and obscure research concepts onto complex public programs and policies. The Part I discussion was useful, but user comments made it clear that the real value was in the cases themselves. The cases clearly voiced the necessity of a distinct and articulated framework for producing more applicable policy research. The last two decades have produced advances in thinking about problem complexity, messy and wicked problems, hierarchical systems thinking, mixed-methods analysis, advanced qualitative analysis (e.g., pattern matching and its variations), alternatives to experimental designs for causal attribution, natural variation designs, and more. Many of these ideas and tools are very useful in analyzing real-world policy problems, though their interconnection in advancing policy research theory and method has not been articulated in classroom texts.

The result of our reflections on these advances in policy research is a completely new Part I for the second edition. The Chapter 2 through 4 titles and subtitles convey the logic and content of this new material.

- Chapter 2, *Be Real: Navigating the Policy Research Terrain* points to the importance of understanding three interconnected perspectives being engaged within the context of the policy problem in each policy research project: the problem context, the user context, and the context of the researcher. It draws on developments in applied research theory and practice to suggest what to look for in these contexts, why these features are important, and how they should shape the design and implementation of the research project.

- Chapter 3, *Be Creative: Policy Research With the Artisan's Touch* emphasizes the creative role of the researcher in making the data and analysis conducted in a policy research study correspond as closely as possible to its specific problem and user realities. This chapter introduces guiding concepts in thinking about making a problem "researchable," identifies the data sources available to the policy researcher, provides guidance on how to organize data from multiple sources into analyzable measures with high correspondence to the problem at hand, and introduces techniques for framing concepts and data to guide relevant analysis. This chapter emphasizes the importance of the researcher's ability to creatively align data to the problem at hand.

- Chapter 4, *Be Credible: Using the Policy Research Toolbox* provides an overview of the quantitative and qualitative data collection and analysis tools available to the policy researcher. These tools are often the emphasis of texts on policy research, but truly gaining expertise in individual techniques requires whole courses, not chapters in texts. The emphasis in this chapter is to introduce different categories of data collection and analysis tools and how to optimize correspondence of tools to different types of policy research problems. The discussion articulates scholarly acceptance and applications that strengthen credibility of perspectives policy researchers have used for some time.

- Chapter 5, *Be Useful: Developing and Delivering Actionable Information* explores reasons why some policy research is used and some sits on the shelf. The chapter addresses the process of transforming technical data and analysis into useful guides for making and implementing policy decisions. Specific topics include data visualization techniques, demonstrating internal and external validity, linear and agile approaches to evidence-based practice, and emerging developments in bridging research and practice.

In summary, we have rewritten Part I to incorporate the latest developments in applicable policy research design, implementation, and products. We are confident that this revision will convey a useful framework for understanding the perspectives and skills necessary to conduct useful policy research.

The Part II introduction presents a matrix (Table II.1) that crosswalks each of the fifteen case-study chapters with concepts and topics presented in Part I. Checks indicate the concepts that are clearly applicable to a case, providing a guide on where to look for a specific real-life example of a given topic or concept. The crosswalk also provides an overview of the diversity and similarities across policy research projects. Each case is drawn from real instances of policy research that provide students with the opportunity to consider and learn how to grapple with the challenges posed by the information needs of public programs and agencies. Each case study focuses on a distinct type of information need and a distinct type of public agency. The case studies are designed to be of value both as examples of how to conduct policy research and as opportunities for students to advance their own knowledge, skills, and experiences with such research.

Although the great majority of employment (and applied research) opportunities for public administration students are at state, local, and nonprofit agencies, many texts use federal government agencies and national policy problems as examples to illustrate concepts and theories. The information needs and resources for research of state and local governments differ markedly from those of the national government. The cases described here arise from broadly representative backgrounds, including local, state, and nonprofit agencies as well as federal-state-local intergovernmental "hybrids."

Each case-study chapter includes (1) a detailed description of a policy research problem; (2) a discussion of the unique challenges posed by the problem; (3) a description of the policy research techniques used; (4) a summary of the outcomes or conclusions associated with the research as it was conducted; and (5) conclusions about the implications or lessons for policy research. Additionally, each case study chapter includes exercises and discussion questions for classroom use.

These cases will walk the reader through fifteen situations, each representing a different type of information need and decision-making "client." The case studies are designed to facilitate the reader's ability to apply what has been learned to real life. Hopefully, they will also convey a sense of the creativity, challenges, and accomplishments that have made this such an engaging career for the authors and their colleagues.

Acknowledgments

This text reflects the encouragement, support, and contributions of many people. First, the authors want to thank the many educators who continued to use the first edition in their classrooms despite the fact that it was clearly getting a bit long in the tooth. This second edition, and the addition of Allan Porowski as a third author, reflects our commitment to maintain and strengthen its value in the classroom. This edition updates and broadens the case studies past users valued so much. We also want to thank Taylor & Francis, and particularly Brianna Ascher and Misha Kydd, our editorial assistants, for their support, guidance, and patience in producing this second edition. The manuscript could not have been produced without the advice and contributions of Sydney Springer's help in preparing the manuscript and Joan Guelden's wizardry with graphic presentations.

Throughout the text, we refer repeatedly to the interest, challenge, fulfillment, and enjoyment we get from our professions in policy research. We must thank the many colleagues and friends that make this rewarding career possible. These colleagues include the contributors to case studies in this text, and many others. Joël L. Phillips, founder of Evaluation, Management, and Training, Inc. (EMT) requires special recognition. His vision of "management-based" evaluation, commitment to making evaluation relevant and useful, and his ability to fashion strong collaborations with practitioners are at the core of the approach to policy research espoused in this text. Other mentors and colleagues have contributed immeasurably to our personal professional growth and the lessons reflected in this volume. Peter J. Haas wishes to acknowledge the inspiration, support, and guidance supplied by Steve Van Beek at San Jose State University; Harold I. Haas, Professor Emeritus at Lenoir-Rhyne College; Larry Baas and Albert Trost at Valparaiso University, Steve Brown and John J. Gargan at Kent State University, and Gordon Whitaker and Deil S. Wright at the University of North Carolina at Chapel Hill. J. Fred Springer thanks Denny Putt of California State University Sacramento; Soledad Sambrano at the Center for Substance Abuse Prevention; Carol Kohfeld and Eugene Meehan at the University of Missouri–St. Louis;

Lloyd Musolf at the University of California, Davis; and Jack Hermann formerly of Macro International for making this career so rewarding. He especially thanks Richard W. Gable at the University of California–Davis as both mentor and friend. His professional and personal example has been a beacon of commitment and caring in all aspects of life. Allan Porowski wishes to acknowledge the influence of Heather Clawson at Communities In Schools; Rose O'Conner at ICF International; Susan Siegel at the AARP Foundation; Seri Irazola at the U.S. Department of Justice; and his colleagues at Abt Associates for their continued inspiration, support, and random hallway conversations.

Part I

Principles of Policy Research

J. Fred Springer, Peter J. Haas,
and Allan Porowski

1 Introduction to Policy Research

How is policy *really* made? Popular views of the workings of American government are characterized by diverse and sometimes contradictory stereotypes—politicians cutting deals in back rooms, bureaucrats putting rules before public interest, and technocrats who coldly pursue numbers and logic to the exclusion of people. This book addresses policy analysts' role in this process, painting a realistic picture of what applied research brings to policy making. It cuts through the stereotypes that policy research is a purely technocratic endeavor and portrays the important place that analysts play in the give and take of policy making in American democracy.

Although policy analysts may not top the list of visible government workers, policy research has some harsh critics. Former U.S. Senator William Proxmire's political calling card was his Golden Fleece award, awarded from 1975 to 1988. The senator often made the award to what he saw as particularly useless publicly funded studies. For example, the first award was to the National Science Foundation's $84,000 study to find out why people fall in love (http://content.wisconsinhistory. org/cdm/ref/collection/tp/id/70852). From a different perspective, advocates for data-informed innovation still lament the "chilling effect on research" that the Golden Fleece Award exerted (Catmull and Wallace, 2014). Political criticism of policy-relevant research has not abated in the nearly thirty years since the Golden Fleece awards. Senator Tom Coburn recently ridiculed the National Science Foundation's funding of a study concerning the impact of climate change on sea life. The study measured the effects of water temperature on the stamina of shrimp trudging along a moving surface. While this study produced important scientific results on climate change and ocean ecology, widely disseminated criticism made "shrimp on a treadmill" shorthand for government waste.

As is frequently the case with public debate, selective understanding of evidence and facts are in part responsible for contradictory positions. One of our major purposes in writing this book is to provide a more balanced, practical, and realistic understanding of how policy research is conducted and how it influences public decisions. This discussion may not enflame passions in the same way as incendiary commentary about politics, but it will lead to a more realistic understanding of the role that policy research plays in public decisions. This perspective should be particularly useful to students and practitioners of politics and public administration.

To provide a balanced discussion of ways in which policy research is actually produced and used in public decision making, we will include case studies that focus on policies and programs at the local and state levels, as well as studies that encompass the workings of the federal government. Multimillion-dollar studies by the federal government make excellent fodder for critics of policy research, but they are not typical of most policy research activity. The work of the policy analyst is usually done at a more modest level, financed by a small budget and limited resources in less visible settings: in state, county, or municipal government or even in the nonprofit sector, which implements many policies. The case studies and discussion presented in this text reflect the diverse programmatic milieu in which public employees and decision makers operate.

This chapter is the first of five that define policy research and introduce a framework for understanding its purpose, methods, and application. We begin by addressing five fundamental questions:

1. *What is policy research?* We will discuss how policy research differs from other social research and introduce common terms used to describe policy research.
2. *How is policy research conducted?* We will discuss basic procedures and methods that are used in policy research.
3. *Who does policy research?* We will discuss the kinds of jobs that policy researchers hold and the kinds of skills their work requires.
4. *Why do policy research?* We will discuss the purposes, mandates, and incentives that motivate policy researchers.
5. *Does policy research improve public decision making?* We will discuss who uses policy research, why it is used, and how it may help.

What Is Policy Research?

Although it is referred to in different ways, many employees (and consultants) of public agencies engage in policy research. "Policy research" is a catch-all term used to describe the many information-gathering and processing activities that public agencies engage in to facilitate decision making. It is both a skillful process and an evidence-based information product (Majchrzak and Markus, 2014, p. 2). Policy research may be referred to as policy analysis, program evaluation, needs assessment, performance monitoring, or other terms depending on the context in which it occurs. For example, policy analysis typically refers to the analysis of policy during the decision-making process, while program evaluation typically refers to the analysis of a program that puts a policy in place. More will be said about these distinctions, how they differ, and what they share in the pages ahead.

Policy research can happen at any point in the policy cycle, which has five steps (Fischer, Miller, and Sidney, 2006):

- *Agenda Setting:* Before a policy can be formed, the problem that is to be addressed by the policy must be defined and balanced against other competing priorities. Policy research can be conducted at this stage to assess the severity of the problem to be addressed, to assess which competing policy issue needs to be addressed first, or even to establish whether the problem exists in the first place.
- *Policy Formulation:* Before policies are passed, they must be formulated to address the problem in question. Policy researchers may do comparative research to assess the different costs and effects of each policy alternative (policy analysis) or research the key components of the policy to ensure that it is specified and will be implemented with fidelity.
- *Decision Making:* The actual passage of a policy may be guided by policy research—or it may not. While decision making is traditionally a political process, policy researchers may be drawn in to testify on pending legislation or help guide a bureaucratic process. The decision *not* to enact a policy can be considered policy making as well.
- *Implementation:* Once a policy is agreed on, there are a multitude of opportunities for policy research to assess how well it is being put into action. These implementation studies may assess how closely the policy as enacted conforms to policy intentions, examine how efficiently it is being put into action, or monitor performance benchmarks, such as the number of clients served.
- *Evaluation:* Using scientific methods to determine whether policies or programs actually produce their intended effects is a common type of policy research (Rossi et al., 2004). Evaluation takes many forms and is often required when policies are put into effect. Policy or program evaluation can assess short-term outcomes of a program, such as determining whether a new preschool program results in stronger reading readiness. It can also assess the long-term impacts of a policy—for example, whether the preschool program results in better reading performance among students in grades K–12. It can also assess the balance of costs and benefits of some programs. For example, the evaluation of a new business tax incentive can involve the calculation of its total economic benefit and comparing that figure to the total cost of public investment in the incentive.

Policy research must take many forms because policies take many forms, including statutes, laws, regulations, decisions, and government programs (Birkland, 2015). Despite the complexity of defining policy research, it has two clear distinguishing factors:

1. **Policy research is problem driven** (Birkland, 2015, referring to the work of Peter May). In other words, policy research is initiated by real-world problems that need to be solved.
2. **Policy research is designed to produce actionable results** (Hakim, 2000). Because policy research is expected to help solve real-world problems, the information it produces must have clear implications for what can be done—it must be "actionable." Policy researchers do not *make* policy decisions. They do provide information that elected officials and public personnel can consider along with other inputs and considerations (e.g., politics, cost, feasibility, credibility of the research, effects of alternative strategies). This role in the decision-making process makes policy research particularly exciting—and complex.

Throughout this volume, you will see that the utility of policy research findings is not determined by the rigor of the underlying research or even the magnitude of impacts detected. Its usefulness also depends on framing and delivering findings in a way that helps decision makers formulate and deliver their arguments and ultimately to make decisions.

How Is Policy Research Conducted?

"Real-world" problems are complex. People respond differently to the same situations, and programs may be implemented differently across states, communities, or even agency offices. Outcomes may differ dramatically in different contexts, and differences in outcomes across contexts may be attributable to multiple interwoven influences. The good news is that the tools and methods available to policy researchers to account for this complexity are constantly improving—and their number is expanding. Aspiring policy researchers should be prepared to embark upon a lifetime of learning as methods and tools evolve. While the full scope of prominent methods and tools available to policy researchers cannot be conveyed in this introductory chapter, the following examples hint at their diversity and evolution.

- *Experimental research:* Experimental research is a long-standing pillar of scientific rigor in policy research. Experimental designs require random assignment of individuals or groups (e.g., classrooms) to either receive services or benefits enacted by a policy (the treatment group) or to not receive the intervention (the control group). By comparing data on subjects randomly assigned to the treatment or to the control group before and after the treatment is received, policy researchers can provide strong evidence on whether the intervention had an effect. This rigorous research method provides a model for determining whether policies or programs produce their intended impacts.

- *Quasi-experimental research.* By requiring the random assignment of the intervention, the experimental model clearly requires more control of the study setting than can be achieved in most policy settings. Quasi-experiments overcome ethical, legal, and logistic barriers to randomizing people by forming a comparison group similar to the treatment group. Comparison groups can be developed prior to the start of the study in a number of ways not requiring randomization, including recruiting clients on a wait list, selecting students in a similar school, or matching persons on demographic or other characteristics of treatment group members. The point of both experimental and quasi-experimental methods is to establish a comparison group to ascertain what *would have happened* in the absence of the intervention and compare that result with the outcomes of those who received an intervention. Quasi-experimental designs are far more common in policy research than experimental methods because they allow for adaptation of experimental logic to the realities of conducting studies in the real world of policy making and implementation.

- *Rapid-cycle evaluation:* To be useful in the rapidly changing world of policy setting and revision, information must be available when decisions need to be made. Rapid-cycle evaluation is a framework for conducting a rapid sequence of experimental or quasi-experimental research that tests whether operational changes improve results (Gold, Helms, and Guterman, 2011). Unlike traditional experimental and quasi-experimental studies, rapid-cycle evaluations typically take months rather than years to complete, and they tend to focus on incremental changes in operations instead of measuring the effects of entire programs. These rapid-cycle evaluation methods are gaining in popularity, since they get answers into policy makers' hands much more quickly, which in turn increases the likelihood that the research will influence decisions.

- *Nonexperimental research:* Nonexperimental methods involve gathering information on intended policy effects before, during, and/or after an intervention from a single group of participants with no comparison group. Though this type of research is considered to be less scientifically rigorous than experimental or quasi-experimental research, it is still often used and can produce actionable information. This is especially true when quantitative (numeric) data is combined with qualitative (nonnumeric) information gathered in the field to help stakeholders understand why or how a policy or program has—or does not have—desired effects.

- *Secondary data analysis:* Using data already collected by programs or regularly collected for other purposes (e.g., surveys conducted to measure unemployment), policy researchers can assess changes in outcomes over time. These secondary data analyses can sometimes support quasi-experimental policy research (e.g., matching program participants to available data on nonparticipants before an intervention started and following their outcomes over time), or these analyses can be nonexperimental (e.g., drawing upon program records to assess trends among program participants only).

- *Survey research:* Policy researchers may survey beneficiaries of a program to determine whether the program had the intended outcomes. Surveys are popular and relevant because they can be tailored to nearly any situation. They provide direct answers to a variety of questions about how policy impacts individuals (e.g., "customer satisfaction" questions to determine how programs can better serve the public). This ability to get information straight from the source makes survey research widely used among policy researchers.

- *Systematic reviews:* Policies are much more defensible if they are grounded in evidence-based research. Policy researchers may review evidence across multiple studies to identify whether compelling evidence exists for the adoption of a program, policy, or practice. Meta-analysis is a commonly used statistical technique for combining findings across multiple studies. In recent years, many systematic reviews and repositories of evidence have been sponsored by both federal and private organizations, including the U.S. Department of Education's What Works Clearinghouse (WWC), the U.S. Department of Labor's Clearinghouse for Labor Evaluation and Research (CLEAR), and the U.S. Department of Health and Human Services' National Registry of Evidence-Based Programs and Practices (NREPP).

- *Site visits:* When trying to understand the inner workings of a program or a policy, there is no substitute for seeing it in action. Site visits to interview the "front lines" of staff involved in service provision are nearly always enlightening experiences. "Ambient observation," a fancy term for getting the feel of a place, can contribute significantly to the policy researcher's understanding of how and why a program is shaped by its context. Whereas quantitative research can be useful for measuring the magnitude of a program or policy's effect, site visits add important information for understanding how, why, and in what situations effects are being produced.

- *Implementation studies:* The field of implementation science is growing rapidly, and it is often coupled with experimental, quasi-experimental, and qualitative research to determine both whether the program being evaluated was implemented with fidelity (i.e., as intended), and what core components of the program are most important for achieving intended outcomes. Early implementation science focused on programs, but it is increasingly being applied to achieving systemic policy objectives such as integrating services and collaborating across agencies.

- *Cost-benefit or cost-effectiveness analyses:* A logical focus of policy research is to determine the "bang for the buck" that a certain policy or program will have. Whereas cost-benefit analysis focuses on the economic benefit of a program by quantifying the dollar value of all costs and benefits, cost-effectiveness analysis compares the costs of a program with the raw outcomes produced (e.g., cost per life saved). The difference between cost-benefit and cost-effectiveness analysis, then, lies in how benefits are quantified. A newer form of cost analysis called social return on investment (SROI) analysis is also gaining momentum. It is related to cost-benefit analysis, but unlike more traditional cost-benefit analysis that focuses on benefits that have a market value, SROI puts proxy values on unvalued benefits to capture the entire social impact of a particular policy alternative or program.

Seems pretty complicated, even confusing, doesn't it? That is because providing useful information that helps solve policy problems is an inherently complex process requiring the policy researcher to define problems, identify fundamental research approaches that may fit the situation, and make the inevitable adaptation that will be necessary to get the most from the available research methods and techniques. Indeed, most studies will require unique combinations of different methods. Though we will return to most of these examples at some point in the next three chapters, a full discussion of each of these methods is beyond the scope of this chapter or even this book. These diverse examples have been chosen to make a few fundamental points. First, it should be clear from this list that policy researchers have a wide array of tools at their disposal (Hakim, 2000; Lipsey and Freeman, 2004; Shadish, Cook, and Campbell, 2001). Second, this variety of tools presents both an opportunity and a challenge. While these tools offer an opportunity to provide nuanced approaches to answer a diversity of policy questions in a variety of circumstances, they can present a challenge because the key to conducting policy research is identifying the proper mix of tools given the purpose, time, budget, and data available—and the research questions that underlie the study. Third, effectively using the many tools of policy research requires creativity. Succinctly stated, "The policy research process . . . is not formulaic; it demands creativity. At the same time, it is systematic, . . . disciplined, rigorous, and, in a word, professional" (Majchrzak and Markus, 2014, p. 5). A primary intent of this book is to help you understand the context and factors to consider when making creative choices about methods, data collection, and the interpretation of results.

In most cases, the information needs associated with a given policy problem or issue will require the use of multiple methods rather than the exclusive use of one method. One common mistake of the inexperienced analyst is to rely too heavily on the technique one knows best. Surveys, for example, are frequently overused because they are a straightforward way to reach a lot of people. For many policy questions, they are too *obtrusive*. This means that respondents can easily recognize the purpose of survey questions and tailor their responses to reflect their self-interests rather than answering the question objectively. This is a frequent source of positive bias in survey findings; the respondents put on their best face. Policy researchers should pick tools with careful consideration; "the problem should dictate the methods, not vice versa" (Patton, Sawicki, and Clark, 2012, p. 78). In fact, the problem should dictate the entire approach to the research process. As we shall see, different kinds of problem situations or policy issues connote a different research process and result in different products.

Who Does Policy Research?

One of the surprises that may face students of public administration is that nearly every kind of public employee engages in policy research at one time or another. Multiple perspectives and skills are needed not only to conduct policy research but also to understand its implications and formulate solutions to problems. And these solutions must be politically, administratively, and financially feasible.

Although their titles may differ across different agencies and organizations, policy researchers can be readily found in:

- *Government.* The most obvious examples of public administrators engaging in policy research occur in federal agencies with such names as the Government Accountability Office and Congressional Research Service. But these relatively large research-focused agencies are the exception rather than the rule. In fact, students seeking employment as policy researchers should know that, without doubt, the greatest number of opportunities exist at the state and local levels. Nearly every state government boasts an equivalent to these federal agencies, and some city governments also have this type of analytic capacity (e.g., the City of San Jose, CA, once had an Office of the Policy Analyst mandated in its city charter). Moreover, nearly every legislator, legislative committee, and task force relies on the work of policy research staff. Often these policy researchers have titles like legislative analyst, program analyst, or management analyst, but an understanding of policy research is a strong asset for employees at all levels of government policy making and implementation. The ability to understand and make informed independent judgments about whether and how to use policy research findings is essential to giving them their appropriate weight in public decisions.
- *Consulting firms.* Because the demand for the information generated by policy research is so great, and because the need for independent

sources of information is so frequent, a great deal of policy research is contracted out to consulting firms, private research organizations, or consultants. When contracts are awarded to conduct policy research on behalf of a public agency, public administrators or managers become the clients and consumers of policy research. Although some public administrators typically find themselves on the consuming end of the research process, they cannot be informed consumers if they have not developed policy research skills of their own.

- *Think tanks.* Think tanks are comprised of independent scholars who are thought leaders or advocates for particular issues. These think tanks may be housed within universities (e.g., the Earth Institute at Columbia University), foundations (e.g., the Kaiser Family Foundation), or as independent entities (e.g., Human Rights Watch, the Brookings Institution, or the Cato Institute).
- *Institutions of higher education.* Academics from colleges and universities often engage in policy research. Although we often think of academics as engaged in the development of theories, they can often be found on the front lines of policy research, either as partners to consulting firms, providing testimony to legislatures, or operating their own policy research institutes within universities (e.g., the Center for Evaluation & Education Policy at Indiana University).
- *Public policy stakeholder organizations.* Public policy in the United States is influenced by a broad range of stakeholder organizations that influence policy decisions directly or indirectly in a variety of ways—lobbying lawmakers at all levels, filing court actions, advocating publicly, testifying to policy makers, and more. These may be registered lobbying organizations, nonprofit interest or advocacy groups (e.g., AARP, Planned Parenthood), labor unions, trade or business associations, or more. Staff in these stakeholder organizations often engage in policy research, both to explore opportunities for improvements in policy and to determine the effectiveness of the policies that they advocate.

Given the multitude of organizations engaged in policy research, it won't come as a surprise that an enormous amount of policy research may be produced on a given topic. Legislators and government administrators must be informed consumers of this research, which requires a great deal of knowledge about how to sift through mountains of research to identify the most rigorous studies, the most pertinent findings, and the most appropriate opportunities for policy changes. Not every public administrator must excel at policy research, but few can perform at their best without a general understanding of it.

Our discussion to this point has emphasized the breadth and diversity of policy research. We have briefly introduced the roles that policy research can play throughout the policy cycle, the diversity of research approaches and techniques it may use, the variety of policy areas it may inform, and the various organizations and interests it may serve. From an individual point of view, practicing policy research will require a similarly diverse set of skills. Those who produce policy research must possess a considerable amount of technical skill with respect to social research and inquiry. Policy research draws on a broad spectrum of techniques for information collection and analysis, including adaptation of the scientific model of experimentation, applications of economic analysis to program costs and benefits, surveys of individuals, statistical analysis of large data sets, personal observation, and more. Students planning careers in policy research–related fields should plan on acquiring skills and experience in as many techniques, methods, and approaches as possible and learn how to appropriately apply and synthesize them in multiple contexts.

Policy research also requires knowledge of public policy, the institutions and processes that produce it, and how policy decisions are made. Producing and delivering information that will be useful requires understanding of the context in which that use will take place. Policy researchers also require communications skills. If information is to be credible, convincing, and useful, it must be delivered in clear and understandable ways. If a researcher has a solid grounding in research methods, a creative mind, and the ability to communicate research results in compelling ways (both in written reports and orally), his or her future may be very bright indeed.

Whether a particular research project is undertaken directly by a public agency, a think tank, a university, an interest group, or by a consulting firm, policy research—except for the very smallest projects—is frequently the product of a team of researchers. This cooperative effort is often achieved by division of research tasks according to the expertise of the team members. For example, a research project might include a leader with lead management responsibilities, a statistician/methodologist, a subject-matter expert, data collectors, IT specialists, and research assistants or graduate students who frequently round out the team. Working on a policy research team is a challenging yet enjoyable experience. A typical project is conducted according to tight deadlines, which impose an atmosphere of pressure and the need for long hours of work. Policy research teams often develop an exhilarating esprit de corps as they get to know one another's personalities, strengths, and weaknesses and work on a collective mission to improve policy.

Why Do Policy Research?

The introduction to this chapter demonstrated that there are differences of opinion on the value of policy research. As policy researchers, we clearly believe it can have great value, but we also believe that its value is oftentimes not immediately clear. Indeed, this text grapples with the reasons for these differences of opinion and how policy researchers can make their product more valuable and useful. Though there is plenty of room for improvement, policy research is a growth industry that has become part of the fabric of public policy making. Here are some major reasons that policy research is here to stay and why many, including us, find it a compelling and fulfilling career.

Policy Research Is the Law

Many public programs must be evaluated at legislatively mandated intervals. The Government Performance and Results Act (1993) mandated that federal agencies set performance targets and report annually on the attainment of those targets. In January 2011, the Government Performance and Modernization Act of 2010 was signed into law, which replaced annual performance assessments with quarterly performance assessments (Public Law 111–352, January 4, 2011). Legislative mandates for evaluation generally reflect a concern about accountability for expenditures, but they are also intended to provide information that will improve programs and policies. These legislative mandates mean that careers in public administration are quite likely to draw individuals into policy research as either planners, participants, and/or consumers of such research. Many of the state and local research projects described in the case studies in Part II were initiated as the result of some legislative requirement.

Policy Research Is Interesting

Granted, it may be an acquired taste for some, but most policy research is conducted at the cutting edge of some of the most important challenges that modern governments face. Because these challenges are complex and typically have a human element that cannot be ignored, there is a wealth of innovation taking place in policy research to better measure and tackle some of our most pressing social issues.

Policy research frequently tackles questions like:

- Are drug treatment programs effective in addressing the drug problem?
- What are the direct and indirect outcomes of instituting agricultural subsidies?
- Do workforce development programs improve employment rates and help decrease generational poverty?
- Do early education programs like Head Start offer a solution to educational inequities?
- How should government deal with the increasing cost and declining availability of health care?
- Will raising the gas tax help reduce the effects of climate change?

If you are interested in these types of questions and interested in mitigating social challenges to improve the quality of life, a career in policy research may be right for you.

Policy Research Can Be Influential

If policy research is indeed influential, then so are those who conduct it. The unspoken goal of many involved in policy research is to have a positive impact on public programs and policy. That is a legitimate and honorable motivation, but it begs a question: Just how influential is policy research?

When policy research became widely applied to public policy issues, particularly in the 1960s and 1970s, some observers felt that techniques like cost-benefit analysis would supplant the democratic political process. They feared that policy research technocrats, using quantitative methods, would make important policy decisions at the expense of the influence of elected officials and citizens. For a variety of reasons, policy research never achieved the kind of influence its supporters envisioned and its detractors feared (Putt and Springer, 1989, pp. 14–16). Perhaps the most important reason was that the American political process proved to be much more resilient and adaptive than anticipated. Policy research has taken its place in the political give and take that characterizes our pluralist democracy. It does not dictate decisions, but neither is it ignored.

The apparent inability of policy research to change public policy quickly and decisively led some cynics to question its overall effectiveness and usefulness. They argue that policy research typically produces reports that sit unread on the shelf. Our response to these critics is this: Asking whether policy research improves public decisions is a poorly phrased question. If the implied criterion for effective research is whether study recommendations were adopted wholeheartedly and implemented immediately, the answer will almost invariably be no. Public decision making, of course, is more complex than just following the research. Such a pessimistic outlook overlooks the impact that policy research often has.

The role of policy research in affecting policy is frequently subtle; its impacts incremental. Policy research is perhaps best regarded as "facilitating policy decisions, not displacing them" (Putt and Springer, 1989, p. 64). Policy researchers need to bear in mind that they are but one source of information for decision makers. Optimizing the influence of that valuable source requires conscious and specific effort. The case studies in Part II are intended to highlight how policy researchers can develop useful information that will affect decision making, and the principles in the next four chapters lay the groundwork for an understanding of those cases.

Policy Research Can Contribute to a Fulfilling Career

For those who want to pursue a career in government, a canny strategy might be to acquire policy research skills and experience. Policy research skills are nearly always in demand, and an individual with such skills can frequently find desirable employment with state or local government. In an era of shrinking government resources and increased reliance on data-driven decision making, the need for policy analysts to determine the most efficient strategies to achieve policy goals is more pressing than ever.

In government as in the private sector, information is valuable, and those who can help procure and analyze it are often in demand. It is not uncommon for erstwhile policy researchers to jump from agency to agency when their skills and experience become evident to the managers of those agencies. It is no accident that the career of many a department head or director has begun in the ranks of the analysts.

Because policy researchers may be hired by governments, consulting firms, think tanks, universities, nonprofit agencies, foundations, or associations, it wouldn't be fair—or accurate—to describe a "typical" career path. In choosing a career path, policy researchers will need to decide whether they want to specialize in a single policy or become a generalist, whether they want to be an advocate or an impartial researcher, and whether they want to enter the public, private, or nonprofit sector. Each research project will shape a policy researcher's reputation and ultimate career path.

Does Policy Research Improve Public Decisions?

For many, the bottom-line question concerning policy research is "Does it improve public decisions?" Are decisions more discerning and more effective when policy research is available? Research unquestionably consumes resources, and cost-conscious decision makers and citizens want to know if they get any bang for their research buck. Even many policy analysts would agree that research findings and recommendations that are ignored are wasted tax dollars.

We agree that public policy decisions should not be dictated by technical studies and reports. Information is, of course, a necessary ingredient in public decisions, but different actors and interests will interpret and value it differently. Policy research is but one ingredient in a complex decision-making stew that includes the biases inherent in institutional procedures, the influence of cultural norms, political clout of specific interests, policy developed in response to a tragedy or a scandal, and more. Therefore, a more realistic assessment of the impact of research on decisions must be based on a more subtle understanding of the influence process than whether a given recommendation is adopted or rejected.

We do argue that well-done policy research improves public decisions in many ways, including the following:

- *Policy research reduces the uncertainty in public decisions.* For example, public decisions often involve judgments about how large groups of people will be affected by a policy or what large groups need. This information is beyond the personal experience or knowledge of any one decision maker or group of decision makers. Research is necessary to inform decisions that otherwise would be guesses or based on personal preferences.

- *Policy research contributes to decision makers' understanding of policies or programs.* Public decisions are often characterized by drift that occurs when decision makers lose sight of the overall policy purpose or program design in the heat of day-to-day decisions and situations (Kress, Koehler, and Springer, 1981). Performance monitoring and other policy research can keep the purpose of policies and programs in focus and keep implementation decisions more in line with a policy's original logic and intent.
- *Policy research can bring new perspectives.* Policy research can improve understanding of public problems and introduce new solutions and responses to decision makers.
- *Policy research can improve the quality of public debate.* By making evidence a part of the decision calculus, policy research can help resolve political differences. An enlightened public is more likely to support conclusions consistent with the findings of policy research.
- *Policy research can fuel continuous improvement of existing policies and programs.* Even after public decisions are made, policy research can help inform their implementation and management by providing performance monitoring, staff and consumer feedback, and other useful information for continuous program improvement.

In summary, policy research leavens the dough of public decisions by bringing evidence and clarity to the decision-making recipe. The process of influence is not simple or straightforward: "Policy research . . . is not expected to produce solutions, but to provide information and analysis at multiple points in a complex web of interconnected decisions [that] shape public policy" (Putt and Springer, 1989, p. 16). Doing this well requires a number of skills. Technical skills are a crucial ingredient, as is an understanding of a policy's purpose, context, feasibility, and the perspectives of stakeholders.

Remember This . . .

As you go through the chapters and cases ahead of you, it will become clear why policy research is an art as well as a science. There is no perfect formula or plan that will fit all, or even any one, policy research projects. However, there are criteria for policy research that when carefully addressed will produce useful products. A brief statement of these criteria provides a summary of important themes that run through this introductory chapter and that will be explicated in the chapters and examples of actual policy research that lie ahead. Good policy research will be:

- *Credible* because it is transparent, systematic, informed by evidence, and understandably presented;
- *Unbiased* because it uses objective methods to the extent possible and acknowledges inevitable differences in value and meaning in political decision-making processes;
- *Meaningful* to and engaging of representatives of stakeholder groups who may be making, implementing, or being affected by decisions resulting from the policy research;
- *Responsible* in considering the contextual circumstances and both positive and negative potential consequences of project findings;
- *Doable* in both process and product given available time and resources; and
- *Creative* because every project must accommodate its unique problem and context while optimizing the preceding criteria.

Overview of the Book

Applied Policy Research is organized in two complementary parts. Chapters 2 through 5 complete Part I, which is titled "Principles of Policy Research." Part II, "Case Studies in Policy Research," presents sixteen examples of actual policy research projects. The title of Part I was chosen for a reason. Principles are fundamental propositions that define the foundation of an approach to behavior or a system of thinking. Applied to the policy researcher, principles can be fundamental guides to professional intention and behavior, to being committed, skillful, and responsible in conducting policy research. The importance of the *policy researcher* as the designer and implementer of actual studies is central to our discussion. Conducting policy research is rather audacious when you think about it. The policy researcher presumes to "speak truth to power" (Wildawsky, 1979) with the potential of influencing decisions that affect lives. Each of the four chapters in the remainder of Part I defines and conveys the importance of a simple principle. The objective is to portray the intentions, perspectives, and skills that will make the work of policy research worthwhile.

Chapter 2, "Be real," is an overview of three important spheres of reality that orient the policy researcher's work: problem reality, user reality, and researcher reality. The objective is to highlight elements in each area that (a) the policy researcher should consider in designing and implementing a useful product and (b) may present challenges in conducting policy research. Chapter 3, "Be Creative," presents a perspective on how to organize complex, real-world problems so that they are amenable to systematic, flexible, and credible analysis. The chapter makes it clear that there is no formula for doing this; it requires creative application of policy research principles to each study. Chapter 4, "Be Credible," introduces the policy researcher's toolbox and options for collecting, analyzing, and designing studies that make a strong argument for credible and useful information. Chapter 5, "Be Useful," covers the ways in which policy researchers can make their study products relevant to real-world policy making and implementation.

The cases in Part II were chosen and organized by a common logic and outline that explores the application of these principles with real-world examples. The studies were not selected to represent "textbook" examples of idealized study designs or data collection and analysis techniques. They were selected to provide a variety of examples that vary in budget; types of policy researchers and clients; level of government from local to national; and policy area including public services (e.g., education, behavioral health, child and family services, criminal justice), planning and environment, and governmental management. This diversity allows for the demonstration of policy research themes in different contexts and the agility policy researchers need in order to accommodate these themes in different contexts.

Discussion Questions

1. What are the differences between policy research and "hard science" research? What part might each play in the process of making public policy?
2. Identify a well-known example of policy research related to national policy. Who conducted it? Why was it initiated? What impact, if any, did (or may) it have on decision making?
3. Repeat the earlier discussion for a well-known policy research project in your state or community. Speculate about how different the policy research project might be at the national and local levels. In which environment might it be more effective? Why?
4. How important do you think policy research is in influencing government programs? What major considerations led to your conclusion? Cite an example supporting your conclusion.
5. Do you think policy decisions would be better if there were more resources for policy research? Why or why not?
6. Discuss what you think the advantages and disadvantages might be of working in different policy research organizations. Which do you think you would like best?

Assignments and Activities

1. Pick one government agency with which you are familiar. Find out which unit conducts policy research for the agency and what

job titles are given to individuals who engage in policy research activities.

2. Have a conversation with someone who works as a policy researcher in some capacity. What do they see as their major responsibilities? Do they think their work makes a difference in policy decisions? What do they like best about their work? Least?

2 Be Real

Navigating the Policy Research Terrain

What does it mean when someone asks you to "be real"? Actually, it depends on who is saying it, who is hearing it, and the circumstances in which the message is delivered. Indeed, "be real" can mean "I don't believe you," "get serious," "quit dreaming," "don't put me on," "pay attention to the actual situation," or more. The admonition to "be real" clearly has many shades of meaning. However, the kernel of similarity running through them makes the case for why "being real" is a critical priority for policy researchers who want their work to be used. The information policy researchers create and present must be *transparent and believable* in the eyes of those who are expected to use it. It must be practical and attainable—not "pie in the sky." It must be balanced and objective in its presentation to be useful in a policy argument. It must have clear relevance to the actual situations in which it must be used.

In this chapter, we will explicate the importance of being real when conducting applied policy research. First, we will explore the complex terrain of the actual situations in which policy researchers find themselves. Three major contours within the policy research terrain are identified and discussed—problem reality, user reality, and researcher reality. These contours overlap to different degrees and in different ways and require different degrees of attention for each policy research project. The researcher must navigate them with care. We will identify practical steps a policy researcher might take to negotiate the policy research terrain. Careful attention to these interrelated realities is a strong start on the path to useful policy research.

Before we begin this trek, we must post caution signs. First, the terrain we are mapping is not simple—it is varied and unstable, shifting with each policy problem, each institutional setting in which it will be used, and each policy analyst who develops and provides information. This is reality! Second, we cannot provide one best way to view and traverse the terrain; indeed, its undulations are a fundamental reason that policy research cannot be formulaic. We can provide a framework for assessing the realities of an applied research project and making informed, creative decisions about how to understand it, study it, to provide valid and transparent information, and to communicate it in a useful and responsible way. Third, many of the most used and even most recommended trails across these regions may reach dead ends in the search for your objective. Although the policy research terrain can be bumpy, each bump provides a new learning opportunity and an opportunity to apply a new skill. These bumps can be puzzling and frustrating. They also ensure that policy research is seldom boring.

Policy Research Terrain: Problem, Use, and Research Environments

Terrain implies more than the physical appearance of a landscape or geographical region. Historically, military strategists have assessed terrain for the opportunities and challenges it presented for particular strategies and tactics. Policy researchers must also strategically assess the terrain of each project they undertake. Careful assessment is important to identify opportunities and challenges to conduct useful research.

Figure 2.1 pictures the major contours of the policy research terrain. This simple map depicts several defining features of this terrain. First, the terrain includes three primary regions. The problem region includes the multiple factors that define the problem the research will address. The user region includes the individuals and organizations that intend to use, or oppose the use of, the information the researcher will produce. The policy research region includes the tools and practices that the researcher may use, along with the professional considerations that may guide that use.

The reality of each region has its own distinct features; however, as depicted by the overlapping areas in Figure 2.1, these regions are also interdependent. The applied policy research region overlaps substantially with the problem and user regions. This large overlap represents the crucial importance of understanding problem and user reality if policy research tasks are to be successfully designed and implemented. The

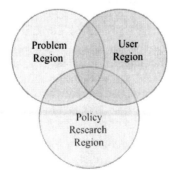

Figure 2.1 The Applied Policy Research Terrain

interconnections and complex pathways between these three regions are central to producing useful policy research. To use the regional map analogy, a storm in the problem region may cause flooding on a river that flows into the user region. This will in turn affect the route the researcher takes and the means of travel necessary to successfully reach a destination in the user region. Identifying the features of each terrain that are important to a particular policy research project, identifying how they interact, and selecting the appropriate route and means of getting there are central to producing useful policy research. The following sections will discuss important considerations for successfully completing this journey.

Problem Reality

Problems come in very different forms. For a student, "problem" may conjure up thoughts of homework or tests—puzzles to be solved using the tools and skills they are learning. In other contexts, problems are negative circumstances that require action to improve them or get rid of them entirely. Policy researchers must see their problems both as conditions requiring change and as puzzles that must be solved. These perceptions of a problem shape each other. For example, California's decades-long policy battles over water, and particularly how to quench the Los Angeles area's growing thirst, were seriously exacerbated by the extreme drought that began in 2012. A $15 billion project, popularly known as the Delta Tunnels, centers around two pipes 150 feet below the ground, 40 feet in diameter, and 30 miles long. They were proposed to transport water from the Sacramento River in the north to the southern central valley and Los Angeles.

The problem is complex, including the competing water needs of millions of people in Southern California, endangered species and fish populations in the delta above San Francisco Bay, vast agriculture industries in the state's central valley, and taxpayer concerns about the cost of the investment. Multiple studies of the problem side have produced information on environmental impacts, both positive and negative, depending on criteria including benefits to water users and cost estimates. The multiple stakeholders impacted by the problem and its planned resolution have shaped the user environment, expanding and shifting emphases in multiple agencies and jurisdictions. A prime example is renaming the tunnel project Water Fix and initiating Eco Fix, an additional $8 billion initiative for construction and watershed restoration and enhancement. The conflicts will not end soon and will produce an ongoing need for information.

Understanding the complex interaction of problem conditions and stakeholders with information users (e.g., advocates, decision makers, and implementers) is important to policy researchers who are trying to produce relevant information. To produce useful lessons, it is important to understand the genesis of a policy problem and the factors that may have shaped it. How and why did it emerge? Who is calling for resolution of the problem and why? What are the feasible leverage or intervention points that policy makers can use to promote improvement?

The coming chapters and case studies will show how decisions about data collection and analysis require a point of view for framing problem and user issues and interactions. Increasingly scholars and practitioners concerned with policy problems are recognizing that they emerge from a complex, evolving, social and environmental system. While not completely controllable, the evolution of societies and environment is "quite different from . . . a self-steering system requiring the government to play no role" (Colander and Kupers, 2014, p. 5). Societies develop internal control systems that make them work—government is an important one.

In our experience, the need to understand and not oversimplify complexity is a key to successfully traversing the problem region. We are all familiar with complexity as "an ordinary noun describing objects with many inter-connected parts" (Holland, 2014, p. 1). The following sections will explicate policy research implications of several important dimensions of complexity (Hester and Adams, 2014, p. vii ff). Discussion will draw from complexity science, which is positioned "on the edge of order and chaos" (Waldrop, 1992, p. 1). *Just right for applied policy research!*

Many Things to Consider

Complex settings are composed of many factors that must be considered in understanding a problem and how to address it. Simply put, all else equal, the more relevant factors there are, the more complexity there will be. This characteristic of complexity is basic. Yet as demonstrated in the Post-3 Rs example it already gives an inkling of the public policy challenges posed by complexity.

Post-3 Rs Education Policy: The Growing Complexity of Public Education

Take the most commonly shared policy responsibilities in most societies, such as basic public education. In early nineteenth-century America the three Rs (reading, writing, and arithmetic) provided a broadly shared understanding of the basic skills education needed to support. Teaching the three Rs and enforcing discipline completed the traditional education package.

Slowly and in steps, understanding of the process of learning advanced beyond cognition to include social, emotional, learning style, cultural, and other differences. Educators saw the inadequacy, indeed harmfulness, of the simple three-Rs-and-classroom-discipline formula. Deeper understanding of the cognitive skills required in industrial, then postindustrial employment made it clear that the three Rs were insufficient content—problem solving, relational thinking, and creativity needed a prime place in public education.

In addition, research and experience pointed to the importance of a safe and supportive school environment. Studies clearly demonstrated the inadequacy of traditional school disciplinary practice; out-of-school suspension and expulsion were shown to accelerate individual behavioral problems, coining the term "school-to-prison pipeline." Public policy responded. Federal initiatives have been undertaken to support improvement in school climate and create a safe and supportive learning environment. The inescapable presence of persistent demographically and socioeconomically based gaps in educational achievement created an urgent need for solutions to the underlying reasons for these gaps. Clearly, the number of factors shaping educational policy has mushroomed, and the range of policy objectives has increased. Education policy makers struggle to accommodate this complexity. Many citizens understandably yearn for the simplicity and comfort of the three Rs formula, and feeding that desire becomes a political strategy. Welcome to modern problem reality!

Lots of Connections

Complex terrains are *interconnected*. It is not simply the number of relevant factors that make a complex problem reality. The patterns of connection between factors within and across regions of the policy terrain pose several challenges to clarifying a given problem. The most basic is determining which factors are associated with others (i.e., tend to occur and vary together). Is positive school climate actually associated with stronger academic performance? It is also important to know the strength of the tendency to vary together. How much difference does a positive school climate make in academic performance? The shape of the association can also be important. Does the association between school climate and academic performance get stronger as the climate gets more positive?

Similar to the nostalgia for manageability and comfort seen in the three Rs, problem solvers may yearn for simple settings with fewer factors and less chaos. The current challenge posed by climate change is a good example. From one perspective, some believe that human influence on climate change is not proven. Reasoning for this view may be that nature is a self-steering system essentially separate from the artificial constructs of human activity. From another perspective, human activity is seen to have a direct impact on changes in the Earth's temperature. Jedediah Purdy, in a brilliant discussion of current challenges in environmental law and policy, clearly states how in the current era (i.e., the anthropocene), environmental policy must recognize the connectivity of human activity and the natural environment. "Climate change makes the global atmosphere, its chemistry and weather systems, into Frankenstein's monster—part natural, part made" (Purdy, 2015, p. 15). To tame the monster, humans have no choice but to attempt to understand this colossally complex connectivity and make intentional policy decisions to move forward.

Layer Within Layer

Nesting is a third important feature of complex terrains. Nesting refers to the tendency for complex settings to be organized by layers of smaller, interconnected systems that operate within each other. An example might be classrooms inside schools, schools inside districts, districts inside state school systems, and state departments of education within the U.S. Department of Education. Other examples might be work groups (e.g., project teams) within offices, offices within agencies, agencies within departments, friends within neighborhoods, neighborhoods within communities, and so on.

Nested realities are typically *hierarchical*, with those higher up encompassing those that are lower down (Springer, 1976). These hierarchies are pervasive in public policy problem settings. Think of the intergovernmental system from national to state to county to community to neighborhood. These hierarchies shape activities such as setting policy, interpreting it, and implementing it as it works to direct impacts on citizens at the street level. Though lower levels are usually constrained by higher levels (top-down effects), the activities of lower levels may influence higher levels (bottom-up effects). These features of nested systems mean that the analyst can and in most cases must distinguish between interactions within subsystems and interactions among subsystems.

What happens within a county or other subsystem, is partly explained by how it is influenced by other subsystems (e.g., counties, or the state) and partly by what happens inside the county. Both must be considered to gain full understanding. The implementation of laws or policies is a ubiquitous example of the interplay of external influences and internal dynamics on how well the law or policy is achieving its purposes. Differences in local implementation across counties may make big differences in how well a state law reaches its intended objectives in different parts of a state.

Hierarchical settings are also characterized by the *emergence* of features in subsystems at different levels. Emergence may be roughly described through a paraphrase of a common saying: "the action of the whole is more than the sum of the actions of the parts" (Holland, 2014, p. 2). "Inclusiveness," for example, may be measured as a characteristic of a community coalition or some other group. It cannot be ascribed to an individual member of that group.

Hierarchical, complex settings have important implications for analysis. *Context* is a critical component of understanding how problems arise and can be resolved. For example, many problems related to individual behaviors are strongly influenced by contextual factors. Recall the Three Rs example. Early study of early education focused primarily on the interaction between teacher and students, surely an important consideration. As understanding of knowledge grew, the critical importance of school climate as a context was recognized. If complex settings are to be understood and resolved, context is "the essential element that modern . . . problem solvers . . . need to include in each problem formulation" (Hester and Adams, 2014, p. 25).

On the Move

Complex social systems are *dynamic* and *adaptive*. Their components, subsystems or individuals, can be thought as "agents (that) learn or adapt in response to interactions with other agents" (Holland, 2014, p. v). This means that problems may grow or resolve, new problems may arise, and none of this can be predicted simply by looking at past events. The dynamic nature of complex settings increases the need for more information and more recent information to assess the dynamics of a problem and the appropriateness of intervention. This dynamic quality also has important implications for analysis. "Analysis of complex systems almost always turns on finding recurring patterns in the system's ever-changing configurations" (Holland, 2014, p. 9). Finding patterns that hold across time and place is important to identifying underlying principles of policy process and action.

Summary

The importance of complexity in understanding the settings in which policy problems emerge and are engaged has remained largely in the background in policy research. The tendency has been to make the implications of nesting, for example, explicit only when data and analysis technique (e.g., hierarchical modeling) are designed for that purpose. The Safe Schools/Healthy Students State Program example that follows identifies how complexity concepts are important in studies even though they cannot be fully represented in a statistical model. The importance of clearly understanding the nature of problem reality is to understand how to frame the questions that evidence can answer. How to gather that evidence is the subject of Chapters 3 and 4.

Collaborative Decisions as an Emergent Property of SS/HS Coalitions

For more than two decades, the Safe Schools/Healthy Students (SS/HS) grant program (U.S. Department of Health and Human Services) has helped local schools improve mental and behavioral health services to students. Community coalitions of stakeholders (education, behavioral health, families, social services, and law enforcement) collaborate to achieve grant objectives. In 2013, the SS/HS state program was initiated to promote state support of local community collaboration in planning and implementing SS/HS programs in schools. At both state and local levels, collaboration was the expected procedure through which stakeholders would problem solve, negotiate, and, most importantly, make decisions. A fundamental part of the SS/HS program theory of change was that collaborative decisions would provide more appropriate action based on the complex realities of the grant context and objectives.

The funding agency of this grant program commissioned a multisite evaluation of the State Program to develop evidence-based lessons for dissemination to states throughout the nation. The complex, hierarchical nature of the evaluation sample (twenty-one districts, within seven states) led the evaluation team to use a complexity perspective. One focus of their comprehensive evaluation was to treat collaborative decisions as an *emergent concept at the coalition level*. Coalitions themselves are complex settings, with diverse internal structures and processes through which collaborative decisions may emerge. Meetings provided a structural focus for collaborative activities. The analysts identified three types of meetings that provided distinct opportunities for collaboration. Leadership meetings involved managers and supervisory staff; steering meetings were regular, formal coalition membership meetings; and partner meetings were meetings that were initiated and sustained through the initiative of coalition members.

The evaluators collected quarterly data on the degree to which meeting types focused on deliberative functions (information sharing, review and approval, recommendations) or decision-making functions (decision input, policy decision making, task design, and implementation). Table 2.1 displays an analysis of patterns

Table 2.1 Deliberation and Decision-Making Emphasis in Coalition Meetings

Collaborative Emphases	State Coalition Meetings (n = 7)				Local Coalition Meetings (n = 21)			
	Leadership	Steering	Partner	All Meetings	Leadership	Steering	Partner	All Meetings
Deliberation (% of coalitions)	50%	69%	29%	49%	55%	43%	35%	44%
Decision making (% of coalitions)	26%	20%	14%	16%	25%	23%	24%	24%
Decision/Deliberation Ratio	.52	.29	.48	.33	.45	.53	.69	.55

of functions across nested contexts: meeting types, coalition levels (states and districts), and state contexts. The first two rows are the percentage of the top three meeting activities in the seven states (row 1) or twenty-one districts (row 2) that identified either deliberative or decision-making activities as one of their top three functions. So, for example, in state steering meetings, 69 percent of the activities receiving most attention were deliberative, and 26 percent were decision making. The third row is the ratio of decision to deliberation emphasis—higher scores mean greater decision-making emphasis in the setting.

The analysis reveals two important patterns concerning collaborative decision making. First, the relative emphasis on decision making versus deliberation is greater in districts than in states (.55 for all district meetings compared to .33 for all state meetings). Second, member meetings tend to be relatively more involved in decision making than other meeting types. The exception to this is state leadership meetings, and interviews provide a clear reason for this. These meetings, uniformly across states, include a small group of program managers who make decisions about grant administrative decisions; they are not collaborative in purpose. Third, local partner meetings clearly have the greatest relative level of decision-making activity. Collaborative decision making is strongest in the most "grassroots" setting—local partner meetings.

Most important, this analysis provides information that is quite actionable. The hierarchical analysis identifying distinct contexts at state, district, and meeting levels suggests important influences of contextual differences in how collaborative decision making can function:

- The degree to which participants have discretion and authority to make the type of decisions relevant to the setting. For example, representatives to state steering committees typically are managerial-level personnel in large agencies. Their authority and discretion concerning any agency commitments is typically minimal. They can share information and shared concerns, and that is what they do.
- The degree to which participants have the knowledge and experience to make reasoned decisions in the decision setting will affect decision-making emphasis. Again, participants in the work group setting are likely to be knowledgeable about the operational decisions they more typically face.
- Third, the degree of contextual constraints concerning decision options will affect the emphasis on decision making. At the

> state level, for example, the ability to make directive decisions can be constrained by laws, the authority of state agencies in their intergovernmental system, and the broad implications of relevant decisions.
>
> In this example, the emphasis on setting, contextual circumstances, and patterns in complex settings led to conclusions about where collaboration can be most decision oriented. This finding would not have emerged in a single site, single level, or aggregated analysis. The analysis suggests that the widespread assumption that collaboration itself will improve social services needs refinement. Training, for example, should focus less on collaboration as a generic cure-all and more on the contexts and conditions in which it can make a difference. Collaboration or other policy options are not simply good or bad, effective or ineffective. It is more complex than that, and useful policy research must supply evidence that recognizes that complexity.

So What?

Before we go on, let's reflect for a minute. Some readers may be wondering what all this discussion about complexity and contexts and hierarchies and emerging properties has to do with learning how to do policy research. We are *not* suggesting that every policy research project must use statistical techniques and research designs that faithfully model the full complexity of the problem setting under study. "Complexity science" is a developing field in mathematics and the natural and social sciences.

While complexity science does not yet focus on practical application, relatively recent developments in statistical analysis do engage complexity. The hierarchical modeling identified earlier (Raudenbush and Bryk, 2002), for example, allows analyses that take into account the interconnections within and among subsystems that are nested. These kinds of analyses, of course, depend on expansive, multisystem data sets with data at more than one level in a complex hierarchy. While all social systems are complex, we often do not have data that adequately represents that reality or the exact tools needed to analyze it.

Still, public policy decision makers, policy researchers, and implementers deal with complex issues and scenarios on a daily basis (Miles, 2009). This is the nagging reality. If policy research is to provide lessons that reflect this reality and that are useful within it, analysts must understand it. Furthermore, though they typically must focus their analyses on some small part of a complex reality, it is important to put that piece of reality into context. Considering focused analyses within the larger picture means policy researchers are less likely to oversimplify, to ignore important caveats, or to deliver information that does not correspond to the realities in which users *must operate*. The following section elaborates how this critical border crossing between problem understanding and user reality is so important and how it can be effectively traversed.

On the Border: Where Problem and User Realities Meet

Coming up with useful policy research findings and recommendations depends as much on insightful assessment of the ability to use the findings as it does upon skills in analyzing the data itself. This requires understanding of user reality, in which there are inevitably "humans in the loop" (Hester and Adams, 2014, p. ix). People see problems from different points of view, they have different values, they have different degrees of tolerance for uncertainty—they will have different end goals in mind when they think about resolutions to complex problems. From an analyst's perspective, "even when we think we have it all figured out, humans enter the equation and blow it all apart" (Hester and Adams, 2014, p. ix). To provide a framework for thinking about the reality faced by intended users of policy research information, we will discuss the importance of issues that always accompany systems in which humans are agents.

This aspect of making policy research useful is not emphasized in most textbook discussions. It is, though probably unintentionally, left up to experience, a professional understanding that grows with time. Too often, in our experience, it becomes sink or swim. This section will introduce aspects of shared reality that persons in the problem environment and persons considering changing that environment see from different viewpoints. Specifically, we will begin with differing perspectives on "meaning," an essential feature of human understanding, the ability to communicate, and the will and capacity to take collective action. The discussion will then turn to the contexts that both enable and limit policy making and implementation. Contexts will include stakeholders, institutional settings, the policy process, and the user information environment.

Meaning

If problem reality shapes input to the policy research process, user reality shapes the path to acceptance, discussion, and interpretation of that information input. In addition to providing *evidence* (e.g., facts about behaviors, conditions, events) through their data collection and analyses, policy researchers must give them *meaning* that intended users of the information can fit into their understanding and decision-making processes. In the words of a bygone TV detective, evidence is typically thought of as "the facts, ma'am, just the facts." But building evidence is more than just the facts. Facts must carry meaning to influence action.

This may seem evident, but meaning is a subtle and often challenging bridge between evidence and decisions to act. It can be one of the most difficult challenges to making evidence useful. Again, the policy challenges presented by climate change, for which there is so much evidence, are a prime example. Different understandings of nature strongly influence readiness to reduce human contributions to climate change. One view, what might be called an ecological perspective, is that humans have impacted the entire spectrum of nature from the running of its rivers to the chemistry of its plants and animals to the acidity of its seas. From this perspective, nature has irretrievably become part of human intention and action: "there is no more nature that stands apart from human beings" (Purdy, 2015, p. 2). From another point of view, nature is completely beyond human influence. There are a variety of positions in between. Facts about climate have different meaning with respect to human responsibility and action depending on where a person (e.g., decision maker, stakeholder) is or professes to be on this continuum.

In sum, facts are interpreted within meaning constructs (Schwartz-Shea and Yanow, 2012). Some of the elements of user meaning particularly important for policy researchers include assumptions, intentions, competitiveness, values, and worldviews. A brief discussion of each follows.

Assumptions

We have all heard the statement "assuming for the sake of argument." In academic discussion of a logical argument, this can be helpful so that the discussion can get to a particular point. However, when the objective is to provide useful information to deal with real problems, it is easy to overlook what is not said but is accepted as true as a premise for the argument. In policy research, it is important that unstated assumptions be transparent and that their implications for the credibility of the argument they underpin be considered.

All assumptions are conceptual in the sense that they are not *based in* new empirical information on the problem at hand. They are imported from past practice, theory, or analysis and used as a more or less credible starting point for a policy question. The careful policy researcher must consider and weigh two types of assumptions: those that frame the policy problem and those that guide the choice of the data and analysis most appropriate to solving the problem. We will address the former here; the latter is a topic for the section on researcher reality.

All potential solutions to policy problems will entail some assumptions necessary to simplify the unbounded complexity of reality. This is necessary to create starting points for understanding. In some cases, these assumptions are explicit and transparent. In others, they are not. Assumptions may be conceptual, involving theories concerning underlying "laws" of social processes. Examples might be assumptions about market mechanisms or other economic choice mechanisms that are important to many policy problems. In their insightful discussion of complexity and public policy, Colander and Kupers (2014, p. 31) distinguish between "pure laissez faire" economic assumptions in which government is seen as a "controller" and "activist laissez faire" in which government is seen as a "natural partner." These assumptions create different boundaries for legitimate and effective public action. Careful, unbiased analysis must at least make fundamental underlying assumptions transparent so they can be considered in the assessment of conclusions.

The more encompassing and formalized the conceptual assumptions, the more likely it is that additional assumptions will be embedded within the argument. These systems of logically connected but unsubstantiated assumptions are often found in political discourse as ideologies that have widely assumed credibility. For example, laissez-faire market assumptions are generally closer to a "complexity" (Colander and Kupers, 2014, p. 31) perspective, but a necessary *sub*assumption of "pure" laissez faire is that agents in the system make rational, individual utility-maximizing choices and that adequate information is available to do that. Many embedded assumptions persist because they are part of widely accepted understandings of reality, often of long standing. They may have once corresponded more closely with reality but become much less empirically verifiable over time. For example, embedded assumptions in pure laissez-faire thinking are clearly less applicable in the anthropocene. The implications of unrealistic assumptions may have some heuristic "what if" value, but they are not well suited for practical lessons useful to practitioners.

Some assumptions will always be necessary in discussion of complex problems. The point is to be aware and on the lookout for the lurking assumptions that may lead to biased interpretation in designing or presenting research results. An important corollary for the policy researcher is to be transparent about the assumptions that lay the foundation for their view of the policy problem they perceive. A "user beware" approach that leaves known and important assumptions unidentified is not responsible policy research.

Intentions

In user reality, policy actions are meant to accomplish something. They are intentional. Policy research stakeholders have objectives they are working to achieve, and those intentions often differ. Some will see benefits from resolving the problem as it is framed, and some will see costs. Intentional agents in the user environment are also competitive and strategic. They will assess the actions of stakeholders who have different or opposite intentions and develop strategies and counterstrategies to gain influence in the decision-making environment. In the complex user environments of current policy making and implementation, the development of useful policy research will be enhanced if the policy research seeks to understand the interplay of supportive and competing intentions in problem and user realities. The agnotology vignette that follows provides an extreme and very influential example of competitive strategy in the policy problem and user environments that focuses on denying the credibility of policy-relevant evidence.

Agnotology and the Merchants of Doubt

What is agnotology? It is a new field of inquiry concerning culturally produced "zones of ignorance" (Bonneuil and Fressoz, 2016, p. 198), usually related to the conscious manipulation, distortion, or suppression of scientific evidence. This seemingly arcane field of study is important to user reality in applied policy research because the zones of ignorance are driven by intentional, competitive, humans in the loop that develop strategies to obfuscate and prevent use of thoughtful analysis of reality. These strategies can range from simple adversarial issues to complex policies impacting the health of whole populations and the welfare of future generations.

Simple Agnotology. An administrative magistrate asked advice on why expert witnesses (statisticians) came up with diametrically opposed conclusions based on statistically significant results of the same data. The case in question was whether a promotion test for firefighters was racially discriminatory. Test results placed firefighters on a ranked list largely in the order of their scores. The witness for the plaintiff found that the test was discriminatory based on the statistical significance criterion set by law; the witness for the defendant found it was not discriminatory. The explanation was the choice of statistical tests, which was not prescribed by law. The plaintiff's witness used both a "means test" and a "ranks test," which used more precise measures of score differences (raw scores and score rank) in calculating significance. The fire department's witness used a "pass or fail" test that compared test scores only on whether they were passing or failing. In neither case were the calculations wrong or the scores rigged; they made different (probably strategic) assumptions about the criterion that would encourage a decision favorable to their client.

Complex Agnotology. Policy regulations to protect public health provide high-stakes historic examples (Michaels, 2008) of obfuscating scientific evidence. The "tobacco strategy" RJ Reynolds and other tobacco giants initiated in 1979 is a particularly egregious and blatant example. The initiative included enlisting a cadre of lawyers, public relations experts, and even scientists "willing to hold the gun and pull the trigger" (Oreskes and Conway, 2010, p. 6). The strategy did fund some legitimate and important research and required that RJR have access to findings. Findings were then selectively used to keep alive the argument that there was no clear scientific evidence that tobacco causes cancer or other disease. This strategy focused on attacks on scientific findings. Many other efforts to influence policy have used strategies to obfuscate scientific evidence. These included blaming the messenger (accusing the Environmental Protection Agency of cooking the books on secondhand smoke health effects); creating a counternarrative concerning the ozone hole; and proactively sowing the seeds of doubt concerning the causes and consequences of acid rain—to name a few (Oreskes and Conway, 2010, p. 6). Undoubtedly, climate change is the most pervasive threat for which scientific evidence is being denied. All of the previous strategies are being employed, including direct attacks on climate scientists themselves. Climate scientists warning of global warming have been accused of collusion, incorrect interpretation of data, and even data fabrication.

Values

Values are clearly part of policy dialogue. Doing what is right, defending "American" values such as liberty or equality, or being responsible with taxpayers' dollars are examples of value-laden statements. They are often part of arguing for a particular policy objective or intention. The relation of values to scientific analysis, however, is murky. Not long ago, the "fact/value" dichotomy was widely discussed topic in philosophy of science or social science methods courses. Simply stated, the argument was that science can measure and prove empirical facts; it cannot prove value judgment (e.g., right or wrong). The implication was that the rightness or wrongness of a policy (or whether a policy did or did not represent more or less freedom or liberty, etc.) could not be analyzed. Only its empirical outcomes were subject to proof. For theory-based social science, this set a boundary around what could or could not be scientifically studied, but for applied policy researchers, the intention to create useful information that can support argument and implementation makes this strict boundary untenable. Policy researchers must grapple with values if they want their information to be useful.

The last several decades have seen a softening of the fact/value dichotomy throughout the social sciences (Putnam, 2002). Academic arguments for this change often hinge on the notion of "thick concepts" that have both empirical and judgmental components (Kirchin, 2013)—for example, words like "courageous," which carries positive valuation but only makes sense in particular factual contexts. In policy research, "effective" and "efficient" are examples. Efficient in terms of *what*? Effective in achieving *what*? These are the kinds of legitimate requests for clarification that make thick concepts empirically testable. The interweaving of facts and values is a big issue for policy researchers. Meaning in policy research is heavily value laden—no getting around it. Policy decision criteria themselves are typically thick. Appeals to values are often at the crux of strategies for advocating or opposing policies, bringing tangential but difficult-to-oppose assumptions into the discussion.

There are three central issues that the policy researcher must keep in mind concerning values. First, pretending that "the facts, ma'am, *just* the facts" is a realistic boundary for policy research is an unreachable mirage. Second, an individual's values are not the primary issue in policy research. It is supporting, advancing, or revising shared values that form the values core of public policy. It is innate in our public policy system that making policy involves weaving a fabric of shared values—*tough stuff!* Third, given the first two points, the policy researcher must engage the task of unearthing and disentangling value assumptions, intended or not, that are part of a policy problem. If they are important to problem understanding, shine a light on them. If they are important to determining criteria for policy choice, make that clear. The need is to embed value meaning into a larger fabric that will hold relevance for a substantial group of people and help drive collective action.

Culture

Culture is an increasingly important consideration in an increasingly multicultural nation like the United States. Cultural sensitivity, cultural competence, and cultural acceptance are all nuanced needs for building effective and shared policies across cultures. This is incredibly important to the policy researcher trying to facilitate society's ability to improve policies and practices and better achieve social goals. It is clearly related to the "larger fabric of value meaning" identified in our discussion of values and their relation to policy research. Culture is encompassing, emphasizing the connections between meanings, emotional and creative expression, behavior, and social institutions. It is a concrete expression of complexity in daily life. Like all expressions of complexity, multicultural societies offer richness of experience and foster creativity—a strong celebration of a country that takes pride in being a melting pot. They can also pose policy challenges; witness the struggles for civil rights that accompany social progress. Citizens may recoil from accepting and understanding other cultures and long for the simplicity and certainty of a single, unquestioned cultural norm. We see a repeating lesson here: seeking simplicity is often avoiding or even fearing reality.

Again, an example may help articulate the importance of culture as a pervasive expression of complexity—an important but challenging concern for policy research. Cultural competency is a particular concern of decision makers and implementers in designing, adapting, or implementing educational or behavioral programs for youth from different cultural communities. The concerns are several. First, policy implementers are concerned about outreach and program access for youth from diverse cultures. Cultural concepts of family and child rearing may, for example, generate skepticism about "outsider" input to these issues. Cultural context may also have important implications for the degree to which a program is able to achieve its objectives for youth. To what extent do intervention messages or services have to be tailored to specific cultures in order to be effective? The high-risk youth (HRY) culturally specific programming example shows how one study engaged this problem, with a potentially useful result.

Are Culturally Specific Programs More Effective?

The National Cross-Site Evaluation of High Risk Youth Programs (see Chapter 10) was designed to generate lessons about effective substance abuse prevention programs for youth in high-risk environments (SAMHSA, 2002). Of the forty-eight programs that were included in this quasi-experimental study, half emphasized culturally specific programming appropriate to their participant populations. The study included more than 10,000 youth from 12 to 18 years of age. Ten study programs served African-American youth; five served Hispanic/Latino youth; five served American Indian Youth; and four served Asian youth. Examination of the content of these programs identified two major components of cultural specificity. The first was incorporation of culturally specific ambiance and tradition (e.g., posters, food, clothing, recreational activities). The second component was a focus on the ways in which protective factors (beliefs and behaviors associated with preventing drug abuse, such as positive self-concept) were specifically manifest in their culture.

Statistical comparisons between study youth in each cultural group in culturally specific programs and those in nonspecific programs produced new information about the effectiveness of culturally specific programs (Springer, Sale, et al., 2004). First, youth in culturally specific programs were more engaged with the program. They were significantly more satisfied and saw the program as more important and meaningful to their lives than youth of their same culture in nonspecific programs. Differences were statistically significant for all five cultural groups. Findings concerning reduced initiation or continuance of substance use (alcohol, marijuana, and tobacco) were different across cultural groups. Youth in culturally specific programs did report less substance use than those in other programs for all cultural groups, but effects were significantly larger for programs that emphasized the second component of culturally specific programming identified earlier. The most successful were programs using the African-American Kwanzaa program that "brought a coherent approach to program activities that combined cultural content with positive identity, skills development, positive social norms, and other recognized protective factors with respect to substance abuse" (Springer et al., 2004, p. 21). These analyses provided lessons that practitioners could adapt to their own cultural context. They also demonstrated the importance of policy researcher awareness and creativity in engaging the complexity of culture.

Culture is typically thought of in terms of national, religious, or other demographically defined populations (e.g., youth culture). However, the term applies to any identifiable group that develops shared and recognized values, norms, understandings, and behaviors. Organizations, professions—any durable and relatively institutionalized group—can develop a culture. While there is a whole literature on organizational culture, for instance, the definitional and functional details are not of particular importance to the policy researcher. As one author put it, in commonsense terms, culture refers to "how things are done around here." Part of the creativity required of the applied analyst is determining what "ways things are done" matter (if any) and why.

While culture includes values, basic beliefs, habits of behavior, and other things that are seen as attributes of individuals, culture itself is an emergent group quality. The "culture" then becomes a systemic concept that influences the behavior of individuals that are "nested" within it. It is an example of how porous the boundaries within complex systems can be. It is also a segue to our next section, which focuses on elements more clearly within the user context.

User Reality

The utility of policy research information is strongly influenced by characteristics of the environment in which potential users work. Important contextual factors influencing the capability of policy makers and implementers to use policy research information and recommendations include stakeholders, the institutional environment, and the availability of necessary resources. If use of policy research in the decision process is the goal, information must be delivered in a form that conforms to the capacity to use it. This capacity will be shaped by the preferences, strategies, and influences of stakeholder groups, by the decision processes and criteria in the institutional environment, and by the information perspectives of individual users.

Stakeholders

Stakeholders are a major part of user reality. In a broad sense, stakeholders are any person, group, or organization that has an interest in another organization or policy—in our case, the organization or policy that is the subject of policy research. Why are stakeholders important for policy research? Simply put, it is because they organize and articulate the various differences in perspective, meaning, and intention that will compete in the decision environment. Anticipating these positions helps policy researchers produce and present information that cannot be dismissed out of hand.

Individuals are stakeholders in the sense of being impacted positively or negatively by policies and their implementation, but individuals work most powerfully through organizations to influence policy decisions. There is no question about whether organized stakeholders (often referred to as "interests") actually are involved in policy decisions and implementation. However, there are great disagreements about when or whether this involvement is helpful or harmful. Witness disagreement over the impact that "Wall Street" interests have on fiscal and economic policy or the influence of environmental interests. Within this jostling for influence, distinctions between different categories of stakeholders may help the policy researcher identify which stakeholders are important to a particular problem, and how.

- *Primary stakeholders* are those that may be directly affected by a policy. Beneficiaries receive direct positive effects, such as homebuyers in mortgage deduction tax policies, or the economically disadvantaged or chronically ill under the Affordable Care Act. Other primary stakeholders may feel that a policy, program, or service will hurt them directly, such as members of the energy industry subject to Environmental Protection Agency regulations.

- *Secondary stakeholders* are those that may indirectly benefit from or be negatively affected by a policy or action. For example, emergency room staff may indirectly benefit from the Affordable Care Act if it reduces overuse of ER services; patients in true need of emergency care may also benefit from improved care. Private insurance salespersons may lose employment opportunities through increased use of online exchanges to purchase more insurance options under the Act.
- *Advocacy stakeholders* are those who have an interest and position with respect to particular policy areas, but they may not directly or indirectly benefit other than seeing a position they believe in gain policy support. Environmental groups, prolife and other social issue position advocates, early childhood issues advocates, and many more public interest groups are examples.
- *Key stakeholders* are those who are most able to influence decision making and implementation in a given policy area. Key stakeholders may be primary or secondary, beneficiaries, or those who feel harmed. Their influence is clearly on a sliding scale, and it is impacted by many contextual factors.

Strong stakeholder influence is often seen as undemocratic or even corrupt. An extreme version of policy "capture" by key stakeholders is the "iron triangle" of (1) key stakeholders with strong direct (usually economic) interests in a policy area; (2) Congress or other law-making groups (e.g., state legislators); and (3) governmental agencies, particularly those making regulatory decisions. The dynamics of the system involves money, information, and lobbying in a symbiotic relation to laws, regulations, programs, and procurements beneficial to the interests. This symbol of captured government for the benefit of the few is the stuff of great investigative journalism (Briody, 2003) and a challenging playing field for policy research. The merchants of doubt introduced in the agnotology example are frequent agents in the iron triangle.

Though the visible image of stakeholders—evident in media stories, political rhetoric, and critical analyses—often focuses on powerful pursuit of self-interest, the presence of organized interests of all types is central to the user environment in a participatory, pluralist democracy. They are particularly important to promoting a clean environment, healthy food, adequate public infrastructure, and other public goods that affect everyone. Organized stakeholders are also particularly important for representing the interests of high-need groups such as young children, cultural minorities, the homeless, and others without political power. A study of the benefits of stakeholder participation has shown that participatory involvement of stakeholders in policy deliberation strengthens the amount and quality of information considered in decisions, broadens the different perspectives considered in deliberations, and makes decisions more likely to concern long range needs as opposed to short-term concerns about feasibility (Bijlsma et al., 2011).

For a policy researcher trying to develop information that can be effectively used, it is important to remember that "stakeholders can help or hinder . . . efforts to solve a policy problem, so at the very least, you'll need to understand their views" (Majchrzak and Markus, 2014, p. 29). As part of understanding the user reality in which findings must be useful, it is important to map out the degree of influence and issue positions of major stakeholders (Majchrzak and Markus, 2014, pp. 29–32). This map should begin with "focal" stakeholders surrounding the decision points in the policy process for which the policy research information is most clearly intended. For example, is the intended information for a particular local governmental unit, state unit, or federal unit? Within this *focal unit* (Majchrzak and Markus, 2014, p. 29), who are the most important direct and indirect beneficiaries? Who are the key stakeholders in the focal unit? What will their positions most likely be? Are there important stakeholders outside the focal unit? For example, if the focal unit is a local school district, are there state or federal agencies, interest groups such as teachers' unions, or other interests "up the hierarchy" that may be influential? On the other hand, are there stakeholders at lower layers within the local district environment that will be important? Examples here might be individual school PTAs, school service providers, or community interest groups. In sum, developing information and deciding how to deliver it should anticipate the information needs and interpretations of the stakeholders that will be involved in or be considered in the decision process. To do this effectively, stakeholder points of view must be incorporated into understanding user reality.

Before we move on, it is important to note that for policy researchers, not all stakeholders are created equal. *Applied* (as distinct from academic) policy research is almost always client based—requested and paid for by an interest or institution for a specific purpose. Client based implies that the goal of policy research is to serve the expressed needs of the person or agency who has requested the information. Policy researchers must bear in mind that *"the ability to respond to information needs of others is a central skill in policy research"* (Putt and Springer, 1989, p. 80, emphasis added). The principle to remember is: *successful policy research begins with and depends upon recognizing the information needs of the client.*

Institutions

"Institutions are the kinds of structures that matter most in the social realm: they make up the stuff of social life" (Hodgson, 2006, p. 2). Policy research information is most often applied within and between complex institutions. In the most encompassing terms, "we may define *institutions* as systems of established and prevalent social rules that structure social interactions" (Hodgson, 2006, p. 2). These institutions come in different forms. Most obvious are the *organizations* in which social agents work. These include public agencies, businesses from multinational corporations to mom-and-pop small businesses, nonprofit organizations meeting a broad range of service and advocacy activities, and less formal organizations such as coalitions, councils, and associations. Less apparent but no less important are service and regulatory institutions such as legislation, criminal law, contract law, the court system, the financial and tax systems, and consensual behavioral norms.

Institutions have the recognizable features of complexity that define both the problem and user terrains. They tend to have hierarchical architecture, with lots of interconnections, and are, at different rates, dynamic. "Modern societies display a multiplicity of institutional terrains, with most actors involved in many of them simultaneously" (Room, 2011, p. 73). What is crucial to our topic is that, in whatever form "[I]nstitutions articulate and enforce rules of interaction; . . . shape the patterns of action and group formation that typically emerge; and . . . (shape) the organization of competence and knowledge that can then be deployed" (Room, 2011, p. 66). They are fundamental to the capacity of decision makers or implementers to use policy research information.

Importantly, institutions are diverse in the degree and rigidity with which they set and regulate the interactions of actors within and across nested and overlapping boundaries (Room, 2011, pp. 67–74). Scholars focusing on institutional implications for policy research have identified different types of institutional regulation and identified implications for actor strategies, interactions, and cooperation (Scharpf, 1997, pp. 39–40). For example, institutions have been distinguished by "agent sensitivity," meaning the degree to which the actions of actors (e.g., leaders, members, groups) are constrained by institutional environments and context. Put differently, to what degree are decisions and outputs determined by institutional constraints, and how much are they determined by participants within the institution (Hodgson, 2006, p. 16)? Before we get too deep in the haze of abstraction, read the SS/HS Revisited example in what follows. It relates agent sensitivity to the Safe Schools/Healthy Students analysis presented earlier in this chapter.

SS/HS Revisited

One policy research objective in the Safe Schools/Healthy Students (SS/HS) initiative is to identify where meaningful (policy or resource) collaborative decision making took place in the hierarchical institutional structure of coalitions at state and district levels. These coalitions had complex membership patterns across and within institutional sectors and organizations. The coalitions also had internal work group differentiation (along similar lines because of similar grant and outcome responsibilities) that had distinct decision-making roles. Comparative analysis of these decision settings revealed a pattern of institutional constraints related to agent sensitivity measured as the relative ability of collaborative groups to make meaningful decisions. Despite the expectation that creating a state coalition would be a central component in taking SS/HS program principles to scale statewide, the state steering committees had the lowest emphasis on meaningful decision making (decision/deliberation ratio of .26) among the six different coalition meeting settings examined in the study. Membership in this setting was heavily driven by grant requirements for sector representation, the expectation that members "high up" in the organization would be most productive, and the assumption that participants had sufficient authority to make decisions. Closer examination of state law and institutional constraints indicated, outside the resources and authority stemming directly from the federal SS/HS grant, most of the sector agents had little discretion to make policy decisions. The setting with the greatest reported focus on policy-related decision making was the community-level member group meetings (decision/deliberation ratio of .69). These groups were largely self-constituted by collaborators, composed of supervisory and staff-level personnel, and focused on making changes in the way local service systems worked. They are working within areas they understand well and in which they have sufficient discretion to agree to changes in the way things are done. In a word, their environment is more agent sensitive. With respect to the SS/HS program, this analysis informs improved understanding of institutional contexts in which collaborative empowerment is likely to be most productive in making decisions. For policy researchers, it reinforces the importance of including context in any analysis of activities in institutions.

Institutions are critically important environments for understanding the user environment. They set rules, expectations, resource availability and resource control, and other critical opportunities and constraints in the user environment. Yet policy research often neglects the pervasive contextual importance of institutions, focusing on anticipated links between problems and interventions (programs and activities) without sufficient consideration of how they are shaped by the institutional environment. Being real about the user environment requires a resetting of this frequent imbalance.

Individual Users

Stakeholder interests and activities help define political considerations in user reality; institutions channel and constrain the available opportunities to access and use information. A third critical component of policy research information use is the "personal factor" (Springer, 1985, p. 492). Part of the challenge of producing useful policy research is to understand decision-maker capacity for, and motivation to, use policy research information in their work. This challenge is exacerbated by the reality that "the 'use' of policy analysis means different things to different people" (Springer, 1985, p. 491). So in scanning user reality, the policy researcher may find it important to consider the perspectives and capacity of users to act on information.

The ways in which data is interpreted and presented may significantly affect its utility for people who are in a position to use it to make public decisions. The reasons are many. First, most public decision makers are not social scientists. They are not formally trained to understand or interpret data. In a consulting experience of one of the authors, the client was a hearing officer in an administrative law court. The consulting task was to explain to the hearing officer how differing technical experts for two sides of a case could arrive at opposite conclusions using the same data. At one point in the proceedings, the judge burst out with frustration, "Please use plain language, I haven't studied mathematics since high school." The point was clear: the judge, who had the responsibility for making the decision in the case, was not technically competent to weigh the differing interpretations of the information. This is often the case in public decision making.

Second, public decision makers often have an intuitive insight into the limitations of the data in their raw form. Public policy is multifaceted. People have varying interests in the outcome of a single policy, and data will most often reflect only some of these interests. Decision makers may sense that the question being answered is not necessarily the one in which they are most interested. Decision makers are often aware of the complexity of the context in which policy is being implemented, and social science methodology (particularly quantitative technique) may not reflect the comprehensive and encompassing concerns of the decision makers and their constituency.

Third, decision makers are often interested in what might be called the human side of research findings. They often want to know how a general pattern of findings (e.g., increased earnings for participants in a workforce development program) translates into real life stories. For example, a statistically significant aggregate increase in income may not make a meaningful difference in the actual quality of life for participants. Indeed, in some instances, the trade-offs in terms of lost medical benefits, requirements for child care out of the home, and other costs may actually produce a reduction in the quality of life for the participants even though they show a statistical improvement in nonassisted income levels. The full human implications of study impacts may not be evident in the data itself.

Fourth, public decision makers are busy people with many demands upon their time. They may not have the time or the inclination to study policy research data closely and draw their own interpretations. In short, they need intermediary assistance between the data and their interest in the data. They need an analyst to interpret the data according to their perspective and interest and to tell them what this data says given their concerns and priorities. This process of translating raw findings or information into meaningful results is the process of transforming data to information, knowledge, and wisdom.

Researcher Reality

A central theme in this chapter is that the problems with which policy researchers are presented arise from a combination of real-world events and the perceptions, capabilities, and opportunities of the agents who are trying to solve them. The extent to which policy research is a success depends on the degree to which it facilitates agent actions that successfully resolve or ameliorate the problem. As the practice of policy research has evolved, it has depended largely on the applicability and credibility of science, frequently social science, to validate the value of their input. Unfortunately, reality intervenes and renders the relation of *applied* policy research to *theory-based* (i.e., academic or "pure") research inexact. This puts the policy researcher in an unfortunate position. The tools they use for data collection, analysis, and interpreting findings are drawn from science, yet they are applied in a setting that does not fully allow the procedural methods or criteria of science. Attaining relevance, let alone credibility, in the problem and user realities we have just sketched is more like arguing in a courtroom than conducting an experiment in a laboratory. "Beyond a reasonable doubt" is a more realistic criterion than "statistical significance," "replicable results," or other theory-based research criteria.

In this section, we address major challenges of the realistic terrain that policy researchers must traverse to reach the objective of producing applicable information and knowledge. To do this, we begin with a sketch of the kinds of challenges that problem and user realities pose for the policy researcher. These are not exactly the kinds of technical issues that are typically stressed in the professional education of policy researchers, but they are critical to policy researchers' success at their craft. First is a perspective on types of research problems given the complexity and human involvement in the real-world problem context described earlier. Second is the relation between these problem types and the *technical* complexity of policy research. Third is the relation between problem types and the *behavioral* complexity of policy research.

Problems, Messes, and Wicked Messes

Not all problems are created equal. Our daily experience tells us that some problems are easily defined, with potentially straightforward solutions. Let's say, what shall we have for dinner? Others are inherently complex, requiring information and consideration of alternatives to resolve. We also know that, depending on exact intentions, problems can be made more or less complex. Dinner decisions become much more difficult if the intention is to cook a healthy, gourmet meal on a limited budget. It can tick further up on the complexity scale if the in-laws are coming for dinner.

What does this have to do with policy research? Everything! While mapping the problem terrain, we provided a low-resolution overview, emphasizing the complexity of the reality from which problems emerge. We pointed out that this terrain shapes the problems that emerge in policy deliberation and that what is or is not a problem can be viewed from many different perspectives. While a full awareness of the reality from which problems emerge is critically important, policy researchers do not need to, indeed cannot, analyze problems in their full complexity. They must define a policy research perspective that is useful for addressing the essential actionable features of the real-world problem, feasible within available tools and resources, and avoids unintended negative consequences. Examination of that question "is where you really start the policy research process: by starting to frame the policy research question and then iteratively getting more and more precise about the question so that it can be addressed by existing evidence" (Majchrzak and Markus, 2014, p. 20).

Tame and Messy Problems

Figure 2.2 outlines a set of distinctions that are increasingly used to discuss the characteristics of problems and their analysis. The distinction between problems and messes dates from the late 1970s, when it was recognized that the assumptions of system simplicity implicit to most policy research (and other applied analysis disciplines) at the time were "mathematically sophisticated but contextually naïve" (Hughes and Hughes,

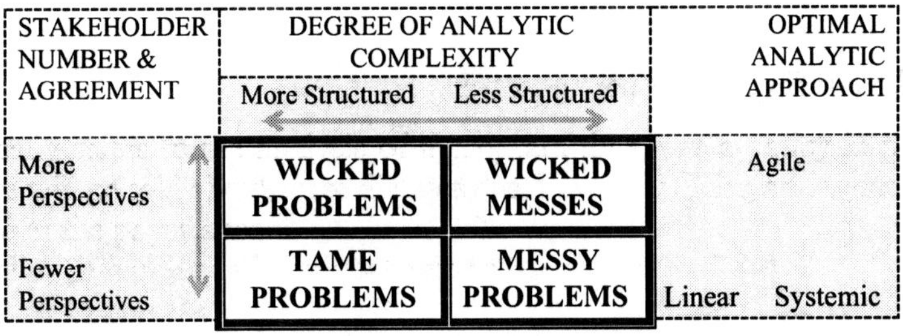

STAKEHOLDER NUMBER & AGREEMENT	DEGREE OF ANALYTIC COMPLEXITY		OPTIMAL ANALYTIC APPROACH
	More Structured ←——————→ Less Structured		
More Perspectives ↑	**WICKED PROBLEMS**	**WICKED MESSES**	Agile
Fewer Perspectives ↓	**TAME PROBLEMS**	**MESSY PROBLEMS**	Linear Systemic

Figure 2.2 Problems, Messes, and Implications for Analysis

2011). The distinction between tame problems and messy problems is technical. Research design and analysis (e.g., statistical) procedures are readily available for tame problems. They are relatively "simple" in being static, having relatively few variables, few connections between variables that require analysis, a single perspective framing the problem (e.g., theory, conceptual map), and no important contextual effects. As the attributes of complexity become more and more present in problem definition—that is, more variables, more connections, less linearity, more contextual effects, and more dynamism—the problem becomes messier and messier.

Another way of saying this is that tame problems are "well structured" and messy problems are "ill structured." One optimal (best) solution may be a reasonable expectation for a well-structured problem. Multiple suboptimal solutions are the norm for ill-structured problems. This means there may be several solutions that could be preferable depending on other circumstances in the system. Let's return to our "what's for dinner?" example. As long as it is just the cook, this problem can be very tame. What do I like, what ingredients are in the house, how much time do I have? As conditions get more complex, additional considerations come into play, such as making ingredients last to reduce cost (use half the chicken tonight, half tomorrow night), cooking something healthy, doing something quick, and not making a mess because friends are dropping by after dinner and we don't know exactly when—it gets messy. Think of the terms used to describe these problems—tame and messy, well structured and ill structured. Which type of structuring do you think would be preferred by most potential problem solvers? Which do you think is most often faced by applied policy researchers? Therein lies the rub, or at least part of it.

For policy researchers, the choice of differential approaches to addressing problems and messes is largely technical. The number of variables being measured, the number of connections being tested, and the relative simplicity of the logic behind connections or even root causes allows application of formalized research techniques, typically quantitative, with accepted decision rules about strength of evidence, such as statistical significance, can be applied. As identified in Figure 2.2, this analysis approach is often referred to as "linear," meaning it proceeds in sequential steps with resolutions at one level being a foundation for the next. This approach to definitive solutions has also been called "waterfall" analysis (Royce, 1970) or "machine age" (Hester and Adams, 2014, p. 25). As problem definition moves toward the messy end, challenges of measurement and analysis increase. Technical advances in meeting challenges have increased with development of multivariate and hierarchical statistical techniques. In addition, "systems methods and modeling, focusing on processes, and interdisciplinary approaches" (Hancock, 2004, p. 38) have helped. The appropriate analysis perspective is most frequently referred to as "systemic." The strengths and limitations of the contribution of linear or systemic perspectives on applied policy research projects is a primary theme in Chapter 3.

Wicked Problems and Wicked Messes

Wicked problems and wicked messes share technical distinctions with tame and messy problems, but they add a heavy dose of humans in the loop. These are problems in which human intentions contribute to their formation; the desire for problem resolution, or not; different understandings of what is actually problematic, why, and how it came about; and different, often conflicting preferences for resolution. The fact that wicked problems and wicked messes are works in progress means they are dynamic—on the move. Wickedness of this type raises particular difficulties for applying analysis designs and tools developed for tame problems. And these designs and tools constitute most standard practice in the policy analysis profession. For example, the experimental model has long been identified as the gold standard of program evaluation design, with the goal of "proving" the effectiveness of programs and practices. As we will explore in Chapter 3, it is not safe to assume this gold standard applies in a wicked, Bitcoin world.

Consider how our dinner problem, once so simple, could progress from just messy to wickedly messy. The first step toward wickedness is the addition of more stakeholders. Let's say that in addition to the in-laws as guests, one of the host partners has a sister who will be coming with the family. She is a vegetarian, while dad-in-law loves meat and potatoes. Oh, and the sister has two children, notoriously finicky eaters. All the guests are rabid local team fans, and the game may linger on through dinner—the formal room is out, but the political argument may be avoided! We could go on, but the wickedness is evident. More stakeholders, more diversity in desired outcomes, blurring of clear intent (from good, affordable, healthy food to ensuring a good time, covering different tastes, avoiding conflict), uncertainty and change (how long will the game last? will the kids get bored?); and defining multiple suboptimal solutions (separate food for the kids, buffet-style serving, informal seating, choices in food to meet different tastes). Of course, this all wreaks havoc with the technical questions (e.g., groceries, cooking, and setting the table).

For policy researchers, the degree of wickedness in a problem stems from behavioral and dynamic complexity (Hancock, 2004) as distinct from simply technical issues. It relates directly to intention, strategy, and values that are an undeniable but complicating (and sometimes frustrating) part of that reality. As exemplified in the example presented that follows, policy problems related to the definition, supply, and management of public goods (e.g., environmental issues, transportation, education) are prime examples of potentially wicked messes.

Public Goods and Wicked Messes

Policy decisions about public goods are a prime field for contexts with wicked characteristics. Public goods are classically defined as goods that can only be shared. A lighthouse is a classic example, suggesting the age of the concept. Once built, a lighthouse is "non-exclusionary" (it is visible to any ship within sight), and it is "non-rivalrous" (ships in the area cannot compete over a view or sell it). Classically, it could be argued that private goods (exclusionary and rivalrous in character), such as a loaf of bread, are the province of the free market, and public goods require public regulation and political decisions on production and distribution. Of course, it is not that simple. A road on which everyone can drive is a public good requiring public decisions, unless it is a toll road. Television news is a public good, unless it is delivered over cable. The growing importance of public goods or the public goods perspective on commodities (air quality, water quality, education, information, healthy food, mosquito abatement) is a big reason that policy researchers must be increasingly aware of and agile at addressing complexity. The pace of technology changes classic definitions of public goods in several ways, such as ways to make public "technologically" private. Cable TV is a realized example; elite citizens living in environmentally healthy domed cities is a science fiction example. These are fascinating, challenging, and important policy problems that are part of policy researcher reality.

The analysis problem posed by public goods cannot be solved through modeling the entire wicked mess to allow a purely technical solution. Generally, it is becoming recognized that the productive approach to analysis of wicked messes must be *agile*. The agile analysis idea emerged primarily in software engineering and development of software systems that met the needs of consumers in wickedly messy situations. Seventeen innovators in software development got together in 2001, created the *Agile Manifesto*, and launched a project-management approach that places priority on a product that is useful to the user, a process that values communication and consumer (stakeholder) involvement over formal procedure, and an emphasis on responsiveness to change. While the agile concept was developed by software engineers, it has clear application to the policy researcher facing wicked messes.

To realize these priorities, agile processes have distinguishing features. They "explore and illuminate the problem space" (Iyer, 2006) by focusing on the project stakeholders' needs for problem resolution and emphasize shared understanding of these needs among project participants. Agile analysis is incremental and iterative, meaning that it recognizes that wicked messes are not going to be resolved in one fell swoop. The agile project manager will be able to prioritize achievable "chunks" of the problem, anticipate their interconnections with other parts, conduct analyses to inform solutions for the component being addressed, and pass on lessons for the next iteration in an ongoing process. In other words, the agile process allows identification of what needs to be done first, including informed compromise among stakeholders when necessary. Another trait of agile analysis is that it should be *communication rich and highly interactive*. Analysts need to be transparent about their procedures and activities and include stakeholders in the project decision-making and analysis process. Personal interaction, in person or facilitated through conference calls or virtual meetings, is important because it enriches the exchange. Finally, agile analysis generates products that are "just good enough" (Iyer, 2006) to provide solid guidance for action. Remember that the environment for determining utility of the product is more like a courtroom than a laboratory. Functionality, not proven truth, is the agile analysis objective.

As noted, agile analysis has become a buzz in IT and business environments. For policy researchers—not so much. Why is this? The priorities and traits identified in the preceding paragraphs are certainly consistent with the problems that policy researchers face, particularly if the priority is information products that can and will be used. The need for agile priorities and traits has been identified and argued for by some policy researchers. We believe that the lack of buzz in policy research circles is due to some persistent points of view. First and most pervasive, it is clear that agile analysis is as much about managing an analysis process as it is about technique. Policy researchers have not focused on the interconnection of project process and analysis technique in shaping a useful product. It wasn't that long ago that "objectivity" was seen as a primary policy research value that could be best ensured by the "independence" of the analyst. In the agile analysis framework, isolating the analyst and limiting idea sharing with the client is a very bad idea. Agile policy researchers will see interaction with stakeholders as an essential part of their role. It will help them better understand client intentions and incorporate them into research design and implementation.

A second reason that agile analysis is sometimes viewed askance is the sanctity of the scientific method (emphasis on method) in the policy research tradition. It has served as a rock of credibility and objectivity, allowing the analyst to claim authority through conformity to method. This haven is often used even when, unfortunately, credibility is purchased at the cost of relevance to reality.

Taming Problem Reality

A key issue for policy researchers is redefining a problem in a way that is feasible for analysis and action while keeping it relevant to problem reality as we have discussed it. It is clear that policy researchers must define a problem that can be "worked"—that is on which data can be gathered and analyzed to answer questions relevant to the real-world circumstance. The primary criteria have usually focused on *how to define the problem in a way that will meet the requirements of analysis logic and technique rather than how to shape analysis to conform to the real-world problem*. For example, a director of evaluation for a division within the U.S. Department of Health and Human Services once told one of the authors, "I cannot tell if this program worked or not if your evaluation does not include a valid comparison group." From a different perspective, we sometimes hear skeptics dismiss statistical results because "people lie with statistics." The first opinion errs on the side of insisting on rules of analytic method; the second errs in dismissing the contribution of analytic method.

A major premise in this text is that the policy researcher must achieve a *balance* between rigorous technique and information that actually helps policy practitioners make decisions and take action. This requires posing research questions that are relevant within the decision-making context—that is, research questions that recognize what is feasible within the constraints of the context and that address the policy objectives that are held by relevant decision makers.

Figure 2.3 provides a high-level graphic depiction of three major tightropes on which the policy researcher must maintain balance between the typical complexities of reality and the understandability and action orientation that comes with taming a problem through structure and logic. Part of the policy researcher's contribution to information is this

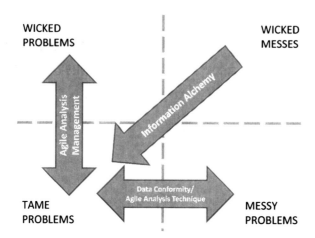

Figure 2.3 Balancing Problem Reality and Solution Usability

thoughtful simplification. The balance is to tame the messiness and wickedness of problems without losing relevance and utility to the real world. Before going into detail on the graphic, some big-picture discussion will be helpful. The three arrows in Figure 2.3 represent those tightropes the policy researcher must walk.

A client may make a request for analysis that is already tame. In these cases, the issue for the policy researcher is to do a reality check that ensures this problem has not been rendered largely irrelevant to its intended need. This is a tricky but not infrequent circumstance in policy research. If the request does not have reasonable correspondence to the real-world situation, the task is to point out assumptions or simplifications in the request that need more careful consideration, if feasible. More often, the major task for the policy researcher is to tame a complex problem to make it more solvable, understandable, and useful. Agile analysis will help balance technical and systems approaches appropriate to the level of complexity (messiness) in a problem. Agile management is necessary to promote interaction and considered accommodation of stakeholder positions and other meaning-related facets of more or less complex problems (Cobb, 2015). Information alchemy is necessary to meet the policy researcher's responsibility to maintain relevance to important elements of messiness and wickedness in problem reality *while generating and delivering* technically credible and sociopolitically usable information relevant to problem resolution.

A completely detailed discussion of Figure 2.3 is beyond the scope of this section, so we will elaborate briefly on the points made earlier and foreshadow upcoming chapters in which more detail is provided. Policy makers and implementers cannot avoid the messy and wicked elements of problem reality; they live within them. Policy researchers can and often do retreat into the relative safety of tame problems and technical solutions. This can allow a claim of authority through conformity to method. This haven may be used unintentionally; credibility may be unwittingly purchased at the cost of relevance to reality. To avoid this, the skillful policy researcher must do the work to understand the real-world problem. This problem awareness is a prerequisite to achieving balance. It is the positive kernel of truth that is missed in the old joke that a consultant is someone who asks you for your watch to tell you what time it is. The skillful policy analyst cannot assume that what the client says they want will meet their actual needs. They may not really know what time it is.

It is important that the policy researcher develops an overall understanding of the problem as it is emerging from the sometimes wicked, nearly always messy real world. The diagonal arrow represents this underlying theme. It relates directly to a core component of policy researcher reality—the need to perform information alchemy (Eisenberg, 2012). Information alchemy is the process of transforming raw data into understandable information and using analysis and application to move further into understanding and knowledge. Chapters 3 and 4 will provide greater detail on how policy researchers can stir technical competence, problem awareness, and user understanding with agility to accomplish information alchemy.

The analyst's need to balance technical competence with relevance to the technically challenging information needs of messy problems was depicted in Figure 2.3. Policy researchers are sought primarily for their technical expertise and credibility. It follows that technical competence is the exclusive bailiwick of the analyst in many circumstances, and the responsibility to make these decisions with care and competence is high. Consumers of the information will not question the policy analyst's choice of techniques in most instances because they are not trained in these technical areas. However, they may question conclusions when they do not turn out as hoped. Chapters 3 and 4 will focus on how policy researchers can balance problem understanding and technical competence with agility. This requires the skill to select tools for collecting data that conforms to problem reality and user need. It also requires the analytic agility to select appropriate analysis techniques to meet user information needs in complex decision realities. Chapter 4 in particular addresses the process of articulating and selecting the analytic chunks that have priority in a given problem setting.

The vertical arrow represents balancing the analytic advantages of a static, simple, and agreed-on problem and a wicked problem environment that is dynamic, complex, and seen from multiple perspectives. The management and stakeholder interaction skills necessary to facilitating this balance are important skills for policy researchers. Balancing agreement on problem definition and stakeholder intentions necessary to support feasible analysis requires these skills. Policy research that places the discovery of objective facts as the priority draws a line between the determination and shaping of the research product and its implementation by practitioners. By contrast, agile analysis management sees the practitioner as a partner in shaping useful analysis products. Insistence that effective use of evidence-based programs depends on "fidelity" to "proven" interventions is an example of drawing this line. As we shall see in Chapter 5, fidelity is often seen as exact replication of a program that has been scientifically tested and found to produce the intended outcome. In its rigorous application, fidelity has been described as "delivery of a manualized . . . intervention program as prescribed by the program developer" (Castro, Barrera, and Martinez, 2004, p. 41). The notion of a "proven program" is a very formal application of a belief in the applicability of static analysis by researchers as the best blueprint for implementation decisions. It is also a clear (if unintended) implication that "adaptive" decisions by practitioners cannot be trusted to produce improvements in intervention effectiveness. Implications of strict fidelity standards for evidence-based practices will be discussed further in Chapter 4.

The suggestion that the use of policy research will be improved by thinking of the users themselves as part of the application decision process is an important if not novel idea. The strict fidelity standard outlined earlier implies that adaptation of tested programs to make them "responsive to the cultural needs of a local community" (Castro, Barrera, and Martinez, 2004, p. 41) would require multiple program evaluations across culturally diverse dimensions to test the elements of adaptation. The number and variety of contextual conditions that may block a program's effectiveness renders this approach to be not viable. Possible confounders of program effects include, at least, language, ethnicity, socioeconomic context, urbanicity, the relative presence of risk factors, characteristics of program staff, myriad community factors, and other factors of program context. Reality suggests another option. Studies should be designed that identify contextual factors important to program adaption, provide recommendations in the form of principles behind a program's effectiveness that should be maintained in adaptation, provide implementer training and information on how to make adaptation decisions, and empower implementers to make adaptation decisions in their program settings. Policy researchers and implementers are sequential team members in the applied policy research process, and a strong hand-off from researchers to implementers is a necessary objective.

How to empower implementers to make effective adaptation decisions is also a topic for Chapter 4. However, we should note that this is a point at which the artisan dimension of the policy researchers' role comes to the fore. Policy research findings will be more useful if they are developed with sensitivity to the roles and circumstances of the users, phrased with respect and empathy for their intentions and motivations, and formulated to recognize and rely on their competency and knowledge of the place, people, and time of application. It must trust them to translate the knowledge passed on by the research artisan into action. This cannot be done well without tapping into the artisan element of policy research, for both researchers and implementers. In his classic discussion of science and human values, Brounstein (1956, p. 94) alludes to the similarities of applying science and poetry's relation to values. "Poetry does not move us to be just or unjust. It moves us to thoughts in whose light justice and injustice are seen in fearful sharpness of outline." Policy research does not dictate the precisely correct decision or action. It gives the decision maker knowledge to more clearly see what to do.

In quick summary, this section has put forth the general argument that policy researchers must balance the frequently wicked messiness of real-world policy problems with the necessity of developing simplified models of these problems that permit analysis. To do this well, policy researchers must take care to identify the "right" questions most relevant to the need for real-world application. At the same time, they must identify the proper balance of technical precision and conformity with real-world understanding that will produce information that both is technically sound and conforms to realistic decision needs. These are major challenges and a delightful opportunity for creativity and learning. Chapters 3 and 4 provide a more systematic outline of the technical and interpersonal skills the policy researcher brings to this challenge.

Project Capacity and Resources

Policy research is not a one-person endeavor. As we have seen, policy problems and identifying their solutions are typically very complex undertakings. It has been observed that "the Boeing 777 is often described as four million parts flying in close formation. No single person—of the over 5,000 engineers who worked on it—have complete knowledge about how it all works" (Arias et al., 2000, p. 113). This is a revealing statement about the importance of human teamwork, what it can accomplish, and why it is essential for complex problem solving.

The simple lesson for persons entering into the policy research profession is that you will frequently be working in teams. As we will see, the cases in Part II vary widely in size and cost, but they all involve a team of colleagues. Teams typically include members who provide overall expertise and direction in the technical research (e.g., principal investigators, research directors); those specializing in project management (e.g., project directors); those with specific technical specialties (e.g., statisticians, data managers, qualitative specialists, IT specialists; production staff); research implementers (interviewers, research assistants); and product developers (e.g., writers, speakers, website developers). Furthermore, team members often are from different organizations and form project-specific work groups. This reality means that clear communication, collaboration, openness to other perspectives, meeting deadlines, being assertive when necessary, recognizing others' points of view, accepting the contributions of others—all of these teamwork skills and more—are crucial to produce usable policy research.

The resources available to policy researchers are almost always quite limited, and this often constricts the realistically available options. The bottom-line resource that first comes to mind is budget. However, appropriate expertise, necessary equipment (e.g., computers), and an organizational environment that encourages creativity are other examples of resources that are critically important and can lessen a reliance on budget as the difference maker. Frequently, the "perfect" or most desirable approach to analyzing a policy or program may be unavailable to policy researchers due to a lack of available resources. For example, an evaluation of a statewide program with sites across a state may call for site visits to every site. Yet travel and staff time to support this activity may be too expensive. Policy researchers must frequently compromise ideal data quality and amount to stay within the limitations of their resources. This reality places an even greater premium on the policy researcher creativity that is a primary theme in the next chapter.

Reality Check

An academic researcher seeking to make contributions to scientific knowledge provides a review of existing scientific theory and literature to identify the increment of knowledge their work may be contributing. On the other hand, an applied policy researcher seeks to make contributions to decisions and actions that will ameliorate public problems. To create a solid foundation for this contribution, policy researchers need to review the problem, user, and researcher realities of each specific project they launch. Figure 2.4 is a high-level summary of the flow of issues that should be included in that reality check. The figure summarizes major complexities in problem reality that will impact problem understanding, potential solutions, and how the policy researcher will frame the problem environment to best address it. That problem environment will include meaning-related issues and dynamics that will link the full complexity of the problem to the user context. The mix of problem and user complexities creates research problems that range from tame to wickedly messy, and the policy researcher must identify the optimal research perspective to address the degree of complexity the problem presents.

To reiterate, before completing a research plan and initiating data collection, it is important for the policy researcher to systematically walk

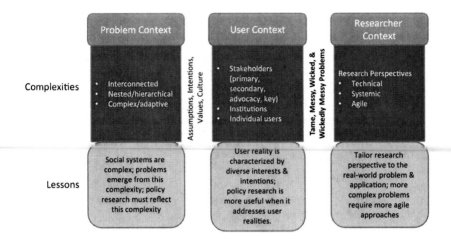

Figure 2.4 Reality Check Framework

through this *reality check*. This process will help build a firm grounding in the problem, an understanding of how study information may be used, and an orientation to what is necessary *and* feasible in the research itself. This check may include the following questions:

- Has the policy research team fully vetted the policy problem that has produced the need for their project?

    - Has the policy research team developed a sufficient under-standing of the conditions that produced the problem, includ-ing contextual circumstances? Is there a sense of the number of important conditions (variables) that need to be considered and their interconnections? Is there a sense of the pace of change, direction of change? Of the stability of these patterns?

- Has the policy research team identified the stakeholders who are or may become engaged in the policy research design, implementation, and use?

    - Is there a perception of the degree of consensus or conflict between stakeholders? Of the degree of engagement with the issue by different stakeholders?

- Does the team have a clear sense of the most important audiences (e.g., potential users) of the information they develop in this task?

    - Do they have an understanding of the range of options the deci-sion makers are motivated to consider?

- Has the institutional terrain relevant to the problem been mapped and explored?

  - Has the hierarchical structure of the institutional environment of the problem decision making been identified? Have the resulting implications for decision-making constraints and opportunities been identified?
  - Has the institutional timeline for use of the information been considered? How does it impact the timeline for the delivery of the policy research information?

- Have the project's own constraints and opportunities been mapped and explored?

  - How do the resource and decision contexts constrain what is feasible for the policy research project?

- Given this reality check, what is the best approach to achieving information alchemy—an optimal process of transforming data concerning the problem into user wisdom on how to take action?

  - Does the reality check confirm that the major client(s)/audience(s) for the policy research has a strongly grounded understanding of the problem, or would some redefinition of the problem be useful in helping them better reach their policy objectives?
  - Given the reality of the information need, what is the best approach to balancing technical complexity with technical feasibility and rigor as conventionally understood?
  - Given the reality of policy intent and stakeholder context, what is the best approach to balancing focus on one interpretation of the policy objective and providing information that consciously addresses multiple perspectives?

These reality-check questions exemplify the nature and range of the questions the policy research team should ask about the reality of the problem and solution realities they are about to engage. The understanding reflected in these questions provides the essential background for creatively designing and implementing useful policy research. Chapter 3 presents practical reality approaches to designing and implementing a credible and useful policy research effort appropriate to the reality portrayed through these questions.

Remember This . . .

Policy research is a potentially high-impact endeavor that can help make a difference in the future of the nation and in the lives of individuals—if done well. Competent and dedicated policy research professionals are important to making this impact as valuable as possible. Several key points to keep in mind from this chapter include:

- **Start grounded and stay grounded:** A basic theme in this chapter and in this book is that policy research is an *applied* practice. The primary purpose is not to develop theory that applies to problems *generally*; it is to develop empirically and logically credible lessons that can help guide action to ameliorate problems *specifically*. The objective is to go beyond generating knowledge about how to think about solving a problem and provide information that informs action to fix the problem. Keeping this fundamental intention at the fore will help us make good decisions about just how to design and implement a policy research project.

- **Keep emerging ideas and observable reality at least somewhat in sync.** It is important that the policy researcher keep the conceptual development of a study as close as feasible to the real-world situation they are studying. To keep these close to reality, it is important to repeatedly compare the concepts you are using with the reality you are observing in your study setting. As you observe the study terrain and begin thinking about how it all fits together, you are conceptualizing the variables, contexts, interrelations, intentions, conflicts, and more that will be important to your study. In later chapters, we will discuss how policy researchers clarify, organize, and analyze these concepts to produce useful information. At the early stages of understanding the reality you are working with, it is important to develop the habit of iteratively checking concept against reality and vice versa. It will help keep your study real.

- **Context! Context! Context!** A fundamental reality of social interaction is that it is nested within complex environments. We have demonstrated that for analytic purposes, it is valuable to know when these contexts have a hierarchical structure and that contextual conditions influence what happens (e.g., how individuals interact within them). These interactions are often the focus of policy research. Do speed limits influence traffic deaths? Does gun control reduce gun-related deaths? We have also seen that, too often, policy researchers do not pay sufficient attention to context and its potential influence on the focus of their study. Always consider the context of the problem you are studying, and be sure you are incorporating its constraints and opportunities into your policy research project.

- **Recognize and tame wicked messes.** Remember that more complexity (variables, connections, layers, change) makes bigger messes; and more humans in the loop (interests, motivations, values, intentions) makes things wicked. Wicked messes are tough to conceptualize and analyze, but treating them as if they were tame from the get-go creates irrelevant findings. To produce useful information, you must engage the mess and create an analyzable problem by identifying and organizing critical variables and connections, and you must confront the wickedness by identifying, working with, and effectively speaking to stakeholders. Taming wicked messes means understanding the core, actionable components that offer the opportunity for progress in addressing these types of problems. It is one of the toughest challenges in policy research. It is also a major reason policy research can be so much fun.

Discussion Questions

1. Identify at least three reasons that it is important to understand the problem region in order to produce useful policy research. Do the same for the user region and the applied policy research region.
2. Look at question 1 a bit differently. Discuss ways in which a policy researcher might go wrong if they had inadequate understanding of the problem region . . . the user region . . . the policy research region.
3. Identify a policy issue in the news and identify the potential stakeholders for that problem. Discuss what their interests and motivations might be with respect to the issue. How contentious do you believe the issue would be, and why? How might policy research help resolve the issue?
4. Why do you think the authors discuss wicked messes under the policy research region rather than the problem region?
5. Discuss the ways in which a policy researcher can "tame" a messy and/or wicked problem.

Assignments and Activities

1. Identify a pending policy decision that is currently in the news (national, state, or local) and describe major elements of the problem reality and user realities of that case. Explain why you would consider this decision to represent a tame problem, messy problem, wicked problem, or wicked mess. Be specific about why.
2. Identify an example of a public decision that was influenced by policy research. Write a paper on how policy research influenced that decision. What about the policy research itself, the decision-making process, or the political context contributed to or limited that influence?

3 Be Creative
Policy Research With the Artisan's Touch

To be a happy policy researcher, it really helps to enjoy the process of solving problems—putting together a puzzle. We cannot overemphasize the importance of the reality exploration that was the subject of Chapter 2, but we also recognize that the outcome is often a better understanding of a very unclear reality. It is like getting ready to solve a thousand-piece picture puzzle. The pieces may be separated into border pieces, single-color pieces, and pieces that look like they may generally go together, but the real puzzle solving—putting it all together—is yet to come. We do not yet see the puzzle solution, the finished picture. The picture puzzle solver has the great advantage of having the finished picture on the cover of the puzzle box. They have a clear blueprint for what they are building. In most cases the policy researcher does not have that advantage and must envision what the picture may look like.

This chapter is about moving from the raw materials of puzzle solving, the pieces of reality loosely organized on the table top, to a clarified vision of how a solution can actually be constructed. Of course, the solution the policy researcher must build is much more complex than a picture puzzle, and fortunately the policy researcher has a large selection of tools to help build a solution. Chapter 4 focuses on the policy researcher's box of tools and how to use them. This chapter focuses on approaches to closer examination of the raw puzzle materials and on tools for organizing puzzle pieces into a systematic analysis. More specifically, we will address the following topics.

- *Guiding concepts* convey a broad perspective to figuring out how to work with the raw material, the jumble of pieces on the table, available to build a problem solution and on identifying and combining research tools and designs for that building process.
- *Materials for policy research* are data relevant to policy research analysis and conclusions. Just as puzzle pieces may be large or small, jagged or smooth, and so forth, data have distinct characteristics—harder or softer, new or used, specific or general, individual or collective—that must be fit to project needs.

- *Logic models* are flexible maps for organizing the pieces of the solution. They are visual representations of the logic of the puzzle solution appropriate to the study's purpose and materials. They provided a speculative version of the picture on a puzzle box.

Guiding Concepts

Policy researchers often have areas of focused technical expertise. For example, the contributors to this text include an expert in economic analysis and statistical regression techniques; several experienced program evaluators with varied focused expertise including highly technical skills such as randomized controlled trials (RCTs), hierarchical modeling, multisite evaluations, and natural variation designs; experienced case study analysts; and a variety of policy area experts with expertise including environmental policy, criminal justice, education, mental and behavioral health, transportation, and planning. However, no one of these skills or areas of domain expertise provides the full range of perspective that makes an effective policy researcher. The need for in-depth technical understanding of analysis technique is a strong reason for team research when complex techniques are needed. But to effectively produce and deliver information that is useful and used, the team must include members who have the policy research understanding to provide the necessary vision.

The Need for Creativity

Creativity may not be what you would expect as a first canon of policy research. However, as you will see in many of the cases in this text, creativity, to a greater or lesser extent, lies just below the scientific/technical surface. There are several reasons creativity is such an imperative in policy research. Think back on Chapter 2 and the complexity, moving parts, and dynamics of problem and user realities. When the surface reality is constantly changing, simple replication of existing programs or policies is not sufficient. Even when "past experience is the starting point, . . . creativity is required, . . . (because) differences in time and space . . . make impossible a carbon copy" (Rose, 1993, p. 30). Policy research is about unearthing new understandings and solutions. Creative thinkers have the capacity to put things together in new ways, detect hidden patterns, perceive connections between seemingly unrelated issues or events, and generate solutions. Policy research is about building foundations for moving forward. "[T]he more the product stimulates further work and ideas, the more the product is creative" (Sternberg and Lubart, 1995, p. xx).

While creativity has a clear fit with the task of assessing and improving public policy, how do we encourage policy researchers to be creative? Isn't creativity something you are born with, a function of way of thinking and personality? Students of creativity would agree that these are factors. As an example, the HRY evaluation case in this text required lots of creativity, and it made some evaluation team members very nervous. In a discussion of abandoning conventional criteria of "statistical significance" for a specific "meaningful" level of effect size (discussed in what follows), a research associate on the team balked. The objection was "I cannot find a definitive argument for that threshold anywhere in the literature!" The project's principal investigator responded, "Remember, *we are writing the literature.*" Scholars do suggest that "one has to be willing to stand up to conventions if one wants to think and act in creative ways" (Sternberg, 2006, p. 89). To press this point, you will find text boxes throughout this chapter that identify "traps of conventional practice" that can deter useful work. Creativity is necessary to avoid them.

Psychologists studying creativity agree that a need for certainty and closure can discourage creativity. They also agree that creativity benefits from "willingness to overcome obstacles, willingness to take sensible risks, . . . and self-efficacy" (Sternberg, 2006, p. 89). The good news on these helpful personality attributes is that you do not have to be born with them. They are learnable, and one can decide to learn and put them into practice. "To be creative one must first *decide* to generate new ideas, analyze these ideas, and sell the ideas to others" (Sternberg, 2006, p. 90).

A takeaway message for readers of this text is that creativity can be learned and practiced. Creativity can be developed by working on redefining problems, questioning assumptions, encouraging the generation of multiple ideas, working collaboratively, identifying and surmounting obstacles, seeing things from others' points of view, taking responsibility for failures as well as successes, and continuing to grow intellectually (Sternberg, 2001). Revealing ways to be creative in policy research is one of the consistent themes in this text.

Context, Correspondence, and Pragmatism

While creativity is central to our discussion of the choice of policy research tools and their design or use, it is not without direction or boundaries. Remember, useful creativity leads to useful products—not fantasy. Three concepts that help guide creativity will be brought to mind as we move through this chapter. First, "given the importance of purpose, creative contributions must always be defined in some context" (Sternberg, 2006, p. 95). *Context* defines the bounds of the problem and the factors that will be considered in analyzing it and proposing solutions. One of the critical roles in leading a policy research project is identifying the boundaries and importance of the "big picture" of contextual factors important to analysis. Setting this context distinguishes what is important to analyze inside it, for example, identifying the constraints of the context (e.g., laws, budgets) so that one can focus on the factors that can be influenced within those constraints. The importance of context has been emphasized earlier in our discussions of policy research, and it cannot be forgotten.

Second, *correspondence* with reality is another important criterion in the selection of research tools and the design of their use. Correspondence relates to the "truth value" of policy research results. Put a little differently, it has to do with the degree of confidence the researcher, and thereby the user, can put in the applicability of conclusions and lessons drawn from policy research findings. The term is associated with a "correspondence theory of truth" (Greener, 2011, p. 109) that identifies research *findings* as true when they correspond to reality. In the following discussion, we will discuss approaches to affirming correspondence, particularly with respect to measurement tools.

Third, creative policy research can be guided by *pragmatism*. Scholars have articulated a pragmatic view on social research that does not focus on any "reality" criteria but accepts that "something is true if, for us, it 'works'" (Greene, 2006, p. 109). This view has particular appeal for a utility orientation in program evaluation, in which a primary interest is that the tool be effective in helping achieve the users' intentions. One of the most useful guides in being pragmatic is the *parsimony* criterion. From a scientific perspective, parsimony means "reducing the infinite plenitude of reality into a carefully framed argument from which unnecessary dross is removed" (Gerring, 2012, p. 66). From a more applied perspective, it means "we need to bring . . . (information) together in reasonably compact form in order for that knowledge to serve a useful purpose" (Gerring, 2012, p. 67). Either way, parsimony brings many benefits to the pragmatic policy researcher who emphasizes utility. For choosing design, it suggests *staying close to the user's view of the world and keeping it simple*. "The best research designs require the fewest, and least problematic, assumptions about the world" (Gerring, 2012, p. 323).

Learning how to make decisions that produce a strong product in the simplest way is a tremendous advantage in the constantly resource-strapped policy research reality. But possibly the greatest advantages come in communication. If an argument is "not summarizable in a compact form, its impact is diminished" (Gerring, 2012, p. 66). If the policy researcher cannot produce a clear executive summary stating the crucial takeaways from their study, it probably does not meet the parsimony criteria. Overall the guides in this section point toward a flexible and mixed use of research tools and designs that are pragmatic and appropriate to context and purpose.

Policy Researcher as Artisan

It is often said that social inquiry, including policy research, is art and science. This statement may at first feel freeing—a kind of "anything goes" impression. In fact, the message is that it needs to be both—and this may be more challenging than being just one or the other. The science side of this duality is associated with objectivity, for example, observation of measurable facts, consideration of multiple points of view, careful application of validated procedure, building on what is known. The art side is associated with subjectivity, such as emotions, perception, empathy, and expressive ability. This chapter demonstrates how policy research draws on both. Successful policy research cannot be formulaic. Every real-world policy problem and solution environment is different, and the research approach must be designed appropriately. Yet it cannot be based on personal opinion or belief. Briefly put, policy research "demands creativity. But at the same time, it is systematic, so that it is disciplined, rigorous, and, in a word, professional" (Majchrzak and Markus, 2014, p. 5).

In brief summary, we find it useful to think of the policy researcher as an artisan. An artisan is skilled in the tools of a craft and uses them to create products that are not mass produced but fitted to the constraints and opportunities of the material being used. Each product is a unique application, often functional, with an artistic touch. The artisan is ideally suited for one of the most challenging and enjoyable characteristics of policy research: the need to blend creativity and function. The raw material of policy research never stands still. Every study brings a new challenge that requires investigating an emerging problem, developing new insights and understandings, and putting together a relevant and creative research design. The remainder of this chapter presents major considerations that the policy researcher must pull together in designing a study that meets problem and user needs.

The Materials of Policy Research

The policy researcher works with raw materials and multiple tools. Knowing the characteristics of the raw material and the capabilities and limitations of the tools and having the ability to foresee how they will interact are central to the quality of the resulting product. For example, a finish carpenter must know the relevant qualities of the wood they may use (e.g., density, malleability, tensile strength, durability, grain, color) to best know how to work it. This is critical to choosing exactly which tools will be used to create a quality product. In this section, we provide a very brief overview of particularly important qualities of the materials with which policy researchers work and an introduction to some major compartments in their toolbox. The focus of this section is to provide an understanding of basic characteristics of the most frequently used materials for policy research.

The basic material for policy research is *data*, generally defined as facts brought together for reasoning or analysis. The term "facts" implies that data refers to the external world; indeed, the singular form, "datum," is a Latin noun meaning "something given." Data is not made up or intellectually fanaticized; it is received from the outside world—reality. The accepted philosophical definition of data is things *known or assumed* as facts, creating the basis of reasoning or calculation. As philosophers are wont to do, the phrase *known or assumed* points to the begged question. How are the bona fides of a set of data (facts) established? As bureaucracies are wont to do, the U.S. Office of Management and Budget, which passes on government-funded research plans, provides a definition. For their review purposes, data means "the recorded factual material commonly accepted in the scientific community as necessary to validate research findings" (OMB Circular 110). In this section, we will see just how crisp and helpful this definition may or may not be. To start, we will identify a major distinction in the sources that "give" the policy researcher their data and fundamental issues posed in the process of receiving it.

Harder or Softer Data

One of the most commonly assumed dichotomies in research is between quantitative data and qualitative data. The terms link data to very different, some have argued incompatible, approaches to social research. Quantitative data is, in the most concrete sense, data that is represented in numbers. For the social sciences in particular, quantitative analysis can tap into a wide and growing array of statistical analysis techniques. When users want very specific answers to highly structured questions, statistical findings can be very powerful. Qualitative data is nonnumeric. It is expressed in "words or images or anything that is not presently in numeric form" (Greene, 2011, p. 3). The positive side of qualitative data is that it allows human subjects to use their own words and to express their own ideas and perceptions. It is important to note that this is closer to *their experience of reality*, which has advantages in developing applicable knowledge. (These advantages will be highlighted later in our discussion.) Qualitative researchers will be quick to point out that socially applicable knowledge is "often contingent and contextual" (Greene, 2011, p. 3) and that quantitative analysis does not easily reflect that aspect of reality.

In the halls of science, it is almost taken as a given that quantitative data is *better*. A clear and understandable reason for this is that numbers are the window to the precision and power of statistical analysis. This, in turn, is a big step toward meeting the OMB criterion that scientific data be commonly accepted in the scientific community as necessary to validate research findings. However, from a perspective that places high value on usability, it is important to realize that this critical attribute of data is as much a researcher's *decision* as it is a *given*. The distinction is not so much whether data *is* quantitative but the degree to which it is *treated as* numeric or not. The truth is that "it's possible to convert just about any non-numeric phenomenon into a number" (Greene, 2011, p. 3). The entire field of psychometrics, for instance, is about converting attitudes, feelings, emotions, psychological states into numbers.

For these reasons, we will substitute the term *harder* for quantitative and *softer* for qualitative when discussing decisions about creating and using these types of data. The use of harder (more quantitative) or softer (less quantitative) puts decisions about data on a continuum that corresponds to reality much more than the implication that it is mutually exclusive. Looking at this distinction as the degree of hardness or softness clarifies why considering qualitative and quantitative in better-or-worse terms is not helpful.

The challenge for the policy researcher is to determine just how hard or soft they want their data to be. The "harder" the data, the more precisely defined it must be. For example, parametric statistics and its impressive array of analysis techniques technically requires that data values have all the properties of the number system that allow the full range of mathematical computation. This type of data is referred to as *continuous*, and it is rare in social research. This means that technically its use would be restricted to variables based on counts of numbers of units with precisely the same value on some metric, such as dollars, pounds, time units. When policy researchers use truly continuous data, it is usually as a proxy for some related concept of more direct interest (e.g., poverty, social class, the elderly, young children, perceived value).

People do not think or behave in standard units, so complete correspondence of the subject of most policy research to the real number system is not possible. For example, in questionnaire items that include a statement then request responses from 1 (strongly disagree) to 5 (strongly agree), the numbers clearly do not indicate equivalent units of "agreement." This type of forced choice response pattern is called a *Likert item* after the researcher who developed it. In statistics, the type of data they produce is called *ordinal*, meaning it has the property of rank (i.e., higher or lower) but not of unit equivalence. So, technically, it cannot be used in the powerful analyses allowed by statistics that require continuous measures. The truth of the matter is that policy researchers and social scientists frequently assume that ordinal data is close enough to meeting the assumptions of parametric statistics and go ahead and use them. We acknowledge that this is often a sensible tradeoff and do it ourselves when the tradeoff is worthwhile. Knowing rank order does support a whole class of *nonparametric* analyses that we will say more about in the upcoming discussion of analysis tools.

Transcripts of debates in congressional hearings might be an example of data at the softest (qualitative) end of the continuum. A transcript will provide an exact replication of what happened in a policy-relevant discussion. It will not come close to meeting the OMB criterion for acceptable data. To make it useful for analysis, it must be hardened up to some extent. For example, to use a transcript to help determine the exact legislative intent behind a law, an analyst must develop some criteria for deciding what phrases in the transcript are relevant to conveying intent. In the case of a single qualitative analyst, these criteria may not be clearly articulated; the analyst is using a variety of cues concerning what is relevant. If multiple analysts are looking at multiple transcripts to develop comparable information that can be used to determine intent, the criteria for what "counts" must be clarified and articulated, or hardened up. An harder example would be the use of "key words," such as used in qualitative software. Indeed, what qualitative software does is harden up qualitative data.

Conversations with respondents, interviews, that is, are a primary source of soft data in policy research. The resulting data is a product of interview questions that are posed by the researcher/data collector. Before use in analysis, they are typically categorized in some way, again hardening them up sufficiently to be useful for description, comparison, or other analyses useful for communicating concepts and conclusions. As we will see in Chapter 4, interview questions themselves can be structured, semistructured, or unstructured—introducing varying degrees of hardness prior to analysis. One of the advantages of qualitative data, however, is that the data that has been categorized for analysis remains in the data record. Often, quotes, paraphrases, or perceived themes in the qualitative raw data may be used to convey the degree of diversity in meaning within a category of responses to which a number has been assigned.

Put a little differently, categories harden up the qualitative data sufficiently to label it in relation to other categories with an ordinal number. The narrative discussion softens the category by showing the complexity of its content. More importantly, the discussion may enhance the communication of information about context, nuances in meaning, and other variance around the core of shared meaning necessary for the category. This adds important information that can make the concept more understandable and useful to practitioners. For example, it may help how well the concept fits in their immediate situation or how it may be made to work better in their situation.

This introductory statement about harder or softer data will get clearer as we say more about its application in coming discussions and in our real-world cases. The central points are straightforward. Harder data is more precisely defined and is presumably comparable across multiple observations. It produces variables that are assumed to represent reality with sufficient uniformity to be used in statistical analyses as a continuous or ordinal number. Qualitative data is nonnumeric, providing discussions of concepts and interrelations. It produces themes, categories, and contextual discussions that can help consumers of findings see application to their needs and circumstances. Quantitative data is not all at the same degree of precision (hardness), and some qualitative data has been organized and labeled to be less soft than a simple descriptive narrative. For now this is enough. As we introduce measurement and analysis techniques, it will become clear why the degree of hardness is not better or worse in itself; it all depends on its use. For now, the guiding principle is that the decision before a policy researcher is not typically whether to use hard or soft data. Rather, they need to consider how hard the data needs to be to best meet the needs of their study and just what mix of harder and softer would be optimal.

Theory-Based Knowledge or Applicable Lessons

More than three decades ago, a team of applied researchers in the very specialized and very applied field of "consumer research" drew a distinction with laser-beam relevance for policy research—and applied research in general (Calder, Phillips, and Tybout, 1981). The distinction they made was between *theory application* and *effects application*. Both of these approaches to producing applicable information live side by side in policy research, yet they are not clearly distinguished or recognized. Effects application has the research goal "to obtain findings that can be generalized directly to a real-world situation." Theory application, on the other hand, seeks to contribute to development of "scientific theory that can be generalized through the design of theory-based (actions) . . . that are viable in the real world" (Calder, Phillips, and Tybout, p. 198).

From a methods perspective, theory application poses a mediating step between studying action in real-world situations and applying action in real-world situations. The underlying belief is that research conducted in one real-world context at one time needs to support abstract theory to become knowledge. It can then be applied to new situations. This concept lies behind the formal application of evidence-based practices (EBPs) discussed in Chapter 5. Effects application seeks to eliminate the process of affirming a mediating theory in order to create lessons applicable elsewhere. While both approaches seek to generate useful findings, they have very different implications for methods.

Theory application places a major emphasis on formal scientific method, including tests of theory to serve as a basis for designing policy and programs, and formal evaluation of interventions to test whether applications work. Calder and his colleagues (1981, p. 200) refer to research methods for theory application as falsification procedures and to research methods for effects application as *correspondence* procedures. Correspondence procedures emphasize selecting samples representative of real-world populations under study, measuring concepts so they parallel meanings in the real-world setting, choosing study settings representative of contextual variation in the real world, and choosing a design that preserves correspondence to the processes taking place in the real-world setting.

The effects application approach articulated by applied researchers, and particularly the correspondence concept, foreshadowed methods applications and designs being increasingly used by applied researchers today. Natural variation designs, capitalizing on the variation produced by correspondence rather than theory falsification procedures, are becoming increasingly well articulated (Springer and Porowski, 2012). Examples of the use of correspondence procedures will be pointed out in coming sections of this chapter and will be evident in some of the cases in Part II of this text. The most important point for the student of policy research is that the methods and criteria that make policy research its own discipline and not just a compromised application of academic social science is being more and more clearly articulated.

Primary or Secondary Data

From an academic science point of view, data would most often be thought of as what it produces in the laboratory or in the field. New data created by the scientist in the field to meet the purposes of their study is usually classified as *primary* data. Policy research often creates and uses primary data. For example, if the project is a program evaluation, the evaluators would collect primary data from program managers, participants, and other stakeholders. However, policy researchers also use old or current data from databases, record systems, and existing documents relevant to the organization, program, or policy need under study. This is *secondary* data that has been collected by someone else for some other purpose and is available for reanalysis at some level.

For a number of reasons, secondary data is an important data source to produce useful information for policy decision makers. Policy research typically takes place within organizational settings and often focuses on questions about organization function, activities, and effectiveness. In this environment, secondary data is often available in a variety of forms. Some of the most common and useful include client data (e.g., demographics, background, needs assessment or diagnosis); service delivery data (e.g., numbers of clients receiving different service segments, service quality indicators); procedural and policy manuals; and fiscal information systems.

Public policy institutions are required to be accountable, document their activities, and communicate substantial amounts of information to the public. This creates a large amount of documentation that is potentially useful for policy analysis. Prominent examples are census data, laws and legislative proceedings, annual reports and other descriptions of activities, and the media. The explosion of sophisticated web technology allowing powerful search and access makes much of this information readily available to researchers. Policy researchers must carefully consider the resource and comprehensiveness advantages of secondary data in planning their data collection.

To more fully understand decisions relating to primary and secondary data, it is helpful to make a distinction between tasks for creating the data (e.g., instrumentation and collection) and the task of measuring and analyzing the data. Table 3.1 focuses on questionnaires and interviews

Table 3.1 Primary and Secondary Data Sources and Analyses

| | | *Data/Instrumentation* | |
		Primary	*Secondary*
Measurement/ Analysis	New (Primary)	*Questionnaires/ Interviews* Questions designed specifically to correspond to optimize relevance and applicability. Reliability/ validity established in study sample. *Records* Items, forms, administrative processes for data collection are developed specifically for the current study.	*Questionnaires/ Interviews* Whole instrument or select items adopted from existing instruments. Measurement structure, validity/ reliability checked for study sample as necessary. *Records* Existing items, forms, public records in accessible database. New measures may be constructed using existing items; existing data may be reanalyzed.
	Old (Secondary)	*Questionnaires/ Interviews* Old instruments, measures, and analyses replicated on newly collected information. *Records* Old analyses replicated on more recent data from record systems used in prior analyses.	*Questionnaires/ Interviews* Whole existing instruments judged to be usable for current study with no adaptation. *Records* Reports prepared by agencies may be re-interpreted in new study context. (This quadrant is not typically considered in discussions of secondary data.)

as primary sources of data directly gathered from people, and records as primary sources of documentation of organizational procedures and performance. Other documentary sources can be very useful for establishing context and history for policy analyses and are discussed elsewhere. The table summarizes four potential combinations of primary and secondary data collection and data analysis.

For the top left quadrant, data instruments and collection procedures (including sampling) are created specifically for the policy research project being conducted. Of course, questions may be adapted from prior instruments, but the finished data collection instruments are designed with an eye to best meeting the needs of the study in ways that are feasible. The SS/HS study that was introduced in Chapter 2 provides an example. One objective of that study was to document and analyze the different ways in which coalitions in the seven study states and twenty-one districts were organized, collaborated, and acted. Regularly kept records on organization structure, membership, meetings, meeting attendance, resource, and intervention events were important to answer study questions. While this is the type of information that many agencies may have at least some of, it was not available in comparable form across the multiple agencies in this study. States and districts collect different pieces of information, define variables differently, and use different data collection systems. In many cases, privacy or technical issues make the data inaccessible for new analyses.

To gain this valuable information, the SS/HS evaluation team had to create a new (primary) instrument to produce the data set they needed. They worked with state and local project grantees to have the data provided online on a quarterly basis. This data was the basis for the "Collaborative Decisions as an Emergent Property" example in Chapter 2. This upper-left quadrant defines most policy research and is the focus of most textbook discussions of policy research. However, as we will see, awareness of the other quadrants is important. They provide preferable options in some projects.

The upper-right quadrant includes studies for which secondary instrumentation and/or data is used for current analysis. This is common in policy research, and has clear advantages with respect to resources. If data being produced in existing record systems suits study needs, it saves research costs and reduces burden for the organization or individuals being studied. With respect to questionnaires and interviews, it is less likely that there will be ongoing surveys in a study setting that will closely meet the needs of a new policy research inquiry. Nonetheless, many policy researchers insist that existing questionnaire instruments should be used, particularly if they have passed rigorous tests for reliability and validity. The argument is that these instruments have proven quality and that they measure concepts more likely to be incorporated in the growing theoretical knowledge about the field.

Other policy researchers argue that it is usually better to borrow and adapt items from existing surveys that more closely reflect the actual meaning of individual-level or contextual variables in their real-world study context. If necessary, it is best to create new items that more closely reflect the questions being asked in the study and the characteristics of respondents. As demonstrated in the Starting Early, Starting Smart example, this difference in perspectives is aligned with knowledge-development and lesson-drawing approaches to using policy research to influence practice. Policy researchers should closely consider instrumentation and data from the upper-right quadrant, especially records, when planning a study. They should also closely consider ways to optimize correspondence to the real-world situation being studied in making decisions about what to use and how to adapt it to study purposes.

Starting Early, Starting Smart: Committing Instrumentation Battery

The *Starting Early Starting Smart* (SESS) initiative is a twelve-site national collaborative investigation of integrating behavioral health services in early childhood and primary health care service settings for children aged 0 to 5 years and their families and caregivers. This four-year applied research initiative was developed and implemented in twelve geographically and culturally diverse cities and brought together a multidisciplinary team of academic and applied (evaluation) researchers who spent a year collectively designing the study (Iida, Springer, et al., 2005). The process benefited greatly from the mix of more formal and applied perspectives, with the exception of whether instrumentation should be largely primary (in the sense of borrowing, tailoring, or creating items and measures with high correspondence to the study setting) or use intact recognized and published instruments. The applied researchers tended to argue for the former, the academics for the latter. The applied side emphasized reducing respondent burden, the ability to measure more factors, and the ability to achieve greater correspondence with program reality. The academics tended to emphasize scientific rigor, ability to contribute to the literature, and precise measurement of key variables. In the end, with some compromise and good cheer, the academics prevailed. The result was an instrument package with more than 400 items. As one researcher asserted in a team meeting, "We have given the term 'battery' of instruments new meaning."

The lower quadrants have limited utility for policy research. Research in the lower-left quadrant applies most clearly to replication studies. Replication is particularly important in the formal knowledge development approach in which testing the same theoretical approach in different contexts is a preferred design for establishing external validity. In this approach, using old instrumentation, measurement, and analyses on new data is required. The lower-right-hand quadrant is the least directly applicable. The takeaway point concerning primary or secondary analysis is that the policy researcher must carefully consider the resource savings and opportunity that are afforded by the secondary instruments and records that are often available and balance that with the need for correspondence to their study questions and setting.

Units and Levels of Observation and Analysis

In Chapter 2, we identified *hierarchy* and *nesting* as central concepts in understanding policy, programs, and practice. Hierarchical structures of legal and procedural rules, public and private authority, and political power are core elements of our intergovernmental, pluralist, and democratic system. An important part of the creative thinking for the policy researcher is to choose methods and tools that adequately reflect while bringing order to this complex hierarchy of constraints, opportunities, and influences.

Clearly mapping important *units and levels of analysis* is an important starting point for policy researchers to get a handle on important contextual and unit-interaction influences in a hierarchical system. *Units* are "bounded entities such as individuals (subjects), organizations, communities, or nation states, which may be observed spatially and/or . . . through time" (Gerring, 2012, p. 75). If they are large and complex (e.g., communities) that are the object of intensive study, they are usually called cases. Individuals under study may be referred to as subjects, respondents, informants, or participants depending on the study design and method. Units of analysis are those units about which analytic statements will be made. For example, in a study of school quality, analytic statements (e.g., descriptions, comparisons) will be made about schools.

Units of observation are units from which data is gathered, such as individual respondents to a survey questionnaire. While this distinction may seem trivial, it is anything but. Some characteristics of school quality may be measured through surveys of students or staff. In this case, the students and staff are units of observation, and the school is the primary unit of analysis.

Many technical analysis issues accompany this quite frequent use of units of observation and units of analysis at different levels in a hierarchical structure. We will encounter these issues throughout this chapter. The point here is that when a study setting is hierarchical, using units at one level to do analysis at another, sampling and instrumentation choices must be made with hierarchical analysis clearly in mind. A simple example would be the use of surveys or interviews to describe organizational processes or functioning. Respondents in this case should be selected carefully to represent multiple relevant perspectives (e.g., management and line staff). When using individual respondent data to infer organizational characteristics, the matching of intent and method can go further. If inferences are to be based on personal *experience*, samples must be larger and more *representative* (because individuals' own differences in expectation, interpersonal skills, perceptiveness, and more will effect their responses and must be "smoothed" to get an accurate estimate of the organizational characteristic). If they are to be based on respondent judgments and characterizations, samples can be smaller but more *purposive* (i.e., intentionally selected for their knowledge about organizational procedure). Being attentive to the hierarchical complexity of real-world policy reality, how it impacts the information and analysis needs in a project, and creatively assessing how to represent it for analysis is a key policy research task.

Multiple-Level Analyses

The analysis of collaborative decisions as emergent characteristics in SS/HS state and local coalitions presented in Chapter 2 was an example of a hierarchical study design. The national SS/HS State Program Multi-Site Evaluation (SS/HS MSE) was initiated in 2013 to assess the potential role of states to (a) strengthen local SS/HS school programs in their states and (b) generate lessons that might be useful in other states with interest in improving mental and preventive services. The focus of the SS/HS MSE was to provide findings that would support strong dissemination and implementation practices to take SS/HS to scale through state and local collaboration. Table 3.2 summarizes the levels of analysis, units of observation and potential analyses at each level in that study (2014–15 data).

This summary table portrays a relatively common multisite evaluation scenario. It also provides a great framework for discussing the importance, utility, and challenges of precisely defining units of observation and analysis and of carefully considering implications for what these analyses can and cannot tell you. We will go level by level. The federal grant program itself is at the top point of the hierarchy. As noted, a large volume of past research at the local level supports a conclusion that on average, over a great diversity of local contexts and implementation diversity, the SS/HS approach helps schools improve the mental and behavioral health of students. Of course, there are big differences in how much they help, and some don't help at all. The general conclusions based on aggregating local results to the national program level do not provide detail on differences in performance that may be linked to different state-of-community

Table 3.2 Levels of Observation and Analysis in the SS/HS Multi-Site Evaluation

Levels	Units of Observation	Units of Analysis	Analysis
Program	SS/HS State/ Program as defined at national level	SS/HS State Program	Document program objectives, requirements, resources, supports
States	7 state contexts, 22 key informant interviewees, 117 collaborator survey respondents, 7 event/activity reports	7 state contexts, 7 state programs, 7 collaborations	*State Level:* Document relevant state laws, education systems; analyze state grantee planning to attain objectives, organization, collaboration, and actions; identify/explain differences across states *Hierarchical:* Document and explain state differences in interactions with districts
Districts	51 collaboration interviews, 47 implementation interviews, 225 collaborator survey respondents, 7 event/activity reports	21 programs, 21 collaborations	*District Level:* Analyze grantee program planning to attain objectives, district organization, collaboration; document district program diversity in program elements, collaboration, activities by state *Hierarchical:* Assess differences in district structure and function (aggregated at state level) in relation to state differences
Schools	310 school implementation survey respondents	21 district program implementations in schools	*School Level:* Document school-level achievement implementing intended outcomes of the program related to school capacity and procedures *Hierarchical:* Assess differences in school implementation (aggregated at state level) in relation to differences in district program, collaboration, and activities

contexts or to program design or implementation. In other words, they say nothing about how to improve SS/HS effectiveness in a particular context. By including information on state and local contexts and on program support and implementation at state, district, and school levels, this study provides information that may provide lessons on how to strengthen program design and implementation in different settings.

Entries in the first column of Table 3.2 summarize units of observation at state, district, and school levels. Interviews and surveys make staff members and collaborators units of observation. However, the units of analysis identified for states and districts in column two are not staff or collaborators, they are contextual (described through documents or interviews) or organizational (i.e., program design, collaboration functioning). The organizational units of analysis are measured through a combination of individual-level observations and reported events and activities.

At the district level, a similar combination of units of observation and analysis was used. Interviews with respondents more familiar with actual service implementation (as distinguished from planning and administering) are added to gather detail on field implementation. The formal documentation of context dropped at the district level because state context is more important to the state program intent, as well as practical considerations of resources and analysis complexity. Planned analyses will document differences in the degree of variance in program design and collaboration between districts by state but will not focus on explaining that variance. This is both a practical decision (budget and complexity) and a decision based on potential utility for lessons application (largely focused at the state level). Finally, units of observation at the school level are limited to school staff, who will report the degree to which school capacity and procedures reflect the SS/HS program framework and the degree to which that changes over the three years of program implementation. District and school analyses will be aggregated to the state level, allowing assessment of the degree to which district-level implementation varies with different measures of collaboration function, program strategy, and supports at the state level.

This brief summary is an example of how units of observation and analysis are organized in a current hierarchical evaluation. This type of evaluation design is limited in application because it is costly, covers multiple layers of context, and suits the direct policy interests of federal or state governments interested in influencing public problems through the complex intergovernmental system. For the purposes of this text, however, it is a useful example of what it takes to actually operationalize the complex realities in which all policy studies take place.

POLICY RESEARCH AND AWARENESS OF CONTEXT

The great majority of policy research studies take place at state or local levels. They have limited resources, and the potential users who commission and pay for the studies typically have focused problem and decision needs. They cannot fund and do not want to wade through extended analyses of contextual constraints and conditions. Still, and maybe especially in these situations, it is important for the policy researcher to carefully identify conditions in the context that should be considered to create findings most useful for taking positive action. The tendency in policy research, particularly concerning behavioral change (e.g., substance use, violence, social-emotional development, mental health), has been to emphasize individual-level variables. Interventions often focus on educational or experiential services to mold individual awareness, knowledge, attitudes, skills, and ultimately behaviors. A more systemic approach will at least consider influences of context (e.g., family, peers, schools, communities) in identifying constraints, incentives, and supports of current behaviors. Without this, interventions may be left working upstream against unrecognized currents. In some cases, policy makers may need to shift focus to changing contextual influences because they overpower individual change. The following case concerning the emergence of school climate as a school-wide intervention is an important contemporary shift from an individual to a contextual intervention focus.

From Safe and Drug Free to Safe and Supportive Schools

In the last half of the twentieth century, substance use and violence, even at school, became major concerns for many Americans. As part of the public response, the Safe and Drug Free Schools and Communities Act of 1986 provided funding to states for substance abuse prevention programs in schools. In the early years, these programs emphasized education and skills for "positive youth development" and resistance to drug abuse. Schools were often encouraged to use manualized EBPs that teachers could deliver. These programs were widely used and popular with communities concerned about school safety and drugs. However, educators were sometimes concerned about losing valuable time for academic education, researchers questioned the evidence for effectiveness of these programs in changing youth behavior, and behavioral health professionals were concerned about the focus on changing individual behaviors to improve school safety and substance use. In more emotive terms, they saw this as a gussied-up "just say no" approach and argued for a perspective that recognized it "takes a village to raise a child."

Growing research concerning the importance of the school environment for educational quality as well as youth social and emotional development supported the idea that the school was not just a convenient gathering place where students could be taught to change their behavior, it was a primary socialization environment in which youth would experience and be supported in positive development (Thapa et al., 2013). Just as a safe and supportive family environment promotes social/emotional development, a safe and supportive school environment does also. Research has also shown that a safe and supportive school environment improves academic achievement.

In 2010 the U.S. Department of Education (ED) funded eleven states to implement statewide programs to help school districts develop and implement Safe and Supportive Schools efforts. Figure 3.1 displays the Safe and Supportive Schools (S3) model of school context concepts that have been empirically linked to improved school safety, less substance use, more engagement with school, and improved academic performance. The emergence of school climate as a key consideration in educational thinking is a concrete example of the increased recognition of systemic complexity in solutions to educational policy problems.

For policy researchers in school climate, there is now a significant set of evidence-based concepts and instrumentation (e.g., the

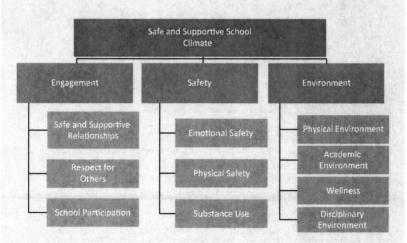

Figure 3.1 The Safe and Supportive School Climate Model

Tennessee School Climate Survey, which was developed by authors and contributors to this text) for use in structuring studies of school behavior and performance that incorporate contextual factors in single-site studies. The capacity to conduct studies from a systemic perspective has been increased by the experience of evaluating S3 programs.

In summary, the points made in our discussion of the material of policy research forms an important a priori step in planning the actual work required to conduct a useful policy research study. Considerations concerning how hard or soft the data need to be, the relative importance of context, what kinds of context (e.g., legal, organizational, interpersonal) are important in building a strong bridge between an understanding of problem and user realities. These are important considerations in selecting the tools and design of a policy research study. In the next section, we introduce logic modeling as a process of building a big-picture framework for appropriate data collection, measurement, and analysis.

Logic Models: Blueprints for Tool Selection

The logic model is a simple technique that has become a widely used design tool for policy research. A logic model is typically a graphic representation of an interconnected system that is designed to achieve a policy or program goal. It can describe real-world events, plans, or theories. Logic models are visual representations that take many forms. However, they share two common characteristics. First, they are composed of shapes that represent components of a system (e.g., concepts, structures, participants, actors, activities, conditions, contexts). Second, they contain (or imply) arrows that more or less specifically connect components. These arrows are typically directional and may represent a variety of transactions between components (e.g., information, services, resources, participants/clients), theory-based or hypothesized influences (e.g., causation, moderators, implementation), or simply chronological progression. Generally the arrangement of components and arrows will show some logical flow, which may be left to right, cyclical, top to bottom, or multidirectional. The simplicity and flexibility of logic modeling underlie its utility.

Logic models were first developed as a tool for program management. A *program* logic model can be defined as "a picture of how your organization does its work" (Kellogg Foundation, 2004, p. iii). "A program model links outcomes (both short and long term) with program activities/

processes and the theoretical assumptions/principles of the program" (Kellogg Foundation, 2004, p. iii). More generally, logic models are typically a series of "if-then" statements about the logical relation of program processes and desired outcomes. By focusing attention on these logical relationships, policy researchers can identify weak (or strong) links in the design of a program or policy.

Table 3.3 is an example of a program model for an AmeriCorps program that was intended to work with high school students in high-need schools. While the model is clearly focused at a detailed program level, it also demonstrates the flexibility of the model. The components in this example are a progression of planned inputs, activities, and outputs (first three columns) and short-, medium-, and long-term outcomes (last three columns). While the arrows are not drawn, arrows are implied between columns as a whole. For example, the inputs in column one are intended to produce the activities in column two, which are intended to produce the outputs in column three, and so on across the model. So while this model does indicate a general conceptual base and loosely hypothesized expectations about relations, it does not specify these in either theoretical or operational terms. Detail about how to use the resources, what skills will be learned, and so on will be provided elsewhere, or left up to the users of the model. In this example, levels of detail vary substantially across the columns. Inputs and particularly outputs are very detailed. The outputs column provides an explicit set of quantitative indicators suitable for monitoring the work that has been accomplished in the program. Other columns, particularly in the outcomes portion, describe general intentions consistent with a theoretical approach that focuses on individual skills and attitude change to produce behavioral success.

The AmeriCorps example also shows how logic models can serve multiple purposes. It reflects common expectations from funders of grant programs displaying a plan for resource use and specific indicators to hold the grantee accountable to the numbers of persons served and the services they would receive. A logic model of this type gives multiple audiences (e.g., staff, stakeholders, interested parties) a quick picture of what the program intends to accomplish, what it does to do this, and what resources are required. For the policy researcher seeking to do an evaluation (process or outcome) of the program, it provides guidance, more or less specific at different points, for specifying concepts, developing data collection and analysis needs, and selecting appropriate data collection, measurement, and analysis tools.

Logic models are used for purposes beyond program representation. They are, for example, used to represent *theories of change* that underlie a policy or program (Funnell and Rogers, 2011). In this case, the intent is to provide a more conceptual understanding of the reasons the program is expected to promote intended outcomes. One of the key differences

Table 3.3 Logic Model for AmeriCorps (NCCC) Life After High School Program

Inputs	Activities	Outputs	Outcomes		
Project Resources	*Core Project Components*	*Evidence of Project Implementation & Participation*	*Evidence of Change*		
			Short-Term	Medium-Term	Long-Term
What we invest (# and type of AmeriCorps members)	*What we do*	*Direct products from program activities*	*Changes in knowledge, skills, attitudes, opinions*	*Changes in behavior or actions that result from new knowledge*	*Long-term meaningful changes, often in condition or status in life*
Cash and in-kind project support 1 Program Director 10 AmeriCorps S/N Members Seniors report feeling more confident in their ability to compete for college admission or career opportunities 2 VISTA members Seniors interview for college, a job or internship,	Provide individual case management to high school seniors to include: tutoring sessions, organizing and chaperoning college campus visits, training in financial aid, researching scholarship opportunities, developing college and career plans with students, mock interviews and résumé writing assistance. VISTA members develop a system for	# of high school seniors tutored # of campus visits completed # of high school seniors completing at least one campus visit # of mock interviews completed # of résumés reviewed # of dollars raised # of mentors trained in student engagement curriculum # of individuals trained to use data collection system	Seniors report feeling more knowledgeable about their postsecondary opportunities. Seniors report feeling more confident in their ability to compete for college admission or career opportunities.	Seniors submit applications for one or more of the following: job, internship, college, financial aid, scholarships, military service. Seniors interview for college, a job or internship, or military or national service opportunities. Volunteers take over implementing major components	All graduating seniors know their immediate next step in life, as they either have a job opportunity or internship or are enrolled in the military, AmeriCorps or a postsecondary institution. Trained volunteers augment AmeriCorps member activities and assist NCCC

or military or national service opportunities
1 NCCC team (10 members)

data collection and analysis, for resource development, student engagement, and curriculum design. The VISTAs also develop and strengthen volunteer and mentoring program opportunities. NCCC carry out the logistics for a newly developed annual "Life After High School" Fair.

# of volunteers engaged
# of partnerships established (with business, military branches, colleges, and local AmeriCorps programs)
# of individuals engaged as presenters at fair.

of the student engagement curriculum, mentor training, and Life After High School Fair.

teams with logistics for the Life After High School Fair.

between a theory-of-change model and program models is a shift in emphasis from the components of the model (the boxes) to the transitions from one component to another (the arrows). Modeling theories of change focuses on "how and why an event (in one box) appeared to have produced a subsequent event (in the next box)" (Yin, 2008, p. 161).

Figure 3.2 looks quite different than the AmeriCorps program logic model, and that difference again demonstrates the flexibility of the logic model format. There is a story behind this "theory of change," which was originally developed by the SS/HS evaluation team and presented to the program manager (client) as the project evaluation logic model. The SS/HS training and technical assistance (TA) contractor, who was participating in the meeting when the model was presented, objected to calling it a logic model because (a) it did not reflect the step-by-step outcome logic of a program model and (b) they already had a generic version of an SS/HS program logic model that was being used to guide grantees in their program planning. Their model was pages long, depicting a sequence of planned activities that each state- and district-level grantee (and subgrantee) would go through to implement their program. The resolution of their complaint was simple; Figure 3.2 became the SS/HS State Program Theory of Change Model.

The name change was fine because the model in Figure 3.2 depicts the interactions between levels of the state/district/school system, focusing more on the arrows showing the complex collaborative interactions in this system. The idea was to picture the major components, particularly the multiple, reciprocal interactions and influences (bidirectional arrows) involved in evaluating a multilevel collaborative system. The primary

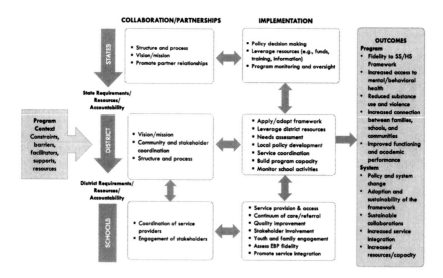

Figure 3.2 Safe Schools/Healthy Students Theory of Change Model

evaluation questions were (1) how and to what extent do states, districts and schools develop collaborative systems? (2) how do these collaborative systems differ in the way they are organized and function? (3) do these collaborative systems affect the performance of programs and systems? and (4) are some collaborative systems more effective in changing performance and why?

The first (far-left) component of the SS/HS State Program theory of change model refers to the context of the study. Even a cursory initial consideration of the potential differences between states with respect to opportunities for collaboration and system change at the local level indicates that context is paramount in this multiple-level, multiple-state study. For example, some of the grantees have strong state departments of education with considerable policy influence at the local level; in others, there is almost no policy influence. In the extreme case, any state policy that will not be left to the discretion of districts must be legislated. Many other differences, for example, some states have operating school climate policies and grants while others do not; some have much stronger early childhood programs than others, and on and on. It is clear that any meaningful analysis of the development and effectiveness of collaboration in district and local schools must be placed in the context of state differences.

In the SS/HS State Program case, this need is evident. With respect to contextual conditions generally, "not only are these conditions likely to be important . . . they may overwhelm the case being studied" (Yin, 2008, p. 162). In the SS/HS example, one state required districts that received a subgrant to implement a specific program, leaving no discretion for the school–community collaborations to make this decision. State context overwhelmed the local collaboration dynamic being studied. Still, "many logic models—only barely attend to contextual conditions" (Yin, 2008, p. 162). In the legal, intergovernmental, and institutional environment, policy researchers need to be sure that context gets the appropriate degree of attention.

In brief summary, logic models are constructed to represent specific intentions and objectives and specific portions of larger systems of interaction. While not all policy research studies are addressing a problem that requires a logic model, they are all guided by some conceptualization that bridges reality to a research-ready understanding of study problem and purpose. The next chapter provides a quick overview of the kinds of tools policy researchers have at hand to turn these conceptualizations into concrete and useful studies. By itself, conceptualizing or modeling program theory or activity "does not provide (sufficient) guidance on gathering the evidence for monitoring and evaluation; it needs to be combined with evaluation expertise to draw appropriately from methods for research design, data collection, and data analysis" (Funnell and Roberts, 2011, p. 39). Chapter 4 provides an overview of the expert considerations that go into decisions about the tools for data collection and analysis that are appropriate for a specific study.

Remember This . . .

- **The artisan's perspective.** The policy researcher's job description is not that of a scientist or an artist or an engineer, but it borrows from all three. Policy research combines the theory, analytic, and evidence-building skills of the scientist, the insight and creativity of the artist, and the functional application skills of the engineer. This combination of technical skill, artistic vision, and functional product is the job description of an artisan, as well as a policy researcher.

- **Data correspondence is a bottom line.** Data quality must be a priority concern for anyone using the tools of science. Much of the discussion of data quality focuses on the empirical characteristics of the data itself, for example, distribution of values, patterns of association, missing data, or reporting errors. Criteria such as reliability, validity, and meeting statistical assumptions all rely on tests of these characteristics. These clearly are important; unreliable data cannot tell us much. However, *the correspondence between measure properties and the real-world phenomena being studied* is also critical. Developing measures that are carefully designed or demonstrated to reflect the policy mechanisms and context under study is more important than selecting reliable and valid measures developed and tested in other settings.

- **In reality, many labels become a matter of degree or context.** Remember our discussions of data-related concepts that are often discussed as different types—qualitative or quantitative and primary or secondary are prime examples. In building data with correspondence to reality, we saw how these distinctions become fuzzy. The data that are useful for analysis are more accurately thought of as harder or softer, with good reasons for developing measures that share quantitative and qualitative content. A strong reason is that analysis precision and applicable interpretation can be balanced. What is a context at one level of hierarchy can become a unit of analysis at another. Hard distinctions break down.

- **There is more than one way to do it.** There is more than one reasonable and productive way to conduct a study. The quest is not for the one best study design; this leads to a search for certainty that too often is resolved by a retreat into conventional wisdom. It is much better to trust your ability to identify the important features of the reality terrain, to carefully structure the data and an analysis logic that reflects it, and to pick a lane and drive in it—being willing to alter the route for good reason of course. You will be better served and will provide a better product when following a course you developed and you understand well.

The next step in the implementation of a policy research project is to pick appropriate tools, and use them. This is the subject of Chapter 4.

Discussion Questions

1. Why is creativity important to policy research? Discuss some characteristics of a policy research problem that might make creativity more important. Why is this? What are the downsides of creativity that the policy researcher should be careful to avoid?
2. Why do the authors suggest that the policy researcher is an artisan? From your perspective, does that make the profession sound more or less appealing? Why?
3. What makes data harder or softer? What are the advantages and disadvantages that come with data being harder or softer?
4. What is the difference between primary data and secondary data? What are the advantages and disadvantages of each from the perspective of a policy researcher?
5. What is the difference between a unit of observation and a level of observation? Discuss how these concepts help the policy researcher organize the complexity of a policy research problem.
6. What does a logic model contribute to a policy research project? How important is this contribution in your estimation? Why?
7. What is the difference between a program logic model and a theory of change? For what purposes is each more or less appropriate?

Assignments and Activities

1. Identify a program or policy that interests you. It can be one you have access to, have read about, or can collect information on in some way. Create a logic model for it, and write up a discussion that describes how the policy or program is expected to work. Refer directly to the components and arrows in the model as they relate to your discussion.

4 Be Credible

Using the Policy Research Toolbox

To this point, in the text we have been largely concerned with the processes of developing big-picture understanding of the problem and user terrains in which a policy researcher will be working and with building conceptual frameworks that help convert this understanding into workable research tasks. These are critical preparatory skills. At this point we turn to the concrete tasks of identifying and using the policy research toolbox. Policy researchers have an ever-increasing set of options among research tools. Their toolbox is full of methods and techniques from political science, economics, sociology, psychology, and multiple fields of applied study. They increasingly borrow and share tools and designs with business, health, and even software researchers and analysts. Advances in computing technology have brought the ability to use highly complex statistical techniques to every desktop. Increases in the ability to collect, store, and access data have made information and analysis a central component of decision making. The richness of these options and the need to bring order to their use are the focus of this chapter.

We do not pretend to explain the technical aspects of these tools or the nuances of analysis designs the tools may support. From a technical research perspective, these topics are expansive, requiring semesters of coursework to address in detail. Techniques of analysis (e.g., sampling, measurement quality, statistical inference—to skim the surface) are the kind of knowledge to which the old saw "knowing enough to be dangerous" is apropos. Thus we leave the technical detail of this topic to other courses. The intent here is to provide an overview of the major attributes of different data collection tools, different analysis techniques, and major differences in the ways in which these tools may be used to draw conclusions. This is centrally important for policy research because technical sophistication, important as it can be, does not solve policy problems unless it is developed and applied in the right way.

The rest of this chapter will include the following topics:

- *Tools for data collection and analysis* provides an overview of interviews, focus groups, surveys, documents, records, and site visits as commonly used and flexible approaches to collecting policy research data.

- *Designs for useful application* presents a discussion of research design in the context of answering four common types of research problems: exploratory, descriptive, effectiveness (causal), and choice. Policy researchers must focus more on creatively designing analysis approaches that answer these questions rather than picking an "off-the-shelf" research design.
- *Concluding comments on policy research methodology* notes the increased attention to mixed methods as a recognized and credible methodological perspective in social science. The discussion acknowledges the value of this increased attention to the eclectic and pragmatic use of multiple methods that has long been standard practice in policy research.

Tool Selection and Use

So, given the introductory caveat, what can we tell you about choosing tools for data collection and technique? To return to our carpentry analogy, these are the hammers, saws, files, knives, levels, rulers, and other tools of the trade. The approach we are using here is more about which tool might be best for a given material, with a particular outcome in mind. If the objective in carpentry is to build the frame of a house, which will never be visible to the user, a power ripsaw may be the best choice. If the task is finish carpentry, the molding on the cabinets for instance, a saw with a fine-toothed blade might be best. The point is that the detailed understanding of how to put the tool into action is not the only or even the primary consideration in choosing which tool to use. Understanding how tools fit the problem context and the reality of the research context and how to flexibly use multiple tools in the same project are important policy research skills.

To portray the choices that face the policy researcher rummaging through the toolbox, we will highlight the roles that a few select data collection techniques can play in a policy research study. In each of these examples, we briefly trace the choices a policy researcher must make and the options that require creative application when a particular data collection choice is made. We will follow these choices from data collection itself to the creation of measures to analyzing these measures and creating findings and to adding touches of interpretation that will make results relevant in presentation to potential users (the topic of Chapter 5).

This approach helps to emphasize a few basic points. First, data collection is only the start of a process in which the tools of policy research are progressively selected and used to shape the information for further analysis and eventually for more effectively informing real-world application. The data initially collected in applied research will often require working and massaging to make it appropriate for measurement and analysis. In Chapter 3, we briefly introduced data collection tools in relation to their fit with different data sources. In this chapter, we revisit data collection tools from a different perspective. We provide more attention to the relation of the information produced by a tool to the analyses it can support. This includes how the same data may be transformed to perform different measurement functions that are often complementary in a mixed-methods approach. For example, qualitative data may be transformed into quantitative data through coding it into categories. It can then be used for comparative or statistical analyses. The qualitative detail within these categories can be used to enrich the understanding of why certain quantitative patterns emerge. More on this later.

Second, the policy research toolbox is not divided into clear trays or sections that hold tools with distinctly different functions. It is more like the authors' desktops, a jumble of tools and materials that will be used in different mixes to produce the desired product. The ripsaw leaves rough edges that must be smoothed by a file when needed. Mixing the use of tools and materials effectively is a critical policy research skill. As argued in the last chapter, many of the academic distinctions between methods (e.g., qualitative and quantitative) do not well serve policy research. Mixing methods as required for correspondence to the reality of the study setting is an overarching requirement of useful policy research.

Third, these scenarios again demonstrate the needs for flexibility and creative problem solving in policy research. Fourth, thinking about making choices in data collection will highlight the importance of laying the foundation of data collection in an understanding of problem and user realities. We will see that understanding the problem reality has particular importance in thinking about how to collect data initially, and thinking about user reality will gain added importance as the process of shaping the data for understandable and useful communication proceeds.

We present only a handful of data collection examples, but these are by far the most widely used in policy research. We treat them in their generic form, and each has many specific variations. The overall points made in the discussion will apply to most of these variations. To demonstrate the adaptability of generic techniques, we sometimes detour into specific examples.

Interviews: Conversations With a Purpose

One unheralded yet truly vital data collection technique for applied policy research is the interview. In fact, interviews with knowledgeable officials, line and staff agency employees, agency clientele, and other relevant individuals are the bread and butter of nearly every piece of policy research, particularly those with fewer resources. Interviews are a convenient source of information about such important topics as policy or program background and history, relevant elements of institutional context, political factors, and other important big-picture information that would be beyond study resources to gather from disparate documentary sources, if they even exist. "It is hard to get away from the fact that interviews, when organized well, can be an efficient way to conduct research" (Greener, 2011, p. 77).

Important considerations in preparing to conduct interviews include developing instrumentation (i.e., questions) and targeting respondents (who will be interviewed). Interview research is primary research; there are no reliability-tested and validated interview questionnaires out there. One of the great strengths of interviews is that they are primarily intended to learn about the particular setting and allow systematic exploration of diverse points of view, interests, motivations, intentions, and other "humans in the loop" topics that make problems wicked. Interview questions open either a set of useful options or a can of worms, depending on how well the policy researcher has thought through what problem and user environments and objectives of a study require from interviews.

Interview instrumentation is typically described in three categories: unstructured, semistructured, or structured. A structured interview consists of a standardized schedule of interview topics and questions that is administered in a similar way to each respondent. Semistructured interviews are designed to give the interviewer more latitude to explore topics of interest as they emerge. In unstructured interviews, the respondent is given maximum leeway in structuring their own response to general topics. If the policy researcher knows the topics and questions for which information is desired or wants uniformity in responses so they can be comparable across respondents or contexts, a more structured instrument is needed. As the label implies, it will provide data more readily shaped for pattern analyses down the line. If the researcher wants to hear what the respondent has to say about a general question without prompting, a less structured instrument is the answer.

For most policy research uses, interview data will be hardened up a bit for use in analysis. This means that the raw narrative material produced by interviews will be interpreted in relation to more general concepts. An example of a relatively small amount of hardening is the development of common themes in the data. In the SS/HS example we have used before, key informant interviews at state and district levels produced information on how much policy direction the state could give schools. The fact that information came from both guiders (state) and guides (district) improves ability to check how clear this component of the system is (e.g., how much agreement there is across perceptions). This thematic analysis can then be used to support ratings of the balance of state authority and local discretion there is in each of the seven states under study.

This general process of using soft (qualitative) data to identify themes, grouping those into categories, and as we shall see when we discuss making an argument, using them in comparative and other analyses, is the process of data analysis that is associated with measurement. The narrative has been turned into higher levels of nominal or ordinal measurement—it has been hardened a bit. A great thing about this is that, if the data is well organized and maintained, the narrative, or at least tidbits in the form of key quotes, will be available in its softer form. This is a major advantage for communicating applicable information at the user level that is temporarily invisible in the hardened measure. For example, the degree of state authority in different SS/HS states is attributable to different characteristics of the state systems (e.g., state constitution or legislated policy, institutional arrangements, state culture). If state authority turns out to be associated with clear differences in producing desired system changes, a policy researcher can use detailed narrative to identify any actionable changes that may allow improvements in specific states. The detail in well-done interviews can play an important role in creating high-correspondence measures in the early stages of analysis and in identifying actionable information at the end of analysis. The often-minimized value of qualitative information becomes a powerful, flexible tool when used with skill.

To support this kind of utility, interview (or other qualitative) data must be produced and *documented* in systematic ways. In many study settings, interviews are used because they can allow a lot of information to be collected relatively inexpensively. If important information from the interview is accurately and fully documented, it can produce valuable understanding. For example, a few interviews can produce a useful description of program context, identification of program challenges, or other topics that can be summarized and reported without further analysis or data manipulation.

If interview data is to be manipulated (e.g., coded) or used to augment other quantitative information, it needs to be systematically stored in an accessible way. Recording is one answer, but it creates cost issues in analyzing a lengthy qualitative data set. Using qualitative software can be useful when resources are available and the analytic objectives are clearly developed. In many instances, an optimal solution is to use interviewers as informed observers who can complete structured interview reports in which they can use notes, sometimes with recorded interviews to reference, to document specific points of information the interview was intended to address. This, of course, requires skilled interviewers who are knowledgeable about study purposes. Again, we see the policy researcher balancing resources, correspondence with reality, and utility for analysis. Depending on how it has been shaped to become more appropriate for analysis, interview information can be important to a variety of analytic objectives. We will go further into this in our discussion of answering analytic questions.

Focus Groups: An Interview Riff

The use of *focus groups* has a certain cachet. They are prominently used in the media—to debrief groups of listeners after a political debate or event, for instance. Policy research reports often cite focus groups as a data collection method. However, the term is often misused. A focus group is a kind of group interview, but it is a special kind developed largely through commercial product testing or advertising in which the objective is to learn how consumers interpret and respond to advertisement messages or what they look for in a product. In focus groups, "the emphasis is on group interaction and the production of shared meaning" (Greener, 2011, p. 77). The interviewer becomes a facilitator, rules are set for group interaction (e.g., do not hog air time, be courteous), and a "script" is used to introduce a few general topics or questions to which participants are expected to react. Groups are small, no more than ten is ideal, and cross-talk is encouraged. The idea is to minimize interviewer guidance and allow participants to interact. The emphasis is to document point of view on a topic and reasons for these points of view that may be revealed in discussion of the topic with others that may have other points of view and to assess changes in point of view and what brings them about. Insight into participants' criteria for making judgments is the kind of information for which focus groups are particularly effective. Focus groups concerning reactions of patrons of a community science center, for example, can identify not only what features they like but why.

This technique is useful in seeing how stakeholders view issues or getting a better understanding of user views of reality, that is, in addressing needs for exploratory information. Focus groups can be very valuable in policy research, but the term is too often misused to describe a semistructured or structured group interview in which responses to specific interview questions are posed to a group of respondents instead of asking for discussion. This not only negates the true value of a focus group, it poses real dangers of biased information because of groupthink or timidity about the quality of one's "answer" to a question from the policy researcher. Each data collection technique has its own strengths and drawbacks, and selecting the right technique for a particular information need requires careful consideration.

Survey Research: An Old Favorite

Survey research can be thought of as an extreme version of the structured interview. In the most common use of surveys, the items are closed ended. This means that all desired responses are provided, and the respondent is asked to simply indicate the response that comes closest to their point of view. (Surveys sometimes contain "open-ended" questions that ask respondents for a narrative response, but the ease of opting out and the burden of a written response will introduce bias into open-ended responses.) The use of simple closed-ended response items is a major advantage for researchers to gather information from large populations, particularly when researchers have strong conceptual reasons for the exact questions they want answered (de Vaus, 2013).

Surveys also have the advantage of tremendous flexibility in the ways in which data is collected. The High Risk Youth program national evaluation (Chapter 10) administered more than 40,000 paper and pencil surveys to adolescent youth across the country. These were administered at four points in time. When literacy was an issue, a survey administrator read along as youth completed the survey. They were administered in schools, in programs, and, after youth left the program, they were often administered in group pizza parties to get respondents together. If respondents had moved, surveys were mailed or sometimes administered over the phone. In the SS/HS study, surveys were completed online, giving the respondents the ability to do it when convenient. The ability to select respondents randomly (when resources and access permit), purposively (when specific knowledge, position, or contrasts are needed), or opportunistically is an additional advantage. All these advantages make survey research a major data collection technique for policy research.

As noted in our discussion of survey use of Likert items earlier in this chapter, this closed-ended technique allows researchers to harden up data for advanced statistical analysis. Combining multiple item responses to create single scores on scales is a common way of increasing the precision of measures and of increasing correspondence to clearly identified real-world concepts. That is why survey research data produces quantitative measures. The powerful techniques of psychometric measurement theory offer ingenious processes for shaping soft human perceptions and opinions into measures hard enough for valid statistical analysis. The major point we want to emphasize regarding survey research is the care that must be taken to ensure that the hardened survey items maintain correspondence to the contexts, actors, and practices under study.

Producing data that has high correspondence with natural settings requires systematic grounding of instrument items. The process should include mapping data items, from existing instruments or original items created by the project, against the evaluation concepts and process models appropriate policies or programs in each study. This process often requires substantial modification of information items adapted from existing instruments and the development of specific items reflecting the setting under study. To the extent feasible, instrument wording or item description should be guided by document review (e.g., record keeping in programs), focus groups, elite interviews, and more focused refinement of items to meet setting through techniques such as cognitive interview labs to refine survey or interview questions (Presser et al., 2004). This due diligence is important to maximize usefulness of the survey tool. The discussion of the Individual Protection Factors Index presented in what follows is an example of instrument development designed to maximize real-world correspondence in a widely used instrument. While survey instruments developed for specific projects will not be able to go to this level of effort, they can take the steps of literature review, input from practitioners in the study setting, and pretesting through cognitive labs (Presser et al., 2004) or pilot administrations.

Documents and Records: A Hidden Treasure Chest

Documents and records are one of the most plentiful and potentially useful data sources available for policy research. The distinction between documents and records is that documents include primarily qualitative information such as laws, policies, procedural manuals, meeting minutes,

The IPFI: An Example of Correspondence-Focused Instrument Design

The Individual Protective Factors Index (IPFI) is a seventy-one-item instrument for evaluating interventions designed to promote adolescent resiliency. It includes short-scale (six-item) measures of ten attitudinal orientations in three domains (Social Bonding, Social Competence, and Individual Competence). The IPFI is an example of developing an instrument with high coherence to the real-world practices being measured. The developers (J. Fred Springer and Joël Phillips at EMT Associates) began with a literature review that provided a list of attitudinal orientations associated with adolescent resiliency; review of existing instruments provided potential items. To ground the instrument in real-world settings, the authors conducted group sessions with staff at four adolescent programs serving different populations. A set of behavioral and attitudinal items thought to represent important features of adolescent resiliency were presented and discussed. Topics included the extent to which constructs and items represented the service needs and objectives that were being concretely addressed in their day-to-day program activities, the appropriateness of item wording and content, and suggestions for addition or improvement. A pilot, 120-item instrument was administered to 2,479 adolescents of diverse ethnicity in twelve relevant programs nationwide. Resulting data was analyzed using exploratory and confirmatory factor analysis in the full sample and in individual program settings. The final IPFI retained the most robust domains, attitude scales, and items that showed evidence of reliability and validity across the programs. Since its development, this IPFI has been used extensively as an instrument and as a source of items in evaluation of adolescent resiliency. Users report they chose it because of its relevance to their programs, its face validity, and its understandability to both staff and participating youth. It has been used by dozens of graduate students, educational and service agencies, and evaluators worldwide (translated into at least seven languages). Its robust generalizability is evidenced by this widespread adoption and by consistent reports of its demonstrated reliability and validity (Aganji, Honarparvaran, and Refahi, 2012).

monthly reports, past evaluative reports, and other similar documentation. Records are more quantitative, typically creating systematic documentation of activities, events, and outputs of organizations. Examples would include court records, prosecutors' case files, intake records for any organizations serving clients, attendance records, personnel records—you quickly see the potential vastness of this category of data. Of course, many documents and records lie somewhere between these descriptions containing more and less systematic information. Public institutions produce documents and records to meet accountability as well as management needs. This adds to their potential as a treasure trove for policy research.

"[T]he documents that an organization or research site produces can tell . . . a great deal about it" (Greener, 2004, p. 78). Not only do they contain basic descriptive information about the context of the policy setting, they can provide a base of data for qualitative assessments. Meeting minutes are an example. How organized and productive are meetings? What is the nature of the deliberations that take place? Is it inclusive? Is it informed? Is it contentious? This qualitative information requires measurement and analysis approaches that parallel those described for interviews.

Records produce more closed-ended data, allowing the use of statistical techniques. In some cases they are convenient and informative sources of secondary data ready for analysis. In other research settings, such as the record systems described in the SS/HS environment, differences between organizations or even between subunits or different record systems in the same organization sometimes require instrumentation to be developed to standardize the data being collected across settings. A prime and fascinating example from the authors' experience was a national, multisite study of career criminal prosecution programs funded by the National Institute of Justice. The study was designed to document how focused career criminal prosecution units made a difference in performance indicators such as charging patterns, plea bargaining frequency and outcome, conviction, and sentencing. Additional process questions addressed issues such as time in process. All of this information was available in prosecutors' case files, but it was not uniformly organized across sites. The study team developed a uniform data collection form and spent hundreds of hours going through prosecutors' case files on-site.

Documents and records provide data for a variety of measurement and analysis needs, but one of their strongest features can be the opportunity for producing empirically precise and qualitatively rich information. In the Career Criminal Prosecution study, we referred to the empirical data from the records as the skeleton of the analysis, with the narrative case notes and interviews with staff as the muscle. Their close attachment in the case file allowed us to trace the ways in which the career criminal unit procedures drove the changes identified through records. Together they provided a comprehensive understanding of the nature and degree of differences made by career prosecution units and how those differences were made.

Site Visits

Another underrecognized tool for policy research is actual observation of programs in action in the field. Site visits can be more or less formally organized and be more or less intensive in the kinds of data collection they entail. Site visits range from a few hours of on-site interviews and observation to intensive visits in multisite studies. The latter can last for several days, often involve two or more visitors, and include multiple on-site data collection tasks. A mix of individual interviews, focus groups, records review, observation of services or events, and distribution of brief surveys to select populations may be used. These intensive site visits require careful previsit planning and assistance from local participants. They often include multiple locations on-site. In smaller studies, such as single-site local studies, spending time on-site can also be very valuable. Not only can it facilitate data collection, it provides the chance for "ambient observation"—seeing the program in practice and staff interactions with participants in their natural setting.

Policy researchers can tell you how much these visits enrich understanding. They often come in from the field energized and with new insights. However, many studies do not capture or systematize this holistic information, and it is not sufficiently incorporated into analysis or reporting. Site visit reports are often more like descriptions of what was done rather than what was learned about the site. In multisite studies, well-designed site visit data collection and analysis can identify important shared themes across site contexts. A technique used in multisite studies conducted by the authors (Chapters 9 and 10) fully utilizes the mix of ambient observation, interview, focus group, and other information that may be gathered in a site visit. This approach treats the site visitors themselves as key informants who have gained rich knowledge through the site visit experience. Before going into the field, site visitors are provided a detailed template of characteristics and questions about the site and program as units of observation. On-site, they follow semi-structured interviews that are uniform across sites and are keyed to the template. They also summarize notes and observations by topic, and assign ratings of the strength of themes as they emerge in each site. This provides a systematic database on observed, often emergent, characteristics of the sites and provides a doorway to quantitative comparisons based on this mixed-method data. These site visit summaries are very useful in interpreting systemic characteristics impeding or strengthening program implementation and performance.

Designing for Useful Application

"Research design" is a prominent term in the lexicon of social research. Generally, it refers to the logical structure of the analytic inquiry component of a study. To make this more concrete and understandable, textbooks may contain sections on types of research design, but the list of "types" will typically be different: explanatory, experimental, quasi-experimental, case study, longitudinal, cohort, descriptive, cross-sectional, semi-experimental, exploratory, comparative, confirmatory—the list could go on. All of these terms were pulled from one or another list of types of social research. The reason there is no consensus is that there are no clear and agreed-on criteria for exactly what a research design is—no clear set of attributes that define the term.

Focusing on logical or structural attributes of the design—control groups, measuring change, sampling procedures, and so on—is not particularly salient for policy research purposes anyhow. As we have emphasized, identifying the policy research information needed to address a problem comes first. The problem comes first, not the design. Building designs that will answer the right question(s) is the key issue. From this perspective, the multiplicity of design variations that makes it so hard to develop a consensus design typology is a good thing. It provides a lot of choices that can be used or combined to answer questions relevant to the problem at hand. Accordingly, our definition of design focuses on its purpose. A strong research design will effectively use collected data to logically and accurately address the research problem. In other words, the strength of a design is situational, depending on the questions that need to be answered to solve the problem under study, as well as the feasibility of methods and techniques in the study setting.

There is no consensus typology of the types of questions that drive policy research, and many if not most policy research projects will blend more than one of the questions we propose. Based on perceived frequency of occurrence and relevance to making choices among traditional design elements, we will briefly discuss four general categories of research problems encountered by policy researchers: exploration, description, causation (effectiveness), and choice (Putt and Springer, 1989, p. 86). In making choices about how to design analysis for a policy problem, it is helpful to consider the research problem in the context of one or more of these categories. Thinking them through is a useful way of defining information priorities and linking them to design and analysis techniques.

Exploratory Research Problems

Even with the glut of information that now pervades many public policy issues, public agencies confront problems that are inherently unclear or about which there is little reliable information. Decision makers sometimes are even uncertain whether they truly face a problem that can be addressed by means of public action. In such situations, policy researchers may be confronting *exploratory research problems*. From a design perspective, exploratory research is very broadly defined, and it is acknowledged that it draws a broad range of data sources and analysis approaches. In fact, it has been suggested that exploratory research is more of a perspective or point of view than a design (Stebbins, 2001). The objective is induction, using raw information to describe and develop understanding of a subject of interest.

Qualitative data collection techniques such as minimally structured key informant interviews, focus groups, or document reviews are typical of exploratory policy research, whether the objective is to improve the client's understanding of a problem area or to improve the policy researcher's understanding of how to design a relevant study. These qualitative approaches and inductive analyses to identify themes, categorizations, and plausibly important explanations requiring more analysis are particularly useful when understanding is minimal and the subjects are broad.

When concepts needing exploratory examination are more structured, harder exploratory techniques are appropriate and available. For example, concept mapping is an exploratory technique that has multiple applications such as developing "logic models of implicit program theories of stakeholders, developing measures, . . . linking data from different data sources in a mixed method evaluation, and creating pattern matching analysis" (Kane and Trochim, 2007, p. 174). It is a flexible process that begins with group brainstorming and ends with cluster analysis and interpretable maps and data displays. It has been called an example of "integrated mixed methods" (Kane and Trochim, 2007, p. 1). Exploratory factor analysis and cluster analysis are other generic techniques that can be used to identify linear dimensions or distinct groupings from pools of variables. In other cases, they can identify the internal structure of a group of measures. There are numerous versions of both factor analysis and cluster analysis that will shape the exact output. These techniques can be powerful exploratory tools, but they make assumptions about the data and the logical structure that must be well understood and carefully considered to ensure a credible and useful product.

Descriptive Research Problems

Descriptive policy research addresses a plethora of information needs. First and foremost, descriptive research helps answer the question "What's going on?" Indeed, it has been suggested that the simplest distinction in research designs is between descriptive designs that address "what" and explanatory designs that address "why." We will see that, in the complex world of policy research, this distinction has limited utility. For our purposes, it is more useful to think of descriptive research as the collection and analysis of data on the world as it is. In descriptive studies, the data is not manipulated to allow application of a research design, it is collected to represent the observed situation with as little bias or control as possible. The value of descriptive research for helping researchers meet the correspondence criterion is evident.

Descriptive information is particularly important for potential users of policy research because "descriptive research provides [decision makers] with information about phenomena they cannot possibly observe themselves" (Putt and Springer, 1989, p. 92). Descriptive analysis can describe situations as they are seen in as much complexity as the structure and measurement qualities of the data will allow. Units of observation at different levels in a hierarchical system can be described, changes over time can be described, associations and correlations between variables can be described, groupings of observations can be described. Since correspondence to real-world circumstances and events is so fundamentally important for research that is understandable and useful for decision makers and implementers, descriptive design is an important foundation for all policy research.

Describing *patterns* in data such as greater or less, similarity or difference, or strength of association can be the basis of significant analyses for policy research. The ability to describe patterns in data that have high correspondence to realities of problems and actions designed to address them is critically important. Indeed, it has been argued that "all social research is based on pattern-matching ideas. A pattern match involves a correspondence between a theoretical or conceptual expectation pattern and an observed or measured pattern" (Trochim, 1985, p. 575). Developing a clear conceptual or statement of an expected pattern is a fundamental beginning point for descriptive studies that produce useful results for policy action. Indeed, the presence of some expected pattern in findings is probably the clearest demarcation of the difference between exploratory and descriptive studies. Exploratory studies look for unknown patterns in data; descriptive studies look for expected patterns.

"Policies imply theories" (Pressman and Wildavsky, 1975, p. xxiii). For disciplinary research, searching for risk factors that contribute to behavioral health problems, the relation between social emotional development and school performance, and many other issues relevant to public policy, the conceptual guide to pattern matching is typically called "theory." It is characterized partly by relatively abstract concepts that are expected to be highly generalizable. For policy research, the conceptual patterns are typically more concrete—a policy specified in law or organizational procedure, a plan for implementing a program, an evidence-based practice, a logic model. To utilize the full power of descriptive analysis, it must be teamed with some variation of pattern matching—of conceptually designing what needs to be described and why.

As we noted earlier, entirely dismissing the ability of descriptive research to answer "why" questions is an oversimplification. The potential of rigorous pattern matching was identified decades ago, and it has taken time for it to really catch hold in the professional and practical literature on policy research. Today, pattern matching is the core analytic strategy in a broad range of design approaches including lesson drawing (Rose, 1993), realist analysis of causal mechanisms in the CMO/context–mechanism–outcomes framework (Pawson and Tilley, 1997), case study analysis techniques (Springer and Phillips, 1994; Yin, 2008), and "process-tracing" (Beach and Pedersen, 2013).

In an early summary of "pattern-matching design issues" (Trochim, 1989, p. 580), it was pointed out that full analysis of a program requires several levels of pattern matching. The *program pattern match* assesses the correspondence between "the program as it is theoretically conceived and the program as it is operationalized" (Trochim, 1989, p. 580). This is what we now call fidelity. The *measurement pattern match* is the degree to which the empirical measures being taken actually identify distinct variance between the concepts, as expected. This is what we call measurement correspondence in this text. Finally, it was argued that there is the effect or *outcome pattern match*. This would be the degree to which an expected condition that a policy or program was designed to produce matched with the observed condition. This third analysis objective, assessing the relation between expected and actual outcomes, is discussed further in the following section.

Causation (Effectiveness) Research Problems

Policies and their constituent programs are often designed to create change, solve problems, improve conditions, save the environment, make people smarter, make people healthier—for just a sample. In more scientific terms, government is expected to *cause* things to happen. When we ask whether a school or a program or government itself is *effective*, we are using asking whether it caused what it intended to or, more likely, what we wanted it to. Causal policy research is intended to disclose how effective a policy or program is in achieving its stated purposes, goals, and objectives. Unfortunately, that undertaking can be quite problematic. Policies are implemented amid an active environment of other forces, including social, economic, administrative, and political influences that may also have an impact on the target of public policies. Nevertheless, causal research seeks to disentangle these outside influences and measure the impact of policies and programs as precisely as possible.

The prototypical research design for producing valid findings on cause is the randomized controlled trial (RCT), also known as an experimental study. Through random assignment of subjects to a treatment condition (to receive a given intervention) or a control condition (to not receive the intervention), researchers can balance these groups on both observable and unobservable factors prior to the intervention being delivered. In doing so, researchers can eliminate many sources of bias from the research (e.g., motivation to participate), and therefore the conclusions of the research will be credible—assuming the research doesn't suffer from other threats to internal validity. For example, since subjects must be measured over time in an RCT, they can drop out, creating an attrition problem. The study may no longer be truly random, because attrition occurs for a reason, and that may interject bias into the remaining sample.

The reason that a control group is such a strong design feature is that it establishes an observable *counterfactual* that allows researchers to measure *what would have happened* if treatment (in our case the policy or program) had not taken place. By comparing subjects that receive an intervention to subjects that do not, we can not only establish the effects of the intervention but also establish what would have happened if the intervention was not delivered. The difference between these two estimates is the treatment effect.

Oftentimes, policy research does not have the funding, the timeline, or the availability of a control group to allow for strong, internally valid designs. Random assignments frequently cannot be made because of legal, ethical, or moral prohibitions on treating clients unequally. Therefore policy researchers must work with diverse methods to establish or estimate the counterfactual. Quasi-experiments (Thyer, 2012) are typically the favored option because they too create an observable, though less clearly comparable, counterfactual. Though there are many specific quasi-experimental designs, the great majority use a comparison group—which serves the purpose of a control group but is not randomly assigned. Comparison groups can be created in myriad ways, often using matching or other means of approximating comparability to the group receiving the intervention. Quasi-experiments can be improved by identifying differences between treatment and comparison groups and making statistical adjustments. Of course, this can only be done with measured variables and is an approximate correction.

Quasi-experiments are a powerful design approach, producing credible findings on effectiveness, when they can be used. But they require resources and time and access to the intervention and comparison participants and do not in themselves establish the implementation practices necessary to produce the observed treatment effect. Policy researchers have strengthened both quasi-experiments and pre-experiments (e g , single-case pre-post studies, multisite pre-post studies without comparison groups, single-site studies with clear outcome objectives) through use of the pattern-matching techniques that focus on creating clear process models with articulated contributions to achieving the outcome.

An observed treatment effect using an observed and credible counterfactual is a highly desirable criterion for assessing effectiveness. However, there are many other logical "cues" (Cordray, 1986, p. 13) to causality in assessing effectiveness that can be incorporated into the conceptual and observed patterns in a pattern-matching analysis. The standard causal criteria of temporal sequence (cause precedes effect) and covariation (causes and effects vary together) can be built into a pattern without a counterfactual observation. Beyond these standard criteria, additional criteria that are part of causal logic but not the experimental design can be applied. One that is basic to pattern matching is the complexity of the causal chain, that is, the detailed logic linking multiple steps in the policy or program pattern model. The greater the detail and specificity of the expected pattern, the stronger the causal implications when the observed pattern fits.

Contiguity and congruity of hypothesized causes and effects are additional logical cues (Einhorn and Hogarth, 1986, p. 10) that increase the credibility of evidence for a causal inference. Contiguity refers to the closeness of identified steps in a hypothesized pattern of causal events. When posited cause and effect are close in space and time, attribution to external intervening causes is less plausible. Congruity refers to the logical strength of the explanation for how and why an observed link is causal. A documented step in a credible evidence-based practice should have high congruity, a strong theory of change.

Natural variation design (NVD) is another approach to effectiveness analysis that is gaining currency in policy research. NVD mixes the reality correspondence of descriptive research, the contextual sensitivity of systems thinking, and the counterfactual comparison logic of experimentation. The NVD label first emerged in large multisite studies in which the natural variation between sites could be used to create contrasts. They might cluster schools into groups according to the degree to which they use traditional punitive disciplinary approaches (e.g., out-of-school suspensions, expulsions) or more restorative approaches (e.g., behavioral support groups, school service projects). These groups can be used to contrast measures of outcomes for which the different policies were expected to make a difference (e.g., disciplinary problems, dropout rates, school performance). Of course, statistical assessment of potential confounding differences between the contrast groups on other variables can strengthen these designs. Other applications (Springer et al., 2005) have drawn on the logic of comparative inquiry (Przeworski and Teune, 1970) to assess the capacity of observed and putatively causal relations to survive over a large number of diverse contexts. Ironically, using this approach, the more diversity in the sample the better. NVD can expand the "most different systems" design from comparative politics (Przeworski and Teune, 1970) to a generalized multisite setting. The logic is that a statistical relationship that is consistent across diverse contexts demonstrates external validity, which in turn provides evidence of internal validity.

Recently, the articulation of NVD has progressed, and it has become a credible design for successful policy evaluation proposals. For example, the national evaluation of the Office of National Drug Control Policy's (ONDCP) National Evaluation of Drug Free Communities (DFC) utilizes an NVD perspective. The DFC program evaluation collects data from 300 plus community coalitions each year. Introducing their NVD approach, the national evaluators noted that this coalition sample exemplifies

> the complexity and diversity of social initiatives operating in their real world environments. Researchers often treat this fundamental reality as a threat to generating knowledge and develop designs and techniques to control the diversity. A constant theme in our proposed design and analysis plan is that we treat this complexity as an opportunity to generate findings that are more relevant to real-world application. Accordingly, our design and methods are built to account for and explain the effects of this complexity, rather than to control for them.
> (Springer and Porowski, 2012)

When experiments, quasi-experiments, or careful pattern matching are all not feasible, policy researchers may have to resort to less powerful alternatives, with appropriate caveats. Pre-post designs among a single group of subjects receiving an intervention, focus groups that identify the opinions of a subset of stakeholders, or user surveys are among the alternatives. Carefully presented information concerning what would have happened in the absence of the intervention can help put it into perspective. For example, policy researchers may compare trends in dropout rates before and after the adoption of a dropout-prevention program in a single school system—but the credibility of findings from this analysis would be stronger if those trends were compared to statewide trends. Although this is not an ideal comparison, it nonetheless provides context for the findings. Policy makers and program implementers must act on the best information they have, and the policy researcher must keep that imperative in mind.

Choice Research Problems

When decision makers face a clear choice among a number of future policy or program alternatives, they may ask researchers to provide an analysis that will enable comparative assessment of their alternatives. Of course, good evaluation studies, studies of social or environmental conditions that may require public action, or other credible policy research products should provide decision makers with useful information for making choices. While this type of research problem is not associated with any particular data collection or analysis technique, it does pose challenges. What makes choice problems different is that they require the explicit analysis of options that provides comparable information on a common metric.

In highly constrained, tame problem realities, engaging choice problems can be fairly straightforward. What if, for example, a community recreation department wanted to choose among three optional designs for a new city park? They worked with neighborhood councils to identify shared criteria for what might be considered. Quite a laundry list was developed, for example, safety, a venue for neighborhood events, water recreation (pools, wading areas), playground, skateboard area, health trails for adults, and so on. A successful bond election made the budget for the parks clear, but some fundraising opportunities were identified if stakeholders could be attracted. The charge to the policy researcher is to provide data-informed alternatives for the department to prepare an eventual proposal to the city council. Depending on the available resources, the policy researcher could develop a systematic process for getting public and stakeholder input (e.g., focus groups, telephone surveys, key informant interviews), identify potential tradeoffs structuring alternatives, and identify options for enhancements that would be achievable with additional funding. And this is a tame choice problem.

The problematic nature of choice research comes partly from the need to establish a basis of comparison, particularly when the need is in the kinds of wicked messes that characterize major policy issues. Cost-benefit analysis is a quintessential and highly technical form of choice policy research. Today, it "is a touchstone language of American policy and lawmaking" (Purdy, 2015, p. 39). Cost-benefit analysis achieved this status in the 1980s as a way to resolve the technical and contentious decision making that accompanied setting and implementing more stringent environmental legislation and regulation. As noted in Chapter 2, environmental issues can be the epitome of a wicked mess for policy researchers. The appeal of cost-benefit analysis in this case is clear. While stakeholders have drastically different positions on the issue, cost-benefit analysis uses monetary value as the criterion for making comparisons. The assumption is that monetary value will have at least similar salience for stakeholders on all sides of an issue and has clear salience for public decision makers who are making decisions about what to do with taxpayers' investments.

Cost-benefit analysis has multiple versions, refinements, and adjustments to make it more applicable to different problems (Fuguitt and Wilcox, 1999). However, the basic concept can be described in three steps. First, estimate the cost of implementing a policy or program choice. Second, estimate the multiple benefits that will be produced by the project and estimate their monetary value. Third, create a cost-benefit ratio (benefit value divided by cost of the policy or project). The clarity of the result, a single measure of how much more value is produced compared to how much it cost, is a clear aid to choice.

Nonetheless, critics of cost-benefit analysis argue that the "would-be objective technique cannot provide a judgment of whether laws are good or legitimate" (Purdy, 2015, p. 39). Some of the reasons are technically rooted in the cost-benefit algorithm. For example, the "smoothing" inherent to the technique, narrowly applied, does not empirically reflect distributive impacts of a policy or project. The benefits of a water project may be heavily weighted for specific stakeholders (e.g., producers of water-intensive agriculture); and the process of assigning monetary value is fraught with issues of differential human values. Valuing a human life is the iconic example used by critics of cost-benefit analysis. It is an example of how hardening a wickedly messy issue into a technical-managerial solution can add a revealing perspective, but it does not resolve the underlying differences in values and interests that motivate the problem in the first place. Even with such an elegant technical solution, the underlying issue for researching choice problems remains finding criteria that are at once measurable, practical to collect, and politically acceptable.

Consistent with the theme of this chapter, the process of designing a policy research study is rarely a simple matter. It is not a matter of making the right choice of packaged designs in the blueprint tray of the toolbox. It is more realistically and productively seen as a process of creating the right mix of design elements to most effectively answer the research questions in a particular study context. Frequently this process itself requires taking a mixture of tools from the policy research toolbox. The cost-benefit example reinforces the value and frequent necessity of a mixture of technical and agile analysis. The job of the policy researcher in a pluralist democracy like the United States is to facilitate and empower optimal resolutions, not to dictate a decision.

Policy Research and Mixed Methodology

When the first edition of this text was published nearly two decades ago, the term *multiple methods* was commonly used to describe studies that use both qualitative and quantitative data and analysis methods. Typical discussions centered on how to use them side by side. For example, it was commonly stated that qualitative data was useful for elaborating or providing narrative examples of findings that quantitative analysis had produced. In that first edition, we argued for the value of a more complex view conveyed through the term *mixed methods* that was particularly suited to policy research. The argument drew heavily on an emerging methodological perspective called critical multiplism (Shadish, 1986). *Critical multiplism* makes the point that simply using multiple methods does not necessarily improve an argument. Clear, rational reasoning about *why and how* the particular mix strengthens the argument is necessary. For example, multiple methods can be used to *triangulate* different sources of method-based bias so the researcher can account for it. This only works if methods are thoughtfully selected "that have biases operating in different directions" (Shadish, 1986, p. 78). This requires critical thinking that includes understanding biases in the selected multiple methods, identifying how these biases potentially affect the measures or arguments being made in the study, and understanding how the use of multiple methods will help.

Using mixed methods through the thoughtful strategies articulated by the pioneering critical multiplists has many benefits for the quality and usefulness of policy research (Cook, 1985, pp. 46–47):

1. Increasing the validity and objectivity of research findings by promoting multiple perspectives to problems and issues.
2. Providing more comprehensive pictures of how policies work (or don't work).
3. Promoting value-conscious, debate-centered research that is more useful because it acknowledges differences in perspectives and values among stakeholders.

In the last two decades, mixed methods has become an increasingly recognized and recommended practice in policy research. Indeed, it has been called "a new star in the social science sky" (Mayring, 2007, p. 1). The multiplists were plowing new ground in what have been identified as the "paradigm debate" and "procedural development" periods for mixed methods (Cresswell and Plano Clark, 2011, p. 23). Today mixed methods are passing through an "advocacy and expansion" to a "reflective" period (Cresswell and Plano Clark, 2011, p. 27). As the mixed-method perspective has matured, it has also broadened from a focus on mixing data types to mixing research designs developed as singular approaches. The term *patched-up designs* (Cordray, 1986) has emerged to indicate that applied researchers, particularly policy researchers, had to borrow from one or more types of research design because a single one could not adequately answer the study question. They use components of different research methods to create a research quilt necessary to correspond to the patchwork reality of complex policies and the actions necessary to resolve them.

Mixed methods and the broader term *mixed methodology* have become standard practice in policy research and can now be critically reflected upon to ensure continued evolution and improvement in the application of research to policy problems. This may be partly due to the fact that mixed methods "is an intuitive way of doing research" (Cordray, 1986, p. 1). Skilled policy researchers sense that decision makers need more expansive information than that which one method or data source can usually provide. When problems are not amenable to solutions that can be simply proved or disproved, building a case through systematic evidence reflecting multiple perspectives is a strong way to meet the decision maker's need for useful information. It follows that mixed methods are increasingly incorporated into policy research education and practice.

The cases in Part II will provide strong evidence of the ubiquitous use of mixed methods. Examples will include:

- Perceiving that the information needs of decision makers required multiple types of information in a single study (and planning research to meet those needs).
- Incorporating multiple types of data collection efforts (methods) in a single policy research project.
- Incorporating multiple measures of key policy variables into the research process, either from multiple data collection methods or from multiple indicators in a single data collection instrument, or both.
- Utilizing the same data (e.g., interview transcripts) at differing levels of hardness (e.g., narrative examples, coded categories) to meet the varied information needs (e.g., perceptions or meaning, comparisons across contexts) of complex policy problem resolution.
- Conducting literature reviews that seek to synthesize the findings of past policy research.
- Incorporating the perspectives of important stakeholders into the planning, implementation, and presentation of research findings.

. . . to name a few.

All of this demonstrates the desirability—no, the necessity—of mixed methods throughout policy research. We have talked about harder and softer data and analysis, incorporating contextual awareness into even single-site studies and demonstrating distinct and complementary strengths of precise statistical findings, logic, and evidence-informed discussions in creating useful information. This is the way policy research is now done and taught. Two decades ago, it was still necessary to argue that policy research was not just compromised science; today policy research has a voice of its own.

Remember This . . .

- **Select data collection to fit underlying criteria.** The policy researcher can choose from numerous options for collecting data. These choices set fundamental limits on what kind of data can be collected and have very different resource implications. A thoughtful choice often requires tradeoffs between desirable characteristics of different tools. Underlying criteria include at least the degree to which the research team knows precisely what they want to know from the data source (e.g., respondent, document); the degree to which hard instrumentation will have to be developed; the degree to which the information they need is likely to be fully available through the source; the need for data corresponds to a challenging reality (e.g., one about which there is little knowledge); the degree to which soft data will need to be hardened to fulfill its purpose; the level of analysis for which the data will be used; the resources (time, money, skill) required collect the data *and make it useful for analysis.* The point is the choice should be made on the basis of careful identification of criteria and thoughtful consideration of how optimal data collection sources can be assembled.

- **Select research designs based on their usefulness and fit with the policy problem.** A research design organizes data and analysis to support the desired interpretation and utility of findings. Remember that the policy researcher wants to choose design tools that perform the analytic functions they need, not as off-the-shelf packages. One way to do this is to focus on the degree to which the logic of a design corresponds to the particular type(s) of research problems that need to be solved. Though they are not definitive, we have identified four widely applicable research problems: exploratory, descriptive, causal (effectiveness), and choice. This approach expands the credible design options available to the policy researcher. An important example is the increasing use of pattern-matching techniques to provide evidence on program or policy effectiveness. This approach to design provides increased flexibility in balancing the sometimes competing constraints and needs of problem, user, and researcher realities.

- **Policy research inherently uses mixed methods.** Good policy research has always required mixed methods. Since it is grounded in the understanding of immediate realities, exploratory and descriptive methods are required. Since it requires extensive understanding of context, including institutional constraints, documents are important. Since it often is assessing services and their outputs, records, interviews, focus groups, and sometimes surveys are needed. Since policy and intervention questions often provide input to decision makers, effectiveness and choice problems are central to many studies. When actual practice is examined, policy researchers have used mixed methods for a long time. As mixed methods is maturing as a professionally and scientifically recognized methodology on its own, policy researchers have more opportunities for putting credible mixed methods into practice.

Discussion Questions

1. What are the major advantages and disadvantages of each of the general data collection methods identified in this chapter (interviews, focus groups, surveys, documents and records, site visits)?
2. If you had to identify one of these data collection methods as most valuable to the policy researcher, which would it be? Why?
3. What distinguishes focus groups from interviews? Identify a policy research problem for which you think focus groups would be preferable. Why would that be?
4. What could you learn on a site visit that you could not learn through any of the other data collection methods? How important is that? Why?
5. What are the major differences between exploratory, descriptive, causal, and choice policy research problems?
6. What is pattern matching? Why has it been said that it is the basis of most analysis?
7. Why is increased attention to mixed-methods social research important to policy research? Do you think it could make policy research more useful for decision making? Identify at least three ways in which this might be true.

Assignments and Activities

1. Get ahold of a policy research report (there are many available online) and identify what data collection methods were used and describe the way the data they produced was used in the study. Identify the types of research problems that were addressed and briefly summarize what was reported about each.
2. Find a media story (or other source) that describes a policy problem that you believe could benefit from some policy research. Identify the research problems that should be addressed. Would a mixed-methods approach be useful to informing decisions on this problem? Indicate how and why.

5 Be Useful
Developing and Delivering Actionable Information

Ultimately, there are two primary types of policy research: research that is used and research that sits on a shelf. In this chapter, we identify strategies to ensure that policy research does not become a "shelf sitter" and strategies to move research more effectively into practice. This chapter will cover the following core topics:

- The policy researcher's role in applied research
- How to effectively communicate research findings
- How to define useful research and define the strength of the research evidence
- How to apply research to policy and practice

Few things are more satisfying to a policy researcher than seeing their research affect policy and the lives of thousands if not millions of people. In this chapter, we will demonstrate how research can be optimized for application to practice. At the most basic level, this involves working closely with policy makers to ensure that the content of the research and the information needs of the policy maker align as closely as possible. The case studies presented in Part II provide examples of how research can be packaged and applied to policy and practice, as well as examples of when research did not fulfill its intended use.

The Policy Researcher's Role in Applied Research

Policy research can be an incredibly satisfying career; however, some perspective is in order. Policy researchers are not typically in a position to make important policy decisions themselves, but they are in a position to influence policy by conducting credible research that builds knowledge and leads to informed decisions. It is incumbent upon the policy researcher to communicate findings clearly, to provide the necessary cautionary guidance on the interpretation of the research findings, and to ensure complex research findings are understandable to a lay audience.

This is no easy task. Sometimes, hundreds of pages of research findings must be distilled down to a few key talking points. While this can be challenging—and frustrating—it is a policy researcher's job to convey the "so what" behind research findings while also protecting the integrity of the research. Policy researchers have the responsibility to convey weaknesses in research methods that may compromise the utility of the findings. They also have the obligation to convey the most salient findings in a clear manner.

Above all, the policy researcher must maintain objectivity. A researcher's reputation is their single biggest asset, and any researcher should never feel pressure to produce results that are pleasing for a client or stakeholder. After all, research is designed to provide a learning experience. If positive results are found, it can be a wonderful feeling because hypothesized relationships between processes and desired outcomes are confirmed. If negative results are found, the onus is on the policy researcher to explain *why* findings were not favorable. In fact, less-than-favorable research results can be a wonderful thing if they lead to changes in implementation, target populations, or program focus that improve the program, policy, or practice in the long run. The point of research is to optimize investments and to make programs, policies, and practices more effective.

Effective Communication of Research Findings

Policy Research Products

Policy research can be presented in a number of different types of products, and the variety of products has been growing rapidly in recent years. The most common format for reporting remains the traditional report. The report may help decision makers choose whether further research, action, or inaction is the most appropriate response to the identified problem. It is beyond the scope of this book—or any other—to prescribe report formats. However, there are a few broad concepts that will make nearly any report better.

- **Know your audience.** Before you start writing, find out who the consumers of the policy report will be. If the audience is comprised of stakeholders who are more technically inclined, ensure that the methodology is written up thoroughly and presented centrally. If a broad, nontechnical audience is targeted, the methodology section can oftentimes be included in an appendix. The point of report writing is to meet the audience "where they're at" and convey findings in the most clear, accurate manner possible.
- **The policy cycle can provide a good organizing framework for a report.** Depending on where one is in the policy cycle, report writing

can logically be organized around the policy cycle by outlining a statement of the problem, the agenda-setting process (what alternatives were considered?), policy formulation (how was the intervention designed to solve the problem?), decision making (who made the decision to enact the policy?), implementation (where and to what extent was the intervention implemented?), and evaluation (was the intervention effective?).

- **Use a clear, narrative style.** A narrative style will enable the researcher to "tell a story," dividing the larger issue into its constituent parts and providing clarity for the reader. The narrative style is usually ideal for mixed-methods research, where qualitative data such as focus group findings is woven together with quantitative findings.
- **Analyze data.** Researchers are often tempted to simply present data and not analyze the results. The researcher should outline what the data mean in a real-world context and take care to ensure that assumptions or methods to draw those conclusions are clearly presented.
- **Define the "policy envelope" of an issue or problem.** The policy envelope refers to the boundaries of an issue (Patton and Sawicki, 1993): which aspects of the problem, for example, are policy manipulable, and which are beyond the scope of the decision maker's authority or influence?
- **Recognize the limitations inherent in the methodology.** Research is more usable when a candid assessment is made of a study's strengths and limitations. A transparent presentation of the limitations of the research will provide context for policy makers to make their decisions with confidence and provide insurance that research findings will not be overinterpreted.
- **Focus on the "big picture."** The best policy reports provide the "so what?" early and weave in data throughout the report to show why the core conclusions are indeed the most salient ones.
- **Identify next steps.** A policy report should ideally include next steps. The policy researcher is in the best position to identify the appropriate next steps (for either the intervention or future research) given the strengths and weaknesses of the report's findings. While a policy researcher cannot be guaranteed that these next steps will be followed, a prescription for next steps can shine light on the researcher's professional opinion and ensure that it is considered in the decision-making process.

Results of policy research can be communicated in myriad ways, including in-person presentations, informal communications, webinars, brief reports, memos, infographics, podcasts, videos, social media feeds, blogs, journal articles, videoscribes, and books. With advances in technology, the number of available presentation options is sure to increase.

In recent years, policy reports and products have been getting shorter, due in part to the platforms used to convey results. Using an extreme example, the traditional size of a "tweet" on Twitter is only 140 characters. It would be extraordinarily difficult to convey the core findings of policy research within that space. It becomes literally impossible if caveats or explanations are required. When brevity is necessary, hyperlinks and references to companion products can help ensure that methods and limitations are given the attention they deserve. This trend toward shorter presentation formats portends a greater role for policy research in the decision-making process, since shorter products are more appropriately tailored to decision makers' needs than large report volumes. The challenge for the policy researcher is to ensure that pertinent details necessary to interpret the findings are clearly and succinctly presented.

Data Visualization and Presentation Techniques

Data visualization is an updated term for a very old idea—a picture is worth a thousand words. A bar chart, a pie chart, and a line graph are simple examples of data visualization techniques. With the advent of more sophisticated technology to process and display data, this field is growing rapidly. The core purpose of data visualization is to tell a story with data, and given that researchers routinely have to distill data into a narrative, it is no wonder that much attention has been given to data visualization techniques in recent years. The central challenge with data visualization techniques is to present multidimensional data in a two-dimensional format that can clearly draw conclusions. For example, a researcher may need to present key findings that include a comparison of two groups, break down data by multiple subgroups, and present changes over time for a select number of subgroups. An infographic from the Annual Homelessness Assessment Report (AHAR) to Congress is included in Figure 5.1 that accomplishes these objectives (U.S. DHUD, 2014).

This infographic provides two points of reference to measure homelessness: on a single night in January 2013 and throughout the year. Each point of reference is presented separately, yet a comparison between these reference points is facilitated through a side-by-side comparison. Key subgroup findings are presented for states where homelessness is particularly prevalent, for minority populations (including African Americans), and for sheltered versus unsheltered locations. Trends from 2012 to 2013 are also presented at the bottom right side of the infographic.

By taking a large amount of data, distilling it down to a few key findings, and weaving together a technically accurate narrative of those findings, this infographic is able to convey a wealth of data in a visually impactful format. Most important, this presentation of data is accessible to a nontechnical audience. The use of infographics is rapidly gaining popularity, and the beauty is their simplicity. Although infographics are

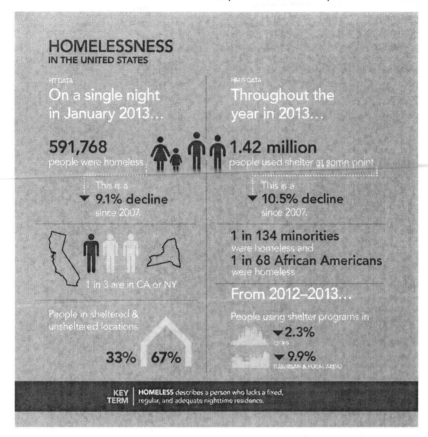

Figure 5.1 Infographic from the 2013 Annual Homeless Assessment Report (AHAR) to Congress

easy to interpret, they are very difficult to develop because the researcher must identify core findings and then incorporate visual cues to weave together a narrative.

The advent of geographic information system (GIS) mapping software has also greatly expanded the use of maps as a data visualization technique. Researchers routinely use maps to identify "hot spots" for particular social issues in communities (e.g., crime), to identify the location of community resources (e.g., health care facilities), or to locate and recruit community volunteers, among many other uses.

The following core ideas can help you produce high-quality, impactful data displays:

- **Choose the appropriate display.** Stephen Few (2004) asserted that there are seven basic types of quantitative messages to be conveyed in graphical displays: (1) nominal comparison, (2) time-series,

(3) ranking, (4) part-to-whole, (5) deviation, (6) frequency distribution, and (7) correlation. Each one of these messages is optimally displayed with a specific type of graph (Figure 5.2).

- **Bar charts** are ideal for displaying nominal comparisons of two categories, to display rankings (ordered by highest to lowest), part-to-whole comparisons (stacked bars are ideal for showing the parts of an entire category), frequency distributions (known as histograms), and deviation (using a reference line to show how far each bar's value deviates from the reference point such as the mean).
- **Line graphs** are ideal for displaying time series data (i.e., data tracked at multiple points over time).
- **Scatter plots** are ideal for showing correlations between two variables, preferably with a trend line to show the directionality of the relationship.

- **Highlight the most important data.** If you use different colors or symbols to show the most important data points, salient findings can literally pop out of a graph with the right design technique.
- **Add small multiples.** Edward Tufte (1983) introduced the concept of small multiples to introduce small, repeated variations in a graphical display. For example, a single line graph displaying monthly trends in crime rates in 2016 would provide far more useful information if it was accompanied by separate, smaller graphs showing trends from previous years (e.g., 2015, 2014, and 2013). These small multiples improve the ability of the audience to interpret how trends in 2016 compare to those in previous years, in terms of both within-year trends and between-year trends.
- **Use symbols to help users make connections.** The use of symbols can help the user make connections between concepts in data displays. For example, in the infographic in Figure 5.1, the authors enclosed the percentage of homeless who were sheltered in a symbol of a house—which facilitated interpretation of the "sheltered" versus "unsheltered" descriptors.
- **Put the magnitude of data or relationships into context.** By scaling the size of symbols (e.g., points in a scatter plot) to represent larger populations or samples, an additional dimension of data can be displayed. For example, using circular "bubbles" that are scaled relative to the size of a community's population can help an audience better understand the differences in outcomes between larger cities and smaller cities.

Exciting new advances in data visualization techniques continue to emerge. Some displays now use animated bar charts to show changes

Bar Chart

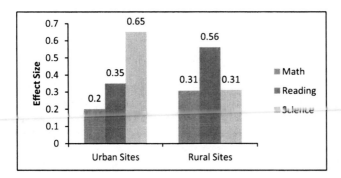

Line Graph

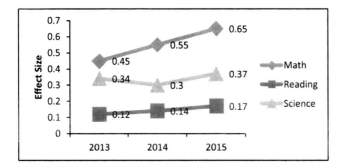

Scatter Plot

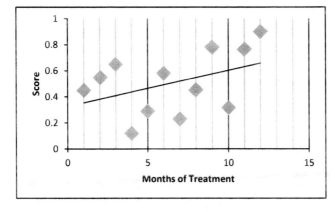

Figure 5.2 Common Data Displays

over time, and interactive data displays can engage the reader in a hands-on exploration of results. By engaging audiences with visually attractive formats, data visualization techniques can help ensure that policy research will be noticed and ensure that the data convey a true narrative about the findings.

The Policy Maker's Role in Applying Research

In order to properly engage in data-driven decision making, policy makers should have some capacity to understand research. They certainly do not need to be experts in complex research methods, but they should understand how to be effective consumers of research. It is sometimes up to the policy researcher to educate the policy maker on the appropriate use of evidence, such as how to assess the credibility of multiple (often contradictory) research reports, the meaning of statistical significance, how to interpret effect sizes, and how to spot weaknesses in research methods. It is not enough to assume that the policy researcher's job ends at the conclusion of a research report; the policy researcher must also help create conditions that enable the policy maker to make the right decision.

One of the major implications we have put forth in this section is that information is much more useful if it empowers the user. Rather than coming across as "here is what you need to do," research reports or presentations should provide concepts, information, and perspectives that help users make better intentional decisions in their environments. While we do not want to overdraw the simile, the empowering communication of policy research information can be compared to Bronowski's insight about poetry and the empowering capacity of the arts. "Poetry does not move us to be just or unjust, in itself. It moves us to thoughts in whose light justice and injustice are seen in fearful sharpness of outline" (Bronowski, 1956, p. 94). Policy research does not dictate the precisely correct decision or action. It gives decision makers information and perspective to more clearly see what they need to do.

How Do I Avoid My Research Being Misused?

Once research is opened to the public domain, findings can be misinterpreted, misrepresented, and misused. The policy researcher's best defense against these risks is to document findings clearly, address limitations of the research transparently, and understand their audience thoroughly. A policy researcher can avoid a lot of potential problems by anticipating how results may be misinterpreted by key stakeholders and anticipating stakeholders' incentives to willfully misrepresent findings. Unfortunately, these misinterpretations can weigh heavily on a policy researcher's reputation, so it is incumbent upon the policy researcher to counter these misperceptions before they become taken as givens in public debate.

As our introduction to agnotology in Chapter 2 demonstrated, there are researchers who will use the tools of the trade, sometimes with skill, to discredit sound research with which a client disagrees or to make an argument for an interest or ideology from which they benefit through misrepresentation or half truths. These merchants of doubt or deception are not true policy researchers. Being socially responsible in presenting and communicating findings is a central principle of policy research (Majchrzak and Markus, 2014, p. 140). This means, above all, "being sensitive to the potential harm you can do to people" (Majchrzak and Markus, 2014, p. 5). The policy researcher must take affirmative steps to be a responsible and trustworthy partner in making policy decisions, including being transparent about the application of methods, providing cautions concerning limitations of findings, presenting consideration of alternatives, identifying assumptions, and clearly communicating what is found rather than what a client might prefer to hear. Policy researchers cannot enforce the responsible interpretation of findings on all purveyors of policy influence, but we can lead by example.

Defining Useful Research and Evidence-Based Practices

Of course, to be useful, research must actually be used in the decision-making process. It may not be the case that decisions are ultimately made based solely on research results. Other factors identified in Chapter 1 such as political considerations, feasibility considerations, and cost can lead research findings to be relegated to the shelf in someone's office. We cannot guarantee that research will be used, partly because these factors are beyond the control or the responsibility of the policy researcher. However, there is another component to being useful that is more clearly within the policy researcher's bailiwick. Policy research findings are truly useful only if they are effective in guiding policies or programs that achieve their intended objectives. The policy researcher must deliver information that has credible evidence of effectiveness and convey that to the user in a way that meets their needs for the information and sets forth a course of action. While achieving this credibility was a major theme in Chapter 4, it is worthwhile to reiterate some parameters of credible evidence and their application. Ensuring and emphasizing these parameters are essential parts of communicating research that is optimally positioned to be both useful *and* used.

Internal and External Validity as Considerations for Effectiveness

As discussed in Chapter 4, internal and external validity are touchstone criteria for establishing that a policy or program will help decision makers reach their objectives. Internal validity refers to the ability of the research to establish a relationship between cause and effect, that a policy or program actually caused specific intended results, for instance. Put another way, *internal validity* is a term used to describe the credibility of policy research claims that a program works. If research is based on strong methods that eliminate sources of potential bias, it is described as having strong internal validity. Strong internal validity is nice to have in policy research; after all, if a researcher can use a strong design to establish credible findings, then a policy maker can proceed with confidence that the research design—and the resultant impact estimates—were solid.

As explained in Chapter 4, the prototypical research design with strong internal validity is the randomized controlled trial (also known as an experimental study). Oftentimes, policy research does not have the funding, the timeline, or the availability of a comparison group to allow for strong, internally valid designs. Researchers must therefore work with less-than-ideal methods such as pre-post designs among a single group of subjects receiving an intervention, focus groups that identify the opinions of a subset of stakeholders, or user surveys that may be subject to sampling error or low response rates. Although these designs technically do not provide a counterfactual, it is incumbent upon the researcher to frame findings in terms of what would have happened in the absence of the intervention being studied.

External validity describes the extent to which research findings can be replicated across people, places, times, or settings (Sparks, 2016). If research findings on policies or programs are generalizable, these policies or programs provide models for scaling up to new settings that will achieve similar results. But how can we tell if research has strong external validity? It's not easy. The generalizability of research is often in the eye of the beholder. A school principal, for example, may not believe that positive research results from a reading program in Philadelphia can be replicated locally—even if the principal is in a setting very similar to Philadelphia.

There are multiple ways that researchers assess and try to improve external validity. Replicating an experiment that produced strong evidence across diverse settings is a rigorous approach but is often impractical in terms of time, resources, or coverage. Large-sample studies encompassing multiple, diverse settings and proper analysis can also help, with the necessary investment. Less rigorous designs include cross-context comparison designs such as the "most different systems" designs developed in comparative politics (Przeworski and Teune, 1978).

Acknowledging the lack of clear and rigorous tests to meet the need for assessing external validity, Donald Campbell (1986) asserted (quite convincingly) that there are numerous potential variables and interactions that are controlled for in experimental settings that may limit the ability of research findings to be replicated in nonexperimental settings. Campbell's attempt at relabeling the concept of external validity to *proximal similarity* represents the notion that findings are most likely to be generalizable when the setting to receive a new policy or program is similar to the setting of the original research in time, subject characteristics, and setting.

In any case, the truth is that expert intuition is typically needed to assess the degree of proximal similarity between the research setting and the setting to be tested. Unlike rigorous tests of the statistical significance of treatment effects, there are no agreed-on "definitive" tests of whether a finding is externally valid. The U.S. Department of Education's What Works Clearinghouse has developed an "Extent of Evidence" rating in its research reviews that combines the size of the study sample and replication as contributors to external validity. The extent of evidence is classified as "medium to large" if more than one study is conducted in more than one setting, and the findings are based on a total sample of at least 350 students or fourteen classrooms. This does provide a standard metric but it is restricted to studies with student samples. While there is no definitive, prospective test for external validity, it is nonetheless a critical factor in a policy maker's decision making. Without evidence of external validity, implementing an existing program in a new setting is a shot in the dark.

Internal and external validity are widely misconstrued as being mutually exclusive concepts. In fact, they can be thought of as a process: first and foremost, research must produce credible findings. Then, if research produces credible findings, it can be assessed to determine whether results are generalizable to new people, places, times, and settings. More accurately, internal and external validity can be thought of as virtual bookends in a progression of questions that are necessary to a full understanding of a study's credibility. These interim steps between internal and external validity include the following: (a) *proof of effect* is assessing whether the degree of certainty (proof) that the findings of internal validity are strong enough to be accepted; (b) *magnitude* is the actual size of the effect measured in the study; (c) *fidelity* is the degree to which the actual policy or program being studied conforms to the model offered for replication; and (d) *utility* is the degree to which the potential realization of intended benefits of the intervention justifies moving forward. Table 5.1 provides a step-by-step framework for matching tools the policy researcher can apply to answer the logical questions for each step. While it is virtually impossible to capture all of the political, moral, and financial considerations that also factor into a policy maker's decision making, these questions and concepts for assessing research can be highly informative and help put the decision maker at ease about the credibility and strength of the information they are receiving.

While we will not provide a detailed narrative on the design and analysis tools that are entered in Table 5.1 (all of them have been touched on to varying extents in Chapters 3 and 4), several observations are important.

Table 5.1 Policy Research Tools for Assessment of Study Strength and Credibility in More- or Less-Structured Problem and Research Settings

Concept/Question	More-Structured		Less-Structured
Internal Validity: Does the research provide credible evidence of effectiveness?	Randomized controlled trials	Quasi-experimental studies	Single-group designs
Proof of Effect: Was there a real difference between intervention outcomes and what could have happened without the intervention?	Statistical significance	Effect sizes; assessment of practical significance	Strength/ likelihood of pattern correspondence
Magnitude: How big were the effects?	Effect sizes	Statistically adjusted group differences	Raw group differences (qualitative or quantitative)
Fidelity: Was the intervention implemented as intended?	Fidelity measures	Core component fidelity	Context-adjusted correspondence
Utility: Is the intervention effect worth the investment?	Cost-benefit analysis	Cost-effectiveness analysis, professional opinion	User assessment of the value of findings
External Validity: Will the results of the intervention be similar when I implement it here and now?	Experiment replication, large and diverse samples, representative sampling	Nested comparisons, natural variation designs	Proximal similarity of people, places, settings, and time

First, the placement of tools on the continuum of more-structured to less-structured problem and research contexts is not fixed. It may be helpful to think of this placement as the place in which each tool is most ideally suited—but they can be moved, with some adaptation, to preserve their strong qualities when they are needed in less ideal settings. The quasi-experiment is an example of transitioning experimental designs into less ideal environments that was so frequently used it became a recognized method of its own. At the structured end of this continuum, the techniques tend to have advantages of professional consensus on strength of design, the precision and power of advanced statistical methods, and clear decision criteria based on hard (quantitative) evidence. The less structured the reality of the problem and research environments, the more compromises must be made in these ideal characteristics, and it becomes even more important for the researcher to address these complexities. The policy researcher must make judgments concerning the optimal balance of tool strengths and problem/research information needs. Technical and agile analyses are themselves not distinct categories but join in different optimal mixes at points on the continuum.

The decision context portion of Table 5.1 provides an overview of selected policy research settings and the relative need for tools at different points on the continuum. These positions reflect the matching of tools to a decision setting that faces the policy researcher. For example, the first scenario is a decision environment in which the stakes are high and policy decisions are being made (e.g., a decision on environmental legislation that will impose high costs on select industries and produce incremental but widespread environmental and health benefits). In this environment, debate is likely to be highly contentious. Strong technical analysis with precise findings and precise criteria for validity are key here because of their strength in representing real results and withstanding criticism from those with preferences not substantiated by the data.

If the research is based on credible methods, if it provides definitive conclusions, if findings are of sufficient magnitude, if the program studied was delivered with fidelity, and if results are generalizable, policy makers will have far more confidence in applying research to policy and practice.

Defining Evidence-Based Practices

The prior section described a process of assessing the strength of evidence produced by policy research. One of the core reasons for making such an assessment is to determine whether the policy, program, or practice warrants use elsewhere—whether it can serve as a model for other decision makers seeking to achieve the same outcome. The propagation of knowledge about theories, methods, and the evidence underlying interventions has been enormous. In 2014, there were about 28,100 peer-reviewed English-language journals, collectively publishing approximately 2.5 million articles a year (Plume and van Weijen, 2014). The research produced by a policy researcher can become part of this enormous and ever-growing evidence base, or it can emerge in unpublished reports (known as "grey literature").

Clearly, research has produced a tremendous source of documented ideas that can and do help professionals meet policy and service objectives. However, it is safe to assume in most cases that policy makers do not regularly read peer-reviewed literature. Even if they did, it would be unreasonable to expect them to go through a study-by-study assessment process described earlier to see if they should trust the evidence before them. The onus is on the policy research field to distill, synthesize, and repackage this evidence base for practical use. As grant-funded program-evaluation proliferated in the 1980s, the value of systematically making evidence-based practices (EBPs) available to policy decision makers and program implementers became evident.

A key challenge was developing infrastructure to distill all this potential evidence down to the most salient, credible pieces of information—and to draw lessons from this down-selected body of work to apply to policy and practice. With a growing number of evidence repositories such as the U.S. Department of Education's What Works Clearinghouse (WWC), the U.S. Department of Labor's Clearinghouse for Labor and Evaluation Research (CLEAR), the U.S. Department of Health and Human Services' National Registry of Evidence-Based Programs and Practices (NREPP), and the U.S. Department of Justice's CrimeSolutions, methodology for conducting systematic reviews and presenting their results has emerged. These evidence repositories apply a peer review process to each study using at least some of the review criteria introduced earlier. These repositories provide a study rating that provides an objective assessment of the strength of the research and/or an assessment of the magnitude and direction of the findings (e.g., strong positive effects). The synthesis of findings across studies can then be made among the studies that pass a minimum rating to provide a summary measure of the average effects found and the rigor of the research underlying the intervention. These evidence repositories provide users an opportunity to compare findings across different interventions, which can help identify the most appropriate evidence-based practices for their needs.

Supporting Implementation of Evidence-Based Practices

Evidence-based practices have become a widely accepted foundation of good program planning and implementation, particularly in helping services including medicine, education, child development, and behavioral health. The underlying reason for using EBPs does appear to be widely accepted and is eminently sensible. Nevertheless, the ways to best put EBPs into daily practice is not evident. A recent advisory panel meeting concerning a national education program makes the point. The grant program promotes use of a program approach identified as an EBP, which requires local collaboration to develop and implement mental and behavioral health programs suitable for local community conditions. In a discussion about local resistance to some elements of the model, one of the panel members stated, "If we allow flexibility of the elements, how do we then say that this is an evidence-based model?" (This question provides an excellent example of the need to apply implementation science in assessing evidence.) Proponents of evidence-based practices tend toward one of two contrasting positions in answering this question: a linear approach or an agile approach. Figure 5.3 contains a simple graphic representation of these positions. As is predictably the case with models of complex social processes, neither is typically put in place exactly as depicted, and actual implementation draws on both. This is actually good, because each demonstrates underlying and inherently conflicting truths about a common goal. The goal is to use *demonstrated knowledge* on how to achieve a shared objective as *effectively as possible* in a new and distinct setting. The linear approach on the left of Figure 5.3 emphasizes the importance of demonstrated knowledge *in the form of a precisely defined program.* The agile approach on the right emphasizes the importance of factors in the implementation environment that may require adaptation of the model to be as effective as possible.

The linear model begins with an EBP that has been rigorously evaluated. The standard is based in the use of research techniques found at the well-structured end of the continuum presented in Figure 5.3. These are the criteria typically applied (in slightly different ways) for achieving a place on the most rigorous EBP registries. Granting agencies, particularly those federal agencies associated with creating registries, increasingly encourage (sometimes require) the selection of EBPs by their grantees. This expectation implies that interventions that meet scientifically approved standards provide blueprints for applying research findings. This is not the case in research reports themselves, so EBPs in this model are typically "manualized." Indeed, some registries independently

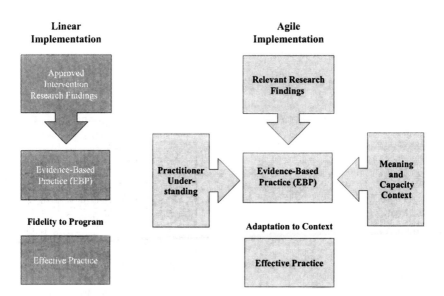

Figure 5.3 Alternative Views of Evidence-Based Practice (EBP)

rate the quality of guidance documentation to ensure that the blueprint implicit in the research findings is made clear.

Fidelity is the central criterion communicated in guidance and trainings for practitioners using EBPs. For example, a monograph on implementing EBPs prepared for the U.S. Department of Justice defines implementation fidelity as

> the degree to which a program's implementation in any real-world setting matches what was stated in the original program model . . . the goal should be to achieve the highest degree of implementation fidelity possible. In other words, an organization should always strive to deliver all program parts and activities precisely as they were prescribed in the program model.
> (Przybylski, Orchowsky, and Woodhams, 2015, p. 3)

To drive the point home, the guide goes on to state that "deviation from the model can not only degrade program effectiveness, it can actually create a situation where the program does more harm than good" (Przybylski, Orchowsky, and Woodhams, 2015, p. 3).

The agile approach places a greater emphasis on the importance of the immediate implementation setting for achieving effectiveness. This emphasis has long been part of the perspective on EBPs in medical practice. From this perspective, EBPs are "the conscientious, explicit and judicious use of current best evidence in making decisions about the care of the individual patient. It means integrating individual clinical expertise with the best available external clinical evidence from systematic research" (Sackett et al., 1996, p. 71). While this approach states that the best evidence "is usually found in . . . research that has been conducted using sound methodology" (Sackett et al., 1996, p. 71), it also recognizes the need for individual practitioner expertise.

Adapting a patient-centered approach to evidence-based practice developed by the Duke University Medical Center, the agile implementation approach is based in research but incorporates understanding of the practitioner's needs to apply the evidence-based practice (and adapt as necessary). The criterion for adopting the EBP includes relevance to the specific problem at hand, not the exact method used or the subject of study.

Implementation research can also provide support for the application of an evidence-based practice. For example, research has demonstrated the effect of practitioner skill and engagement with participants as a significant influence across diverse intervention models (Sale et al., 2008). Relevance of implementation research as a useful guide to evidence-based practice will be determined by both the policy researcher(s) involved in creating and demonstrating the potential relevance of the findings and the practitioner(s) who will use them. The application to actual practice will depend on adaptation of the research-supported evidence to the situation as seen by the practitioner and as constrained by stakeholder values and preferences in the local situation.

Implementation research has also provided specific tools and concepts to support the agile approach. One of the most important is the identification of EBP "core intervention components" (Blasé and Fixsen, 2013). The concept has also been referred to as a program's "active ingredients" or "behavioral kernels" (Embry, 2004). The idea underlying core intervention components is to identify the "essential functions or principles, and associated activities" (Blasé and Fixsen, 2013, p. 4) that are most important to producing program effects. The components concept also reflects the agile model by identifying principles rather than a prescribed set of activities to identify evidence-based practices. Principles are clearly guides that *require* interpretation and adaptation to specific contexts and populations. The culturally specific program example in Chapter 2 is a good demonstration of the core-component and principles approaches in action. While culturally specific ambiance and activity was engaging to participants, it was the incorporation of core principles of effective prevention into shared cultural traditions that drove outcomes.

Another brief example might help make the implications of these models more concrete. We have talked about the importance of external validity, or generalizing beyond the specific context in which a study is conducted, in making the lessons produced by the policy researcher more broadly useful. The linear and agile models imply very different approaches to addressing this issue. The linear model provides very specific guidance to action and would require replication to test findings' generalizability to different contexts. The agile model would provide guidance in less precise terms: first, identify the core (i.e., most important) parts of an intervention or action, and second, identify potential contextual considerations to the extent possible. Then it would rely on the practitioner to "generalize" the program or practice to its context as feasible. Put another way, the linear approach uses the replication model to address external validity, while the agile approach uses the proximal similarity model to address external validity.

Neither of these views about how to use research evidence to improve practice will define what is best or even feasible in all situations. The linear model will be more applicable in well-defined and structured contexts; the agile model will apply best in more messy and wicked situations. Actual applications will most often be a hybrid of some sort. Still, the models are useful and have important implications. The linear approach minimizes the need for policy researcher interaction with the client; the agile approach depends on the policy researcher and practitioner working closely together. The linear model limits information input to what is learned through the data; the agile model opens input up to more realistically incorporate what "makes sense" to the implementer and what may be allowable or supportable by key stakeholders. This understanding also hinges on the ability of the practitioner to understand the implications of the EBP and its relation to context. Agile implementation of EBPs will require greater investment in policy research products that make sense to practitioners; and practitioners must be given more education and training in how to make sense of research findings.

These concepts of EBP development have been in part borrowed from the field of software development. The use of traditional linear development techniques (also known as "waterfall"), in which a software program is conceptualized, developed, and assessed in its entirety, is increasingly being replaced by "agile" development, which focuses on an incremental approach. Agile development processes use cross-functional teams to develop incremental improvements in "sprints," and those incremental improvements are assessed with quick-turnaround feedback. The idea underlying agile software development is that by working in incremental sprints and rapidly evaluating success, products—and programs—can evolve more quickly and effectively.

The Future of Assessing Programs, Policies, and Practices

For many years, interventions were planned, developed, and implemented—then evaluated—as entire bundles. For example, a typical elementary school reading intervention might involve teacher professional development, a curriculum, "manipulatives" (i.e., objects that can be manipulated to help students learn concepts), a computerized tracking system, whole-group instruction, small-group breakout sessions, and a battery of tests. When we evaluate such a program, exactly *what* are we testing? The answer, of course, is the entire bundle of intervention components. This is the classic "black box" evaluation, which considers the reading intervention as a bundle of components without considering the incremental effect of each component. In recent years, momentum has been building for a new paradigm in which programs are "tweaked" incrementally in their development to identify and optimize the most effective components. These "tweaks" or "nudges," which are akin to agile development, have been used to improve programs substantially at very low cost. In an era of shrinking budgets, these types of approaches are naturally gaining in popularity. For example, Castleman and Page (2013) found that college matriculation rates increased among at-risk students when they were provided (low-cost) customized text messages in the summer preceding college that included reminders about prematriculation tasks (e.g., signing up for classes) and connections to counselors.

These types of behavioral nudges or program tweaks have opened up momentum for a new field of research in sequential and rapid-cycle research. Rapid-cycle evaluation techniques use rigorous methods to assess whether modifications in interventions produce positive, actionable results. Drawing upon frequent data collection and quick-turnaround analyses, rapid-cycle evaluations provide low-cost alternatives to traditional long-term evaluations. For example, whereas a traditional five-year federal evaluation may produce findings in the fifth year, the rapid-cycle framework calls for the evaluation and modification of programs to move research to practice more quickly, often multiple times per year. Although findings from rapid-cycle evaluations may be granular in detail since they focus on a particular incremental tweak or time period, they can nonetheless provide an agile method to improve programs at lower cost than traditional studies. Another outgrowth of agile approaches is the sequential multiple-assignment randomized trial (SMART), in which tailored treatment regimens are randomly assigned based on a subject's response to a previously delivered intervention component (Almirall et al., 2012). For example, a student in need of substance abuse treatment can be randomly assigned to one of two types of treatments, and after the completion of the treatment, students will be randomly assigned to a second type of treatment (e.g., two types of more intensive programs for students who don't respond to the first phase of the intervention or two types of step-down programs for students who positively respond to the first intervention). These "adaptive interventions" have the potential to produce better results at lower cost than traditional interventions—assuming the evaluation produces positive results.

How Is Research Applied to Policy and Practice?

Facilitating and speeding up the translation of research to practice has been a preoccupation of many researchers, especially for the last two decades. Morris, Wooding, and Grant (2011) reviewed twenty-three studies to track the amount of time it took to move research findings into practice. Even though the authors found it difficult to estimate the amount of time it took to translate research to practice, they note that in health, the literature has converged on an estimate of seventeen years. Needless to say, that fact is a bit discouraging.

Moving research findings into practice, which is known as "translational research," can be divided into two phases. Type 1 translation involves the conversion of knowledge from basic research to an intervention that can be tested. Type 2 translation involves moving the components of the intervention into standard clinical practice (Morris, Wooding, and Grant, 2011). With a turnaround time of seventeen years (in health care, at least), it is no wonder researchers and practitioners alike are searching for solutions to this conundrum.

Several solutions to moving research into practice have been identified, and they can be classified into the following approaches:

- **The evidence repository approach.** A number of evidence repositories have sprung up that are designed to provide practitioners a prescreened and repackaged presentation of research evidence. The U.S.

Department of Education, for example, established the What Works Clearinghouse in 2002 to be a "central and trusted" source for what works in education. The What Works Clearinghouse has developed research standards and established protocols for reviewing research against those standards. By identifying the most credible research and presenting results in clear, easy-to-use formats, the What Works Clearinghouse has taken an important first step in facilitating the movement of research to practice. Other evidence repositories that have been initiated by federal agencies include the Clearinghouse for Labor Evaluation and Research (CLEAR, U.S. Department of Labor), the National Registry of Evidence-Based Programs and Practices (NREPP, U.S. Department of Health and Human Services), and CrimeSolutions (U.S. Department of Justice). A review of research standards from these clearinghouses is one of the best primers on research methods a student of policy research can get.

- **The participatory approach.** Participatory research involves the conduct of research with the people whose experiences are under study (Bergold and Thomas, 2012). By involving community members, for example, in the conduct of research, the inquiry and research questions for a given study involve the convergence of scientific and practice perspectives. The two most common types of participatory approaches are *participatory action research* and *community-based participatory research*. Participatory action research involves four steps: (1) *reflecting*, in which community members and external researchers meet to define the problem to be researched, (2) *planning*, in which the research team designs the research to be carried out, (3) *acting*, in which the research is actually conducted, and (4) *observing*, in which the research team consisting of researchers and community members analyzes data and draws conclusions. In community-based participatory research, a "reference team" is created that is comprised of several community members who represent the community on the research project. The research follows the same general steps as in participatory action research, but researchers operate much more independently in community-based participatory research. The central focus of both of these approaches is on action, as opposed to knowledge building in conventional research. Because community members often collect data in participatory approaches, these studies lack scientific independence that ensures that the research is unbiased. Still, participatory methods are intriguing because the utility of the research is almost preordained—which is hardly guaranteed using traditional approaches.

- **The research partnerships approach.** Research partnerships are partnerships between researchers and government agencies (e.g., local education agencies), nonprofit organizations, or any other entity that requires the capacity to evaluate programs. Research partnerships are distinguished by the collaborative development of research questions between researchers and partner staff, the focus on capacity building throughout the project, and the dialogue between researchers and partner staff in reviewing research results. By coopting the people who make programmatic decisions on both the front and back ends of the research project, researchers are able to develop both research designs and findings that are optimized to be put into practice. The Regional Educational Laboratory (REL) program of the U.S. Department of Education is a good example of the research partnerships approach. RELs operate in ten regions throughout the U.S. in partnership with school districts, state departments of education, and others to use data and research to improve academic outcomes for students. The University of Chicago Consortium on School Research (UChicago Consortium) is another excellent example of a research partnership. The UChicago Consortium makes its research accessible to local stakeholders by hosting events for local practitioners, policy makers, and the media to discuss research findings and their implications (https://consortium.uchicago.edu).

- **Communities of practice approach.** Communities of practice (CoPs) are groups of people who engage in shared learning on a particular endeavor. CoPs may include practitioners that have the same job function—or they may include diverse groups of stakeholders who meet together to solve a common challenge. Formal communities of practice are typically held in moderated forums, often online. The moderator is in charge of sending the latest research to participants in the community of practice, who then can discuss opportunities for translating research to practice in their given area of expertise. While communities of practice typically do not engage in empirical research, their focus on collective learning makes them the ideal target audience for research that can be put into practice.

Does Applied Policy Research Really Help Improve Program Effectiveness?

One of the take-home messages in this text is that doing policy research is a challenging endeavor. It requires hard work and multiple skills and can be very frustrating when the cacophony of competing expectations, impossible deadlines, messy data, and disappointing findings grows too loud. On the flip side, it allows the researcher to look beneath the surface of political rhetoric, to see the reality facing dedicated public servants, to exercise creativity in a never-ending set of new and unique problems to solve, and, occasionally, to have the rewarding "aha" experience of a revealing an important finding. Behind all this, however, is the lurking question: Does what we do *really* help design and implement more effective public policies?

Based on decades of cumulative policy research experience on a great variety of topics in diverse institutional settings and at all levels of government, we can point to lots of anecdotal examples of why we *sincerely believe* it helps:

- The state agency that kept a lengthy evaluation report for years as the "best training" their employees could get about how to do the work to fulfill their mission.
- Developing a monitoring instrument for intervention effects on adolescent social emotional development that has been adopted around the world in eight languages.
- The many rewarding discussions with policy implementers who feel they have gotten a handle on problems that had plagued them for years.
- Developing research that catalyzed improvements in program standards that affect more than a million children each year.
- A chance to share the experiences of a focus group who enthused about how a community prevention program had changed their children's lives.

These experiences are personally motivating, but they do not answer the longer-term and more abstract questions about how much policy research helps overall. We do know for certain that there is a strong movement at all levels of government to use research more effectively in the decision-making process. This movement would not be possible if the value of research was considered marginal at best.

Policy research is increasingly understood as a multifaceted profession that requires comprehensive skills in understanding the policy environment, working with policy and practice decision makers and implementers, and creatively matching technical research designs and tools with dynamic problem environments. How does it get any better than this?

Summary: The Policy Researcher as Artisan

The policy researcher is typically charged to answer a simple research question, *Does the intervention work?* Whether the intervention being studied is a program, policy, or practice, this seemingly simple question is oftentimes dependent upon the behaviors of people. And we know that people are not the same—they don't respond in a similar fashion to the same services, offers of assistance, or even the same laws. Adding to this complexity are the behaviors of policy makers in response to research results. These complex real-world conditions require the policy maker to act as a scientist and an artisan at the same time, weaving together a narrative that frames both the findings of a study and the ancillary effects that the research may not have captured. Maximizing the usefulness of research is not simply a matter of finding statistically significant results. It requires rigorous methods, effective presentation of data, contextualizing the findings in light of the evidence base, understanding fidelity of the intervention's implementation, determining whether benefits were generated at a reasonable cost, and understanding the political feasibility of action in response to the findings. Definitive answers are rare in the social sciences, so the researcher must work as a true artisan. Just as an artist needs to capture the right shading of his or her subject, the policy researcher must cast the proper amount of shading on findings through the presentation of study limitations and caveats.

Remember This . . .

In order to produce usable—and actionable—research, a policy researcher should keep the following key points in mind:

- **Be forward thinking by working backward.** One of the key developments in the research-to-practice movement is a greater emphasis on involving practitioners in the design of experiments. Work with practitioners (or policy makers) and identify what they want to get out of a study. By understanding the key information needs of a practitioner or policy maker by the end of a project, you will be in a better position to design research at the beginning of the project to meet those needs.
- **Focus on the story, not on the design.** Impactful visuals in a report tell a story that brings data to life. While it is not a bad idea to ensure that data are presented in a visually pleasing manner, the key underlying motivation for infographics and data visualization techniques is to convey a story about key findings and their implications. If you can tell that story with visually pleasing graphics instead of a long narrative, that's all the better.
- **Internally valid studies are a foundation, not an end goal.** Developing strong causal evidence with rigorous research designs is not an appropriate goal *per se*. The researcher's goal should be to design a study to help stakeholders understand the effects of a program, policy, or practice in the most authentic, reality-focused manner possible. It is tempting to compromise reality to pull off a rigorous design (e.g., by limiting the study solely to sites that can implement a rigorous design), but ultimately, learning opportunities are maximized when the research aligns to reality.

Discussion Questions

1. A recent national study in teacher attitudes toward evidence-based practices (EBPs) asked respondents to indicate the extent to which

several factors would affect the likelihood that they would adopt new interventions in which they had been trained. One of those factors was "if it made sense to you." What would this response mean if you were interpreting the answer from the perspective of linear implementation of EBPs? . . . from the perspective of agile implementation of EBPs?

2. If you were a policy maker, what factors would you consider in determining whether research was "useful"?
3. As a policy researcher, what can you do to ensure that policy makers are using research accurately and effectively?
4. What can researchers do to increase the external validity of findings?

Assignments and Activities

1. Download an intervention report from the U.S. Department of Education's What Works Clearinghouse (http://ies.ed.gov/ncee/wwc). Identify ways this product can provide useful information to a policy maker to assess the strength of evidence. Is any information missing that would help a policy maker implement an evidence-based practice?
2. The University of Chicago Consortium on School Research is a well-known example of a research-to-practice model. Visit the Consortium's website (https://consortium.uchicago.edu/) and identify what type of research-to-practice model is used by the Consortium.
3. Find an example of an effective presentation of data, either from a report or from a website. Why do you think it's effective? What design elements make it effective?

Part I References

Aganji, N., Honarparvaran, N., and Refahi, Z. (2012). Reliability and validity of the Persian Individual Protective Factors Index (IPFI). *Iranian Journal of Psychiatry and Clinical Psychology, 18*(3), 220–226.

Almirall, D., Compton, S.N., Gunlicks-Stoessel, M., Duan, N., and Murphy, S.A. (2012). Designing a pilot sequential multiple assignment randomized trial for developing an adaptive treatment strategy. *Statistics in Medicine, 31*(17), 1887–1902.

Arias, E., Eden, H., Fischer, G., Gorman, A., and Scharff, E. (2000). Transcending the individual human mind—creating shared understanding through collaborative design. *ACM Transactions on Computer-Human Interaction, 7*(1), 84–113.

Beach, D., and Pedersen, R. (2013). *Process tracing methods: Foundations & guidelines.* Ann Arbor, MI: University of Michigan Press.

Bergold, J., and Thomas, S. (2012). Participatory research methods: A methodological approach in motion. *Historical Social Research (Historische Sozialforschung), 37*(4), 191–222.

Bijlsma, R.M., Bots, P.W.G., Wolters, H.A., and Hoekstra, A.Y. (2011). An empirical analysis of stakeholders' influence on policy development: The role of uncertainty handling. *Ecology and Society, 16*(1), 51.

Birkland, T.A. (2015). *An introduction to the policy process: Theories, concepts, and models of public policy making* (3rd ed.). New York, NY: Routledge.

Blasé, K., and Fixsen, D. (2013). *Core intervention components: Identifying and operationalizing what makes programs work.* ASPE Research Brief. Washington, DC: U.S. Department of Health and Human Services.

Bonneuil, C., and Fressoz, J. (2016). *The shock of the Anthropocene: The earth, history and us.* New York, NY: Verso.

Briody, D. (2003). *The iron triangle: Inside the secret world of the Carlyle Group.* New York, NY: John Wiley and Sons.

Bronowski, J. (1956). *Science and human values.* New York, NY: Harper & Row.

Calder, B.J., Phillips, L.S., and Tybout, A.M. (1981). Designing research for application. *Journal of Consumer Research, 8,* 197–207.

Campbell, D.T. (1986). Relabeling internal and external validity for applied social scientists. *New Directions for Program Evaluation, 31,* 67–77.

Castleman, B.L., and Page, L.C. (2013). *Summer nudging: Can personalized text messages and peer mentor outreach increase college going among low-income high school graduates?* Center for Education Policy and Workforce Competitiveness Working Paper No. 9. Charlottesville, VA: University of Virginia.

Castro, F.G., Barrera, M., and Martinez, C.R. (2004). The cultural adaptation of prevention interventions: Resolving tensions between fidelity and fit. *Prevention Science, 5*(1), 41–45.

Catmull, E., and Wallace, A. (2014). *Creativity, Inc.: Overcoming the unseen forces that stand in the way of true inspiration.* New York, NY: Random House.

Cobb, C. (2015). *The project manager's guide to mastering agile: Principles and practices for an adaptive approach.* Hoboken, NJ: Wiley.

Colander, D., and Kupers, R. (2014). *Complexity and the art of public policy: Solving society's problems from the bottom up.* Princeton, NJ: Princeton University Press.

Cook, T.D. (1985). Postpositivist critical multiplism. In R.L. Shotland and M.M. Mark (Eds.). *Social science and social policy* (pp. 21–62). Beverly Hills, CA: Sage.

Cordray, D. (1986). Quasi-experimental analysis: A mixture of methods and judgment. *New Directions for Program Evaluation, 31,* 9–27.

Cresswell, J., and Plano Clark, V. (2011). *Designing and conducting mixed methods research* (2nd ed.). Thousand Oaks, CA: Sage Publications.

Einhorn, H., and Hogarth, R. (1986). Judging probable cause. *Psychological Bulletin, 99,* 3–19.

Eisenberg, M. at TEDxUofW. (2012). "Are You Experienced? Information Alchemy: From Data and Information to Knowledge and Wisdom," University of Washington. Retrieved from http://youtu.be/d1pYbvmpm2o

Embry, D. (2004). Community-based prevention using simple, low-cost, evidence-based kernels and behavior vaccines. *Journal of Community Psychology, 32*(5), 575–591.

Few, S. (2004, September 7). Eenie, meenie, minie, moe: Selecting the right graph for your message. *Intelligent Enterprise.*

Fischer, F., Miller, G.J., and Sidney, M.S. (Eds.). (2006). *Handbook of public policy analysis: Theory, politics, and methods.* Boca Raton, FL: CRC Press.

Fuguitt, D., and Wilcox, S. (1999). *Cost-benefit analysis for public sector decision makers.* Westport, CT: Quorum Books.

Funnell, S.C., and Rogers, P.J. (2011). *Purposeful program theory: Effective use of theories of change and logic models.* San Francisco, CA: Jossey-Bass.

Gerring, J. (2012). *Social science methodology: A unified framework* (2nd ed.). Cambridge, MA: Cambridge University Press.

Gold, M., Helms, D., and Guterman, S. (2011). *Identifying, monitoring, and assessing promising innovations: using evaluation to support rapid-cycle change.* Commonwealth Fund Publication 1512, vol. 12. New York, NY: The Commonwealth Fund.

Greener, I. (2011). *Designing social research: A guide for the bewildered.* London, UK: Sage.

Hakim, C. (2000). *Research design: Successful designs for social and economic research* (2nd ed.). New York, NY: Routledge.

Hancock, D. (2004). Tame problems & wicked messes: Choosing between management and leadership solutions. *The Risk Management Association Journal*, 86(11), 38–42.

Hester, P.T., and Adams, K.M. (2014). *Systemic thinking: Fundamentals for understanding problems and messes.* New York, NY: Springer.

Hodgson, G.M. (2006). What are institutions? *Journal of Economic Issues*, XL(1), 1–25.

Holland, J.H. (2014). *Complexity: A very short introduction.* Oxford, UK: Oxford University Press.

Hughes, A.C., and Hughes, T.P. (Eds.). (2011). *Systems, experts, and computers: The systems approach in management and engineering, World War II and after.* Cambridge, MA: MIT Press.

Iida, E., Springer, J.F., Pecora, P., Bandstra, E., Edwards, M., and Basen, M. (2005). The SESS multisite collaborative research initiative: Establishing common ground. *Child & Family Social Work*, 10(3), 217–228.

Iyer, V. (2006). *Agile methodology and systems analysis.* St. Louis: University of Missouri-St. Louis presentation.

Kane, M., and Trochim, W. (2007). *Concept mapping for planning and evaluation.* Thousand Oaks, CA: Sage Publications.

Kellogg Foundation. (2004). *Logic model development guide: Using logic models to bring together planning, evaluation, and action.* Battle Creek, MI: W.K. Kellogg Foundation.

Kirchin, S. (Ed.). (2013). *Thick concepts.* Oxford, UK: Oxford University Press.

Kress, G., Koehler, G. and Springer, J.F. (1981). Policy drift: An evaluation of the California Business Enterprise Program. In D.J. Palumbo and M. Harder (Eds.). *Implementing Public Policy.* Lexington, MA: Lexington Books.

Majchrzak, A., and Markus M. (2014). *Methods for policy research: Taking socially responsible action* (2nd ed.). Los Angeles, CA: Sage Publications.

Mayring, P. (2007). Introduction: Arguments for mixed methodology. In P. Mayring, G.L. Huber, L. Gurtler, and M. Kiegelmann (Eds.), *Mixed methodology in psychological research* (pp. 1–4). Rotterdam/Taipei: Sense Publishers.

Michaels, D. (2008). *Doubt is their product: How industry's assault on science threatens your health.* London, UK: Oxford University Press.

Miles, A. (2009). Complexity in medicine and healthcare: People and systems, theory and practice. *Journal of Evaluation in Clinical Practice, 15*, 409–410.

Morris, Z.S., Wooding, S., and Grant, J. (2011). The answer is 17 years, what is the question: Understanding time lags in translational research. *Journal of the Royal Society of Medicine, 104*(12), 510–520.

Oreskes, N., and Conway, E.M. (2010). *Merchants of doubt: How a handful of scientists obscured the truth on issues from tobacco smoke to global warming.* New York, NY: Bloomsbury Press.

Patton, C., Sawicki, D., and Clark, J. (2012). *Basic methods of policy analysis and planning* (3rd ed.). New York, NY: Routledge.

Pawson, R. and Tilley, N. (1997). *Realistic evaluation.* London: Sage

Plume, A., and van Weijen, D. (2014, September). Publish or perish? The rise of the fractional author. *Research Trends*, Issue 38. Retrieved from www.researchtrends.com/issue-38-september-2014/publish-or-perish-the-rise-of-the-fractional-author.

Presser, J., Rothgeb, M., Couper, M., Lessler, J., Martin, E., Martin, J., and Singer, E. (Eds.). (2004). *Methods for testing and evaluating survey questionnaires.* New York, NY: Wiley Inter-science.

Pressman, J., and Wildawsky, A. (1975). *Implementation.* Berkeley, CA: University of California Press.

Przeworski, A., and Teune, H. (1970). *The logic of comparative inquiry.* New York, NY: Wiley.

Przybylski, R., Orchowsky, S., and Woodhams, T. (2015). *Implementing evidence-based practices.* Report prepared for the U.S. Department of Justice, Bureau of Justice Assistance. Washington, DC: Justice Research and Statistics Association.

Purdy, J. (2015). *After nature: A politics for the Anthropocene.* Cambridge, MA: Harvard University Press.

Putnam, H. (2002). *The collapse of the fact/value dichotomy and other essays.* Cambridge, MA: Harvard University Press.

Putt, A.D., and Springer, J.F. (1989). *Policy research: Concepts, methods, and application.* New York, NY: Prentice-Hall.

Raudenbush, S.W., and Bryk, A.S. (2002). *Hierarchical linear models: Applications and data models.* Thousand Oaks, CA: Sage Publications.

Room, G. (2011). *Complexity, institutions, and public policy: Agile decision-making in a turbulent world.* Cheltenham, UK: Edward Elger.

Rose, R. (1993). *Lesson drawing in public policy.* Chatham, NJ: Chatham House Publishing.

Rossi, P.H., Lipsey, M.W., and Freeman, H.E. (2004). *Evaluation: A systematic approach* (7th ed.). Thousand Oaks, CA: Sage Publications.

Royce, W.W. (1970, August). Managing the development of large software systems. *Proceedings of IEEE WESCON, 26*, 1–9.

Sackett, D.L., Rosenberg, W.M., Gray, J.M., Haynes, R.B., and Richardson, W.S. (1996). Evidence based medicine: What it is and what it isn't. *BMJ, 312*(7023), 71–72.

Sale, E., Bellamy, N., Springer, J.F., and Wang, M.Q. (2008). Quality of provider-participant relationships and enhancement of adolescent social skills. *Journal of Primary Prevention, 29*, 263–278.

Scharpf, F.W. (1997). *Games real actors play: Actor-centered institutionalism in policy research.* Boulder, CO: Westview Press.

Schwartz-Shea, P., and Yanow, D. (2012). *Interpretive research design: Concepts and processes*. New York, NY: Routledge.

Shadish, W.R. (1986). Planned critical multiplism: Some elaborations. *Behavioral Assessment, 8*, 75–103.

Shadish, W.R., Cook, T.D., and Campbell, D.T. (2001). *Experimental and Quasi-experimental designs for generalized causal inference* (2nd ed.). Boston, MA: Houghton Mifflin.

Sparks, G.G. (2016). *Media effects research: A basic overview* (5th ed.). Boston, MA: Cengage Learning.

Springer, J.F. (1976). Empirical theory and development administration: Prologues and promise. *Public Administration Review, 36*(6), 636–641.

Springer, J.F. (1985). Policy analysis and organizational decisions: Toward a conceptual revision. *Administration and Society, 16*(4), 475–508.

Springer, J.F., and Phillips, J.L. (1994). Policy learning and evaluation design: Lessons from the community partnership demonstration program. *Journal of Community Psychology*, CSAP Special Issue, 117–139.

Springer, J.F., and Porowski, A. (2012). *Natural variation logic and the DFC contribution to evidence-based practice*. Presentation to the Society for Prevention Research, Washington, DC.

Springer, J.F., Sale, E., Hermann, J., Sambrano, S., Kasim, R., and Nistler, M. (2004). Characteristics of effective substance abuse programs for high-risk youth. *The Journal of Primary Prevention, 25*(2), 171–194.

Springer, J.F., Sale, E., Kasim, R., Winter, W., Sambrano, S., and Chipungu, S. (2004). Effectiveness of culturally specific approaches to substance abuse prevention: Findings from CSAP's national cross-site evaluation of high risk youth programs. *Journal of Ethnic & Cultural Diversity in Social Work, 13*(3), 1–23.

Stebbins, R.A. (2001). *Exploratory research in the social sciences*. Thousand Oaks, CA: Sage Publications.

Sternberg, R.J. (2001). Teaching psychology students that creativity is a decision. *The General Psychologist, 36*(1), 8–11.

Sternberg, R.J. (2006). The nature of creativity. *Creativity Research Journal, 18*(1), 87–98.

Sternberg, R.J., and Lubart, T.I. (1995). *Defying the crowd*. New York, NY: Free Press.

Substance Abuse and Mental Health Services Administration (SAMHSA). (2003). *The national cross-site evaluation of high-risk youth: Points of prevention*. Washington, DC: U.S. Government Printing Office.

Thapa, A., Cohen, J., Higgins-D'Alessandro, A., and Guffey, S. (2012). *School climate research summary*. New York, NY: National School Climate Center.

Thyer, B. (2012). *Quasi-experimental research designs*. New York, NY: Oxford Press.

Trochim, W. (1985). Pattern matching, validity, and conceptualization in program evaluation. *Evaluation Review, 9*(5), 575–604.

Trochim, W. (1989). Outcome pattern matching and program theory. *Evaluation & Program Planning, 12*, 355–366.

Tufte, E. (1983). *Visual display of quantitative information*. Cheshire, CT: Graphics Press.

U.S. Department of Housing and Urban Development. (2014). *The 2013 annual homeless assessment report to congress. Part 2: Estimates of homelessness in the United States*. Washington, DC: U.S. Government Printing Office.

Vaus, D. de (2013). *Surveys in social research*. New York, NY: Routledge.

Waldrop, M.M. (1992). *Complexity: The emerging science at the edge of order and chaos*. New York, NY: Simon & Schuster.

Wassertein, R.L., and Lazar, N.A. (2016). The ASA's statement on *p*-values: context, process, and purpose. *The American Statistician, 70*, 129–133.

Wildawsky, A. (1979). *Speaking truth to power: The art and craft of policy analysis*. New Brunswick, NJ: Transaction Press.

Yin, R.K. (2013). *Case study research: Design and methods* (5th ed.). Los Angeles, CA: Sage Publications.

Part II

Cases in Policy Research

Part II Introduction

Part I of this text has provided a broad view of the realities that policy researchers face, the tools and methods they have at their disposal to conduct policy research, and the perspectives they bring to produce useful information. Part II presents case studies in policy research that demonstrate how the skills and efforts of policy researchers play out in real-world circumstances. The cases are not hypothetical; they are descriptions of real policy research, telling how the project came about, how it was conducted, what was found, and how it was or was not used. They were not selected because they were particularly successful or because they demonstrated a particular point. They were selected primarily to reflect diversity in the policy research context, method, and outcomes.

Part I Concepts and Part II Case Studies Crosswalk

Table II.1 provides a crosswalk of topics discussed in Part I with each of the case studies in Part II. This crosswalk is designed to identify which case studies provide a guide for how a particular topic introduced in Part I was applied through real-world policy research. Some topics (e.g., descriptive research problems) are to some degree applicable to nearly every case. Only those cases that clearly demonstrate application of a concept or topic are checked in the table.

The rows in Table II.1 provide the chapter number and a brief name for each of the case studies. The chapters are organized by general policy areas.

- Chapters 6 to 10 address social policies and programs. The first three provide examples of different policy approaches to reduce school dropout; the others concern implementation of state bullying laws and identifying lessons for "what works" in youth substance abuse prevention programs.

Table II.1 Crosswalk of Part I Concepts and Part II Case Studies

	1. National	2. State	3. Local	4. Messy Problem	5. Wicked Problem	6. Wicked Mess	7. Meaning	8. Institutional Context	9. Hard Data	10. Soft Data	11. Hierarchical Data	12. Interviews	13. Surveys	14. Documents / Records	15. Site Visits	16. Mixed Methods	17. Advanced Statistics	18. Exploratory	19. Descriptive	20. Causal / Explanatory	21. Choice	22. Implementation Science	23. Internal Validity	24. External Validity	25. Research to Practice
Ch6. Refining Quality Standards	✓		✓	✓			✓	✓	✓				✓	✓		✓	✓	✓	✓	✓	✓	✓	✓✓	✓	✓
Ch7. Dropout Prevention Mentoring	✓✓	✓✓	✓	✓	✓				✓	✓			✓			✓		✓		✓	✓	✓	✓	✓	✓
Ch8. State Dropout Policy		✓	✓						✓							✓			✓					✓	✓
Ch9. Implementing Bullying Laws			✓					✓	✓	✓	✓	✓		✓	✓	✓		✓	✓			✓	✓		✓
Ch10. Program Effectiveness		✓	✓		✓		✓	✓	✓	✓	✓	✓	✓	✓	✓	✓	✓	✓		✓	✓	✓	✓		
Ch11. Waste Management			✓			✓	✓		✓	✓				✓		✓		✓			✓		✓	✓	
Ch12. Transit Tax Initiatives			✓						✓	✓		✓		✓		✓	✓			✓	✓		✓		
Ch13. High Speed Rail Workforce	✓		✓	✓		✓		✓		✓				✓	✓	✓	✓		✓						✓
Ch14. Climate Change Adaptation		✓	✓	✓			✓		✓	✓		✓	✓			✓		✓	✓					✓	
Ch15. City Housing Sales			✓			✓	✓		✓	✓		✓	✓			✓			✓						
Ch16. Ignition Interlock Pilot	✓	✓	✓		✓					✓		✓		✓	✓	✓	✓		✓	✓	✓	✓	✓	✓	✓
Ch17. Community Policing			✓			✓	✓	✓		✓			✓	✓		✓		✓	✓						
Ch18. Recruiting Foster Families							✓	✓	✓	✓		✓		✓	✓	✓			✓			✓			
Ch19. Public Debt Burden		✓✓				✓✓	✓	✓✓	✓✓	✓		✓	✓	✓		✓	✓		✓				✓	✓	
Ch20. Changing Institutions								✓	✓	✓				✓		✓		✓	✓			✓			

- Chapters 11 to 15 provide a variety of examples of policy research concerning environment, infrastructure, and planning policies (e.g., climate, waste management, transportation, and housing).
- Chapters 16 and 17 concern topics in criminal justice policy.
- Chapters 18 to 20 include cases related to government institutional and procedural practice.

The columns in Table II.1 identify important topics raised in the five Part I chapters. Chapters 1 through 3 have fewer columns because those chapters focus on the overall policy research environment and setting the stage for making more specific decisions about how to carry out a research project. Chapter 4 has many more columns because it is about how the policy researcher chooses particular tools and design features that will tailor the study to a specific problem and setting. These are the decisions that will distinguish one study from another and are more readily applicable to individual cases.

The following descriptions of the column topics help clarify what to look for in cases that are checked.

- *Level of Commission and Application.* The first three columns indicate the governmental level at which the policy research was initiated and commissioned and the level at which the findings are intended to be applied.
- *Complexity of the Policy Problem.* Columns 4 through 6 indicate the degree and nature of the complexity of the problem reality addressed in the study.
- *Meaning.* Column 7 will be checked if unclear assumptions, differences in interpretation, conflicting values, unclear concepts, or other issues of meaning play a central role in the policy study.
- *Institutional Context.* Column 8 will be checked if the institutional setting (e.g., laws, rules, procedures, authority, culture) is a core challenge or issue in the study.
- *Hard and Soft Data.* Columns 9 and 10 will be checked if the case makes substantial use of quantitative data, qualitative data, or both.
- *Hierarchical Data.* Column 11 will be checked if data is systematically collected at different levels, with lower levels nested within higher levels in the analysis.
- *Data Collection Methods.* Columns 12 through 15 indicate the data collection methods that were used in the study.
- *Mixed Methods.* Column 16 will be checked if the study makes substantial use of mixed methods (e.g., both qualitative and quantitative, complementary analysis techniques) in measuring concepts, conducting analyses, or interpreting results.
- *Advanced Statistics.* Column 17 will be checked if the study uses multivariate, longitudinal, hierarchical, or other advanced statistical

analyses (i.e., more than simple descriptive or comparative statistical methods).

- *Research Problem Type.* Columns 18 through 21 indicate the research problem question types (i.e., exploratory, descriptive, causal choice) that are an important part of the analysis and findings in the study.
- *Implementation Science.* Column 22 will be checked if analysis and findings related to the implementation of a policy are an important part of the case.
- *Internal/External Validity.* Columns 23 and 24 indicate the degree to which the case focuses on establishing and communicating strong internal validity of causal analyses or the external validity (generalizability) of case findings.
- *Research to Practice.* The final column will be checked if the case explicitly addresses the application of policy research products as guides to practice (e.g., EBPs).

As summarized in Table II.1, these case studies provide a diverse set of examples. They include national, state, and local studies from different regions of the country; the studies were conducted by a variety of policy researchers; they address different degrees of study complexity (from tame problems to wicked messes); and they demonstrate use of many different tools in different combinations. Some cases were directly applied and produced policy actions; some had less direct effects by contributing to changed perspectives on a problem or policy; some just sat on a shelf.

Case Study Outline

Each case study follows a similar organization that serves to highlight how the policy research exemplifies concepts and topics identified in the previous chapters. The outline follows a fairly consistent pattern that usually includes the following headings.

Introduction . . .

names the study, provides background, and highlights the policy research concepts that the case study best exemplifies.

The Policy Problem . . .

describes the policy context of the research. The discussion typically includes the basic background and history of the policy and/or program that the research addresses. It helps establish why the policy research was necessary and what it may contribute to policy decisions. Some of the case studies address very specific programs, and others cover broader policy concerns.

Initiation of Policy Research . . .

includes discussion of who requested the research, who conducted it, and why. The case studies reflect a variety of contexts for both client and researcher. Clients include local, state, and federal government agencies as well as nonprofit organizations. Policy researchers include government agencies, consulting agencies, and individuals. Additionally, the case studies represent different *mechanisms* for initiation of policy research, including legislative mandates, requests for proposals (RFPs), and more informal means.

The Policy Research Task . . .

presents a general, introductory discussion of the nature and scope of the policy research task implied by the request from the decision maker. This discussion includes the nature, rigor, and scope of the primary research task but also includes tasks related to establishing relations with the client, clarifying study purposes, and communicating the requirements and limitations of the research task to the client.

Objectives . . .

outlines the general purposes of the policy research; what did the policy research team need to accomplish? The decisions can include specific objectives as stated by the client or objectives that were developed by the policy researcher. In some instances, the negotiation of specific objectives is an important part of the overall policy research task.

Challenges . . .

identifies unique conditions, often constraints, that represent challenges for policy researchers. This section helps to clarify how the realities of the research context affect the research process and how policy researchers must be responsive and creative in addressing these realities.

The Decision Context . . .

introduces the decision context in which study results will be applied. The intention to use findings and possibly recommendations directly for decision-making purposes—policy-related, programmatic, or managerial—is a major factor distinguishing applied policy research from other types of research. This section considers contextual circumstances that influence the degree to which this intention is realized.

The Institutional Context . . .

identifies key agencies, organizations, and individuals involved in making decisions pertinent to the case study research projects. Some studies focus on only one organization, whereas in others, many organizations participate in the decisions. Understanding their role is important to fashioning usable policy research.

The Policy Cycle . . .

illustrates the points in the policy cycle at which studies are initiated and the points in the policy cycle at which the results are expected to be used. Each study occurs at a different point in the cycle, with significant implications for how policy research is conducted.

Clients and Stakeholders . . .

describes the clients and stakeholders that may have an important interest in the study and what influence they may bring to bear. The potential information needs, opportunities, and constraints stakeholders may bring to the study context are important considerations in designing and implementing a policy research project.

Research Design and Implementation . . .

provides an overview of how policy research was actually conducted in each case. The emphasis is on how the research was designed, adapted, and implemented to meet the needs and constraints of the realities described earlier in each case study. Some of the key findings derived from those methods are presented, including an explanation of how the methods led to the research findings.

Information Needs . . .

explores the information needs of the client—the driving force behind effective policy research. Because applied research situations virtually always require a variety of types of information, the discussion in some cases identifies the relative priority of different information needs.

Design and Methods . . .

describes the overall research design and the specific techniques or methods used to implement it. The designs range from those that are relatively simple, straightforward, and structured to those that involve multiple methods and complex interpretations. The discussion of design and method includes explication of the logic of the research and the rationale for selection of data collection and analytic techniques.

Selected Findings . . .

presents key excerpts from the findings of each project. Findings are selected to highlight important features of study design and application. This section is the critical bridge between the intention and design of the research work and its application.

Communicating and Using Results . . .

describes the ways in which findings and interpretations are communicated to potential users. Traditionally, this has been done through technical reports, but policy researchers interested in fostering use of their findings are turning to other modes of communication. The story of a piece of policy research is not complete until the resulting policy actions are identified.

Reporting Results . . .

describes how the research findings were organized and presented, including a discussion of how written reports were organized, as well as efforts to enhance the dissemination of the research products. Where appropriate, other means of communicating with stakeholders are discussed.

Selected Recommendations . . .

summarizes significant recommendations that emerged from the research findings if the project requires or allows them. If direct recommendations were not made, other avenues of influence on the decision-making process may be discussed.

Action . . .

discusses how and to what extent the policy research contributed to action by decision makers. Even when this contribution is not direct, the extent and nature of influences on decisions, institutions, or the way a problem is seen may be important.

Lessons for Policy Research . . .

links the specific experiences recounted in each case study to more general themes about how policy research should be conducted in order to best improve the decision-making process. In most instances, these lessons serve both to illustrate and to build upon some of the themes explored in Part I.

Focus on Research Methods . . .

highlights a specific research method, technique, or perspective relevant to the case. Discussion explores the method in greater detail than in the case study narrative and weighs some of the pros and cons of the method as appropriate.

Enjoy the cases. Our hope is that this dip into reality will effectively bring home concepts presented in Part I and give a sense of why we so thoroughly enjoy the day-to-day challenges and accomplishments of our work.

6 Using Research to Refine Quality Standards

The Evolution of Communities In Schools' Total Quality System (TQS)

Allan Porowski and Heather Clawson

Introduction

The Policy Problem

There was an old saying at the Communities In Schools (CIS) National Office that "if you've seen one CIS program, you've seen . . . one CIS program." This was the natural result of a program that began through grassroots efforts designed to meet local needs and build on existing community assets—and this was both intentional and seen as a key benefit of the program. However, with any program that was implemented in manifold ways, concerns remained about the quality and the consistency of support provided by each CIS site. In this case study, we show how our research supported the adoption of CIS's Total Quality System (TQS) standards, an underlying set of principles and standards that now underlie the work of every local CIS affiliate.

Initiation of Policy Research

Communities In Schools was founded in 1977 by Bill Milliken, a youth advocate in New York City who wanted to bring community resources into public schools. CIS works with communities to identify students' needs and connect community service providers to meet those students' needs. For example, if students have trouble seeing the blackboard in class, CIS works with a vision provider to provide glasses or contacts to students. If students are consistently tardy or missing significant days of school (i.e., they are chronically absent), CIS conducts home visits and calls parents or caregivers to identify the underlying cause of the problem and then connects the student and family with any needed supports to overcome barriers to getting to school. The CIS model therefore evolved differently in each community, since needs and available service providers were different. Services are managed by a Site Coordinator, a trained professional placed inside a school to work with school leadership to identify schoolwide needs and establish support plans for the school and its students. Site coordinators guide the delivery of integrated student supports to address identified needs and help schools and students achieve measurable goals. This highly localized and personalized model is designed to engage students to keep them in school and engaged in their schoolwork. CIS operates on a federation model, with a National Office that guides policy, state offices, local affiliates (typically serving a school district), and local schools that have substantial autonomy over their operations. Today, CIS serves 1.5 million students in nearly 400 school districts and 2,300 schools across the United States. It is the largest organization in the United States dedicated to keeping students in school.

The evaluation team's involvement with CIS began in 2001, an era when there was clear momentum building at the federal level for data-driven decision making and using evidence to inform policy and practice. CIS identified this trend early and began plans to design a comprehensive national evaluation plan that would provide a solid evidence base and inform the evolution of program operations. CIS wanted to make sure this was a true learning process and engaged our third-party evaluation team as partners not only in the plan's development but also in thinking strategically about the future direction of the organization. In order to meet CIS's needs, we agreed that this evaluation needed to use "gold-standard" research methods yet also include capacity-building activities that would ensure that evaluation activities could continue after our evaluation contract was finalized.

Like virtually all nonprofits, CIS did not have a government-sized research budget and sought to fund this work through a grant from a foundation. Our first job, then, was to develop a comprehensive evaluation plan for the CIS program. The evaluation plan was developed by Caliber Associates and guided by the CIS Network Evaluation Advisory Committee (NEAC), a group of CIS state office staff, local affiliate staff, researchers, and content experts who met twice each year. The national evaluation plan was designed to be modular in format, such that as money became available from foundations, CIS could conduct a new piece of the evaluation, ultimately building to a comprehensive evaluation that addressed all the research questions posed by CIS and the NEAC.

The CIS National Evaluation had eight components, as shown in Figure 6.1:

1. **Data Inventory:** The first component (component 1.1) was a data inventory, designed to review all data collected by CIS to date, identify gaps in the data, and identify preliminary findings from those data sources to inform subsequent evaluation activities.

National Evaluation

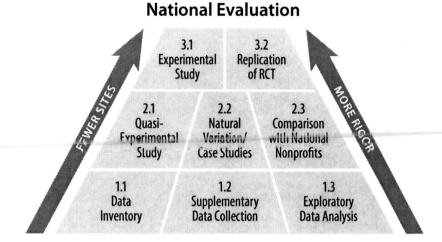

Figure 6.1 CIS National Evaluation Design

2. **Supplementary Data Collection:** The second component (component 1.2) was supplementary data collection, which was to address the gaps in data collection identified via the first study component. This component culminated in the development and administration of a Critical Processes Survey (CPS), which was administered in January 2006 and designed to capture the service delivery and leadership structure in each CIS school. We captured a wealth of data about CIS site operations from 1,894 CIS schools.
3. **Exploratory Data Analysis:** The third component of the evaluation (component 1.3) was an exploratory data analysis. This data analysis was specifically designed to identify a typology of CIS sites. Our rationale was that if we could identify the core models by which CIS services were delivered, we could (a) better define the CIS model, (b) identify key sources of variation in the CIS model, and (c) use this exercise to form subgroups for subsequent evaluation components. CIS underscored that the goal of this typology was not to identify the single most effective CIS model but rather to identify which CIS models worked best in particular situations and contexts.
4. **Quasi-Experimental Study:** The fourth component (component 2.1) was a school-level quasi-experimental study. For this study component, we identified 602 schools first served by CIS between the 1999–2000 school year through the 2002–2003 school year. These schools were then matched to 602 non-CIS schools in the year prior to CIS implementation on a number of variables, including urbanicity,

attendance rate, students receiving free/reduced-price lunch, students with special needs, total student enrollment, race/ethnicity distribution, the percentage of students who scored proficient on the state standardized math test, the percentage of students who scored proficient on the state standardized English test, and for high schools, the dropout rate. Data were drawn from State Department of Education websites, and schools were followed from the year prior to CIS implementation to three years following CIS implementation.

5. **Natural Variation/Case Studies:** The fifth study component (component 2.2) had two subcomponents. The first subcomponent was a natural variation study. Natural variation studies seek to draw lessons from natural variation in processes and outcomes to draw real-world lessons about which approaches are working best in given situations. As opposed to planned variation studies, which seek to engineer interventions (and reality) to facilitate study procedures, natural variation approaches can provide more generalizable findings. For the CIS National Evaluation, we used school-level Site Coordinator Survey data to identify key factors that separated the most successful schools in the quasi-experimental study from the less-successful schools. This was done with logistic regression and simple subgroup comparisons (e.g., we identified schools in the quasi-experimental study that had positive effects on graduation and those that did not and then ran a logistic regression using "success on improving graduation" as the dependent variable and service data from the Site Coordinator Survey as the independent variables). The second subcomponent was the conduct of eight case studies with CIS affiliates. These case studies included interviews with CIS staff, focus groups with students and parents, and interviews with school staff including principals and teachers. This study subcomponent was designed to identify *how* CIS was working, to inform our conclusions from previous study components, and to identify new hypotheses for subsequent study components.

6. **Comparison with National Nonprofits:** The sixth study component (component 2.3) was an External Comparison Study of other youth-serving nonprofit federations. We conducted interviews with eight national nonprofits, which were initially identified based on their success in one or more of the following areas: branding, total quality management, external innovation, public policy, brokering, and internal innovation. This study component allowed CIS to benchmark their performance to other national nonprofits and identify opportunities for further innovation and refinement of their program model.

7. **Experimental Study:** The seventh study component (component 3.1) was a randomized controlled trial (RCT) of the CIS program. Two RCTs were initiated in the 2007–2008 school year: one at six high schools in Austin (TX) and one at two middle schools in Jacksonville

(FL). These studies involved the random assignment of students to either a treatment group (which received case-managed, sustained CIS services) or a control group (which did not receive case-managed, sustained CIS services). RCTs are considered to be the gold standard in research because through randomization, we can balance treatment and control groups both on observable factors (e.g., test scores) and on unobservable factors (e.g., motivation to participate, family structures), which provides the most unbiased estimates possible. Across two cohorts first served in the 2007–2008 and 2008–2009 school years, the final RCT sample in Jacksonville included 164 CIS students and 168 non-CIS students, and the final RCT sample in Austin included 93 CIS students and 58 non-CIS students.

8. **Replication of RCT:** The eighth and final study component (component 3.2) was the replication of an RCT. Replication research is not particularly popular since funders tend to want to study new interventions or fund new evaluations for interventions that do not already have an evidence base. However, replication research is absolutely critical to determine whether results can be sustained when programs are scaled up to new locations. Our replication research involved an RCT at a high school in Wichita (KS), which was initiated in the 2008–2009 school year. The final RCT study sample included 50 CIS students and 40 non-CIS students.

The premise underlying this evaluation "pyramid" was that each successive level involved more rigor but fewer sites. Base-level studies included all CIS sites, and the RCTs—which are expensive to conduct—involved only 9 of CIS's more than 2,500 schools at the time.

As noted previously, this evaluation was designed to be modular in format, so when resources became available, CIS could begin a new module of the evaluation. The base-level components were also purposefully designed to be less expensive, since we wanted to initiate the study with a modest amount of seed money from a foundation. In May 2005, the Atlantic Philanthropies in New York City committed to funding all of the study components at once. This provided the team with a lot more work, much sooner than expected. It was, nonetheless, exciting to have the creativity inherent in this evaluation design validated by a funder that was willing to make such a substantial investment.

The Policy Research Task

This case study will focus on our development of an implementation rubric and the use of that rubric in the school-level quasi-experimental study (components 1.3 and 2.1). These components were the key to validating the need for CIS's Total Quality System (TQS) standards and providing CIS with the data it needed to make a strong case for these standards.

From the mid-1990s until 2007, CIS had in place a set of quality standards for CIS affiliates called the Quality and Standards (Q&S) process. This process included standards related to nonprofit management and best practices identified at the time. The Q&S process also outlined models for serving students, and approximately 60% of affiliates completed this process and were chartered by CIS. CIS saw the need to have 100% of sites meet standards, to more precisely define their standards, and to ensure that the standards were reliant upon a stronger evidence base. Although the Q&S process provided some structure around the CIS model, it was nonetheless resulting in a wide range of business practices and service delivery strategies across sites. The TQS Standards were designed to address these challenges.

The TQS Standards had a number of goals:

* Redefine the stages of CIS affiliate development, culminating in the designation of a Total Quality Affiliate Organization
* Update management standards through CIS organization and business standards
* Define CIS site operations standards, which guide site-level implementation
* Strengthen the CIS brand
* Ensure CIS affiliates receive support at all stages of development; and
* Ensure network-wide accountability (Communities in Schools, 2007).

Whereas the old Q&S standards process was administered at the affiliate level, the new TQS standards were designed to deepen the reach of these standards to govern both local affiliate business operations and site operations related to implementation of the CIS model.

The Total Quality System standards were approved by the CIS National Board of Directors in May 2007. These standards were proposed to provide CIS Affiliates with a common blueprint for establishing and sustaining high-functioning organizations that maximize CIS's chances of having an impact on the lives of students and their families. The TQS standards were developed by CIS National Office leadership and were based in large part on the recommendations of a committee comprised of local executive directors, state directors, state office staff, and national staff.

Objectives

The CIS National Evaluation's school-level quasi-experimental study was also being finalized in mid-2007. With the impending rollout of the TQS standards, the CIS National Office requested an evaluation to determine whether implementation of the CIS model *as intended* was associated with stronger outcomes. If a relationship could be found between adherence to the CIS model and positive outcomes for CIS students, then the TQS standards could be validated, they could be based in evidence, and a stronger case could be made for the rollout of these standards nationwide.

Challenges

There were two primary challenges in our efforts to measure implementation of the CIS model and link implementation fidelity to outcomes:

1. The CIS model had previously not been defined with such specificity. CIS had a logic model in place to describe how the CIS program worked, but the specifics behind implementation were not defined. To overcome this challenge, the evaluation team worked with the Network Evaluation Advisory Committee to help define and refine measurement of the CIS model with the site-level service data that had been collected. Specifically, core components of the CIS model were identified.
2. **Outcomes from the quasi-experimental study were between one and four years older than the site-level service data collected in 2006.** To overcome this challenge, we simply assumed that site-level processes had not changed between the times when the service data and the outcome data were collected. This was a big assumption, but it was the best data at the evaluation team's disposal—and the Network Evaluation Advisory Committee confirmed that site-level processes typically did not change considerably from year to year.

The Decision Context

The Institutional Context

It was no coincidence that the design of the CIS National Evaluation was initiated in 2002, the same year the U.S. Department of Education launched the What Works Clearinghouse. The What Works Clearinghouse was designed to develop standards of research quality and to review the quality of research evidence against those standards. Ultimately, the goal of the What Works Clearinghouse was to provide a central and trusted resource to describe the evidence base of educational interventions. The What Works Clearinghouse standards clearly signaled the need for research to focus on strong research designs (i.e., randomized controlled trials and strong quasi-experimental studies). The CIS National Office wanted to be recognized for developing strong evidence—and they desired strong evidence to make informed decisions about the delivery of services across the network. The CIS National Office also wanted to develop an understanding of what strategies worked and what *didn't* work in order to maximize their effectiveness. In other words, what was needed was a rigorous, candid assessment of CIS to build an evidence base and to maximize effectiveness.

The Policy Cycle

This case study is somewhat unique since the policy cycle within a non-profit organization doesn't necessarily follow a legislative cycle. However, the CIS National Office's decision to adopt new Total Quality System standards largely followed the policy cycle as described in Chapter 1.

Agenda setting began with the CIS National Office identifying the need to adopt new standards and to expand the standards from the affiliate level to the site level as well. This policy shift was assessed against CIS's existing standards at the time (the Q&S process), and the decision was made to move forward in 2006. The *formulation of the policy* began in 2006 and was guided by the work of a committee comprised of local executive directors, state directors, state office staff, and CIS National Office staff. The ultimate *decision making* about the content of the new standards was determined by executives at the CIS National Office in 2007, and the deliberative body ultimately in charge of approving these standards was the CIS National Board of Directors, which meets annually to approve major policy changes. The *implementation* of Total Quality System standards began in 2007 and became official CIS policy in July 2008. These standards were further refined in August 2009. Although a formal *evaluation* of these standards was not completed as part of the CIS National Evaluation, our evaluation activities were designed to support the refinement and validation of these standards with the data already collected. A description of how we conducted this part of the evaluation is addressed in what follows.

Clients and Stakeholders

The key stakeholders for CIS's Total Quality System standards were the CIS network participants. The CIS network is comprised of a system of state offices, local affiliates (that serve one or more school districts), and local sites (i.e., schools). The clients for the policy research were the CIS National Office, the Atlantic Philanthropies (the funder of the evaluation), and the Network Evaluation Advisory Committee, which met twice each year and provided guidance on the evaluation.

The clients in the CIS National Office were in an interesting situation: they needed to move to a stronger evidence base and yet respect the CIS program's tradition of being flexible and grounded in local needs and personal relationships. The National Office was aware that there was a certain amount of risk involved in revising standards, especially among affiliates in lower-resourced communities. For example, CIS's revised TQS standards called for schools with fewer than 1,000 students to provide sustained, case-managed services to at least 10% of students within the school. In rural areas that did not have access to full-time site coordinators, adherence to the standards would require quite a large caseload for each site coordinator. CIS invested $50 million to support the network in implementing these new standards and moving the network toward accreditation. Even with this amount of funding, it was difficult to change practice on such a grand scale.

Research Design and Implementation

Although the complete CIS National Evaluation design is described earlier, this section will focus more deeply on the research that was conducted to support and refine CIS's TQS standards. A timeline of the evaluation is included in Table 6.1.

Information Needs

From a very early point in the CIS National Evaluation, the CIS National Office wanted to know whether a typology of CIS sites could be developed (i.e., a classification of the different types of CIS service delivery models). By understanding the types of implementation processes that were taking place at CIS sites, the CIS National Office would be in a position to understand how to best support these models. It was clear from the outset that the goal of the evaluation should not be to identify the single best model but rather to describe the most appropriate model

Table 6.1 CIS National Evaluation Timeline

2001	Network Evaluation Advisory Committee (NEAC) formed
2002	National evaluation design commissioned
2005	CIS National Evaluation funded by the Atlantic Philanthropies (May)
2006	Critical Processes Survey administered (January)
	Decision made to revise Q&S process (mid-year)
	Implementation fidelity rubric finalized (December)
2007	TQS standards approved (May)
	Site Coordinator Survey administered (June)
	Austin & Jacksonville RCTs started (August)
	Quasi-experimental design finalized (August)
2008	TQS standards became official policy (July)
	Wichita RCT started (August)
2009	TQS standards refined (August)
2010	CIS National Evaluation completed

for a given context. Given that CIS served urban, rural, and suburban schools in a wide swath of the country—with diverse needs and community assets—it was important to ensure that any guidance emanating from the CIS National Office was broadly applicable and generalizable but also effective. The case therefore exemplifies a situation in which multiple information needs required substantial efforts, particularly in the area of descriptive and effectiveness information.

Following the administration of the Critical Processes Survey in early 2006, which gathered data on site-level processes from 1,894 CIS sites, one of the first tasks for the research team was to develop a typology of sites. We began this daunting task by conducting a cluster analysis, which is an exploratory method designed to identify distinct clusters of subjects (in this case, CIS sites) by minimizing variance within clusters and maximizing variance between clusters. By generating clusters of CIS sites based on the types of services offered, structure of service delivery, and context (e.g., urbanicity), it was hoped that distinct CIS models would emerge. However, as with any exploratory statistical method, cluster analysis is only useful insofar as the results made sense. We found that clusters were unstable (i.e., any minor shift in the variables used in cluster analysis resulted in completely different clusters of CIS sites). This actually validated the adage that "if you've seen one CIS program, you've seen one CIS program." A different method was needed to classify CIS sites in a way that would help elucidate findings from the National Evaluation. As noted previously, it wasn't enough to simply evaluate whether CIS was working; we also wanted to know how CIS was working, why it was working, and in what situations it was working. That required some method to link processes to outcomes. Thus this project required an actively creative orientation to the information problem.

Design and Methods

It became clear early on that CIS sites would not fit into discrete categories of program models. We came to an epiphany that since CIS sites would not fit into discrete "buckets," we needed to put sites on a continuum. When we shifted the analysis from *what types* of models CIS sites were engaging in to *how much* of the CIS model was being implemented, this challenge became much less daunting.

The Critical Processes Survey provided a number of data points for the assessment of implementation fidelity. It used a measure of "fidelity" that did not initially focus on a dichotomous (yes/no) indicator about whether CIS sites were implementing the model with fidelity; rather, our goal was to score each site to identify the intensity of the CIS model being implemented.

The evaluation team developed a 19-item rubric to score CIS sites' intensity of the model. This rubric (Table 6.2) takes into account five

Table 6.2 Fidelity of Implementation Rubric

Domain	Question*	Scoring
Needs Assessment Domain	• Does CIS conduct a needs assessment? (L1 and L2)	• Yes: 5 pts.; No: 0 pts.
	• How often are needs assessments conducted? (L1 and L2)	• More than once a year: 5 pts.; Once a year: 3 pts.; Less than once a year: 1 pt.
	• Types of information used for identifying needs (L1 and L2)	• 1 pt. for each type of information used (max 5 pts.)
	• Types of information for prioritizing overall needs (L1 and L2)	• Student and external factors: 5 pts.; Student needs only: 3 pts.; External factors only: 2 pts.; No needs assessment: 0 pts.
Planning Domain	• Does CIS have an annual operations plan? (L1 and L2)	• Yes: 5 pts.; No: 0 pts.
	• What is included in the annual operations plan? (L1 and L2)	• 1 pt. for each type of information used (max 5 pts.)
Referrals Domain	• How are students referred to CIS for targeted and sustained interventions (i.e., Level 2 services)?	• Internal, external, and self: 5 pts.; 2 of 3 sources used: 3 pts.; 1 source used: 2 pts.; No referrals: 0 pts.
Service Delivery Domain	• How many of the 5 basic needs are addressed with Level 1 and Level 2 services?	• 1 pt. for each of the 5 basics covered
	• Percentage of students in school who receive Level 1 services from CIS	• Above 75%: 5 pts.; 50% to 75%: 3 pts.; 25% to 49%: 2 pts.; 1% to 24%: 1 pt.; 0%: 0 pts.
	• Percentage of students in school who receive Level 2 services from CIS	• Above 5%: 5 pts.; 1% to 5%: 3 pts.; 0%: 0 pts.
	• How much time site coordinator spends coordinating CIS services	• 100%: 5 pts.; 76–99%: 4 pts.; 50–75%: 3 pts.; 26–50%: 2 pts.; 1–25%: 1 pt.; 0%: 0 pts.
Monitoring and Adjustment Domain	• How often does CIS review student progress? (L1 and L2)	• More than once/grading period: 5 pts.; Once per grading period: 3.5 pts.; Once per semester: 2.5 pts.; Once per year: 1 pt.; Never/less than once/yr: 0 pts.

* Questions denoted with "L1 and L2" indicate that the same question was asked regarding Level 1 (whole-school) and Level 2 (case-managed, sustained) services. Scoring was conducted separately for each level of service. This rubric was found to have acceptable levels of internal consistency ($\alpha = .834$).

components of the CIS model, which align to CIS's process of delivering integrated student supports:

1. **Needs assessment:** The TQS standards specified that sites should identify and prioritize overall student needs annually based on multiple sources of information (e.g., school assessment data, school improvement plans, surveys, etc.).

2. **Planning:** The TQS standards indicated that each site should have an annual Site Operations Plan that includes site demographic data, student needs to be addressed, objectives related to each need, description of whole-school services to be implemented, description of case-managed services to be implemented, a description of how services will be monitored, and a description of data collection and reporting procedures.

3. **Referrals:** The TQS standards as drafted in 2007 did not specify procedures for referrals, except that students referred to CIS for sustained, case-managed services should have individualized plans. The process of referring students to CIS was nonetheless recognized as a core part of the model. Our rubric recognized that a wide range of referral sources (i.e., where students could be referred by community partners, school staff, or via self-referrals) was congruent with the CIS model.

4. **Services:** The TQS standards indicated that a Site Coordinator should be onsite at least half time, whole-school services should be available to at least 75% of the student population, and case-managed services should be provided to at least 10% of the student body in schools with fewer than 1,000 students, and 5% of the student body in schools with more than 1,000 students. Moreover, these services should be aligned to the "five basics" of CIS: (1) a one-on-one relationship with a caring adult; (2) a safe place to learn and grow; (3) a healthy start and a healthy future; (4) a marketable skill to use upon graduation; and (5) a chance to give back to peers and the community.

5. **Monitoring and adjustment:** The TQS standards indicated that services should be monitored and adjusted as appropriate—and at a minimum, these adjustments should be made each year in the annual site operations plan.

Since the Critical Processes Survey was administered in January 2006 and the TQS standards were approved in May 2007, we needed to update our measures to make them align better to the TQS standards. The CIS Site Coordinator Survey, which was administered only to quasi-experimental study participants to reduce response burden, achieved a 64% response rate (368 valid responses). When Site Coordinator Survey data were available, we used this survey in our fidelity scoring process for each site; otherwise, the Critical Processes Survey data were used. Although we were not able to precisely measure adherence to the TQS standards for all sites, our fidelity rubric was nonetheless widely viewed as a close approximation of the CIS model as it was intended to be delivered at the site level.

The rubric was not designed to capture all of CIS's TQS standards; rather, it was designed to capture the elements of the standards that were closely aligned to service delivery or any other aspect of site operations that could directly affect students. Other elements of the standards (e.g., standards related to branding and financial management) were not incorporated into this rubric. Following alignment of the data, the domains were weighted equally such that the maximum possible score would be 100. This provided an intuitive measure of fidelity for any consumer of the data.

There were two additional considerations needed to ensure that the fidelity scores were sufficiently refined. First, we needed to establish a cut point for an acceptable threshold of adherence to the CIS model. Based on analyzing breaks in the distribution of implementation scores, and through discussions with CIS staff to determine how much tolerance the CIS model had to local modifications, we identified 70% as the natural cut point. "High implementers" were defined as CIS schools that delivered programs with 70% or higher fidelity to the "ideal" CIS program model. "Partial implementers" delivered programs with less than 70% fidelity. Second, we had to recognize that some sites offered whole-school services only (Level 1 services), and some sites offered sustained, case-managed services only (Level 2 services). These sites, by definition, were identified as partial implementers because they did not deliver the full array of CIS services specified in the model.

Selected Findings

A summary of the results of the fidelity rubric is included in Table 6.3. It was evident that just under half of CIS sites (48%) were implementing the CIS model with fidelity. This was an eye-opening figure—and it signaled a need to tighten network operations through the TQS standards.

Table 6.3 Number of Sites (and Percentage of Total Sites) in Each Implementation Category

	Partial Implementer	*High Implementer*
Level 1 Only	195 (13%)	
Level 2 Only	148 (9.8%)	
Comprehensive (Level 1 & Level 2)	453 (29.8%)	713 (47.0%)
Total	796 (52.4%)	722 (47.6%)

After the fidelity of implementation rubric was finalized, the logical next step was to determine whether fidelity of implementation could be linked to stronger outcomes. If it could, this would be tantamount to a validation of the CIS model itself, and it would make a strong case for the strengthening of implementation fidelity across the network through the TQS standards. To test this hypothesis, we used data from the school-level quasi-experimental study. As noted previously, this study involved 602 sites that first implemented the CIS model between the 1999–2000 and 2002–2003 school years. Each of these 602 sites was matched (using a technique called propensity score matching) to a non-CIS site in the year prior to implementation. These pairs of CIS and non-CIS sites were then followed for three years following initial CIS implementation. Core outcomes for this study included dropout rates, graduation rates, and rates at which students achieved state-mandated proficiency levels on standardized tests in grades 4, 8, and 10. We also measured attendance rates for these grades. At the time the data were initially reported, each state used different definitions of dropout and graduation rates, so we developed proxies for these measures. Dropout rates were measured using the promoting power index, which compares the number of 12th graders in a high school to the number of 9th graders three years earlier (Balfanz and Legters, 2004). Graduation rates were measured using the cumulative promotion index, which is a measure of on-time graduation, and represents the steps on a student's way to graduating from high school: promotion from 9th to 10th grade, from 10th to 11th grade, from 11th to 12th grade, and receiving a high school diploma (Swanson, 2003).

Results from this study are presented in Table 6.4. Results are presented for all CIS sites and for high implementers only (i.e., sites scoring 70 or above on the implementation fidelity rubric). Outcomes are expressed two ways: (1) net change, which is the net difference between CIS schools and comparison schools from baseline to three years postimplementation (this is also known as a difference-in-differences measure, since it subtracts the change in the comparison group from the change in the CIS group over the four-year period) and (2) effect size, which is a metric that expresses these differences as the number of standard deviations that separate treatment and comparison group means. Effect sizes are used often in research because they express the magnitude of difference between groups on a standard scale (i.e., in standard deviations). For reference, the U.S. Department of Education's What Works Clearinghouse considers an effect size of .25 to be a "substantively important" effect (What Works Clearinghouse, 2014).

Results from Table 6.4 indicate that with the exception of middle school attendance, high implementers had stronger outcomes than all CIS sites. High implementers, for example, had a 3.6% lower dropout rate than the comparison group (i.e., a positive number denotes stronger

Table 6.4 CIS School-Level Quasi-Experimental Study Results: All CIS Sites and High Implementers

Outcome	All CIS Sites		High Implementers	
	Net Change	Effect Size	Net Change	Effect Size
Dropout Rate (promoting power)	+2.0%	.21	+3.6%	.36
Graduation Rate (cumulative promotion index)	+1.7%	.08	+4.8%	.31
Attendance (elementary school)	+0.1%	.10	+0.2%	.42
Attendance (middle school)	+0.3%	.24	+0.1%	.12
Attendance (high school)	+0.3%	.18	+0.3%	.19
Grade 4 Math	+2.2%	.21	+5.2%	.36
Grade 4 Reading	−0.1%	.08	+2.3%	.31
Grade 8 Math	+2.0%	.16	+6.0%	.53
Grade 8 Reading	−0.1%	−.01	+5.1%	.36
Grade 10 Math	+0.4%	.03	+0.8%	.07
Grade 10 Reading	−0.3%	−.04	−0.3%	−.02

promoting power), while CIS sites overall had dropout rates that were 2.0% lower than non-CIS sites. The net change in graduation rates was nearly three times higher for high implementers than it was for all CIS sites. These numbers provided compelling evidence for the effectiveness of the CIS model and served as a validation of the CIS model itself (Porowski and Passa, 2011).

Communicating and Using Results

The Communities In Schools National Office and the external evaluation team operated as true partners. Although the external evaluation team by necessity had to maintain its independence and not involve the CIS National Office in the collection of data or in the interpretation of findings, there was nonetheless a great deal of internal communication about these findings and their implications for the CIS network. In the view of the research team, this evaluator–client relationship worked incredibly well. Keys to this successful relationship included these key factors: (a) the CIS National Office had a strong desire to learn about how to best serve their network, (b) the CIS National Office requested a number of additional analyses to refine understanding of the results, and (c) the CIS National Office offered access to staff on the front lines of service provision through the Network Evaluation Advisory Committee and an Implementation Task Force, which included state and local affiliate staff who provided candid advice to the evaluation team (e.g., how long surveys could be before they became overly burdensome). This allowed the evaluation to be a true learning process for everyone involved.

Reporting Results

In addition to the informal reports presented during regular meetings, the results of the fidelity of implementation rubric were vetted to the Network Evaluation Advisory Committee, presented in formal evaluation reports, presented in a journal article on results from the school-level quasi-experimental study (Porowski and Passa, 2011), and presented at the National Press Club at the conclusion of the evaluation.

Selected Recommendations

The results of this study provided clarity regarding the core components that made up the CIS model and validated the need for CIS sites to adhere to the CIS model. The evaluation team conveyed this finding to the CIS National Office, and the TQS standards were propagated throughout the network. These evaluation findings facilitated the rollout of the TQS standards, since the research findings demonstrated that adherence to the standards not only tightened up the CIS model and helped define what fidelity looked like, but it also translated into more positive outcomes for schools and students.

Action

The CIS National Office communicated the results of this study to the CIS Network and used them to underscore the importance of adhering to the new TQS standards. Accreditation began in 2007, and a deadline was set for all operating affiliates at that time to become accredited by July 1, 2015. Each affiliate received training, desktop document reviews, on-site preparation, and access to tools/templates aligned with the standards. For each affiliate, two-person teams consisting of a National Office and a network representative conducted on-site interviews with board members, affiliate leadership and staff, school leadership, community partners, and students, as well as conducted data and document reviews to ensure compliance with the standards. Following the review, a report with recommendations either to accredit the affiliate or allow an extension to meet standards was presented to the TQS Governance Committee made up of members from the CIS National Office and state directors. The committee made a final determination regarding accreditation. If sites were unable to meet 100% of standards prior to the July 1, 2015, deadline, support was provided to the affiliate to transition out of the network or merge with an accredited CIS affiliate. For those accredited, they were expected to maintain standards and participate in reaccreditation reviews every three years.

The overall results from the TQS accreditation process were very positive. To date, 161 accredited local affiliates make up the CIS network. Other outcomes of this process include:

- **The CIS network is about 24% smaller than it was when accreditation started.** Rather than pursuing growth at all costs, CIS made the conscious decision to prioritize organizational health and sustainability, quality programming and fidelity to the proven CIS model. Some affiliates had other priorities, and more than 50 left the network rather than seek accreditation.
- **CIS's student headcount has grown by 20% during the same time.** In 2007, there were 217 local affiliates serving 1.24 million students. In 2014, 165 local affiliates served 1.48 million students. The TQS process has made CIS a much more efficient organization, able to deliver more programming with less administrative overhead.
- **CIS's revenues have remained constant.** In 2007, combined network revenues totaled $199 million. In 2014, that figure was unchanged at $199 million. Given that the network shrank by a quarter over that same time period, each affiliate is getting a larger share of revenue.
- **CIS's student outcomes have improved.** CIS's focus on quality implementation of the CIS model of integrated student supports has yielded 35% more graduates than CIS was on track to achieve prior to the adoption of TQS.

In summary, since TQS standards were implemented, more students are seeing better outcomes from a leaner organization working with the same budget.

Lessons for Policy Research

This case study of the research leading to the development and validation of CIS's Total Quality System (TQS) standards provides several lessons for policy researchers:

- **Policy research is practiced in nonprofit organizations.** Policy research is not limited to government activities. This CIS case study provides an excellent example of how policy is made within nonprofit organizations.
- **Implementation matters.** As noted in Chapter 5 ("Be Useful"), research results are more credible and generalizable when we can make the link between processes and outcomes. This case study provides an example of how implementation science can be applied to an evaluation to generate credible findings. Moreover, by unpacking the components of the CIS model, we were in a better position to describe not only whether CIS works but also how it works, why it works, and in what situations it works.

- Building momentum for change based on research findings can be difficult. For an organization with a tradition of using personalized approaches to reach at-risk students, it was a difficult "ask" to systematize operations at CIS sites. This rollout of TQS standards resulted in the contraction of the CIS network. Among the affiliates that remained in the network, the TQS standards—and the research underlying those standards—were seen as an opportunity to improve

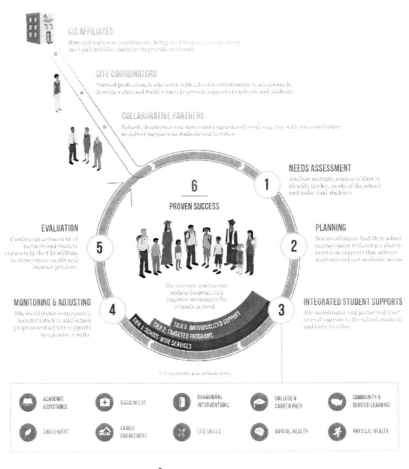

Figure 6.2 The CIS Model

outcomes for students. By appealing to CIS affiliates' core mission to improve the lives of students, the CIS National Office had sufficient leverage to institute these standards.

- **Policy research is ideally an ongoing process.** CIS has continued to conduct research (both internally and with third-party evaluators) to review practice, and, when necessary, change standards. CIS's business and site operation standards have already changed since the first iteration of the TQS standards, and the CIS model now recognizes three tiers of services (school-wide services, targeted programs, individualized support) instead of the original whole-school versus case-managed service dichotomy. Figure 6.2 presents an overview of the CIS model as it is being implemented at the time of this writing.

Due to the TQS standards and the research underlying those standards, CIS has evolved from doing "anything for kids" to a well-defined, evidence-based model. Having standards based in evidence and an accreditation process in place to monitor adherence to those standards has allowed CIS to scale with fidelity and quality.

It is always fulfilling to see one's research result in a positive change; it was particularly satisfying in this case to see policy research affect the lives of more than 1 million students each year.

Focus on Research Methods

Implementation Science

Implementation science is a rapidly growing field that is designed to measure the extent to which an intervention was successfully delivered and to contextualize the role of implementation in the assessment of outcomes. The study of implementation is one key to identifying evidence-based practices, and as shown in Chapter 5, it is an integral component in the decision-making calculus about whether an intervention should be scaled up.

Implementation fidelity is a potential moderator of the relationship between interventions and their intended outcomes (Carroll et al., 2007). For this reason, it is important to study whether an intervention (whether it is a policy, program, or practice) was delivered as intended—and if not, whether deviations from the "ideal" model may have tempered its effectiveness.

The measurement of implementation and implementation fidelity begins with a logic model. These logic models may already be developed, may need to be developed from scratch, or, in the case of CIS, need to be further refined. By tracing how intervention components are related to program outcomes, the logic model provides a sound basis for tracing the pathways that need to be measured in an implementation study. Once a logic model is developed, the key components of the intervention need to be operationalized. In the case of CIS, the five core components of the CIS model (needs assessment, planning, referrals, service delivery, and monitoring and adjustment) were measured and scored using data from the Critical Processes Survey and the Site Coordinator Survey. After each element is scored, a rubric should be developed to synthesize results and provide a measure of implementation fidelity. This is where the art and science of applied policy research meet. Some elements may be considered to be core elements of the model, while other elements may be considered "nice-to-haves." The scoring and weighting of these elements is ideally conducted after consultation with program staff who have knowledge of the inner workings of the intervention.

Measuring fidelity of implementation is but one component of implementation science. Other considerations include the quality of implementation (i.e., measuring how well an intervention was administered, which may focus on intangibles), exposure and dosage (i.e., measuring how much of the program content was received by participants), participant responsiveness (i.e., measuring how participants responded to or were engaged by an intervention), and program differentiation (i.e., measuring how the intervention differed from other alternative interventions) (Dane and Schneider, 1998).

Measures of implementation may be used as contextual information in the presentation of research findings, or they may be built directly into analytic models. In either case, the use of implementation science to inform both findings and scale-up of interventions is quickly becoming standard practice in policy research.

Acronyms and Jargon

Affiliate—A CIS affiliate office guided the implementation of CIS in the lowest-performing schools in a given school district or districts. Affiliates provide annual performance reports to the CIS National Office.

CIS—Communities In Schools—A nonprofit organization dedicated to helping students stay in school and achieve in life. CIS surrounds students with a community of support by placing site coordinators within schools to assess students' needs and connecting students with community resources (e.g., food, school supplies, health care, counseling, or academic assistance) and a positive adult role model.

CPS—Critical Processes Survey—Administered in January 2006, the Critical Processes Survey was administered to all CIS schools to capture the types and structure of service delivery within individual schools.

Domain—An organizing concept to describe a sphere of activity or knowledge. The domains described in the CIS fidelity-of-implementation rubric align to the major types of core activities conducted by CIS sites.

Implementation Task Force—A group of CIS state office and local affiliate staff that provided candid advice to the evaluation team. For example, this task force helped the national evaluation team identify the ideal length for its surveys and provided feedback on the fidelity-of-implementation rubric.

Level 1 Services—Whole-school services provided by CIS. These services could involve bringing in motivational speakers to address students, providing school supplies to students, or any other school-wide effort to improve school climate.

Level 2 Services—Targeted, sustained services delivered to students who were identified as being in need.

Natural Variation Designs—This is a study design that draws real-world lessons from the natural variation in program approaches, settings, and outcomes. The CIS Natural Variation Design included logistic regressions to identify the key factors that differentiated the most-successful sites from the less-successful sites.

NEAC—Network Evaluation Advisory Committee—A group of experts consisting of CIS field staff, CIS National Office staff, academics, and subject matter experts that met twice a year to guide CIS's evaluation plans. The NEAC was formed in 2001 and provided guidance throughout the course of the CIS National Evaluation.

Q&S—Quality and Standards (Q&S) Process—Starting in the mid-1990s, the Q&S process provided an affiliate-level review of standards related to nonprofit management and best practices. The Q&S process also outlined models for serving students, and affiliates that successfully completed the Q&S process were considered to be Chartered affiliates.

QED—Quasi-experimental design—A study that involves the formation of two or more groups, either through formalized matching (e.g., propensity score matching) or through other means to ensure that groups are equivalent on observable characteristics at baseline.

RCT—Randomized controlled trial—Considered to be the "gold standard" in research, randomized controlled trials involve the random assignment of participants to form two or more groups that are differentiated by whether or not they receive the intervention under study. Through randomization, RCTs produce groups that are similar at baseline on both observable and unobservable characteristics. This design allows any subsequent (i.e., postintervention) differences in outcomes between the intervention and comparison groups to be attributed to the intervention, assuming substantial biases are not introduced by overall or differential attrition.

Site Coordinator Survey—This survey was administered in 2007 to schools that were in the quasi-experimental study. This survey was a more detailed version of the Critical Processes Survey and was used in the natural variation study and in the fidelity-of-implementation rubric.

TQS—Total Quality System standards—Approved by the CIS National Board of Directors in May 2007, the TQS standards replaced the Q&S process and were designed to provide CIS affiliates with a common blueprint for establishing and sustaining high-functioning organizations. The TQS standards had two primary components: (1) Organizational and Business Standards, which included standards for identity; boards; planning and implementation; fiscal management; written agreements; and data collection, evaluation, and reporting; (2) Site Operations Standards, which identified standards for service provision. The Site Operations standards guided the development of the fidelity rubric for the evaluation.

Discussion Questions

1. How did the assessment of implementation add to CIS's evidence base?
2. In what ways does policy research differ within nonprofit organizations and within government organizations?
3. Were agile research methods built into this evaluation? If so, which study components built off one another to deepen knowledge about the effectiveness of CIS?
4. What potential conflicts of interest may be present, and what "firewalls" need to be built when researchers and program staff work closely together, as in the case of the CIS National Evaluation?

Assignments and Activities

1. Identify a nonprofit program of your choosing and identify an opportunity to conduct policy research for that organization. What

are your key research questions? What methods would you use to evaluate the program?
2. Find a program logic model online. Identify core components of the intervention and draft a strategy for how you would plan to measure those program components.

7 The Dropout Prevention Mentor Project

Delivering Unexpected Messages Through Policy Research

Elizabeth Sale and J. Fred Springer

Introduction

Policy researchers sometimes have to deliver messages that clients or stakeholders do not want to hear. This case study summarizes an evaluation of a local program in which the client had a major investment, as well as high expectations of a positive evaluation outcome. In this circumstance, getting the client to listen to and act on findings of program deficiencies was a real challenge. The case also demonstrates the importance of integrating the findings of process evaluation and outcome evaluation in policy research. Process findings concerning implementation problems provided a clear explanation for why outcomes had not been as strong as expected, allowing the program director to maintain her faith in the mentoring strategy that lay at the base of the program. The integration of process and outcome findings provided both information on the strengths of the program and guidance on how to improve it.

The Policy Problem

The St. Louis Public School District's Dropout Prevention Program was initially funded in the fall of 1992. A grant of $271,397 by the U.S. Department of Education, under its School Dropout Demonstration Assistance Program, was for a three-year project to explore the efficacy of a mentoring approach of encouraging students to stay in school. The Dropout Prevention Program was to build upon an already successful mentoring model developed by the district, and it incorporated elements of effective mentoring approaches implemented in other school districts.

School dropout is a serious problem in the St. Louis Public School district and in many school districts throughout the country. In St. Louis, dropout rates in some schools approach 50 percent by the 12th grade. The lack of a high school diploma exacerbates the economic barriers facing many of the district's youth and contributes to the syndrome of economic and social problems that characterize numerous city neighborhoods. The mentoring demonstration was proposed by the Office of Federal

Programs within the district as a way of countering dropout before it gets established. The program began with elementary youth and was designed to provide continuing services through middle and high schools. The demonstration targeted schools that experienced high dropout rates or that fed schools with high dropout rates. The program included two elementary schools, two middle schools, and two high schools.

Dropout Prevention Program services were provided primarily by community liaisons and mentors working to strengthen connections with school and improve attendance. Six home–school–community liaisons— one in each of the schools selected for services—monitored attendance; communicated with parents, teachers, and school administrators; assigned mentors to appropriate students; and provided assistance to students during or after school as needed. Liaisons were near–full-time employees located in the schools.

Mentors were volunteers from the community who agreed to be matched with individual youths from one of the program schools. The goal for the program was to have mentors assigned to approximately 1,200 students participating in the program. Mentors were recruited from public agencies, businesses, universities, and other organizations in St. Louis. They were asked to make at least one personal contact with their student each month, at least one contact a week by telephone or mail, and to meet with the student's parents at least twice each year. In addition, mentors were asked to monitor school attendance and performance and to intervene where appropriate.

Finally, the program was to provide citywide awareness of the dropout problem in the city through three awareness and promotional fliers per year. Information gathered during the course of the program would be used to develop a model for other dropout prevention programs in the future.

The evaluation data reported here were gathered in the program's second year, after it had one year to get established and in time to provide some input to program formation in the final year. By the second year, the program had made significant progress toward its implementation goals—specifically, increased recruitment and involvement by mentors, improved retention of home–school–community liaisons, and expanded services to additional students. The number of students served by the program was expanded from approximately 400 in the first year to 800 in the second. At the end of the year, about 530 mentors had been formally recruited, trained, and assigned. The program also had hired a project specialist to assist the liaisons with resources and ideas, and two program specialists were assigned to recruit and retain mentors.

Although one home–school–community liaison resigned in the spring and was succeeded by another, the remaining five were with the program throughout the year. Mentor recruitment met greater success in the second year, though it was still not sufficient to provide a match for each child in the program classrooms. Furthermore, every mentor who signed up did not necessarily provide significant mentoring activity. As indicated in what follows, these issues were addressed in the process-evaluation component of the study.

Initiation of Policy Research

The school district official responsible for designing the program and acquiring the U.S. Department of Education funding initiated evaluation of the Dropout Prevention Program. This official had a primary concern with developing programs to address the many educational, disciplinary, and resource problems that confronted a large inner-city school district. She had launched smaller-scale mentoring programs in the district and was convinced that if it could be expanded sufficiently, the mentoring approach would prove effective for reducing the district's excessive dropout rate. This advocate's personal commitment to the concept was emphasized by her own service as a mentor in the program.

This official saw program evaluation as a tool to document the success of the mentoring program and to secure further funding for continuing a strong mentoring program. The Department of Education funding source did not require a methodologically rigorous evaluation, and it would allow the use of a modest amount of grant money for evaluation. To strengthen the credibility of study findings, the district official sought the involvement of experienced program evaluators in two major local universities. The result was a unique collaborative research effort involving faculty and graduate students in these institutions.

The budget for the study was modest, ranging from $7,500 to $15,000 per year for the duration of the program, but the participation of advanced graduate students from both institutions helped stretch these resources. The study proceeded in three phases, each lasting one year. Phase 1 documented the implementation of the program and piloted outcome-evaluation methods. Phase 2 focused on outcome evaluation, assessing the outcomes of the program for the full range of program participants. Phase 3 was devoted to elaboration, involving more in-depth, qualitative analyses of a small sample of participants. This section focuses on Phase 2.

The Policy Research Task

The task for the Dropout Prevention Program evaluation focused on outcome evaluation. From the perspective of the client, the task was to use limited available resources to produce a scientifically credible study that "proved" the effectiveness and value of the mentoring approach to reducing dropout rates. The evaluation team was solicited with this task in mind, and evaluators brought their own perceptions of an adequate approach to the research task to negotiations about the study scope and method. Given their experience with prevention programs and with mentoring programs in particular, the evaluators argued strongly for a more balanced study that collected sufficient information on program implementation to assess the degree to which the "planned" program had been fully implemented. The final study method described in what follows was a negotiated design with input from the client as well as the evaluation team, which consisted of faculty from two university research institutes.

Objectives

The Dropout Prevention Program in the St. Louis Public Schools was an ambitious attempt to provide mentoring and other services to at-risk students in district schools. As stated in the funding proposal, this program's goals included the following:

- Increasing the number of students who stay in school
- Increasing positive attitudes toward school among participating students in Grades 3 through 11
- Provision of trained adult mentors for each of 1,230 participating students
- Strengthening home–school–community collaboration for dropout prevention through the services of liaisons
- Pilot testing and dissemination of a mentoring model that could be replicated within the district and in other school systems

The data gathered in the evaluation were central to the latter objective. Accordingly, pilot testing would focus on the degree to which the program had met its goals for matching students and mentors, for serving students with home–school liaisons, for reducing tardiness and absenteeism as indicators of staying in school, for improving self-concept, for improving attitudes toward school, and for improving performance in school.

Challenges

The Dropout Prevention Program evaluation brought challenges in several varieties—technical, implementation, and use. From a technical research point of view, the first challenge concerned adequate measurement of program outcomes. Whereas the program was intended to reduce school dropouts and to improve school performance, these ultimate outcomes were difficult to measure. For one thing, the younger students would have a very low probability of dropping out at any time during the life of the study—this benefit would come later in the students' education. School performance was also a difficult outcome to measure, particularly in a short study span. Grades are not a highly precise measure of performance, and they are made less sensitive by measurement "noise" introduced through differences in teachers, changes in class environment, and other sources of extraneous variation. Accordingly, an adequate design had to include other measures of attitudinal and behavioral outcomes that had to be constructed to be relevant for the program's primary plausible impacts.

Studies in school settings bring additional challenges of design and implementation. Typically, experimental design requirements like random assignment are not feasible—or ethically acceptable—in school settings. The resulting quasi-experimental designs, such as that used for this evaluation, raise technical challenges of analysis and interpretation. (These are discussed in more detail later in the design section.) School settings also can raise issues related to study implementation. In this study, for example, the quality of data collected in the first year was severely compromised because questionnaires were to be administered by classroom teachers, and some did not comply because of other priorities. The support of administrators had to be reiterated to improve compliance in the second year. Grade data were dropped as a dependent variable because there was no automated way to gather them in a timely fashion across all schools, and other forms of data collection met teacher resistance.

Finally, the evaluators in this case faced significant challenges in reporting findings that would be used in making program decisions. As noted, the client had a very specific use scenario in mind when the project was initiated. There was little doubt in the client's perspective that the study would produce positive findings and that they would be useful for promoting the program—*if* the evaluation team did a credible job in documentation. If the evaluation turned up anything other than a positive result, the evaluators would have a difficult time getting the client to take the study seriously.

The Decision Context

The decision context in this case is relatively simple. Only one organization was involved in decisions about letting the contract, and its size and funding status did not require involving other actors through a competitive bidding process or extensive review. The school board did have to approve the research, but this was routine because the district office had a strong research responsibility. The focus of institutional attention in one unit meant that the context was not complex and that interaction with stakeholders would depend almost exclusively on the relationship with the primary client.

The Institutional Context

The St. Louis Public School District is a large urban district that encompasses the entire city. The district had an independent evaluation unit, but its function was largely to monitor and make periodic recommendations concerning the quality and effectiveness of ongoing programs. The Dropout Prevention Project was administered through the district's Office of Federal Programs, a major center for responding to external funding opportunities available through federal programs. Since many federal programs are demonstrations that require independent evaluation, the office had ties to the local evaluation community.

Internally, office personnel were experienced not only with policy research but also with its use for purposes of assessment and argument. They were aware of the utility of credible documentation for influencing decisions about program expansion or reduction. Senior staffers were knowledgeable about the general nature of evaluation research, though they were not researchers themselves. In summary, the institutional environment for administering the project was focused within a subunit of the school district, and this subunit was experienced in directing and using program evaluations and planning studies.

School buildings and classrooms are also a relevant part of the institutional environment for this project. Data collection took place in the classroom setting and required the cooperation and support of principals, teachers, and program staff. With the small project budget, the evaluation team was dependent on school personnel to ensure that data collection was organized and implemented. The negotiated contract for the study specified that a member of the office staff would coordinate the implementation of data collection procedures that involved school personnel or that took place in the schools. While this designated coordinator had experience working with evaluation data collection, the project was not always her highest priority, and lapses in data collection did occur in the first year of the study.

The Policy Cycle

The Dropout Prevention Project was ostensibly funded as a demonstration. The expectation was that the Department of Education funding supported a seed program that would provide guidance for development of future programs in the district. Formally, then, the project was clearly situated on the feedback loop between policy evaluation and policy planning. Evaluation research is an expected part of demonstrations so that the implementation and outcome effectiveness of the program can be documented and tested. The formal presumption is that the evaluation research will provide empirically based findings that will guide future action. Furthermore, that guidance may suggest that the approach is not effective and should be dropped, that it is promising but needs modification, or that it is very effective and should be expanded largely as implemented. Evaluation may also find that the program was poorly implemented and that this demonstration does not provide a strong basis for decisions about the core program concept.

In the Dropout Prevention Project, the ideal operation of the demonstration concept as a "neutral test" was somewhat compromised by the realities of the decision setting. As noted, the client was strongly committed to the program and was strongly disposed to discounting anything other than a positive result. Put simply, some outcomes from the evaluation would be more readily used than others if the feedback loop were to operate.

Clients and Stakeholders

The discussion to this point has emphasized that the evaluation team was working with one primary client. While the St. Louis Public School District was the formal client, the role was functionally focused in one small office within the district, primarily in the senior staff person who was the entrepreneur behind the program. The size and nature of the program meant that other stakeholders were distinctly secondary in influencing the project. The program was noncontroversial and had low visibility.

Within this caveat, other stakeholders for the project can be identified. Because school dropout is an important public education problem and mentoring is an intervention that was receiving increased attention in an era of public–private partnership, the project was potentially interesting to a broader audience. The Department of Education could be an audience for demonstration findings, but it would not be an aware stakeholder for program implementation. The school district and professional groups would be in a similar position of potential interest in findings that were effectively packaged and disseminated to them.

The immediate stakeholders with a vested interest in the actual conduct and immediate results of the study were teachers and program staff. Teachers might have had an interest in minimizing any work burden that the project placed on them, and program staff might have had an interest in a positive result. As in many evaluation studies, the dual role of staff as study subjects and interested stakeholders posed a challenge of data interpretation for the evaluation team.

Research Design and Implementation

The Dropout Prevention Evaluation was designed to focus on outcome data and analysis and to collect sufficient implementation data to prevent serious errors in interpreting program effectiveness. As is necessary in any applied research with very limited resources, the evaluation team had to be creative and resourceful in the design of the study and in the analysis and reporting of results. The design features are highlighted in this section.

Information Needs

The client's insistence on a rigorous outcome evaluation meant that this study focused on causal information needs more than is the case with many examples of policy research, particularly those with small budgets. The client was also supportive of a quasi-experimental design that would focus on causal evidence and interpretation. The central information need was clearly to demonstrate the causal relation between mentoring activities and positive changes in attitudes and (less directly) behavior.

As is typical of policy research, the study involved not only exploratory research in identifying the purposes and strategies of the program from the standpoint of implementers but also descriptive research in documenting the program intervention.

Design and Methods

Design

The Dropout Prevention Program used a quasi-experimental design that compared attitudinal and behavioral changes in students participating in the program with changes occurring in similar students who were not participants in the program. The design also employed multiple methods to enhance interpretation and collect information on program implementation. The basic characteristics of the design were the following:

- The design included a treatment group composed of students in selected classrooms in the six schools participating in the program. Students in each of these classrooms were served by a liaison, and the program intent was to match each of them with a mentor.
- To provide a benchmark for identifying the effects of the program, the study also collected data on a comparison group composed of students in selected classrooms in six schools that did not participate in the program. These schools were chosen to be similar to the treatment schools in school and student characteristics.
- The Dropout Prevention Program design includes preprogram and postprogram measures on outcome variables for students in participating schools and those in comparison schools. If the program was effective, it was expected that students in the treatment schools would show more positive (or less negative) change than students in the comparison schools. Measurements for participant and comparison students were gathered early in the fall and late in the spring semesters.
- The participant and comparison samples were composed of intact classrooms (except for the high schools). In other words, students were not randomly (or individually) assigned to participant or comparison groups. Whole classrooms were designated. As is typical of evaluations conducted in school settings, this design had several limitations that had to be taken into account in the analysis and interpretation of the results.
- Most important, the use of intact classrooms raised the possibility of nonequivalence between participant and comparison students. The

logic and power of the quasi-experimental design depended upon the similarity of students who participated and those who did not. Without this similarity, differences between the groups could be attributable to factors other than that of receiving program services. While efforts were made to select schools and classrooms that would be similar, the possibility that youth are systematically different in the two schools was a threat to validity.

Methods

The development of explicit measures of program outcomes is a critical point in any evaluation design. For the Dropout Prevention Program, measures were developed with the full consultation and review of program staff. The pre-post questionnaires were designed to measure several attitudinal areas that the program was expected to affect. These attitudinal dimensions are possible "proximal" outcomes linking intervention activities by mentors and home–school–community liaisons with behavioral change (such as finishing school). In the Phase 2 data, all the dimensions conformed to conventional standards of measurement reliability.

These dimensions included two major areas. First were scales measuring orientations and attitudes related to personal confidence and efficacy (for example, self-esteem, efficacy in planning for the future, or belief in a positive future). These reflected the Dropout Prevention Program's aim to develop a generalized sense of competence and an ability to attain positive personal accomplishments that will motivate a child to stay in school. The hypothesis embodied by the program was that home–school–community liaison contact, mentor contact, and the positively reinforcing behaviors issuing from these contacts would result in improvements in personal confidence and belief in personal efficacy.

Second, the instruments included scales measuring attitudes toward school and education, including school bonding and a sense of belonging at school, perceptions of support and encouragement in school, and belief in the relevance and importance of school. These measures were central to program expectations about motivation to stay in school. The hypothesis was that home–school–community liaison contact, mentor contact, and the positively reinforcing behaviors that issue from these contacts would result in more positive attitudes related to school and education. In addition, the postprogram test included questions asking about (1) the extent and nature of contact with home–school–community liaisons and mentors, (2) the perceived benefits of this contact, and (3) overall satisfaction with the program.

In Phase 2 of the study, 784 students completed preprogram questionnaires in the fall; 594 completed postprogram questionnaires in the spring, and 518 students completed both the preprogram and postprogram questionnaires. Of the students completing both questionnaires, 278 were in the participating schools, and 240 were in the comparison schools. Specific measures of change could be calculated for these 518 students, and they constitute the sample for the outcome results of the study.

In addition to the pre-post student questionnaires, the evaluation design incorporated other sources of data. Evaluation team members personally interviewed all home–school–community liaisons and all program administrative staff. The evaluation team also prepared a survey to elicit the experiences and perceptions of mentors in the program. The questionnaire, accompanied by a self-addressed return envelope, was mailed to 300 mentors in the dropout prevention program. Fifty-four mentors (a response rate of 18 percent) completed the survey and returned it. The survey included a series of closed-format and open-ended questions asking about contact with student partners, satisfaction with participation in the program, and perceived effectiveness.

Selected Findings

The evaluation was designed to test the program hypotheses that improved attitudes toward school and increased self-esteem, greater self-control (or efficacy), and positive changes in attitudes regarding personal behavior will lead to behavioral changes that may result in students remaining in school. The basic analysis to test this expectation was to compare change in attitudes between treatment and comparison groups. A finding of more positive change among treatment youth would tend to confirm program effectiveness.

Statistical comparisons of profiles were conducted to see whether the participant group and the comparison group, though not randomly assigned, approximated each other demographically. Participant and comparison groups were similar in their distributions on age, grade, gender, and race. No apparent problems of nonequivalence between participant and comparison groups would cloud the interpretation of results.

Analysis of Classroom Effects

Table 7.1 displays results of a regression analysis in which postprogram scores for youth were used as the dependent variable. Preprogram scores and membership in the participant group or the comparison group were entered as independent variables. (A positive relation for coefficients in the "Participant Classroom" column indicates that students in participating classrooms showed more positive change on the average than those in comparison classrooms, thus indicating a positive program effect.) Beta coefficients are standardized regression coefficients that represent variables in terms of standard deviations rather than raw scores, thus improving comparability of coefficients across variables with different measurement ranges. The figures in the R^2 column indicate the total amount of variance in the postprogram scores as explained by (a) the preprogram scores and (b) whether the student was in the participant or comparison classroom.

Table 7.1 Multiple Regression of Program Effects on Change in Participant Attitudes ($n = 518$)

Dependent Variable	Preprogram Score Beta	Participant Classroom Beta	R^2
Behavior	−.43*	.001	.18
Academics	.49*	−.006	.24
Hopefulness	.46*	.005	.20
Efficacy	.26*	−.06	.07
Attitude toward school	.47*	−.07	.22
Attitude toward authority	.41*	.001	.17
Total improvement	.55*	−.02	.30

* Statistically significant at the .01 level

Asterisks in the table indicate the level of statistical significance represented by results. A single asterisk indicates a probability level less than .05, the typical standard of acceptance for social science sources.

The results underscore that no statistically (or substantively) significant difference was found between the average change in attitudes for students in participant classrooms as compared with students in comparison classrooms. In other words, being in a participating classroom had no apparent effect on the average change in scores from preprogram to postprogram, as compared with students in a group of comparison classrooms. The results of this analysis provided no evidence for program effectiveness in affecting student attitudes. This preliminary finding did not meet the client's expectations and engendered a very negative response. Indeed, the client immediately sought ways of discounting the null result, focusing on the weakness of measures and the lack of "hard" behavioral data (which were not available).

Documentation of Individual Contact

The evaluation team used additional information on program implementation and participation both to explicate the reasons for this finding of no program effect and to provide useful guidance for the program. The supplementary data gathered from other sources clearly indicated that the actual degree of contact with mentors or liaisons varied significantly between students in participating classrooms. Table 7.2 displays student responses concerning the amount of contact they had with the liaisons and their mentors.

As Table 7.2 illustrates, contacts with home–school–community liaisons were much more frequent than contact with mentors. Comments from the liaisons corroborated this student report. Significantly, more than one third of the students had never met with a mentor, indicating that some students simply were not participating in the mentoring program. Results of the mentor survey were consistent with student reports. One half of the mentors reported five or fewer meetings with students.

Table 7.2 Contact with Liaisons and Mentors

Frequency of Contact	Liaisons (n = 261)	Mentors (n = 278)
"A lot" (6 or more meetings)	48.7%	16.9%
Some (3 to 5 meetings)	29.5	12.6
Only 1 or 2 meetings	12.6	36.0
No meetings	9.2	34.5

Another series of questions asked the students whether they ever met with their liaison or their mentor outside of school and whether the liaison or mentor ever visited the student's home, telephoned the home, or spoke to the student's parents. Table 7.3 displays the responses of those students who indicated having contact with a liaison or a mentor at least once.

The table indicates that many of the liaisons and the mentors became involved in the lives of their students beyond activities or meetings at school. Students reported extensive contact in their homes. In all areas, the liaisons were more likely than the mentors to have had some home contact with the student.

As these data indicate, liaisons and mentors often extended their efforts to contacting students at home. However, when the number of children who never had contact with a mentor was considered, only a small minority of children had a mentor who interacted with their family. Only two in ten (19.8 percent) had a mentor visit their home; slightly fewer than one third (29.5 percent) had a mentor call their home; and just more than one third (33.5 percent) had a mentor talk to their parents. Most children in program classrooms had no interaction between mentors and their home.

More specifically, of 261 students in participating classrooms who provided information in their postprogram questionnaires, just 47 (or 18 percent) remembered having more than five meetings with a mentor, and 127 (or 49 percent) remembered having more than five personal meetings with a liaison. Just 34 (or 13 percent) had more than five meetings with both a mentor and a liaison. These findings indicate that just being in a participating classroom did not mean that a student was a meaningful participant in the program. The evaluation team elaborated on the implications of this issue by examining the effects of intensity of participation on change in student attitudes.

Analysis of the Effects of Individual Contact

To distinguish levels of participation among children in the participating classrooms, the evaluation team constructed intensity-of-participation indices for liaison contact and mentor contact. To construct this measure, students were simply divided into those who had more than five contacts with a liaison or mentor and those who had five or fewer contacts.

Table 7.3 Students' Reports of Contact with Liaisons and Mentors Outside of School

	Liaison (n = 237)			Mentor (n = 182)		
	Yes, more than once	*Yes, once*	*No*	*Yes, more than once*	*Yes, once*	*No*
Question						
Met outside of school?	Not Applicable			21.4%	18.1%	60.4%
Visited home?	15.2%	18.9%	65.9%	14.8	15.4	69.8
Telephoned home?	35.4	18.6	46.0	28.0	17.0	55.0
Talked to parents?	39.2	23.2	37.6	20.9	30.2	48.9

Table 7.4 Average Change by Degree of Intensity (Total Sample)

	Liaison Contact		Mentor Contact		Combined Contact	
	High	*Low*	*High*	*Low*	*High*	*Low*
Hopefulness	.03	−.05	−.04	.05	.04	.03
Efficacy	.02	−.04	.08	−.05	.18	−.05**
Attitude toward school	.01	.02	−.02	.17**	.08	.15
Attitude toward authority	−.07	−.11	.00	−.09	.04	−.08
Total Scale	.02	−.08*	.008	−.01	.08	−.02

*   Statistically significant at .05 level
** Approaches statistical significance at .05 level

Table 7.4 displays mean change between preprogram and postprogram scores on all attitude measures for high-intensity and low-intensity contact with liaisons, mentors, or both. For example, students with high-intensity liaison contact had postprogram scores on the total improvement scale that were an average of .02 points *higher* than preprogram scores. Students with low-intensity contact had postprogram scores that were an average of .08 points *lower* than preprogram scores. The difference between change for students with high-intensity contact and those with low-intensity contact approached statistical significance (probability was between .05 and .10).

The data in Table 7.4 indicate a consistent pattern of more positive pre-post change for students with high-intensity contact with liaisons than for students with low-intensity contact with liaisons, except for attitude toward school. The individual changes were not, however, statistically significant. No clear pattern emerges for mentor contact, and results for several items indicate that students with high-intensity mentor contact experienced less positive change. Combined contact with both mentor and liaison shows a general pattern of positive effect and a significant positive impact on attitude toward school. While these results are not strong, they do suggest a positive impact of high-intensity liaison contact.

Finally, Table 7.5 displays multiple regression results for several independent variables and each attitude dimension. These results do not account for the differences between schools identified earlier, and as interim results, they require more detailed analysis in the final study report. Overall, however, these results indicate the following:

1. Students in participating classrooms in the aggregate did not experience more favorable attitude change than did students in comparison classrooms when intensity of participation is in the equation.
2. Intensity of mentor contact showed no pattern of positive impact on attitude change across the dimensions.
3. Intensity of contact with liaison did show a consistent pattern of slight positive relation to positive attitude change, approaching statistical significance for total improvement and hopefulness.

The suggested importance of liaisons was strengthened through self-report by the program youth. In response to questionnaire items concerning the perceived helpfulness of the program, a pattern of differences emerged in perceived effects between liaisons and mentors. Across the board, liaisons were perceived to have helped more than mentors. The liaisons also appeared to have been more effective in areas directly related to getting to school and getting along at school. This pattern was consistent with the focus of their activities on school-related issues.

The student postprogram questionnaires provided positive self-reports concerning program effects. In particular, these reports emphasized the

Table 7.5 Program Effects on Change in Participants' Attitudes: Expanded Model (*n* = 501)

Attitude	Pretest Score Beta	Participant Classroom Beta	Mentor Intensity Beta	Liaison Intensity Beta	Race Beta	Gender Beta
Behavior	.45*	−.03	−.02	.04	.03	.10
Academics	.48*	−.03	.04	.05	.12*	.03
Hopefulness	.49*	−.06	−.07**	.10*	.10*	.09*
Efficacy	.27*	−.10**	.003	.06	.06	.05
Attitude toward school	.46*	−.11*	.04	.06	.13*	.03
Attitude toward authority	.41*	−.02	.006	.005	.03	.08**
Total Change	.56*	−.08**	.00	.08**	.10*	.08*

* Statistically significant at the .10 level

key importance of liaisons to the program. Liaisons had more contact with students and were perceived to have had a more positive impact, particularly in areas directly related to school behavior. The pattern of pre-post change in attitude measures suggested that higher levels of contact with liaisons exerted a positive influence on attitude change. This pattern did differ significantly across schools, suggesting that some approaches to liaison activities may have been more important than others. Indeed, implementation data were consistent with school differences, documenting that the most skilled and active liaisons were in the schools experiencing the most positive evaluation findings. Providing support to children is an endeavor that depends on personal skill and continuity. The pattern of results for attitude measures supports observations by interviewees that the liaison and mentoring approaches are less suitable and less effective for older students.

In their own perception and in the perception of students, mentors brought strengths with respect to general outlook such as self-concept and thinking about the future. They were less helpful with respect to concrete issues and behaviors related to school. The results of pre-post comparisons of attitude change were thus consistent with a conclusion that mentor effectiveness in this program was limited. Dedicated mentors may have had a very positive impact on children, but the number of these instances was small, and many mentor relations were less productive. The study clearly documented that mentoring programs are difficult to implement. Few students received a level of mentor contact that could have been expected to have much impact on their attitudes or behavior.

The evaluation emphasized the fact that the program does not provide significant levels of contact, particularly mentoring contact, for large numbers of students in the participating classrooms. This shortfall in planned service intensity has occurred for understandable reasons (such as the difficulty of recruiting mentors and the limitations of liaison time). Nevertheless, they seriously complicated the analysis of evaluation results, and they lessened the potential impact of the program on the full range of students in participating classrooms. If mentoring approaches are to have much effect, they must be strongly implemented, with corresponding attention to recruitment, training, and retention of mentors.

Another unexpected result of the study was the suggested importance of the school liaisons. These program members tended to be very committed to students and had relatively high levels of contact with them. They focused on school issues and were on the scene to help and support young people. They were more likely to have contact with the student's home than were the mentors. The study suggests that the liaison role may be a more feasible and effective means of ameliorating immediate school problems in an inner city setting than is the more politically appealing mentoring strategy.

Communicating and Using Results

The evaluation team in this case worked closely with the program staff. Staff members agreed on the design, were involved in data collection, and were informed of emerging findings in face-to-face meetings. Still, the research findings were not consistent with the expectations of a determined client, and this presented an insurmountable challenge to full use of the study.

Reporting Results

Results of the study were presented in three annual reports. These reports were complete, presenting summary tables of analyses with full narratives in a clearly organized format. They did not stop simply at presentation of data. Instead, they reported on a series of analyses that explicated the relation between program implementation, differential exposure to the program for different students, and outcomes. The most comprehensive of these reports was the Phase 2 report that has been summarized in this chapter. This report included not only the basic findings reported here but also much more detail about individual schools and the satisfaction and perceptions of students, mentors, and liaisons. The client showed no interest in producing summaries or less-technical reports suitable for more general distribution, and the audiences for the reports never went beyond the immediate staff and possibly the school district and funding agencies.

Results were also presented and discussed in person through periodic meetings with the client. While the evaluation team repeatedly emphasized the value of the findings for strengthening the program and the suggested value of the liaison position, the client was persistently concerned about the lack of an unequivocally positive result.

Selected Recommendations

The Phase 2 report produced a number of recommendations, some of which were acted on in the third year. Many focused on the necessity for strengthened implementation of the mentoring program. The study clearly demonstrated that, despite impressive numbers with respect to mentor recruitment and assignment, the program had not been meaningfully delivered to most of the participants. Before a fair conclusion concerning the value of mentoring could be reached, it would be necessary to strengthen delivery of mentoring services. Recommendations for increased training and follow-up with mentors were partially implemented.

The evaluation team also recommended several improvements in the working conditions of liaisons. These were potentially important because of the promising findings regarding the effectiveness of liaisons. Indeed, the study suggests that this role is potentially productive independent of the mentoring component. Since liaison employment was governed by the school district, these recommendations went unheard because the program staff was not in a position to influence personnel matters.

Action

The overall use of the evaluation was discouraging. Even though the study's design and implementation provided focused information on the reasons for program weakness, little action resulted in the context of this program. The study's conclusions did not meet the expectations of the client and therefore were not considered suitable for the promotional use that the client had anticipated. Accordingly, the client had no commitment or motivation to disseminate the results, and the reports remained internal documents. While the study produced strong recommendations for management action in the program, the constraints of short-term funding and a large organizational environment prevented aggressive action to implement the recommendations. It may be that, as in many cases of policy research, the most direct effects on action will be in the altered awareness and expectations of decision makers in designing future programs.

Lessons for Policy Research

The Dropout Prevention Program evaluation exemplifies basic lessons in policy research. First, the study demonstrates the importance of balanced outcome and implementation designs in the evaluation of actual programs. A failure to collect adequate data on implementation will often result in a conclusion that a program is not effective when in fact it was never implemented. In this case, integrating information on liaison and mentor contact into the analysis helped explain the flat result of the simple outcome analysis and raised the possibility of further exploration of the liaison role as a countermeasure for school dropout.

The second point this study makes is that it exemplifies the marginal methodological strength of many policy studies. No strong measures of anticipated behavioral outcomes were feasible within the limited resources of the study, so intermediate attitudinal and perceptual measures became the focus. These are prone to measurement error and accordingly yield weak patterns of result. Interpretation of such weak findings must often involve multiple data sources and judgments about what is reasonable in the overall context of the study setting and the pattern of findings.

The third and final point is that the case highlights the importance of the expectations and orientation of the client for the use of the study results. Despite close cooperation between evaluators and the client, and despite careful attention to the concrete explanation of patterns of result, the study was of limited use because it did not fit the initial expectations and plans of the client.

Focus on Research Methods

Measuring the Policy "Dose"

One prominent purpose of policy research is to assess the degree to which some policy intervention achieves its intended effects—thereby providing causal policy information. The study of the St. Louis Dropout Prevention Program indicates how important it is to measure the degree to which targets of a policy intervention (in this case, students) actually receive the planned intervention services (mentoring or contact with liaison). Policy researchers often refer to this degree of actual intervention or exposure to program efforts as the program "dose." Measures of contact are similarly referred to as "dosage data."

For the dropout study, dosage data were gathered through self-reports. That is, students were asked how much contact they had with their mentors or their home–school liaisons. This method of data collection is prone to error (respondents may forget or "selectively remember," based on what they feel the desired response is), but it was still critical to the analysis of program outcomes.

When resources allow, policy research can be strengthened through careful collection of dosage data from primary sources such as attendance records or service logs. Collecting consistent and accurate dosage information typically requires close cooperation with program staff, because policy researchers rely on them to complete data collection forms.

Acronyms and Jargon

Liaisons—School employees who facilitated student–mentor relationships
Mentors—Community figures who served as advisers to school children
Office of Federal Programs—An agency of the St. Louis Public School District that administered the Dropout Prevention Mentor Project

Discussion Questions

1. How did the information needs of the client affect the outcome of this study?
2. In your opinion, how should the policy researcher have dealt with the client's demands?
3. What ethical questions about policy research does this case study raise? Are these questions commonly associated with policy research?
4. How were qualitative research methods used to enhance the usefulness of this study?

5. Why was a quasi-experimental and not a classical experimental design used in this study?
6. How could the use of the policy research findings have been enhanced?

Assignments and Activities

1. Describe a strategy to maximize the use of policy research that contradicts a client's expectations.
2. Assuming that the client ordering this study had not had strong feelings for or against the program, suggest a research design that is more appropriate for this type of policy situation.

8 The Use of Applied Policy Research to Inform and Reform Statewide Dropout Policies

Jill Norton

Introduction

The Policy Problem

In 2004, high school dropout was emerging as a critical national policy challenge. Evidence was mounting that students without a high school diploma were less likely than their peers to secure a well-paying job, less likely to wed, more likely to become parents when they were very young, more at risk of involvement with the criminal justice system, and more likely to need social welfare assistance.[1] Even in Massachusetts, an affluent state with generally high achievement, one in five students did not graduate from high school within four years.

Massachusetts state policy makers, with urging from local and community advocates, began to turn their attention to what, by 2007, many came to refer to as a "dropout crisis." This case study describes applied policy research conducted in Massachusetts by an independent nonprofit, the Rennie Center for Education Research & Policy, and the impact of that research on state policies related to students dropping out of high school.

Initiation of Policy Research

The Rennie Center for Education Research & Policy, an independent applied research and policy think tank,[2] first became involved with informing policies to reduce Massachusetts high school dropout rates in 2005 through its participation in the Youth Transitions Task Force (YTTF), a Boston initiative established the previous year by Mayor Tom Menino. YTTF was Boston focused but intentionally drew in a powerful array of community-based organizations, city and state agencies, and leaders within the Boston Public Schools. Intended to serve as a cross-sector coalition that could tackle issues of poverty that were contributing to Boston youth dropping out, YTTF became the impetus for a city- and statewide movement to reduce the dropout rate.

In 2005, YTTF commissioned research reports that quantified the impact of the dropout crisis in economic and societal terms and served as a rallying cry for YTTF members, attracting attention not only in Boston but across the state. State legislators from Boston and throughout the Commonwealth began to recognize the significant negative impact of students dropping out on taxpayers as well as on students themselves. Compelled by the task force's research, the Rennie Center engaged with YTTF, sending a representative to its monthly meetings and looking for opportunities to increase attention to the dropout crisis statewide.

Early in 2007, the Rennie Center began partnering with YTTF to host a series of statewide meetings on the dropout crisis that featured leaders from the governor's office and the Department of Elementary and Secondary Education (DESE). These meetings also served as a platform for state legislators to present proposed legislation related to reducing the number of students who drop out of school.

As a result of these meetings, an informal partnership began to develop between me (the Rennie Center executive director), Lisa Famularo (Rennie Center research director), Stafford Peat, Jenny Curtin, and Nyal Fuentes (leaders from DESE) and Kathy Hamilton (YTTF director). Late in 2007, the DESE team approached the Rennie Center with a research question. While analyzing state dropout data over the past four years it had been collected, DESE leaders realized that nearly a dozen high schools appeared to be reducing their dropout rates over time. The question was: what were these schools doing to achieve these notably lower rates? The DESE team wondered if the Rennie Center would be interested in conducting a study to find out. Within a week, the Rennie Center research team began designing a qualitative research study to attempt to answer that question.

Meanwhile, momentum to address the dropout crisis continued to build across the state, and in August 2008, the legislature passed an Act to Improve Dropout Prevention and Reporting of Graduation Rates.[3] Among the law's provisions was the creation of a commission—the Graduation and Dropout Prevention and Recovery Commission—to survey dropout prevention and recovery best practices nationwide and to identify promising programs currently in use in the Commonwealth. The legislature directed the commission to provide findings and recommendations on 10 specific topic areas, including developing early indicator systems, examining school discipline policies, and considering raising the compulsory age of attendance. For a complete list of the 10 topics, see Table 8.1.[4]

While the Rennie Center did not have membership on the Graduation and Dropout Prevention and Recovery Commission, Jenny Curtin, Stafford Peat, and Kathy Hamilton were appointed as commission members. After the first commission meeting, these three approached the Rennie Center team to explore interest in producing research targeted at informing the decisions of the commission. According to Stafford, Jenny, and Kathy, it was clear that the commission did not have enough information

Table 8.1 Graduation and Dropout Recovery and Prevention Commission Areas of Focus

1. Setting a goal and timeline for reducing the statewide annual dropout rate
2. Further developing early indicator systems to identify students who are at risk of dropping out or who are not likely to graduate on time from high school without receiving additional support and school policies that exacerbate dropping out
3. Expanding the definition of "structured learning time" to include internships and work-study programs and exploring ways to encourage school districts to incorporate quality internships and work and learning programs into structured learning time to engage all students in relevant and rigorous curricula
4. Developing a reimbursement mechanism for districts sending students to alternative education programs
5. Exploring the connection between school discipline policies and students' level of engagement in or alienation from school, with emphasis on school referrals for discipline purposes and court-involved youth
6. Providing financial incentives for districts that are effective in graduating at-risk students and recovering high school dropouts
7. Raising the compulsory attendance age from 16 years of age to 18 years of age
8. Creating a dropout prevention and recovery grant program to:
   • Provide school districts with funds to implement early indicator systems
   • Create capacity within regions by engaging local workforce investment boards for outreach to dropouts and referral to local school districts and Alternative Education programs; or
   • Provide funds to local districts or nonprofit programs to develop alternative routes to a diploma or its equivalent to prevent students from dropping out and to meet the needs of those returning to education
9. District activities in compliance with Section 18 of Chapter 76 of the Massachusetts General Laws and any regulations or administrative directives of the department regarding required and appropriate measures to identify, locate, interview, and counsel high school dropouts; provided, however, that the commission shall also make recommendations regarding mandatory reporting by districts on activities in fulfillment of statutory requirements and administrative directives
10. Establishing a threshold annual dropout rate for each school district such that rates in excess of threshold levels would establish a mandatory requirement on districts to adopt and implement a districtwide action plan to reduce dropout rates and effectively track students

to make informed recommendations about two areas in particular: raising the compulsory age of attendance and altering school discipline policies. The challenge was that the research had to be completed within six to eight weeks if it was to influence the Commission's decisions.

At the time, the Rennie Center was a small team (four full-time staff). With staff already working to complete the policy brief focused on the 11 districts that were reducing their dropout rates as well as two other projects, committing to another project seemed untenable. But the team agreed that the opportunity to inform the commission's recommendations was too compelling to pass up. So the center took a leap and embarked on two new projects for the Dropout Commission: (1) a rapid-cycle research project on the compulsory age of school attendance and (2) an exploration of state data and school discipline policies.

Policy Research Task

The overall policy research task was to inform the recommendations of the final report of the Graduation and Dropout Prevention and Recovery Commission through three distinct research projects: (1) identifying policies and practices used by high schools that were successfully reducing their dropout rates in order to provide other schools with models from which to learn, (2) conducting a literature review of the empirical evidence base on raising the compulsory age of attendance as well as scanning other state compulsory age policies to explore their impact, and (3) conducting an initial analysis of state discipline data to identify trends and to uncover policies that might be contributing to students dropping out of school.

Stafford Peat, director of secondary school services at the Massachusetts Department of Elementary and Secondary Education, described the overarching policy research task before us: "state policy makers have developed a good understanding of why students drop out. Types of evidence and research-based interventions and level of support services needed to successfully keep students from dropping out and re-engaging those who have made the decision to leave school" are less clear. This was the need the research team would address.

Objectives

In addition to increasing understanding of the topics described already, the primary objective of the research was immediate and tangible: the team had to produce research that would be easily accessible to commission members and would form the basis for their decisions about proposed recommendations. It also tried to look beyond the commission and designed research to inform state legislation and regulatory changes at state education agencies.

Challenges

There were three main challenges to the team's efforts to inform the Graduation and Dropout Prevention and Recovery Commission's decisions:

1. **Quick turnaround.** As mentioned, the research team had a six- to eight-week window during which to complete its research. The commission met monthly and had determined which topics it would address at each meeting. If the research wasn't complete in time for the commission's meeting that focused on that topic, it was unlikely

that it would be incorporated into the commission's recommendations or would inform legislation. So the team's goal was to strike a balance between conducting high-quality research and producing it as fast as possible to conform to the commission's decision-making timeline. For example, for two of the projects, the team conducted scans of existing data instead of embarking on new data collection efforts that would have been prohibitively time consuming and costly.

2. **Limited staff capacity.** With only four staff, committing to such a quick turnaround put additional pressure on an already prolific team. To accommodate the additional workload and free up staff capacity, timelines for two unrelated projects were extended. Policy research resources are always finite, and this exemplifies the kinds of decisions that sometimes have to be made "on the fly."

3. **Uncertainty about the commission.** As mentioned, the Rennie Center had close relationships with several commission members, and the chair of the commission was former Rennie Center president Paul Reville. Yet with no official seat at the table, the research team had somewhat limited influence on the commission's agenda setting and direction. The team was, for the most part, reliant on reports from commission members about its priorities and timelines for addressing each of the 10 policy topics it was charged with examining. The team was able to work around this challenge by staying in regular communication with the commission members we knew well and keeping them and Secretary Reville informed of the progress of our work.

The Decision Context

The Institutional Context

The Graduation and Dropout Prevention and Recovery Commission was chaired by Paul Reville, founder and former president of the Rennie Center, who left the Rennie Center when he was appointed Secretary of Education by Massachusetts Governor Deval Patrick in early 2008. Secretary Reville's appointment made the Rennie Center's role both easier and harder. On the one hand, there was no one in the state who knew the Rennie Center's research better. On the other hand, Reville was keenly aware of the negative perceptions that might come from having his former organization lead the commission's research efforts, and he was therefore careful to keep the Rennie Center at a distance during the commission's meetings and deliberations.

The Policy Cycle

In this case, the determining cycle was the commission's meeting schedule and its charge to publish a report with recommendations fewer than 12 months from the date it was first convened. The Rennie Center's three research projects included several elements of the policy cycle described in Chapter 1, but the research team's work was mostly situated in the agenda-setting phase. While the legislation that established the Dropout Commission had already set its agenda without the team's input, it was positioned to help the commission prioritize and better understand some of the 10 topics on that agenda. The team wanted to inform the commission's recommendations and hoped that those recommendations would then influence state legislation and regulatory changes.

Stakeholders

Members of the commission were the primary stakeholders. However, the team's goal was also to inform the chairs of the Joint Education Committee of the Massachusetts legislature as well as individual legislators as they considered proposing legislation to reduce dropout rates. Finally, it became clear as the team developed its research that some findings would be particularly relevant for the Board of Elementary and Secondary Education as well as for the commissioner and his staff.

Research Design and Implementation

Information Needs

With three separate but related projects developing simultaneously, the team needed three different sets of information, each of which is described separately in the Design and Methods section that follows. All of the projects included an analysis of qualitative or quantitative data, but in addition to reporting on findings related to data, they also included context for that data. For example, in the work on the compulsory age of high school attendance, the team knew it would be important for policy makers to learn what had happened in other states that had raised their ages of compulsory attendance.

Design and Methods

The design and methods of the research that the Rennie Center conducted were largely shaped by the timeline of the Dropout Commission. While longer-term, more rigorous empirical research would have been preferred, the research team didn't have the time or resources to conduct such studies and had to determine what methods could deliver the soundest findings in the shortest amount of time. The design and methods for each project are described in what follows:

- **Promising practices from high schools reducing their dropout rates.**

  School selection. The process for selecting schools for this study involved four steps. First, the team selected districts that have been making steady progress in reducing the dropout rate over at least three of the past four consecutive school years. Next, school districts were rank ordered based on their average change in dropout rate over a four-year period (from school years 2003–2004 to 2006–2007). Twenty-seven districts were found to have an average decrease in their dropout rate of more than two percentage points over that period. Third, from those 27 districts, the team selected the ones with the largest populations of students at greatest risk for dropping out and that were making greater progress than expected. Twelve districts were identified through this process. Of the 12 selected districts, seven agreed to participate, and four of those districts had more than one high school, resulting in a sample of 11 schools.

Data collection. Research for this study was conducted using structured phone interviews with both school leaders and district administrators. Twenty interviews were conducted: 9 with superintendents and/or central office staff and 11 with principals and/or headmasters.

- **Raising the compulsory age of attendance.** For this study, the team analyzed compulsory attendance laws in Massachusetts and conducted an overview of the trends in compulsory attendance laws nationally. Additionally, recent legislative action to raise the age and penalties for noncompliance were evaluated along with a review of research examining the effectiveness of this policy in reducing the dropout rate and increasing the graduation rate.
- **Considering the impact of school discipline practices in Massachusetts.** This study described the purpose of school discipline policies, summarized findings from recent research on the effects of removing students from school for disciplinary reasons, summarized the legal background for disciplinary removal, and analyzed statewide discipline data by student subgroup and by school type (e.g., charter, traditional).

Selected Findings

Promising Practices from High Schools Reducing Their Dropout Rates

This study revealed common themes from these high schools; most of these schools:

- used data to identify students at risk of dropping out (including early indicators of potential dropouts and high school attendance)
- offered targeted interventions such as personalizing the learning environment and supporting the transition to ninth grade

- connected high school to college and careers
- provided alternatives to traditional high school
- formed collaborations and partnerships to bring in additional resources for students at risk of dropping out

Raising the Compulsory Age of Attendance

This study revealed a lack of empirical evidence to support the premise that raising the compulsory age of attendance would decrease dropout rates and increase graduation rates. The analysis of prior research uncovered that the effects of raising the compulsory age diminished over time; that is, the effect decreased over time. The effect of raising the compulsory age was the strongest in 1960, smaller in 1970, and even smaller in 1980. Analysis of another study of school attainment of individuals who were age 16 between 1970 and 1995 exposed that, on average, raising the compulsory age above 16 increased an individual student's length of schooling between .12 and .16 years. In other words, on average, students stayed in school for an additional 1½ to 2 months when the compulsory age of attendance was raised.

Considering the Impact of School Discipline Practices

This preliminary analysis of Massachusetts discipline policies and data revealed that:

- in Massachusetts, education was not a fundamental right—students who had been expelled could be denied a public education
- out-of-school suspension was the most frequently used form of disciplinary removal
- the number of disciplinary removals peaked at 9th grade and declined in 10th through 12th grade
- of 380 school districts statewide, 65 had out-of-school suspension rates higher than 10%, meaning that at least 1 out of every 10 enrolled students received an out-of-school suspension during the 2007–2008 school year
- students from low-income families, special education students, male students, and Black and Hispanic students were removed at disproportionately high rates

Communicating and Using Results

Reporting Results

Because the main objective was to inform the commission's recommendations, the team opted to share its promising practices and compulsory age-of-attendance reports with commission members before we published them—not a typical Rennie Center practice. Once those two reports had been shared with the commission, they were published as Rennie Center policy briefs, and public release events for each were convened.

Selected Recommendations

Each report included recommendations specific to its topic. Each of these is described in what follows.

Promising Practices from Schools Reducing Their Dropout Rates

Based on the interview research with school and district leaders, the reports provided considerations for policy makers and other school and district leaders that included:

- developing a set of interventions to address the diverse range of needs for students at risk of dropping out
- investing in dropout prevention efforts consistently over time
- focusing efforts on student engagement, not just academic support
- engaging with partners and community resources to expand capacity to address students' needs

Raising the Compulsory Age of Attendance

Informed by the team's review of the scant empirical evidence supporting the effects of raising the age of compulsory attendance, policy makers were urged to consider:

- other policies with stronger evidence before raising the compulsory age
- increasing alternative educational options so that if students were compelled to stay in school, they might have the option of enrolling in a nurturing alternative program that was better tailored to their needs
- concurrent policies if they opted to raise the compulsory age, including considering the costs and policies of enforcing such a change, funding outreach programs to reengage young people who left school before graduating, and expanding professional development for teachers to better connect with and support these students

Considering the Impact of School Discipline Policies

The research noted that there was reason for concern when considering the findings from Massachusetts data reported earlier in light of what national research revealed about the impact of disciplinary removal. Policy makers were urged to:

- hold schools and districts accountable for the appropriate use of disciplinary removal
- require districts to report details on the nature of "unassigned" offenses that result in students being suspended and expelled from school
- report school discipline data to the public annually and disaggregate it by subgroup

Action

The actions that took place in response to this research happened over time and in some cases are still occurring. The team's short-term goals for the research were met: the Graduation and Dropout Prevention and Recovery Commission utilized much of the research to inform its recommendations.

In October of 2009, the commission published its report and discussed it at a public convening hosted by the Rennie Center. The report cited the Rennie Center's report on promising practices for reducing the dropout rate and echoed its recommendations for targeting interventions and connecting school to future opportunities. Responding to cautions about raising the compulsory age of attendance, the commission recommended raising the age, but only when coupled "with adequate supportive programming and services to effectively implement and enforce the changes in school attendance law." According to Secretary Reville, "We won't move forward on that until we are confident that we can put in place the service and supports and programs that need to be there to make it possible to get some reduction of the dropout rate through raising the age."[5]

Finally, in line with Rennie Center research, the commission report recommended that the legislature immediately amend the law that allowed school districts to deny an education to students who had been expelled. The commission also recommended that the Board of Elementary and Secondary Education require school districts to develop models that incorporate intermediary steps before the use of expulsion and to require a written explanation from the school district to the Department of Elementary and Secondary Education when excluding a student for more than 10 consecutive days.

Regarding longer-term impact, over the next two years, the legislature engaged the research team to inform its proposed policies on dropouts. For example, on September 27, 2011, the state legislature's Joint Committee on Education invited testimony on pending dropout prevention and recovery bills from Lisa Famularo, Rennie Center research director. Lisa was invited based on "the Rennie Center's body of research on dropout prevention and recovery." Her testimony featured findings from policy briefs on compulsory age, school discipline, and promising practices for dropout prevention published in March 2011 and February 2009.

Lisa's testimony informed the adoption of two bills that were passed by Massachusetts Legislature during the 2011–2012 legislative session—an act relative to student access to educational services and exclusion from school (Chapter 222 of the Acts of 2012) and an act regarding families and children engaged in services (Chapter 240 of the Acts of 2012), each of which included considerations on school discipline and dropout prevention and recovery from the Rennie Center's briefs *Raise the Age, Lower the Dropout Rate? Considerations for Policy makers* and *Act Out, Get Out? Considering the Impact of School Discipline Practices in Massachusetts.*

Even now, the implications of this study continue to inform state policies and state education agency regulations. In January 2016, the Department of Elementary and Secondary Education

> announced that the state's four-year graduation rate improved for the ninth consecutive year, with 87.3 percent of students who entered as ninth-graders in 2011–12—or who transferred into that same cohort at any time during high school—graduating within four years. The state's annual dropout rate declined to 1.9 percent in 2014–15, dipping below 2 percent to the lowest overall rate in more than three decades.

In the Department of Elementary and Secondary Education's announcements of these graduation rates, it noted,

> in October 2009, when the state's annual dropout rate was more than 3 percent, the Massachusetts Graduation and Dropout Prevention and Recovery Commission made some recommendations to dramatically reduce that rate. Some of those recommendations have been fulfilled, including reformed discipline laws to provide continued education for suspended and expelled students. The state, using federal High School Graduation Initiative funds, has also created a dropout prevention and recovery program, which was another of the commission's recommendations.[6]

Lessons for Policy Research

- **Timeliness is key.** In policy research, it can sometimes be hard to compel policy makers, who have a broad array of issues and crises to which they must attend, to pay attention to the topic that you have researched and about which you are eager to advise them. One essential element that ensured the team's research was used and had an impact was that we had an audience—the Graduation and Dropout Prevention and Recovery Commission—which was responsible for making recommendations within a set time frame and needed the evidence and information that we provided.
- **Relationships and connections matter.** While in some ways the Rennie Center's close connection to Commission Chair and Secretary Paul Reville made the role of the researchers more complicated, there

is no question that it benefitted from its affiliation with him; their work was given attention from the commission that it would not have received had it been from a lesser-known organization. Just as important were the relationships that were established with members of the commission before its formation. The team had proved to be trustworthy partners and credible researchers.

- **Tone and delivery are paramount.** Since the team knew its audience and the specific topics it was charged with deliberating, it was able to craft recommendations in a way that was clear and applicable to informing a commission report. The team understood that commission members—all of whom served on a voluntary basis and had "day jobs"—would have limited time to delve deeply into the research or to spend time digesting long reports. So it did the analysis and distilling for them, presenting findings in a simple format with as few pages as possible. The research team strived to make our reports "skimmable" and substantive so that busy policy makers could scan the briefs for key findings and recommendations and quickly find what they needed without missing the nuances of the issue.

- **Even when research makes a compelling case, policy makers may still "go with their gut."** One cautionary tale is related to our research on the compulsory age of school attendance. After our review of the empirical evidence, the team became persuaded that raising the compulsory age of attendance was not likely to make much of a difference in reducing the dropout rate. While the team thought it had made a compelling case not to focus on raising the compulsory age and rather to focus on other policies with stronger evidence, many legislators and policy makers still urged the commission to recommend raising the age. When we talked with one policy maker and commission member about our lack of conviction about that policy, he said, "I know there isn't much empirical evidence to support it, but it just seems like it makes sense." While Massachusetts has yet to raise its compulsory age of school attendance to 18, legislation to this effect has been proposed in nearly every legislative session since the Dropout Commission's report was published.

Focus on Research Methods

Rapid-Cycle Research

Rapid-cycle research has the potential to impact real-time policy decisions but carries with it several risks that must be weighed and balanced. The interrelated challenges of time, quality, and scope are described in more detail next.

1. **Time.** How tight is the turnaround? A judgment must be made about how much high-quality research can be conducted in the amount of time provided. If the timeline is too short, it may not make sense to

engage in a project at all, as the research to be conducted may be so incomplete as to not provide policy makers with adequate information upon which to make a sound decision. It may be better not to engage in a project at all if there is a possibility of missing the window of opportunity to inform a decision, since information that comes to policy makers after a key decision or vote is complete is not likely to be used. Researchers might also consider releasing findings to a key group of decision makers before they are officially published.

2. **Quality.** What is the highest quality of research that can be conducted in the given amount of time? A tight timeline has the potential to weaken the research, and a judgment must be made about the needs related to the research topic and what will best serve policy makers' needs. Researchers must also consider whether there is time for a peer review process and if not, what impact will this have on ensuring the quality of the research. Is the benefit of conducting the research quickly worth the reputational risk of having the research be of low quality?

3. **Scope.** What is a feasible scope for the research given the constraints of quality and rapid turnaround? Rapid-cycle research can constrict the design of a project, so questions must be carefully considered with an eye toward what is feasible. For example, it will be important to gauge whether there is adequate existing research that could be summarized and synthesized or if new research must be conducted. If new research must be conducted, are public data or existing data sets readily available to researchers? With rapid-cycle research, it can be more practical to analyze and synthesize existing research and translate it in a way that makes it easier for policy makers to digest and use than to attempt to collect and analyze new data.

Although this case provides an example of a successful application of rapid-cycle research, and Chapter 5 extols the virtues of rapid-cycle research, these points are important to consider before any rapid-cycle project is started.

Acronyms and Jargon

Graduation and Dropout Prevention and Recovery Commission— Established as part of Massachusetts legislation to make recommendations on 10 topic areas; Commission membership included state legislators and/or their designees, representatives from public school districts, higher education, the Massachusetts Teachers Association, a variety of youth-serving state agencies, and community-based organizations.

The Rennie Center—The Rennie Center for Education Research & Policy is a small, nonprofit, public-policy think tank located in Boston, Massachusetts, that seeks to foster thoughtful public discourse and informed policy making through nonpartisan, independent research and constructive dialogue on key education reform issues.

YTTF (Youth Transitions Task Force)—First convened by former Boston Mayor Thomas M. Menino in October of 2004 and charged with lowering the high school dropout rate, the Youth Transitions Task Force is a broad cross-section of organizations that includes the Boston Public Schools, community organizations, city departments, and state agencies.

Discussion Questions

1. The research team had a close relationship with its client, as several of its colleagues served on the commission it was serving. What benefits and risks did this relationship create for the project?
2. This project had an unusually short time frame of just six to eight weeks. How did this limitation affect the design and implementation of the study?
3. The results of this project seemed to have an immediate and striking impact. How was this achieved?
4. The research team had difficulty convincing decision makers that raising the compulsory age for schooling was of dubious value to reducing dropout rates. How could they have been more successful at this effort?

Assignments and Activities

1. Scan the final report (available online) and describe how it was (or was not) effective in presenting complicated information in a way that was digestible for commission members.
2. Assume that the study had six to eight months rather than six to eight weeks to be completed. How would you suggest strengthening and/or improving the design of the study? Write a brief outline of an alternative research design.
3. Prepare a presentation to a local school board (or similar body) that summarizes the essential findings and recommendations of this research in an effective manner.

Notes

1 Alliance for Excellent Education (2008). The High Cost of High School Dropouts: What the Nation Pays for Inadequate High Schools; Boston Private Industry Council. Summary of Three Reports on the Social and Fiscal Consequences of the Dropout Crisis.
2 The Rennie Center was founded in 2002 by Paul Reville (who served as its president until he was appointed to be Massachusetts Secretary of Education in 2008). With a statewide focus, the Rennie Center's mission is "to

improve public education through well-informed decision-making based on deep knowledge and evidence of effective policymaking and practice."

3 An Act to Improve Dropout Prevention and Reporting of Graduation Rates. Acts & Resolves of Massachusetts (2008), Chapter 315 § 1. Available online at https://malegislature.gov/Laws/SessionLaws/Acts/2008/Chapter315

4 *Massachusetts Graduation and Dropout Prevention and Recovery Commission* (2009). Making the Connection. Boston, MA: Author. Available online at www.mvwib.org/documents/Dropout_Commission_Report_10_21_2009.pdf

5 WBUR (2009). Project Dropout: Revisited. Available online at www.wbur.org/2009/12/29/project-dropout-revisited

6 Massachusetts Department of Elementary & Secondary Education (2016). Massachusetts' Four-Year Graduation Rate Improves for Ninth Consecutive Year. Press release, January 21. Available online at www.doe.mass.edu/news/news.aspx?id=21406

9 Political Statement or Effective Policy? Comparing Implementation of State Bullying Laws

Victoria Stuart-Cassel and J. Fred Springer

Introduction

In the United States, public education has historically been a local issue. States typically set education standards and testing, but much of the policy making rests in more than 16,000 local school districts across the country. Though the national importance of education is increasingly recognized in a global economy, influencing or even gaining information on local education policy and action is challenging. This chapter concerns a study of school policy regarding bullying, a youth behavioral problem that became highly visible across the nation in the last decade. This study documents and develops lessons concerning local district implementation of state bullying laws. It is an example of the federal government attempting to act as a facilitator of state solutions to an education policy problem that has been virtually universally recognized nationwide.

The Policy Problem

From 1999, when Georgia passed the first law concerning school bullying policy, through 2012, 49 states introduced new laws governing bullying in their local school systems. In many states, these laws have undergone multiple revisions as problems with their effectiveness or their implementation emerged (U.S. Department of Education, Office of Planning, Evaluation and Policy Development, Policy and Program Studies Service, 2011). This growth in state legislation has been a response to broadening public concern about the impact of bullying behavior on the social and emotional development and long-term health of bullying-involved youth.

In August 2010, the U.S. Department of Education (ED) and the U.S. Department of Health and Human Services cohosted the first Federal Partners in Bullying Prevention summit, which brought together government officials, researchers, policy makers, and education practitioners to explore potential strategies to combat bullying in schools. This summit highlighted gaps in knowledge concerning the current status of state laws and their key components. It also exposed the lack of information on how laws and policies were being implemented at the local level. This gap was the policy problem addressed by the policy research discussed in this chapter.

Initiation of Policy Research

Following this summit meeting, the ED, Program and Policy Studies Services, awarded a competitive contract to conduct the *Analysis of State Bullying Laws and Policies* research study. EMT Associates, a small but experienced firm in Sacramento, CA, was selected. The study was designed in two phases. The first phase collected and assessed all then-current state laws concerning bullying. The policy research contractor prepared a report (Stuart-Cassel et al., 2011) that identified the extent to which each law, select state school policies, and select district policies covered key legislative and policy components identified by ED as important to bullying policy. Phase two, the subject of this chapter, was to address the question *"How are state laws translated into practice at the school level?"*

The Policy Research Task

The policy research task necessary to answer this question was daunting. The reality of the decentralized process of educational policy making in the U.S. meant at least a three-tiered hierarchical system had to be studied. States and districts were institutional contexts exerting diverse influences on local policy. The policy research task required disentangling the welter of social-emotional issues that impact youth behavior, the dearth of knowledge about local school disciplinary policy, widely divergent opinions about what disciplinary policy should be, and multilayered, nested contextual influences. To add salt to the wound, the client's study question specifies only the "school level," making external validity of findings (i.e., generalizability) a prime concern.

Objectives

The overall objective of the implementation component of the study was to answer the general question identified earlier. The focus was on the process of translating the provisions and intents of state laws into actual practice in the schools. The study was not intended to assess the extent to which these practices actually reduce bullying in or out of the schools—first things first. The initial step was to see whether the laws make a difference in school practice and why or why not. The underlying motivation and hope was two-fold. First, findings should say something about differences in the laws themselves. Do some laws seem to make a bigger difference than others? What does this tell us about why or why not? Second, findings should say something about differences in the degree to which different districts and schools in the same state implement practices. What district or school characteristics explain these differences? Based on these findings about top-down or bottom-up influences, the objective was to develop lessons that may help guide improvements in laws and/or implementation practices.

Challenges

This discussion makes it clear that this policy research task was full of challenges. The diversity and number of these challenges will become ever more clear through discussions of user environment, research methods, and study findings in subsequent sections. The point to make here is that these challenges are not just technical, concerning the selection and use of particular tools. They are fundamental to the kind of problem reality that was being addressed. As defined in Chapter 2 of this text, the diversity of perspectives on bullying, on school role, and on approaches to resolution, combined with the complexity of potential causes and diverse manifestations of bullying behavior, made this problem a prime example of a wicked mess. The challenges to the policy researcher begin there.

The Decision Context

From what you have learned about this project and what you will learn about how it was carried out, the pervasive importance of decision contexts in the study should become evident. With respect to actual design, implementation, and interpretation of findings, the policy researchers' contract relationship with ED made decisions by the department's Office of Planning, Evaluation and Policy Development (OPEPD) very important to the study. As you will see, the internal decision making environment in that unit would have substantial impact on whether the implementation study would produce useful information.

From the standpoint of study content and dissemination, the intended decision context was broad. The decentralized policy-making environment in education meant that study findings would not inform one or a few policy decisions that would change everything. To influence implementation decisions, the study findings would have to be incorporated into a broader discussion among professional audiences who influence nationwide policy and knowledge dissemination such as training programs or interest advocacy. If the study were to have importance for actual practice regarding bullying in schools, findings would have to infuse a complex decision setting.

The Institutional Context

Because the bullying implementation study client was itself a research unit, the institutional context in which the policy research team was working was a step or more removed from the schoolteachers, parents, students, and administrators who had the most direct stake in the study findings and the uses they might have. This creates a very different set of institutional constraints and opportunities than there would be if the client were a local school board or the National Education Association. Put plainly, the immediate institutional context focused more on how the study was done and particularly on the technical elements of study design and implementation. This meant more focus on how findings were stated and given credibility than on the actual implications for end user interests. This was certainly appropriate, but as we shall see, it placed unexpected constraints on the policy researchers trying to deliver a message.

The Policy Cycle

It follows from previous discussion that the implementation component of the bullying laws study was a process evaluation examining the implementation of policy, not the outcome itself. Given the diversity of the laws in the country and the diversity of the schools, there was no "model" law to anchor the study, and implementation environments were diverse. This meant that the focus was really on the challenges that arose in trying to make diverse laws apply in their relevant environments. Those challenges could be in the laws themselves or in the institutions expected to implement them. So the point at which study results could be most useful would be federal agencies, such as ED; agencies inside the Department of Health and Human Services that provide policy guidance information, demonstration grants, or training concerning youth behavior and social-emotional development; and the Centers for Disease Control which identifies bullying as a public health problem.

Clients and Stakeholders

The state bullying laws study had an advisory group that met with the evaluation team annually in Washington, DC, and provided review comment and recommendations at the meeting and on request. The composition of that group reflected the stakeholder interests for the study. Members included noted scholars concerned with school climate, social-emotional development, and their implications for a supportive learning environment and academic performance. This point of view was concerned with developing supportive interventions and services for both bullying perpetrators and victims and with promoting school environments that reduced bullying behaviors. It also included legal experts who represented a concern with issues of liability, cost, enforcement, civil rights, protection of victims, and consequences. Education professionals were concerned with support and reasonable expectations concerning school staff and impacts on the school environment. Bullying victims support organizations focused on socioemotional harm to victims, threats to safety including suicide, and adequacy of protection and support. The complex perspectives and multiple interests were clear, and this was in the relatively insulated research environment, several steps removed from direct conflict around actions and their impact.

Research Design and Implementation

EMT proposed a comparative case study approach to generating the information and analysis necessary to meet the implementation component of the state bullying laws study. The firm proposed an ambitious study that included site visits to 12 school districts and 24 schools nationwide. Though the project officer questioned the feasibility of the design with the available resources, EMT had extensive experience in national fieldwork and argued that this combination of coverage and detail was necessary to address the equally ambitious study objectives. The actual fieldwork, data management, and analysis were implemented successfully. This section tells that story.

Information Needs

Information needs for the implementation study component were guided by the following specific questions:

- How do state laws define bullying in each of the four study states? How do school policies define bullying in each of the school districts participating in the study?
- To what extent were school personnel aware of definitions of bullying outlined in school policies? What was the range of behavior middle school personnel defined as "bullying"?
- How did study middle school personnel implement key components of state legislation and bullying policies, including (1) procedures for reporting, investigating, and assigning consequences for violations of policy, (2) documentation of bullying incidents for program monitoring and accountability, (3) communication of school policy expectations, (4) training for school personnel, (5) strategies to prevent and reduce bullying behavior, and (6) safeguards and supports for targeted students?
- What did school and district personnel identify as the major challenges to and supports for implementing key components of state bullying laws?

Design and Methods

The evaluation team, in collaboration with OPEPD, used a purposive sampling strategy to select four study states. The strategy identified states that represent the regional diversity of the U.S. (i.e., West, South, Midwest, and East) and the diversity of state legislation. This *most different systems* (Przeworski and Teune, 1970) approach maximizes diversity in state contexts, providing evidence concerning the generalizability of findings within these contexts. For example, if a particular implementation challenge is consistent across all settings, it suggests that this challenge is not a product of the law or broad cultural differences between states. If a challenge emerges in one or two states, a closer assessment is appropriate to identify contextual (unique or shared) conditions that may explain the challenge. Findings from the *Analysis of State Bullying Laws and Policies* first-phase report, which profiled the structure and content of state bullying laws, guided the state selection. Specifically, states were chosen to represent variation in the number of key components in laws current through May 2012 and the detail and comprehensiveness of their provisions.

A random stratified sample of three school districts (i.e., one urban, one suburban, one town, and one rural) in each state was selected. Because the sampling strategy called for visits to two middle schools within each district, the sampling frame was limited to medium and large districts with two or more middle schools. The final study sample included 11 districts and 22 schools; the rural stratum for one state was not represented due to challenges with school recruitment. Overall, the study sample included a mix of medium and large districts that was diverse with regard to the race, ethnic, language, and socioeconomic composition of their enrolled populations.

Site Visits

Data collection for the implementation study took place entirely through site visits conducted by two-person teams of carefully trained interviewers. A two-day training was held in EMT's offices in Sacramento, CA. The focus of training was on the site protocol through which visitors summarized all data collected on each site. Site visits were conducted between February and May of 2012. Site visits to each district took four days divided between the middle school sites. Site visitors conducted in-person interviews with a total of 281 school personnel across the 22 schools. The sample of interview respondents included 49 school administrators (principals, vice principals, and deans of students); 30 student support personnel, including school counselors, psychologists, intervention coordinators, and bullying specialists; 134 classroom teachers and physical education instructors; 3 teacher's aides; 41 school resource officers (SROs) or other security personnel; and 24 transportation personnel or bus drivers. When respondents required selection from a larger group, (e.g., teachers, counselors), interviewees were randomly selected from a list of school staff organized by job designation.

Interview respondents were asked to complete a brief survey containing fixed-choice responses that was administered at the beginning of each interview. Respondents completed 17 items rating how frequently they responded to bullying incidents at school (including cyber-bullying), the degree to which bullying was disruptive in their school environment, and their perceptions about how common it was for bullying at their school to be based on specific characteristics of targeted students. The surveys provided a systematic description of the perceptions of school staff in sampled schools and aided in interpreting interview responses regarding the school setting and its possible influences on implementation of bullying policy.

Interview guides were developed with careful review and collaboration with the U.S. Department of Education. These interview guides and the process through which they were prepared for analysis had several distinguishing features. The guide content was designed to focus on features of state law and policy that were identified in the first-phase study report. This meant that they were very structured with respect to the topics covered and the questions asked. They covered 15 specific topics such as local experience with development and communication of district and school bullying policy within the state law, strategies to prevent bullying and to promote positive school climate, cyber-bullying, investigation and documentation, and consequences. A section of the interview that will be focused on in this discussion concerns practice in reporting bullying behavior incidents.

To ensure relevance of questions to the different groups of respondents interviewed in each district and school, separate interview guides were developed for (a) a representative of the state education agency in each selected state who was knowledgeable concerning the state legislation and development of agency policy guidance concerning bullying, (b) a representative of selected districts who has central responsibilities for and knowledge of district bullying policy and activities, and (c) each of the distinct respondent roles and positions interviewed for each school site. Each guide included specific questions and probes that systematically answered major questions concerning awareness, influence, and implementation of key bullying law and policy components; questions that provided guidance to areas in which more detailed responses were appropriate; and probes to guide follow-up issues when needed. Each guide also included space for narrative description, explanations of responses, and interviewer notes and insights concerning notable interview responses. Interviews were recorded with respondent permission. In summary, the interview process was carefully structured to provide systematic and comparable information across sites to answer agreed-on study questions.

Analysis Approach

School interview responses provided a broad range of perspectives on the occurrence and seriousness of bullying in schools and on the implementation of law, policy, and programs to address bullying. These interviews documented perceptions and experience of individual respondents that together with other sources of information on schools (e.g., student body composition, community environment, additional programmatic initiatives in the schools, school resources, related policies such as disciplinary policies, state and district bullying policy) provided descriptive answers to study questions at the school level.

The site visit study analysis started immediately after data collection was completed. The first analysis step was to create mixed-method measures with schools rather than respondents as the unit of observation. School Site Summary Protocols were used to aggregate the multiple interview results and other data about schools into a single source of systematically organized and comparable information that characterized each school as a whole. (The protocols and their use are the subject of the Focus on Research Methods box at the end of this chapter.) To make these measures as accurate as possible, site visit teams completed protocols before or as soon as possible after leaving the site.

These School Summary Protocols document a school-level analysis and summary of each school, and they provide the most important database for the analyses and description in this report. Accurately completing these site summaries was the heart of the analysis process. Once completed, each summary provided 155 items of dichotomous (yes/no) or 1–5 ratings for the extent to which a given site characteristic was reported as present in a site. For example, one item is *Reporting of Incidents—Awareness of Reporting Expectations:* Rate (1–5) the extent to which school personnel are aware of reporting expectations outlined in policy. Site visitors were extensively trained in the rating criteria and made decisions collectively among visitors to that site. These categorizations of interview responses allowed comparison of school ratings on different implementation dimensions reflecting law and policy across all 22 schools in the study or across schools in a district. It also allowed comparisons of aggregated (average) ratings across all 11 districts or across the districts in a state. Finally, comparisons could be made between ratings aggregated to the state level. Patterns of difference are then explained to the extent feasible with the rich qualitative data to which these ratings were attached. The procedure and its resulting information provide a strong basis for establishing similarities and differences in policy implementation, the perceived usefulness in different policy and support strategies, and the perceived challenges of implementing in these different environments.

Selected Findings

The EMT team prepared a detailed (204-page) draft final report and a 12-page executive summary. Early drafts had been reviewed and commented on by the advisory committee, and the team had worked closely with the ED project manager to develop an accurate and useful document.

This section can only address select components of the lengthy report. It will focus on the state law context in the four states, development of a detailed process model for school-level implementation of the bullying laws, some differential influences the laws had on the implementation of bullying policy in schools, and key influences and challenges that emerged across the diverse state contexts.

State Bullying Laws and Policies

The bullying law implementation study analysis design was based in identifying states with contrasting laws concerning bullying in schools and to assess potentially differential influences of these laws on implementation. One of the most important features of these laws and the larger state context was the degree to which each law mandated specific district/school policy or set more general policy expectation leaving detailed policy up to districts. Figure 9.1 arrays states from the strongest mandate and most detailed requirements (State A) to the greatest emphasis on local control (State D). The figure also includes summaries of how states exercise their respective levels of authority. For example, State A's law applies directly to districts and schools; State B's legislation gives the state education agency the authority to write prescriptive policy within parameters required by the law. State C's legislation includes definitions and recommended procedure and requires districts to adopt policies that are consistent with the law. Districts can adapt details to their circumstance. State D requires that districts develop a policy. There are no specific required definitions or procedures.

ED has identified eight core components of bullying policy. States A and B addressed all of these in some fashion; State D addressed none in detail. Table 9.1 compares the four state laws on provisions on three of the most important components—definitions of bullying behaviors in the laws, application of those definitions at the district level, and expectations for reporting incidents of bullying in schools. These summaries are

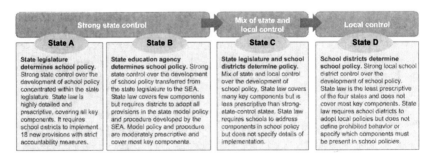

Figure 9.1 Summary of Four State Bullying Laws and Degree of State Control

Table 9.1 Comparison of Select Legislation Content; States A, B, C, & D

Key Components	State A	State B	State C	State D
Prohibited Behavior	State law defines bullying as a single act or series of incidents motivated by an actual or perceived characteristic that disrupts or interferes with the orderly operation of the school or rights of students.	State law defines harassment, intimidation, and bullying as an intentional electronic, written, verbal, or physical act that physically harms a student or damages property, interferes with a student's education, creates a threatening educational environment, or disrupts the orderly operation of the school.	State law defines harassment as a pattern of behavior motivated by characteristics that place student in fear of harm or disrupts the operation of the school.	State law does not define prohibited behavior.
School Policy Definitions	School districts must adopt the definition of bullying outlined in state law.	School districts must adopt the definition of bullying outlined in state law.	SEA model policy definition must conform to definition of bullying outlined in state law, and districts must adopt policies consistent with the state model.	No specific requirements for how bullying should be defined.
Reporting Expectations	School personnel must verbally report incidents to a school administrator or designee on the same day the incident occurred and must report in writing within two days.	Staff must intervene when witnessing or receiving reports of harassment, intimidation, or bullying.	Students and parents/guardians are encouraged to report bullying incidents. Districts must provide standard complaint form.	No district requirements for reporting.

meant to make the degree of difference between these laws more concrete and understandable.

Three of four states in the study defined bullying in legislation; two of these required school districts to adopt these definitions; the third required that they adopt definitions that conform to the state definition. The fourth state allowed schools discretion to define prohibited behavior and provided a definition in the state model policy that schools could choose to adopt. The definitions of bullying found in state laws and local policies often referenced the same criteria used to define bullying in research, including repetition, the intent to harm, and an imbalance of power. However, few formal definitions required all criteria to be present for behavior to be labeled as bullying. Even the most specific definitions in the study states are quite different. The reporting expectations also vary substantially, including immediate verbal reporting and prompt written follow-up in State A, requiring staff intervention in State B, making reporting a student/parent responsibility in State C, and no reporting requirement in State D. The sample states certainly deliver the diverse contexts intended in the study design. It is notable, however, that one feature of legislative action did not vary across the states. None of them provided funding to support implementation of the requirements of the laws.

Implementation Decision Process Model

Since bullying laws are aimed at identifying incidents of potentially harmful behavior, they require a process for recognizing that behavior, substantiating and investigating bullying complaints, and determining appropriate sanctions. In all of the schools in this study, the process involved multiple participants, phases, and decision points. While state laws and policies, district policies, and school policies did help shape this process, other influences were also important. These included community and school norms, the individual perspectives and orientations of involved participants, and the school environment (e.g., resources). The evaluation team constructed a process model (Figure 9.2) that corresponded to the decision processes observed across the sites as closely as possible.

Columns in the process model identify phases in which decisions about incidents of potential bullying must be made. A full discussion of the volume of information the study produced on each of these phases is beyond the scope of this chapter. Accordingly, key findings in three areas will be presented: (1) issues concerning the immediate response; (2) issues related to the second and third columns that concern formal administrative decisions about whether the incident was an actual bullying act that requires consequences; and (3) decisions about what consequences should be applied (fourth and fifth columns). The discussion will briefly describe key issues and identify how they varied under different state laws.

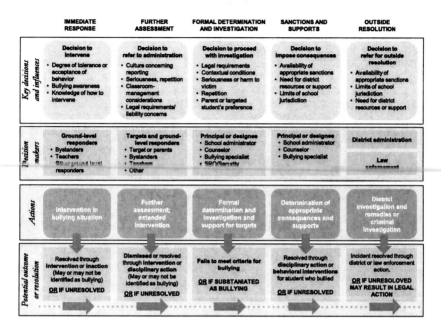

Figure 9.2 Overview of Process for Responding, Reporting, Investigating, and Resolving Bullying Incidents

DECISION TO INTERVENE

The implementation process begins with a decision about whether to intervene in a potential bullying situation. This decision will be made by "ground-level responders" in a position to witness the behavior in question. In schools, this typically means teachers, other school staff, or students. A decision to act would mean intervening to stop the bullying in some way. School personnel in the position to be ground-level responders widely agreed that a broad range of hurtful behaviors, including bullying, should be met with an immediate response. The great majority of site visit respondents described immediate intervention in hurtful behaviors as the first way they addressed bullying. This immediate action was seen as important to setting expectations, helping youth recognize behaviors that were "out of bounds" and providing an opportunity to help them reflect on their behaviors.

Respondents most often felt that an immediate intervention produced positive results. They felt that bringing students' attention to their behavior and warning of consequences usually resolved the immediate situation. This perception was consistent with a view that much of the hurtful behavior that respondents deal with was not part of a repeated pattern or was not deliberate in its intent to inflict serious physical or emotional harm. Instead, this behavior was viewed as more impulsive and reflective of the maturation process in middle schools.

Nearly half of all school personnel interviewed for the study reported responding to what they saw as bullying on at least a weekly basis. Most of the behaviors that school staff described as bullying were perhaps less serious or persistent in nature than the behaviors defined more narrowly in state or school district policies. A telling example is the fact that by far the most frequently perceived reason for targeting victims in the middle schools was personal appearance, such as weight, clothes, hair style, or other physical challenges to "fitting in." The second most frequently perceived reason was dating behavior, clearly a social fit issue in middle school. These target characteristics were not mentioned in any of the four state laws. The protected categories of individual characteristics that were often identified in state laws (e.g., race, gender orientation, religion, disability) were much less frequently perceived by ground-level responders as reasons for bullying. Nevertheless, the "bully-like" incidents in which ground-level responders intervened were perceived to be physically or emotionally hurtful to targeted students regardless of the reasons for targeting.

Respondents reported substantial variation in how they would individually handle an immediate intervention. Many times this simply meant directly addressing the behavior and demanding that it stop. Some relied on admonitions and threats related to the fact that the behavior was an infraction of rules and emphasized the potential consequences. Respondents frequently referenced bullying laws as a useful "tool" for immediate intervention. The seriousness of the behavior and potential consequences defined by law and policy could be referenced to deter future bullying.

The most consistent approach to intervention described by school personnel involved separating victim and bully, often by sending them to separate locations, and talking to each individually to assess the situation and to discuss the seriousness of what just happened and the harm it imposes. Teachers in particular noted that this was a significant disruption in the class environment. The time required was seen as a major constraint on immediate resolution of potential bullying situations.

In the study sample, SROs or security officers were sometimes mentioned as a resource for immediate interventions in hurtful behavior. This was particularly true when SROs were well integrated into the school community and had established trusting relationships with students and school personnel. SROs were included in discussions with potential bullies to reinforce the seriousness of bullying behavior.

The patterns of immediate response discussed were the same across the four states, even though only State B identified individual intervention as a responsibility of ground-level school employees. Across all states, ground-level responders placed an immediate intervention as both a disciplinary act and an opportunity to help students reflect on their behavior. This meant that a lot of what school personnel do to engage and prevent bullying is not mentioned in state laws. In this study, no state or district explicitly set expectations about how immediate intervention should be carried out. Neither did they provide training or other supports for immediate intervention. Indeed, as discussed, respondents reported diverse ways of carrying out immediate interventions based on their individual beliefs about what might work. The ground-level responders volunteered that effective techniques for intervening in bullying incidents and positively engaging both bully and victim were their most important training needs. Given the widespread reported use of immediate interventions, greater attention to training on best practices in intervening appeared important.

Administrative Determination of Whether Bullying Occurred

The next phase of the decision process (column 3 in Figure 9.2) required or implied by the state laws begins with the decision to report the incident to school administrators. The report was usually made to a vice principal, the principal, or, in some schools, a designated staff member such as a counselor. In State A, each school was required to have a designated bullying specialist on staff to whom reports were to be submitted. The follow-up to a report might include a requirement (State A) or expectation (States B and C) of an investigation before a decision on whether the incident is in fact bullying is reached.

Each state had a distinct approach to defining responsibility for reporting a bullying incident for administrative determination. State A made it a legal requirement for school employees to submit a written report of any potential bullying incident they observed or were told about. State B required verbal reporting of an incident if the immediate response did not resolve a continuing problem. State D left policy on reporting up to districts, and state C had a unique approach discussed later in this section.

The study site visits revealed common conditions about staff reporting that were particularly salient for State A and State B. Across all states, school personnel were aware of their school's bullying policies but were rarely well informed about specific details of the district policy, let alone the state's. They typically did not know precisely how state law defined bullying or under what circumstances they should report incidents to the school administration. Speaking of formal academic or legal definitions of bullying generally, they saw challenges in applying them because of the subtlety and complexity of observed student interactions, the difficulty of discerning student intent, and the practical limitations of what staff could observe or what was reported to them. As a result, reporting a "bullying" decision for administrative consideration of consequences, which could often be substantial, was a difficult and ethically challenging action in the eyes of many ground-level responders. This was a particular challenge in

State A, where staff could technically face penalties (up to losing their job) if the did not comply with the legal requirement, which was very difficult to apply in specific circumstances.

As mentioned, State C had a unique requirement. It required that administrators allow and respond to reports of potential bullying from parents, but there was no requirement concerning reporting by staff. These reports, particularly when triggered by parental expectations that the bullying law would require a forceful and quick resolution, created a difficult situation for administrators. Parents had limited awareness of the details of the school policy or of how bullying was precisely defined. In addition, parents often wanted an immediate resolution of the issue. Respondents understood that parents were worried about their child's physical and emotional safety and wanted to avoid any additional harm but had to address many situations in which parents report hurtful behaviors as bullying that did not meet the policy definition of bullying. School personnel in State C used interpersonal discussion or procedures (i.e., written reporting forms documenting bullying criteria) to clarify the use of the term for students and parents before pursuing a formal complaint. Though this skated on the edge of strict implementation when law and policy required full investigation, it was a practical step that administrators felt they had to take.

Parental reports of potential bullying issues highlight the challenges that often arise from broad public use of bullying to describe hurtful behavior relative to the more narrow and precise definitions found in bullying law and policy. Formal reports of bullying set in motion a careful investigative and decision-making process that can produce serious, life-changing consequences. In cases where this process was mandatory for accusations of bullying, this created a potentially difficult job for school administrators or designees that received parental reports and entered into discussion with them. For example, under the highly prescriptive law in State A, any report of bullying behavior required schools to launch a formal investigation within a 2-day time period that had to be completed within 10 days of the initial report. The investigation and its conclusions had to be summarized in writing and reported to the superintendent within two days of its completion, and the investigation had to be presented to the school board within a single board cycle. Because parents were often unaware of the differences between the hurtful behaviors that their child might have experienced and what policy defined as bullying, parents might misreport acts of bullying, placing a heavy burden on school administrators and on budgets. This level of specificity in follow up, requiring a decision using difficult-to-apply legal criteria, also increased concern about possible litigation and the multiple harms that could bring to the school district. The process brought multiple challenges, and the more the state law emphasized holding school personnel accountable, the more challenging it became to school districts.

Deciding on Consequences

Decisions to assign consequences for bullying behaviors as defined by law and policy were made after investigation was completed, and a determination had been made concerning whether the behavior was bullying as described in policy. In three states, legislation required districts to include specification of consequences for bullying in their policy. States A and B required that there be a range of consequences including intervention services as well as disciplinary action. State B required interventions to remediate impact on targeted students. State D's legislation did not require that districts specify consequences in their policies. States A and B required a similar range of consequences for students who bully depending on the severity of the incident as determined through investigation. State A did require that suspension or expulsion be a possible option for bullying behavior.

State laws did allow for a wide range of consequences, including behavioral and socio-emotional interventions such as behavioral or different forms of counseling. Nonetheless, just six of the district policies in the study provided any detail on any consequences other than disciplinary options, such as suspension and expulsion. At the school level nonpunitive consequences were usually available, but respondents were not widely aware of them. Respondents in one school in State B identified an after school group program for skills building and reflective learning as a frequently used consequence for potential bullying. When they were used, behavioral learning and therapeutic interventions tended to be used during the mediation and negotiation processes prior to the formal designation of a behavior as a case of bullying.

Options were also limited by the availability of resources and procedures. In most schools, supportive services for youth involved in hurtful behaviors were limited to counseling services, and in most schools these were very limited. Some schools offered after school group programs. Referral to outside counseling or support services was typically available, but it was not funded in the study sample schools. Two districts used federal, state, or private grants as additional resources that strengthened in-school counseling and behavioral support.

The bottom line was that once an incident was considered to be bullying disciplinary options were the most likely consequence. Respondents in all schools frequently commented that the available consequences for bullying were not adequate. Out of school suspension or expulsion were often identified as inadequate because many of the students who were disciplined for bullying need to be more strongly connected to school. Additionally, suspension and expulsion do not address the environments and learned behavior that led to bullying behaviors. These observations are consistent with the growing understanding that suspension and expulsion has serious negative consequences for future school connection, academic outcomes, and eventual life success for students (Fabelo et al., 2011).

Selected Findings and Conclusions

In the study schools, implementation processes typically produced very few incidents that were in fact confirmed to meet the criteria for bullying under state law. For example, in a State C district, one school initiated investigation of 25 incidents, and 1 was determined to meet the district criteria; the second school investigated 45 incidents and 1 was determined to meet district criteria. In State A, respondents in both schools in a district identified about 10 investigations in each school, and state records indicated that neither school had reported a confirmed case of bullying under the state criteria. In a State B district with very similar communities and student bodies in both its schools, one school identified three incidents that met state criteria; the bullying specialist in the other school reported "approximately" 10, though that number was not confirmed. The study noted that the investigation process was much more systematic and careful in the first of these schools.

The small number of "official" cases of bullying found in these schools could be interpreted as showing that the laws, as implemented, did not have much effect. That would not be warranted for a few reasons. First, while the number of bullying incidents defined in policy was small, these cases often represented serious harm to targets and a threat to other students. Second, the laws did arguably have additional effects. They heightened awareness of and attention to bullying among school district officials, school administrators and staff, students, and parents. In all states, districts, and schools, school employees, parents, and students found it difficult to distinguish between bullying as described by law and policy and a continuum of hurtful behaviors that are easily associated with potential bullying. Respondents also expressed consensus that behaviors along this continuum are harmful to the targets and to the social-emotional and behavioral development of the bullies.

The policy implication that is possibly most important is that the bullying problem is not a problem of individuals who are bullies and is more a problem of socially driven behavioral and social-emotional problems that are endemic to the maturational process in youth. These may best be addressed through more contextual policies such as promoting positive school climate and more supportive policies providing counseling and socioemotional programming in schools. These include the kinds of consequence options identified—but not funded—in many bullying policies. As stated by one state education employee in the study:

> We need to develop a process that's responsive to legitimate concerns that victims may have, but do it in a way that is educational for the

students involved and that will change their behavior—not just trying to impose consequences. From the research we know that bullying is a learned behavior. We need to focus on how to unlearn it.

Communicating and Using Results

The most frustrating part of this study for the policy researchers was their inability to effectively communicate the value of the study for policy application. From their perspective, this was an exceptionally rich implementation study that effectively mixed qualitative data collection and systematic analysis to produce useful lessons and insights into the development and implementation of state laws concerning bullying and potentially for similar behavioral issues. Nonetheless, ED never disseminated any of the study findings. The evaluation team had worked closely with the project officer to identify the lessons produced in this very large and very detailed case study. Members of the advisory committee reviewed the report and provided helpful comments on important findings and how they might be best communicated. A third draft was produced with an executive summary and submitted for approval. The team was confident that it was close to a finished product and felt it provided a lot of insight concerning bullying as a policy issue.

As the third draft was being prepared, OPEPD transitioned to a new director, who had final say on whether a final study project would be accepted and put into a broader review for publication. This director brought a whole new perspective to the review. There was a greater concern for simplicity and clarity of message. The detail and complexity of the report obscured the message. There was a concern about the reliance on qualitative data and the need for caveats that would undermine study credibility. The study had produced very strong qualitative data, a revealing mixed-method analysis, and necessary understanding of a complex reality from the researchers' perspective. From the evolving perspective of the client, it produced unclear information that supported no clear policy conclusions. The budget had been more than expended; the study had produced the widely used first-phase report; and the new director brought a perspective that found the study methodologically and substantively flawed. No results were reported. No recommendations were accepted. As far as the policy research team knew, it was dead.

A few years later, at the request of several federal agencies and foundations, the National Academies of Science published a major study titled *Preventing Bullying Through Science, Policy, and Practice* (National Academies of Science, 2016). National Academies studies have high credibility for policy makers, practitioners, and stakeholders throughout the nation. They are usually intensive literature reviews based on credible research that has been conducted on the study topic. The middle school implementation study report to US ED (EMT Associates, Inc., 2013) was widely cited and quoted, for both method and substance, in the National Academies study volume. Even though US ED had chosen not to publish the report, it had ended up in the hands of the research group that conducted this study. It was resurrected as a contributor to evidence-based policy recommendations that will receive national attention.

Selected Implications

Even though the implementation report was not intended to make specific recommendations, it certainly had implications for areas in which policy development and further policy research were important. It gave voice to the district and school employees who implement at the local level, an area in which little systematic information has been available. Accordingly, the study has documented new perspectives and understandings concerning how state bullying law and policy translate into feasible and practical action within schools and on larger issues of how schools can become more safe and supportive. Areas in which policy development and policy research are needed include the following:

- One of the major themes emerging from the study is that laws and policies tend to define a narrow band of bullying behavior that school employees find it difficult to clearly identify. School personnel expressed a need for follow-up training to review and reinforce knowledge and skills relevant to effective immediate responses to bullying (e.g., knowledge of bullying policy or how to identify bullying behavior).
- State laws and policies differ significantly in the degree to which they prescribe procedures, decision discretion, and decision criteria in determining whether an incident is bullying. Respondents identified differing benefits and challenges represented by more or less prescription. An important area for further study is to improve knowledge of these trade-offs and to identify ways in which benefits may be optimized and challenges reduced.
- Another set of implementer concerns involved the range of consequences for bullying and the widespread perception that there was a need for more options. These options range from interventions to alter both individual awareness and skills and the school social environment to interventions focusing on sanctions. School personnel would significantly benefit from further research on the use of effective intervention strategies in bullying situations that keep students who bully in school while maintaining the safety of targeted students.
- Finally, the study has demonstrated that even in highly prescriptive policy environments, the discretion and skill of individual school personnel is critical to implementation. For example, ground-level responders share the perception that immediate intervention is important to reducing bullying and other hurtful behavior in the school.

However, in the study sites, there was little shared understanding of how to do this, and approaches to intervention differed significantly. The most common training need identified by staff across school sites involved professional guidance on how to effectively intervene in bullying situations. Research and policy development on this continuum of behaviors and effective preventive and remedial practices are important to practical and feasible school policy and practice.

Action

The most visible and powerful potential link between this study and action is inclusion in the National Academies study, which will be a reference for policy analysts and advisors throughout the country. It was also influential in more subtle ways. Years of experience in conducting site visits and working closely with local programs of different kinds has convinced the authors that the very process of thinking systematically about program implementation brings insights and change at the program level. The engagement and thoughtfulness of many of our discussions throughout the site visits makes us believe that those schools benefitted from the opportunity to reflect and systematically consider their program. Another indirect benefit of the unusually detailed comparative information produced by this study might have been its utility to the members of the advisory panel. The members included influential scholars and practitioners with respect to bullying, other behavioral health issues for youth, and school policy. Discussion in the advisory panel meetings revealed ways in which the study reinforced or altered their thinking on these issues, and this will be passed on. Similarly, one of the reasons the authors of this chapter were eager to include it in this text was the hope that it would help future policy researchers or policy research users better tame the many wicked messes they will encounter.

Lessons for Policy Research

Too Many Meanings

This study contains a major lesson about wicked messes and policy research. Different perspectives on what a policy problem means, and therefore how it can be tamed, often lie at the center of a wicked mess. In this case, the various meanings of bullying are at the center of the difficulty of drawing a nice clear policy lesson from this study. In this case, ground-level responders, including teachers and parents, saw bullying in an everyday way with fluid and situational empirical outcroppings, that is an observable range of hurtful behavior that is common in middle school settings. Legislation and policy defined bullying in a much more precise and behaviorally specific way. This type of definition might be thought of as "bureaucratic" because it meets the needs of accountable and enforceable implementation over a variety of circumstances. Many of the key findings in the study stemmed from the tension between and sometimes the incompatibility of these differences. The everyday definition focused on the harm to the victim caused by an act and reducing those acts regardless of the perpetrator; the bureaucratic definition focused on identifying the person who is prone to this type of act and holding them accountable. There are other nuances in what bullying might mean, but these perspectives make the point.

There are other assumptions that lie, explicitly or not, behind the differences in these points of view. The bureaucratic definition implies solutions that identify and punish or "rehabilitate" the bully—the individual perpetrator. The implicit assumption is a form of the "bad apple" theory of crime. In this view, *bullies* are the bullying problem. The policy implications of this approach are quite different than those of the ground-level responders who see *bullying* as the bullying problem. This view implies a systemic social problem that is explained by learned patterns of how to gain status and fit in. It is perpetrated by many youth in many situations—hence the much higher levels of self-reported or observed bullying in schools than implied by the number of policy-defined bullies this study found to be identified through the implementation of state bullying laws. The systemic, social-emotional understanding of bullying implies systemic, preventive, and supportive solutions that help youth find more positive, productive, and fulfilling ways to fit in. These kinds of solutions were mentioned as options in state legislation. However, they take resources, and none of the legislation included funding.

On reflection, the reason that the implementation study died was that the systematic and detailed qualitative research design identified these different viewpoints and the policy misfit between the ground-level view and the bureaucratic solution. It is a strong example of exploratory policy research that revealed a difficult-to-deliver message. The true complexity of this problem is that both of these meanings have applicability, and optimally addressing the problem requires creating complementary policy responses. That message clearly emerged from careful policy research, but it did not meet the user desire for a clean set of findings that focused on the implementation of the legislation without the mess of reality. The policy researchers could not find a palatable balance between problem reality and the users' perspective on usability. The unfortunate and very disheartening result was years of work and resources with little direct application.

Focus on Research Methods

Making Site Visit Data Comparable

One of the biggest impediments to effective use of site visit information in comparative studies stems from the same qualitative detail that can make site visits so useful. In this study, for example, developing findings about the challenges of applying logically constructed concepts to the relative chaos of reality required detailed qualitative data. The ability to deconstruct the ubiquitous but sometimes subtle effects of institutional or social context also required that detail. The problem was how to systematize the volume of mixed-method information that was gathered in site visits so that comparative findings could be developed.

For this study and many of the other multisite studies we have conducted (see Chapter 10), the EMT evaluation team has developed a systematic approach to site visit data collection and measurement. The method begins with recognizing that the common unit of observation to which the site visit data contributes is not the respondents, it is the site itself. The site may be somewhat differentiated into multiple units, for example, community, organization, and program, but this is a simple set of units of observation compared to the many data points within the site visit. So the first step in analysis is to aggregate information to site-level measures. If the objective is comparison, data collected within each site must be used to build comparable measures of site level concepts that are used across study sites.

Experience and familiarity with other policy research told the EMT team that this approach required that the site visit data collection itself be guided by a common set of measures that we wanted to compare site performance. The team also knew that trying to develop these measures through some analytic process (e.g., qualitative software) that was removed from the field experience would lose a lot of ambient knowledge that site visitors get on-site. It would also lose the ability to see patterns within context, another "you had to be there" understanding available only to the site visitors. EMT's answer has been to use the site visitors themselves as informed respondents who fill out a site-level protocol that creates categorical measures of site characteristics. Table 9.2 is the bullying implementation study protocol section on reporting behavior incidents.

To make is data as accurate as possible, site visit teams completed these summary protocols as soon after leaving the site visit as possible. Team members worked together to complete the protocols using their experience on-site, and interview responses, as the primary information base. The protocols are organized according to 17 information areas. In each of these areas, team members completed closed-ended rating questions about the degree to which the subject school experiences bullying, how policy addresses it, and how that policy is implemented. The protocol also has explicit questions and guides to describing and explaining these ratings and provided rich documentation of the site visit information.

Without this informed and systematic reporting of site visit data, much of the information that is gathered would not be used. From a practical

Table 9.2 Example From *State Bullying Law Analysis* Site Visit Protocol

Section 6: Reporting of Behavioral Incidents
The section focuses on documenting expectations for staff to report bullying incidents they may have witnessed first-hand or that are reported to them by students, how decisions are made to report conduct that may constitute bullying behavior, and the procedures that are used to document reported incidents.

Site Summary Topic	Closed-Ended Summary Scores	Narrative Elaboration	Relevant Items	Notable Examples (e.g., quotes)
Reporting of Incidents—Mandatory Reporting Indicates (y/n) if reporting is mandatory for school personnel. Describes specific reporting expectations (e.g., required for staff, required for students, encouraged for staff, encouraged for students)	Y	N	J6a	
Reporting of Incidents—Awareness of Reporting Expectations Rates (1–5) the extent to which school personnel are aware of reporting expectations outlined in policy	1–5		L7d, N6d, O5e, R5e, R5f, R5g	
Reporting of Incidents—Staff Ever Reported Bullying Incident Records the number and percentage (based on the number of staff who responded to the indicated items) of school personnel who *ever* reported a bullying incident to the school administration.	– %		L8a, N7a, M8a, O6a, R6a	
Reporting of Incidents—Reaction to Bullying Observed First-Hand Identifies (y/n) the frequency with which personnel identify the following types of responses with an accompanying description of the range of describe responses to observed bullying-related situation.	NR		L7a, M7a, N6a, O5a, Q7c, R5a	
No immediate response, monitor future interactions	1–5			
Interview to stop the behavior, monitor future interactions	1–5			
Intervene to stop the behavior and report the incident	1–5			
Report the incident to a school administrator or designee	1–5			

Reporting of Incidents—Reaction to Bullying Reported by a Student Describes the range of actions described by respondents in response to bullying-related situations that are reported to staff second-hand.	NR	L7b, M7b, N6b, O5b, Q7d, R5b
No immediate response, monitor future interactions	1–5	
Interview to stop the behavior, monitor future interactions	1–5	
Intervene to stop the behavior and report the incident	1–5	
Report the incident to a school administrator or designee	1–5	
Reporting of Incidents—Intervening in Bullying Description Describes the strategies that respondents report using to intervene in bullying situations with students.	NR	L7c, M7c, N6c, O5c, Q7c, R5c
Reporting of Incidents—Intervening in Bullying—Degree of Consensus Rates (1–5) the extent to which there is consensus among school personnel about how to intervene in bullying situations.	1–5	L7c, M7c, N6c, O5c, Q7c, R5c
Reporting of Incidents—Decisions to Report Describes the processes used by respondents to determine whether student conduct represents a reportable bullying offense.	NR	L8b, M8b, N7b, O5d, Q7e, R5d
Reporting of Incidents—Decisions to Report—Degree of Conformity Rates (1–5) the extent to which there is conformity across respondents in the way reporting decisions are made.	1–5	L8b, N7b, O5d, Q7e, R5d
Reporting of Incidents—Enforcement and Sanctions for Non-Compliance Rates (1–5) the extent to which there are processes in places to enforce staff reporting requirements. Describes enforcement procedures.	1–5	J6b
Reporting of Incidents—Designee—Identification Indicates (y/n) whether there is an individual who has been designated to receive bullying incident reports. Lists the name and position of the individual.	Y	N	J6c
Reporting of Incidents—Designee—Awareness of Designee Rates the extent to which school personnel are aware of who has been assigned as the designee for incident reporting.	1–5	L7e, M7e, O5f

(Continued)

Table 9.2 (Continued)

Site Summary Topic	Closed-Ended Summary Scores	Narrative Elaboration	Relevant Items	Notable Examples (e.g., quotes)
Reporting of Incidents—Procedures—Description Describes school procedures for reporting bullying incidents.	—		J6d, J6e, L7f, M7f, N6f, O5g	
Reporting of Incidents—Process for Anonymous Reports Indicates (y/n/) whether the school has established procedures for anonymous reporting of bullying incidents	Y	N	J6f	
Reporting—Maintaining Records Describes the process used to record bullying incident reports.	NR		J6g	
Reporting of Incidents—Process—Use of Written Records Identifies (y/n) whether the incidents reports must be recorded on standardized forms or documented in writing. Describes reporting format.	Y	N	J6e	
Reporting of Incidents—SRO—Standard Complaint Forms Identifies (y/n) whether the SRO completes a standardized complaint or reporting form. Describes reporting format.	Y	N	Q7f	
Reporting—Process—Degree of Consensus Rates (1–5) the extent to which there is consistency among respondent descriptions of reporting expectations and requirements.	1–5		J6a, L7f, M7f, N6f, O5g	
Reporting—Process—Degree of Conformity to Policy Requirements Rates (1–5) the extent to which school personnel descriptions of reporting processes conform to written policy requirements.	1–5		J6a, L7f, N6f, O5g	
Reporting—Challenges Rates (1–5) the extent to which reporting of bullying incidents presents a challenge to personnel in the school setting. Describes nature of challenges.	1–5		J6h	
Other Notes and Comments:			—	

Notable Examples/Quotes

6a.

standpoint, the process of analyzing the raw qualitative material is simply too resource consuming. This is especially true when site visits are implemented by a number of different researchers. Protocols of this type allow searches for comparative patterns using simple nonparametric statistics; they facilitate interpretation of the information based on qualitative notes on each measure; they allow easy location of original data (e.g., interview recordings) because measures are clearly linked to specific interview or observation questions; and they allow retrieval and use of specific quotes or examples. This is a powerful mixed-method tool that appears daunting in development and application but pays dividends in efficiency and quality of analysis.

Acronyms and Jargon

"Bully-like"—Behaviors that are a normal part of social interaction among children and youth (e.g., teasing, nicknames, roughhousing) but can also be bullying behaviors when they are used to belittle, exert power, or meet other definitions of bullying intent. They complicate the identification of bullying as defined in bullying laws.

Cyber-bullying—Verbal bullying behaviors conducted through social media that can be widely distributed.

Different Systems Designs—A comparative research design involving cases picked because of distinct differences in context (Przeworski and Teune, 1970). This logic is useful for finding policy lessons that are generalizable across jurisdictions and locales (e.g., states, communities, schools).

OPEPD—Office of Planning, Evaluation, and Policy Development is a unit within the U.S. Department of Education that administers policy research contracts addressing current policy questions facing the department.

SROs—School resource officers are law-enforcement officers placed in schools for safety and security. They may be local law enforcement or school district employees. Their roles vary with respect to involvement in disciplinary or supportive services for students.

Discussion Questions

1. Discuss the degree to which you believe this case is a "political statement" or "effective policy." State your reasons.
2. Discuss the differences between seeing the *bully* or *bullying* as the problem. What are the policy implications of each?
3. Using findings presented in this case as evidence, what are the pros and cons of more state-level authority to guide local school district policy or more local school district discretion? How useful is this study for answering this question?

4. Discuss why the evaluation team used the site visit data collection and measurement approach it did. Discuss the benefits and potential problems that might accompany this approach.

Assignments and Activities

1. Find your state's bullying law. Referencing findings from this study, assess its strengths and weaknesses.
2. Referencing your state's law, what would be three important policy research questions you would ask to help understand its effectiveness? Briefly outline a study design that could answer these questions.

10 Intervention Effectiveness in Real-World Settings

The National Cross-Site Evaluation of High Risk Youth Programs

J. Fred Springer and Allan Porowski

Introduction

The National Cross-Site Evaluation of High Risk Youth Programs (HRY evaluation) was an unusual policy research opportunity produced by a perfect storm of institutional commitment from the sponsoring agency (the Center for Substance Abuse Prevention—CSAP), the support of an exceptional project officer (Dr. Soledad Sambrano), guidance from an advisory group that included some of the most creative minds in policy research (including Dr. David Cordray and Dr. Will Shadish), a talented research team staffed by eager and hardworking young policy researchers who loved their work, and a team leader who didn't quite anticipate but was committed to resolving the challenges that would come up. Oh, another unusual opportunity was what seemed like a plentiful budget— more than $8,000,000 for the five-year study. This was quite a large contract for the small business (EMT Associates) that won the competition. In an early team meeting, the principal investigator noted with a touch of chagrin, "If we don't learn anything from this study, we can't blame the budget." What a daunting yet rewarding adventure was ahead!

The Policy Problem

Between launching the High Risk Youth Program grants to local providers in 1987 and the award of the HRY evaluation in 1994, CSAP funded three- to five-year grants for more than 400 local programs. These programs took a variety of approaches to prevention services for youth at risk, many of them home grown or based in "common sense." The funding agency realized that learning from this diverse experience and passing on lessons to other providers was important. Indeed, the "let a thousand flowers bloom" approach to the HRY grants was expected to stimulate new thinking about how to prevent substance abuse among youth. To help identify and document program designs and accomplishments, grantees were required to have local evaluators. These evaluations were as diverse as the programs, using a great range of research designs including case studies, process evaluations, quasi-experimental outcome evaluations, and the occasional randomized controlled trial.

The large number of evaluations gathered across the HRY programs promised a rich store of information. The question was how to extract it and summarize the patterns of program intervention that produced success. CSAP put together a small team of policy researchers (including the eventual PI of the HRY evaluation) to develop criteria for determining whether individual program evaluations had sufficient scientific credibility to identify promising programs. Of the hundreds of evaluations that had been completed and submitted by grantees, just over 30 met criteria for further review, and only 9 were eventually disseminated as promising program models (Brounstein and Zweig, 1999). The local evaluations focused more on providing program managers with formative evaluation information that would help implement or refine the local prevention program. This did not mean that their evaluation work was not useful (Springer and Phillips, 1994); it just meant that the research designs used by the reviewers did not establish internal validity of *outcome* findings.

One approach for generating generalizable lessons about "what works" was to conduct statistical meta-analytic studies of collections of local evaluations. This approach allows statistical assessment of relative program effectiveness by developing effect sizes for evaluations that have comparable outcome measures, meet methods criteria, and have generally similar intervention approaches (e.g., group interventions to prevent substance abuse). Meta-analyses have produced some important lessons for practice. For example, a meta-analysis of 120 prevention programs for youth clearly demonstrated that "interactive" programs were more effective than "noninteractive" programs (Tobler and Stratton, 1997). However, the information base for placing interventions in these categories was minimal and often variable. It was very difficult to obtain the detail to make this categorization. It was nearly impossible to provide the detail for a practitioner to know what activities count as interactive, let alone understand what gives interactive programming its juice. It was clear that lecturing kids was not a great alternative; it was not so clear how to do interactive things effectively.

So the policy problem at the initiation of the HRY evaluation was to draw lessons from the significant number of prevention programs for youth to improve practice. To identify these lessons, our first option was to encourage, find, and disseminate evaluations of single programs (or single-program models) that worked. Indeed, this path had led to registries of evidence-based programs (EBPs) like SAMHSA's NREPP, and a lot of alphabet soup. The shortcoming of this approach was and remains the problem of generalizability and adaptation. Demonstrating that a "program" works in one or a few places does not prove that it, or what part of it, will work elsewhere. The second option was meta-analysis, which established the possibility of finding more general principles underlying effective prevention (e.g., interactive programs) but would provide very little specific guidance on how to implement those principles. SAMHSA's hope in requesting the Cross-site Evaluation of High Risk Programs was to find a middle ground—a study that would generate knowledge about what works more generally and provide sufficient implementation detail to support lessons about how to do it.

Initiation of Policy Research

The HRY evaluation was initiated through a competitive bid process. While the request for proposals (RFP) did not specify a budget, the scope of work it described made it clear that this was a large contract. EMT Associates (a small business in Sacramento, CA) and Macro International (a large research firm in the Washington, DC, area) teamed on a proposal submission. EMT had limited experience with national evaluations but had probably been through the door of more local HRY programs than any other firm in the country. EMT had carried out more than a dozen program evaluations of HRY programs in several states and had done even more monitoring site visits to HRY programs as a contractor to CSAP. The team knew the diversity of both programs and settings that would be encountered in the study. The EMT team developed a proposed design that anticipated the need for strong data on program context, strong program design and implementation data, and a sophisticated multilevel analysis plan. The proposed method was breaking new ground in using the natural variation between sites to produce generalizable findings on detailed program design and implementation practices. The fact that this high-profile evaluation was awarded to a small business outside the Beltway—way outside—was a surprise to the Beltway firms. In fact, one of the favored competitors launched a protest and held up the contract award for nearly six nail-biting months. It was eventually dismissed as frivolous, and the work began.

The Policy Research Task

The EMT/Macro proposal had argued that CSAP's desire to include the full diversity of program approaches and settings in the study sample could actually be an advantage to generating usable lessons. The team claimed that "when the ultimate objective is to develop applicable knowledge that can be applied by practitioners in real world settings, multi-site evaluations of locally-driven interventions may represent a more efficient approach to knowledge generation than multi-site trials of carefully controlled program models" (Sambrano et al., 2005, p. 491). The policy research task before them was, plainly put, to make good on that claim. Essentially it meant fashioning a flexible yet scientifically credible design that would identify and verify effective practices. This verification was greatly needed given the state of prevention knowledge at the time. More detailed discussions in upcoming sections of this chapter tell the tale of how this task was carried out.

Objectives

The HRY evaluation created an unprecedented opportunity to use the experience of HRY grantees to generate lessons about effective prevention for youth at risk. The evaluation was initiated with three major objectives (SAMHSA, 2002):

- Rigorously assess and demonstrate how CSAP–funded HRY programs prevent and reduce substance use among youth at risk for such behavior.
- Provide systematic information about the role of risk and protective factors in prevention programs, including the linkages between risk and protective factors and substance use in the HRY target population.
- Systematically document how prevention programs are delivered and identify settings, designs, and implementation processes that are common to effective programs.

As summarized in the remainder of the chapter, the HRY evaluation successfully fulfilled each of these objectives.

Challenges

The HRY evaluation was challenging at every turn. A brief focus on just three areas of challenge will give a sense of the variety of roadblocks and surprises that are not atypical to policy research. To begin with, the project began nearly six months behind schedule due to the protest, but the study implementation timeline could not shift since it was tied to the grantee cohort that would be studied. To complicate the need to make up for lost time, the team was immediately faced with producing an Office of Management and Budget (OMB) clearance package that is required to approve all instrumentation and sampling plans and to assess the study "burden" on participants to ensure that federal studies fulfill a justifiable need and are not wasteful. The team was warned this could take six months. With determination and careful relationship building, the team wrote a detailed OMB clearance package and cooperated closely with the review process. Clearance was obtained in six weeks.

A second challenge was collecting data in the 48 sites across 22 states that ended up in the program sample, including surveys of participants, detailed implementation records, and qualitative information on programs. To add to the challenge, this had to be done within budget, and the credibility of the study depended on the quality of this work, particularly in keeping youth participants' attrition rate as low as possible across four time points stretching two years. The solution again focused on building relationships. Each site was assigned an evaluation liaison who established regular communication with a site representative, usually the program manager. The evaluation team worked with local evaluators to hire local staff for collecting data, developed a strong intersite and center-to-site communication network, and provided clear procedures, regular feedback, and strong training. This strategy worked remarkably well, producing aggregate survey respondent retention rates of 87% for participants and 83% for the comparison group at program exit; 74% for participants and 75% for comparison 6 months after exit; and 68% for participants and 67% for comparison at 18 months after exit.

The third challenge was being able to obtain the necessary information on field operations and to maintain the necessary flexibility in design implementation to make the many adjustments the team knew were going to be necessary. The team emphasized their experience with this challenge in the proposal and outlined an "error detection and error correction" procedure for continuously monitoring data quality from the field. When a data collection problem was flagged, the team took immediate, positive action rather than wait until the study was compromised. For example, if survey response rates were falling behind in a site, we implemented options to improve it. Pizza parties at which surveys could be completed were a popular strategy that worked. In sum, the challenges were manageable because the team planned for them and because the team was committed to making the data as strong as possible.

The Decision Context

The decision environment to which the HRY evaluation could contribute was diffuse. At the federal level, findings from the study could have implications for the kinds of policy support decisions made by CSAP (e.g., what kinds of prevention programming they want to support through training, technical assistance, or further grant support). The results of a major evaluation such as the HRY study could also be important for supporting agency budget requests before Congress and could provide ammunition for interests in support of prevention spending. The evaluation had another relevant decision context at which more detailed study findings were targeted. Youth program and prevention practitioners could find the results useful for making decisions about program design and implementation. In addition, youth behavior researchers and professionals with access to the study might be part of a chain of influence through which study findings could contribute to improved outcomes. Though there was no focused decision maker for study recommendations, the hope was that study findings would provide important information to improve decisions by a broad range of relevant decision-making audiences.

The Institutional Context

The HRY evaluation was a contract, not a grant. Technically that means that the evaluator is acting as an agent of the government, and the client agency has the power of decision over how the work is done, what is produced, and what is published or made public as an official product. In the case of a large study like HRY, the project officer in charge of directing the contract is a very important institutional actor. As noted, the project officer for the HRY Evaluation was very important to the project's success. She supported the study design when some review officers felt it departed too much from standard research procedure (e.g., focusing analyses on sites with stronger counterfactual designs to establish patterns for confirmation in the full sample, discussed later), and worked hard to disseminate the emerging findings. The four monograph *Points of Prevention* series published by SAMHSA at the completion of the project was faced with some skepticism in agency review, and her strong support was essential to its release.

The Policy Cycle

The HRY evaluation did not fit neatly into any one place in the policy cycle. It did not produce information designed to be useful for a specific decision at a particular point in the cycle. Data were gathered at the evaluation phase of the policy cycle to generate information intended to be useful for future planning and implementation decisions. At the client agency level, it should inform planning decisions related to future grant funding, as well as training and technical assistance support for program design and implementation. For local agencies, schools, and service providers, it should inform program design and implementation decisions. The HRY study was a designed part of the dynamic link between the results of past decisions and the planning of future decisions.

Clients and Stakeholders

As a study more concerned with generating generalizable knowledge to improve interventions for a public health concern, the HRY study generated less intense or contentious relations with stakeholders than more specific studies that relate more clearly to specific actions and interests. Few stakeholders disagree with policy action to help youth avoid substance abuse. However, research focused on more specific policies might generate more stakeholder controversy. For example, research focused on the effectiveness of banning advertising or increasing taxes on "alcopop" (sweet-flavored alcoholic drinks) to reduce appeals to youth has generated more stakeholder interest, both in opposition and in support. The HRY evaluation generated interest and support from policy research and public health professionals, but there were no strong interests immediately at stake. The stakeholder environment could be characterized as low intensity.

Research Design and Implementation

Multisite evaluations (MSEs) are not unusual for large demonstration grant programs intended to "seed" interventions to address education, behavioral health, or other social problems. However, the HRY evaluation was unusual in its size, clear hierarchical structure, and comprehensiveness of data. The 48-site study included several important features: (1) a *common instrument*, the CSAP National Youth Survey, was used to collect youth background, perception, and behavior data across all study sites; (2) there was a *comparison group* in each site; (3) data were collected from more than 10,000 youth (5,934 participants and 4,539 comparison youth) at *four points in time*, including at baseline, program exit, and two follow-up points after program exit; (4) a common implementation monitoring instrument was completed by program staff to provide data on *exposure to prevention services* for each program participant, totaling more than 217,000 coded events; and (5) a common site visit protocol was used to collect data on *program-level* information, including information on design and implementation.

Sample

The sample was drawn to represent the range of strategies, capabilities, and participation in prevention programs funded through the High Risk Youth Initiatives in 1994 and 1995. Thus, the sample represents school- and community-based programs using differing intervention strategies implemented by a variety of organizations with different resources, staffing, and experience. Since no criteria of design or implementation strength were used to select programs, the study provides the opportunity to learn about a range of program experience in actual community conditions and to learn what design and implementation features contribute to effectiveness in reaching prevention objectives.

The High Risk Youth programs were diverse in community setting (two thirds urban, one third rural or suburban), organizational context (two thirds nonprofit providers, one third research organizations, public agencies, or schools), and service delivery setting (nearly one third in classrooms, the remainder in a variety of out-of-school settings). Programs also varied in duration and amount of contact with participating youth. One fourth of the programs were four months or less in length, another fourth were longer than a year, and the remaining half were in between. Half of the programs had an average of 40 or fewer hours of direct contact with participating youth; about a third had between 41 and 80 hours of contact; and the remaining 12 percent delivered an average of more than 80 hours of service to each participant.

The participant sample included 10,473 youth from all 48 sites, with 5,934 participants and 4,539 comparison youth nested within the programs. The programs served youth throughout the adolescent age range, of both genders, and from a variety of ethnic and racial identities. Half of the youth were of middle school age (12–14), and half were older (15–18). The program sample included sites taking part in a CSAP initiative in female prevention programs; 40% of the HRY programs served females only, and two thirds of the total youth sample was female. More than one-third (35%) of the study youth identified themselves as African-American; 26% identified themselves as Hispanic; and the remaining youth are relatively evenly distributed between Native American (13%), non-Hispanic White (12%), and Asian or Pacific Islander (11%). In sum, the High Risk Youth evaluation was designed to be a system-wide assessment to identify the key drivers of prevention effectiveness, not a typical program evaluation that identified entire interventions that were shown to have the strongest effects. The intent was to measure and use this diversity in the analysis, not to control it by focusing the study on model programs or specific target populations.

Measures

Programs within the National Cross-Site Evaluation shared a common outcome goal—to reduce the rates at which participating youth initiated or increased their substance use. Two approaches to evaluating change in substance use rates were taken: changes in individual substance use rates and aggregated changes at the program level. At the individual level, this outcome was a measure of the frequency with which the youth had used cigarettes, alcohol, or marijuana over the last 30 days. In several analyses, past-30-day use for cigarettes, alcohol, and marijuana were specified as separate outcomes. At the program level, effect sizes were calculated to measure the magnitude of program outcomes. Effect sizes provide a variance-adjusted measure that improves comparability of change scores across programs. The effect sizes reported in this analysis express the magnitude of the difference between the participant group and the comparison group changes in 30-day substance use from program entry to program exit.

Program-Level Data

As noted, the HRY Evaluation collected detailed data on the design and implementation of the interventions actually delivered in the study. To do this, the evaluation team (1) conducted structured site visits at which evaluators interviewed program directors, managers, service, and evaluation staff; observed program activities; and completed standardized protocols; (2) collected individual contact data for all participants (i.e., dosage), which included the type of services being offered, the method of delivery, and the amount of contact for each service category; and (3) produced case study narratives and standardized protocol summaries. Systematic coding and mixed-method measurement development produced a comprehensive set of design and implementation measures, which were constructed to help explain potential differences in program effectiveness across study sites.

Some of the most creative and useful process data were measures of the *methods* through which intervention content was delivered. Previous research had shown that programs that engage youth in interactive activities are more effective than noninteractive programs. The HRY team combined dosage data measuring program focus on interactive interventions with site visit data that provided detailed description of what program activities actually occurred during the time that was labeled interactive. Specifically, we identified interactive programs emphasizing group activities involving *building connections* with others (e.g., problem-solving groups, community service activities), programs in which interactive activities focused on *introspective* or self-reflective learning (e.g., facilitated discussion groups, processing videotaped role-plays), and *other interactive activities*. Of the programs analyzed for substance use change, 17 had a strong emphasis on introspective learning methods, and 13 placed an emphasis on building connections with others.

Data were collected on multiple areas of program organization and implementation hypothesized to have a possible relationship to program effectiveness (e.g., staff training, program coherence, program duration, program intensity, and program management). In the analyses reported here, two measures of the implementation of program services in the HRY programs are particularly important. A measure of *program coherence* refers to the extent to which program theory is explicit, articulated, and used to focus multiple activities on achieving program objectives. This program coherence variable is an exceptional example of mixed methods with respect to measurement. The measure structure is explained in the Focus On Methods section of this chapter. Achieving coherence is closely related to adequate and relevant training of staff so that program objectives, procedures, and rationale are understood and put into practice day to day. *Program intensity* is measured as the number of hours per week that youth were involved in the program. Most evaluations of program "dose" use program duration or total hours as measures. HRY site visits had suggested that programs that really engaged the youth and provided meaningful experience were those that had longer sessions that allowed more involved activities. In the HRY programs, intensity ranged from an average of less than 1 hour of service per week to 15 hours of service per week. Programs were divided into two equal groups of 23 sites, those with higher intensity (3.3 hours per week or more) and lower intensity (fewer than 3.3 hours per week) for purposes of analysis.

In summary, the multimethod information gathered in the Cross-Site Evaluation supported development of measures of program implementation through direct indicators (e.g., dosage measures), multiple-item indicators, or coded variables. The specific measures described here have been identified in previous analyses as those most strongly associated with program effect sizes and are used in subsequent analyses to identify strong programs.

Analysis Procedures

For analysis of program participants, the HRY evaluation team used hierarchical linear modeling (HLM) to conduct analyses on the full pool of participants in the program and comparison groups. The HLM procedure made adjustments for nesting that strengthened these analyses, which include comparisons of treatment and comparison groups from program entrance to 18 months after program exit. For the analysis of program effectiveness, the team used a meta-analytic approach to identify, examine, and explain variation in impact on outcome effect sizes across sites.

In summary, the overall analytic strategy used for the findings presented here combines pooled analyses using multilevel statistical modeling and meta-analytic approaches based on program-level effect sizes. The multilevel statistical modeling was important for identifying pooled longitudinal effects of interventions and for describing differences in these effects between subgroups of programs or subgroups of participants (e.g., youth who were already using substances at baseline). The meta-analytic approach was useful for clearly describing the differences in effectiveness between sites and for exploratory analyses identifying the characteristics of programs that attained larger effect sizes. Using both approaches allowed for exploration of the data, identification of variables contributing to effective prevention programming, and testing the longitudinal effects of prevention programming.

Selected Findings

The hierarchical, multisite, quasi-experimental, multimethod design of the HRY evaluation involved the creation of a data set that was very unusual in the degree to which it incorporated detailed measurement of the real-world context of the programs, program intervention design, program implementation, and detailed demographic and outcome data on participant and comparison groups in each site. This presented an incredible opportunity to engage in creative and agile policy research.

A full treatment of the numerous analyses the data supported is not possible here. (The Final Technical Report for the study was delivered in two volumes, one covering findings, the other covering methods. Together they were more than 500 pages in length.) The select analyses and findings summarized here show how the team made complementary use of the analysis opportunities and moved between levels of analysis to identify and confirm emerging findings.

Pooled Sample Analysis Findings

A top-line research question for the HRY evaluation was "Do participants in prevention programs have less increase in substance use rates over time than similar youth who did not participate?" Figure 10.1 presents a growth curve graph comparing rates of increase for tobacco, alcohol, marijuana, and 30-day substance use (all three combined) over the evaluation study period. The answer is "no" for overall 30-day substance use and for tobacco; the answer is "yes"—but barely—for alcohol and marijuana. HLM trend analysis of the pooled participant sample across four points in time for past-30-day substance use produced no statistically significant differences between program participants ($n = 5,605$) and the comparison group ($n = 4,341$). However, as demonstrated in the growth curves, HRY participant youth did report less increase in the use of alcohol (linear trend, treatment interaction = -0.056, $p < 0.05$) and marijuana (linear trend, treatment interaction = -0.060, $p < 0.05$)

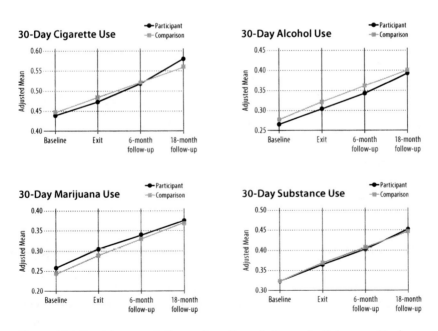

Figure 10.1 Participant and Comparison Growth Curves by Substance Used

relative to the comparison group. Even though statistically significant, these substance-specific differences in trends are very small.

If these results were interpreted from a laboratory science perspective, they would be very discouraging. After all, given the effort and resources put into the study, one would be tempted to conclude that these programs just don't work. However, from the perspective of real-world policy research, they suggest that more work is needed. We are not seeing the whole picture. There are three plausible reasons why the "on the face of it" conclusion may not be warranted. First, even though comparison groups were selected to be "no service" comparisons, some of the communities have higher levels of other (non–HRY) youth programming and services than others. Comparison groups in those communities might not provide as strong a counterfactual as comparison groups in low-service communities. Second, successful programing might need to be focused on subgroups of participants (e.g., different genders), and these focused effects may be "washed out" in the pooled analysis. Third, it is probably the case that some programs are effective, and others simply are not. The reasons for variations in impact might be different (e.g., some program designs may simply be ineffective [as was found for didactic lectures]; other programs may be potentially effective but poorly implemented). In either case, the examples of effective programs within the full sample might again be "washed out" in the pooled analysis. The evaluation team assessed these plausible explanations, and a few nuggets from their findings will be presented in what follows.

Pooled Findings Adjusted for Context

In the HRY study, comparison-group youth might have been exposed to prevention services that had the same objectives as the intervention under study, or they might have received the intervention itself. This "contamination" erodes the distinction between the participant group and the intervention group—and it is even more problematic in longitudinal studies that include follow-up periods, since youth in either the participant or comparison group have more opportunities to participate in additional community services.

The HRY study included data that identified the degree to which youth in the comparison group in each site had the opportunity to participate in substance abuse prevention programming services. This measure, which split sites into two groups, allowed comparisons of outcomes for programs in which comparison youth had "lower" or "higher" opportunity for participation in substance use prevention programs. Comparison group students in the 23 sites with higher opportunity for prevention participation had slower rates of increase in substance use than comparison youth in the 23 sites with lower opportunity for participation. This result is consistent with the expectation that prevention effects in sites with higher availability of prevention services will be underestimated, because comparison youth in these field settings also benefit from these other prevention services.

A reanalysis of the growth curves presented in Figure 10.1, taking availability of community prevention services into account, did indicate greater separation between participant and comparison youth, with participant youth consistently indicating lower substance use rates. Nonetheless, as in the full sample, statistically significant benefits for participant youth across programs are found only for the use of alcohol (linear trend, treatment interaction = -0.075, $p < .05$) and marijuana (linear trend, treatment interaction = -0.070, $p < .05$). Adjusting the sample to account for comparison-group exposure to prevention services strengthens the evidence for the effectiveness of prevention programming in reducing substance use, though the pooled effect across diverse programs in diverse community settings remains small.

For analysis purposes, the evaluation team used this low-service-opportunity group of sites to conduct analyses on this smaller pool that had more distinct counterfactuals, which could yield more crisp findings. One of the most interesting results that emerged from these analyses was the identification of very different program outcome effects for females and males. Figure 10.2 displays the growth curves for this analysis. Gender differences in the HRY sample were evident in the analyses partitioned by low opportunity for prevention services.

The patterns of effects were nonlinear for males (quadratic trend, treatment interaction = 0.049, $p = 0.025$) but linear for females (linear trend, treatment interaction = -0.044, $p = 0.016$). However, both females and males experienced a statistically significant decrease in use relative to comparison youth of the same gender. Even more interesting, the shapes of the growth curves for participant and comparison youth of each gender are dramatically different. The curves for participant and comparison females grow progressively farther apart in the shape of a fan. The effects of programming are small but are sustained and increase over time. By

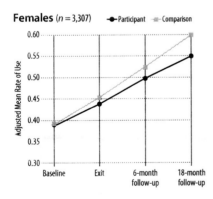
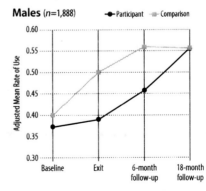

Figure 10.2 Participant and Comparison Substance Use Growth Curves by Gender

contrast, use rates reported by participant males diverge more dramatically from comparison males at exit and 6 months after exit. The participant and comparison trends converge at 18 months after exit, forming a kind of football pattern.

These dramatic differences disappear in the pooled sample. The slow divergence in the female pattern pulls in the more dramatic divergence in participating and comparison males at the middle time points. "The convergence in the males at the final time point mutes the growing difference for females. The result is a non-significant trend, and a masking of two very different, but significant, longitudinal patterns" (Sambrano et al., 2005, p. 498). It is important to recognize just how wrong a conclusion based on the full pooled sample would have been. The programs did work, even in that aggregated sense, for both genders, but differently. More than anything, this suggests a need for further understanding of why this difference existed and what can be done to strengthen results for both genders. The evaluation team planned to answer these implementation questions by taking a meta-analytic approach to analyze program-level effects and detailed process data.

Program-Level Analysis and Findings

Given that some programs work very well, some don't make much difference, and some can have an iatrogenic effect (i.e., a negative effect inadvertently caused by the intervention; see the jargon box), a primary objective of the HRY Evaluation was to generate information about the characteristics of effective programs in natural community settings. Diversity in effect sizes across the HRY evaluation programs and our ability to measure program design and implementation provided an opportunity to identify those program characteristics that correlate with more positive effect sizes. The selection of program design and implementation variables included in this analysis was generally grounded in past literature on prevention programming as reflected in the data collection instrumentation. Many of the specific concepts that ended up in the analysis were developed to reflect refinements of these concepts as informed by intensive site visits that provided detail on program management, theories of change, and the precise activities used to accomplish them. The variables that emerged as most important in the meta-analytic analysis reflect this attention to developing measures that corresponded as closely as feasible to the reality of the HRY program strategies.

Bivariate analyses of a large number of program-level measures of organizational capacity, intervention design, and implementation design resulted in the identification of five program characteristics that produced statistically significant contrasts in average effect sizes between programs that exhibited that characteristic and those that did not. Three are features of intervention design (behavioral skills emphasis, use of introspective learning, and a focus on connection-building delivery methods), and two are features of implementation (coherent program implementation practices and high service intensity).

Figure 10.3 demonstrates average effect sizes for programs manifesting each of the characteristics of effective programming. While these effect sizes are substantially larger than the average overall effect size for all 46 programs in the analysis (average = 0.022), they are still small by usual study standards (i.e., an effect size of 0.20 is a common study standard for a small effect). For the purposes of this analysis, the magnitude of the effect was not the major criterion used to define meaningful results. Indeed, the pooled analyses of participants had identified compelling reasons why there was a small detectable effect at the whole-program level. Effect size could be constrained by downward biases from comparison groups with high exposure to prevention services, the limited ability to detect effects because the great majority of youth were nonusers at baseline (for whom program effects were less detectable), the masking of effects that could be influenced by gender, or other factors in this messy program environment. Furthermore, it is not surprising that no one characteristic of the complex social processes represented in prevention programs would be sufficient to attain strong effects across diverse programs and contexts (Springer, Sale, Hermann, et al., 2004).

It was important that each of these program characteristics made a statistically significant difference in the magnitude of measured effects. Even more important, each of these characteristics provided a conceptual explanation of *why* effects were taking place, which had direct implications for practice.

- Program emphasis on *life skills* was associated with the highest average effect size. This finding is a confirmation of a theme in prior

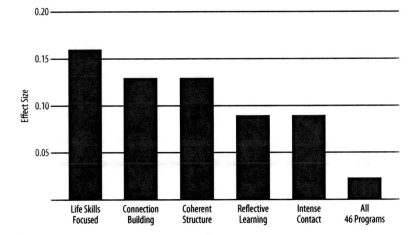

Figure 10.3 Average Effect Sizes by Effective Program Characteristics

evaluation findings for prevention programs. HRY programs with this focus often used cognitive-behavioral approaches to skills develop-ment, focusing on behavior management more than emotive content.

- The *connection-building* and *introspective learning* characteristics elaborate and provide specificity to the established evidence-based finding that interactive programming improves program effective-ness. The evidence supporting these concepts and examples of how to engage in interactive programming provide actionable informa-tion for practitioners.

- The *intensive contact* characteristic adds an insight to what differ-ence "dosage" (i.e., the amount of contact) might make in effec-tiveness. Neither duration of contact (length of program) nor total amount of contact (total hours spent in the program) was related to effect sizes. Intensity (i.e., the number of hours per week) was. Though this finding needed further investigation, the implication was that program activities that require a substantial portion of the participants' time and attention, even for a relatively short duration, were important.

- Finally, *program coherence* is a construct that emerged from the exploratory facet of the HRY evaluation. It is a soft version of fidel-ity that focuses on conveying program purpose, theory of change, and associated principles of practice to staff; working with staff to develop buy-in and enthusiasm about the program; and applying the program's goals in actual activities.

Pooled EBP Programs Confirmatory Sample

Further analyses tested the degree to which programs with multiple posi-tive characteristics produced larger effects. The fact that the five program characteristics were not highly correlated with one another strengthened the potential to detect gains in effectiveness through combinations of strong design and implementation characteristics. The analyses identified a clear incremental increase in effectiveness when programs implemented at least four of the positive program characteristics. The exact combina-tion of these characteristics did not make a significant difference. Eight of the 46 programs were identified as comprehensively strong programs implementing at least four of the five positive characteristics. The median effect size for these eight programs was 0.22 compared to a median of -0.02 for all other programs. This difference was large and highly statisti-cally significant ($p < .01$).

To confirm this program-level analysis with participant data and to test whether these comprehensively strong programs produced lasting effects on the substance use of participants, the HLM growth curve analysis was replicated on participant and comparison youth in the eight comprehen-sively strong program sites. Figure 10.4 presents growth curves contrast-ing trends in substance use for participants and comparison youth in the

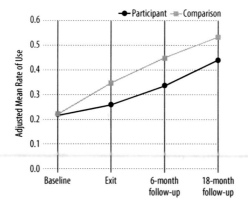

Figure 10.4 Participant and Comparison Substance Use Growth Curves for Programs with Four or More Effective Characteristics

eight comprehensively strong programs. These longitudinal findings support and extend the effect size analysis reported earlier. There were dramatic differences between the findings for the total sample and findings for the eight programs with at least four positive program characteristics. While longitudinal differences in substance use between participant- and comparison-group youth were very small (and not statistically significant) in the full sample, differences between the participant and comparison youth in the eight-program cluster were pronounced and statistically significant (interaction coefficient = 0.032, p = 0.039 [one-tailed test]).

Even 18 months after program exit, substance use among participant youth was significantly lower than rates of use among comparison youth, demonstrating enduring prevention effectiveness. Furthermore, the growth curves for these programs were nearly identical for males and females, suggesting that comprehensively strong programs produce similar and lasting benefits for both genders. These eight comprehensive programs are more effective over time than other programs, and their effects are more equitable between males and females.

Secondary Analysis: Evaluation and Effectiveness

One of the nagging problems contract policy researchers often experience is an imbalance between the resources devoted to data collection and management of one side and data analysis on the other. They know that the timeline-driven analyses that are necessary to meet report deadlines often raise as many questions as they answer. If evaluations were conducted in a manner that explored data more deeply than the original research questions suggested, more robust lessons learned could emerge.

The HRY Evaluation project officer recognized the analysis gold mine presented by this data set and got a modest contract augmentation to allow limited additional analyses. A priority for the evaluation team was to develop a stronger understanding of why some programs were more effective than others. Using a path analysis technique, the HRY evaluation team produced the analyses presented in Figure 10.5. Path analysis produces measures (coefficients) of the degree of association between variables in a plausible path of influence, a sort of logic model. Simply put, it measures the association (-1.00 = perfect inverse association, 0.00 = no association, and 1.00 = perfect positive association) between steps in a process—usually the steps in a hypothesized causal chain between the intervention and its outcomes. The technique adjusts for the degree to which the associations farther to the left contribute forward to those to the right. In other words, it is not assessing the association between each variable in the causal chain (e.g., the negative relation between setting and strong intervention design); it is measuring the independent contribution of each variable to an identifiable path of influence to produce an outcome while adjusting for their sequential interrelation. This is complex but revealing.

In plain terms, what does this tell the producers and users of policy research about influences on program effectiveness in the HRY study? There are a number of lessons.

- Beginning from the left, it shows that program management makes a difference in two ways: (1) supportive management (defined and measured as management that focuses on training, inclusive decision making, close collaboration with partners, and a positive work environment) was associated with greater use of in-school prevention programs, and (2) supportive management was associated with strong intervention design (defined as the number of the five positive program characteristics in the program).
- Interestingly, only one of these influences is positive, because in-school programs are less effective. The negative path from in-school or

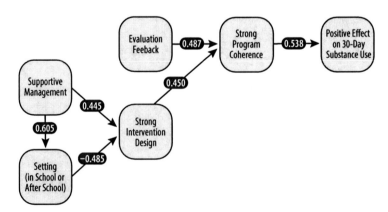

Figure 10.5 Path Analysis of Program Process Factors Contributing to Effective Outcomes

out-of-school context is consistent with earlier HRY evaluation findings that the most effective program practices were those that required more time and a less regimented environment (e.g., self-guided group processes, experiential learning). The in-school environment constrained program options for intense and less-structured interventions.

- The path analysis confirmed the influence of combining effective practices, and very importantly, it demonstrated that these combined practices are much more effective if they are implemented with *coherence*. The importance of program coherence was a prime lesson from the study. It was the mediating variable for all of the major positive influences in this model. Everything worked better when coherently implemented.

- A final finding of this analysis is particularly important for understanding the influence of a local program policy researcher. Evaluation feedback is a measure of how involved local evaluators were in program design, continuous feedback of information on program performance, and decision making. Some evaluators were quite "independent" of the program, collecting and analyzing data and producing formal reports. Others were very involved. They attended program meetings, frequently presented and discussed findings as they emerged, and participated in interpreting and applying findings to program revisions. The degree of evaluator involvement was an important contributor to coherence, the lynch pin between management, context, program design, and activities and attaining outcomes. Evaluator involvement strengthened program coherence. It made a difference.

Communicating and Using Results

Again with the support of their Project Officer, the HRY evaluation team began disseminating the emerging results of the study as early as possible. While the final analyses of the study were still underway, it had achieved enough recognition in the research community to be nominated for and to win the 2000 American Evaluation Association Study of the Year Award. Nonetheless, study findings never received widespread dissemination or recognition from CSAP or SAMHSA, the sponsoring agencies. How the HRY results were reported and the mixed success of their dissemination will be elaborated next.

Reporting Results

The HRY evaluation team reported results early and often. The reporting took the following forms.

- *Reports to the Funding Agency*. Comprehensive annual reports were submitted to CSAP. These included a separate executive summary that summarized take-away findings for wider dissemination, a lengthy findings report providing detailed findings and data displays, and a methods report that provided extensive detail on methods choices and procedures.

- *Professional Meetings.* From the beginning of the contract, the Project Officer and evaluation team presented papers at major prevention and evaluation conferences, often presenting several papers on different topics at each conference.
- *Journal Articles.* The evaluation team published eight articles in highly regarded scholarly journals. The unique data base supported articles with innovative analyses making important contributions to prevention research (Derzon et al., 2005; Sale et al., 2005).
- *SAMHSA/CSAP Monographs.* The study was summarized in a four-volume series of monographs titled *Points of Prevention.*
- *Invited Presentations.* The dissemination of program findings and very positive review commentary in professional publications generated numerous requests for presentations by the study principal investigator (PI) in key addresses at conferences, presentations to policy makers or program professionals, and workshops. Examples included State School Health Conferences in Alaska, California, and Montana; a European Union Preventive Health Directors Policy meeting in Lisbon, Portugal; presentations to provider organizations in the United Kingdom; and numerous presentations to local providers.

Selected Recommendations

The HRY evaluation was not designed to provide specific model program guidance. It was designed to generate findings that identified and demonstrated intervention content and implementation practices that proved to be effective across a range of contexts and participant characteristics. It would also provide guidance on how the effective characteristics interacted with specific contexts (e.g., where might they be more or less effective, and what contextual characteristics are independently important for achieving program objectives?). The *Points of Prevention Monograph Series* (SAMHSA, 2002) provided numerous statements of principles that were guides to intervention policy and strategy, not specific program models. A few examples of principles to make prevention efforts more effective include:

- Prevention programs should be designed to *promote opportunities and skills that build connections to positive social environments* such as supportive schools, healthy families, caring adults, positive peers, community service, and other positive contexts. A corollary to this recommendation was the clear recognition that the importance of connections is strongly related to the presence of positive environments in which the youth can connect. Analyses of HRY data on youth perceptions, for example, showed that in families with low perceived trust and support, stronger perceived parental disapproval was associated with higher reported use. Building safe and supportive schools, healthy families, and supportive communities are necessary complements to youth connectedness.

- Prevention programs should use interactive—not didactic—delivery, and activities that engage youth in thought-provoking and meaningful activities that encourage team building (e.g., community service).
- Prevention programs should provide four or more hours of contact per week. This contact creates a significant presence in youth's time that promotes engagement and the kinds of connection building, thoughtful interaction with peers, and self-reflection that characterize effective interventions.
- Prevention programs should be coherent; that is, they should have clearly articulated objectives, a sound theory of change explicitly connected to program activities, substantial staff training specifically on the program and its rationale, and consistent feedback to program and staff concerning performance.

The study produced many more applicable lessons with direct implications for action. In this regard, it clearly met the intention of providing applicable evidence on how to improve prevention effectiveness.

Action

Despite extensive dissemination of findings in refereed journals and other venues, CSAP itself took very little action explicitly based on the findings of the study. Early on in the study, the agency director was a well-known academic with a strong prevention research background. Analyses of the baseline HRY data produced a path model showing the interrelation of context and individual characteristics contributing to youth substance use (Sale et al., 2003). The director used that model regularly in presentations, and it was the basis for a visible public service announcement asking "Do you know where your kids are right now?" The message was based on items from the measure of family connectedness that was a strong protective factor in the model. The study was an important source in shaping prevention policy in the European Union. However, when the study was complete, it remained barely visible in CSAP policy or training.

While the reasons for this lack of direct connection to action are not clear, there are some plausible explanations. First, a new director was in place and had not been part of discussions that approved methods decisions during study implementation. She relied more on technical review by staff than her own judgment about study credibility. Some staff members involved in technical review had a very formal and conservative view of the study design and were often not enthusiastic about the HRY team's agile and creative approach. In this regard, it might have been an error to disseminate so much of the information through scholarly journals. A closer relation to CSAP leadership might have increased understanding of the study and therefore the utility of its result.

Another reason for the lack of visible use may have been that the study suggested changes in policy and supported positions that countered the conventional thinking in CSAP and the larger prevention community. For example, the study suggested less focus on individual-level risk and protective factors (e.g., personality, attitudes, beliefs) and more on contextual risk and protection. Accordingly, much of the prevention programming based on individual characteristics (e.g., self-esteem, perception of health risk, or value clarification) was found not to be effective focus. It also suggested that in-school programs were less effective than other options. While these findings were not championed by CSAP at the time, most of the practice and policy implications of the study have come into good currency in the last two decades. So as is often the case, the utility of a careful and productive study could have been diffuse and contributory to slow change.

Lessons for Policy Research

This case has demonstrated the importance of multisite evaluations as contributors to knowledge about the effectiveness of substance abuse prevention or other social interventions. Multisite evaluations provide the opportunity to disentangle the complex interaction of context (e.g., exposure of comparison-group youth to prevention services in high-resource communities), differences in outcomes based upon the characteristics of the youth (males/females, users/nonusers), and differences in the effectiveness of intervention and implementation practices. They provide context for understanding the selection, application, and adaptation of program models that the broad evidence base for the models cannot provide. Multisite evaluations have an important and unique place in research to improve prevention interventions and other services designed to improve social conditions.

Focus on Research Methods

Mixed-Methods Measures in the HRY Evaluation

Mixed methods are often thought of as applying to the use of both qualitative and quantitative measures in the same study, the use of multiple types of data collection (e.g., surveys and interviews), or the use of complementary analysis approaches. Mixed-methods measures are not as frequently discussed in the methods literature. However, as argued in Part I of this text, measures are not distinct from analysis. In applied studies, measures are the end of the analysis continuum closest to empirical observation. They are particularly important because they are the point at which the study's correspondence to reality is most explicitly established. In the HRY study, this correspondence to reality was cemented with mixed-methods measurement procedures. The two examples presented next show how.

First, to develop an agile approach to more fine-grained measures of what interactive intervention activities really looked like, the evaluation team developed a two-step measurement process. They developed a monitoring instrument that local HRY Evaluation data collectors worked with program staff to complete. Using attendance records, the number of hours each participant attended was recorded and then categorized as didactic or interactive delivery for educational or skills-building purposes. Using site visit and document review information, the team then identified the interactive time as connection building, reflective learning, and other. This combination of quantitative and qualitative data allowed classification of 17 programs as emphasizing introspective learning activities and 13 as emphasizing connection building. These measures were among the five most important in their effects on substance use and provided greater understanding of why interactive programming was more effective.

The second example is the team's measure of coherent programming. This mixed measure started with qualitative insights that were then "hardened up" to support comparisons. A pattern emerged in site visits, through interviews and observation, and a short questionnaire that staff were asked to complete. What emerged was that in some programs, there was a shared understanding of what the program was trying to accomplish and why and how that related to daily staff activities. One of the triggers for the idea that this was important was that a single item from an opportunity sample staff questionnaire administered during site visits was found to be highly correlated to effect sizes. That item was "I believe that what I am doing will help prevent substance use by participating youth." The team constructed a rating of the degree to which programs had a clear program logic, strong training, and daily implementation of program elements. Based on this, programs were classified as more or less coherent. Again, this mixed-method measure proved important to the creation of effective programs.

Acronyms and Jargon

CSAP—The Center for Substance Abuse Prevention is one of three centers within SAMHSA. It is a leading funder of prevention policy research.

Effect Size—Effect size is a simple indicator of the magnitude of the difference between two groups that has descriptive advantages to tests of statistical significance. It focuses on size of the difference (in standard deviation units) rather than confounding this with sample size.

HLM—Hierarchical linear modeling is a family of hierarchical analysis techniques that use various statistical algorithms to incorporate multiple nested levels into analyses of change. Growth curves are a common visualization of HLM results, allowing comparison of rates of change in treatment and comparison groups.

Iatrogenic Effect—A negative effect inadvertently caused by the treatment. For example, a prevention program may seek to educate parents by publishing a pamphlet about where youth most commonly obtain drugs—these materials may also serve as "how-to" guides for youth to engage in negative behaviors.

PI—Principal investigator is responsible for leading the design, analysis, and interpretation of findings of a research project.

SAMHSA—The Substance Abuse and Mental Health Services Administration is an agency within the United States Department of Health and Human Services. It focuses on issues of behavioral and mental health policy and service provision.

Discussion Questions

1. What were the supports and challenges of CSAP's institutional environment for the HRY National Evaluation? How did they specifically benefit and inhibit the evaluation implementation and use?
2. How did the HRY Evaluation differ from earlier CSAP and other policy research efforts to learn from individual programs? What do you see as the benefits and drawbacks of the HRY evaluation approach?
3. In your judgment, what were the most important concepts/measures in the HRY analysis and why?
4. From a practitioner's perspective, what do you think would be the most important findings from the HRY Evaluation and why?
5. In what ways did the HRY Evaluation demonstrate an agile approach to research?

Assignments and Activities

1. Identify a program for which you think a multisite, hierarchical evaluation would be valuable. Identify what program factors would be important to the study and what individual participant factors would be important. Explain why.

11 What to Do About Scrap Tires? Options for Productive Waste Management

Robert W. Wassmer

Introduction

In this case study, Robert W. Wassmer describes his preparation of a policy analysis on the desirability of instituting a state subsidy to waste tire processors. Professor Wassmer conducted the study as a consultant to the California Integrated Waste Management Board (CIWMB). The study offers an illuminating example of how policy analysts can help steer their clients to a method widely taught to policy students but all too rarely employed by actual policy makers. Wassmer and his study team used a rational analysis method to increase the logical clarity of the CIWMB's decision on the use of subsidies to increase the amount of waste tires diverted from California landfills. They ultimately decided against the use of these subsidies, but going through this process helped clarify the pros and cons of other alternatives that were since employed by the CIWMB (and now CalRecycle) to reduce the extent of scrap tires ending up in California's landfills.

The Policy Problem

> A bulging mountain of scrap tires six stories high caught fire in the northern San Joaquin Valley early Wednesday, spewing a black plume of smoke 3,000 feet in the air and sprinkling soot for miles. Because tire fires are nearly impossible to put out, the blaze is expected to burn for months. Millions of scrap tires are scattered illegally in canyons, quarries and fields throughout the state, and California produces 30 million more a year—the most of any state. In 1989, the state launched a war on illegal tire piles, many of which are "orphan" piles with no responsible party to pay for cleanup. Since then, authorities have made a dent in the state's stockpile of discarded tires, but about 15 million remain and the threat of fires persists.
> —Jennifer Warren, *Los Angeles Times*, September 23, 1999

With no way to put it out, the tire fire described here burned for nearly a month. It has been characterized as one of the 10 worst tire fires in the world, and it resulted in the incineration of over seven million scrap tires that yielded a half-million gallons of pyrolytic oil runoff into a nearby stream. In the terms of Kingdon (2010), this "focusing event" made the low visibility problem of scrap tires a more important policy problem for the people of California, and their elected officials.

In the language of economics, the production and sales of tires left entirely to the free market can generate negative "externalities" to society, meaning here that the cost of tire consumption goes beyond the private cost of material and labor put into their production, sales, and installation. The true social cost of tire consumption should include the potential environmental consequences when they are disposed of in above-ground stockpiles or in ground landfills.

In the early 2000s, Californians generated about 30 million scrap tires a year (the rule of thumb being about nine-tenths of a scrap tire per person per year). Recognizing the need to fund programs that reduce or deal with the negative externality that scrap tires can impose upon others when disposed of, the California Tire Recycling Act required that a consumer pay an additional dollar per tire as a tire-recycling fee. The CIWMB used the nearly $30 million this generated annually to fund a combination of research, market development incentives, public information campaigns, and regulatory activities to try to manage the state's waste tires. California's diversion rate of scrap tires from landfills and tire piles increased from 34 percent in the late 1980s (before an earlier recycling fee of $0.25 per tire that lasted between 1989 and 1999 and rose to a dollar in 2000), to nearly 70 percent by 2000. The diversion occurring in 2000 being about 20 percent of scrap tires being ground into crumb rubber, 15 percent used as fuel, 12 percent used for landfill construction, 10 percent resold as still usable, 7 percent retreaded, and the remaining used for other miscellaneous civil engineering projects. Yet after all this diversion, California in the early 2000s annually added nearly nine million tires to its landfills and tire piles.

Initiation of Policy Research

Originally scheduled to expire in 1999, in 1998, Assembly Bill (AB) 117 extended the California Recycling Tire Act through 2001. Before this 2001 expiration occurred, Senate Bill (SB) 76 permanently renewed and expanded the Recycling Tire Act in year 2000. Nevertheless, in AB 117, the California Legislature required that the CIWMB produce an evaluation of its previous handling of scrap tires. The 2001 report that resulted from this (*Five-Year Plan for the Waste Tire Recycling Management Program*) suggested a need for the sustainable development of a market for scrap tires in California but explicitly lacked an endorsement of the use of a per-tire subsidy to accomplish this. The stated justification for this nonsupport was (1) its likely high expense, (2) the "marginal" processing of scrap tires it would likely generate, and (3) evidence found from other states that end-use incentives damaged the sustainability of markets for used tires that had previously developed.

Following this lack of an endorsement for a per-tire subsidy, stakeholders increasingly attended the CIWMB's public meetings and insisted upon a further reevaluation of the program as a viable policy option to reduce further the percentage of California's annual scrap tires going to landfills. Many of the stakeholders attending these meetings were representatives of crumb rubber producers in the Los Angeles Basin and felt particularly threatened by a recent expansion of Canadian subsidies to crumb rubber producers in British Columbia. They claimed that such subsidies generated an excess supply of Canadian crumb rubber that ended up in the empty cargo holds of ships returning to Los Angeles after delivering consumer goods to the Western Canadian market. The infusion of imported crumb rubber resulted in a reduction in the price paid for it in the Los Angeles Basin and a lower return to Southern California crumb rubber producers that caused them to cut back on production and the amount of California scrap tires purchased. To stakeholders in Southern California's crumb rubber industry, this chain of recent events justified the validity of their request that the CIWMB offer a subsidy similar to the Canadian government.

At this point, the CIWMB contacted Professor Wassmer and asked if he was available to conduct a policy analysis on the desirability of state subsidies to waste tire processors. Wanting to share this opportunity with students in the Master's in Public Policy and Administration program at Sacramento State, he structured the study in the form of a culminating team project for them. Eight students assisted Wassmer in this analysis, with most of them completing their master's thesis on a topic related to tire recycling.

The Policy Research Task

The research task initially requested that Professor Wassmer provide advice on whether California should use funds collected from tire recycling fees to offer a per-tire subsidy to waste tire processors in the state. Before agreeing, Professor Wassmer wrote a proposal to the Board indicating that his team would use a variation of the "eightfold path" and "criteria alternative matrix" (CAM) methods summarized in the *Focus on Methods* box later in this chapter. After reviewing the proposal and meeting with representatives of the CIWMB, the Board accepted this approach.

The first task in Bardach and Patashnik's (2016) Eightfold Path is to generate a concise statement representing the specific public policy problem investigated. After consultations with representatives of CIWMB members, the agreed problem became:

> If stockpiles and landfills are not considered acceptable alternatives, the supply of scrap tires generated in the State of California in 2001

exceeds the uses for these tires by about 25 percent. Are there solutions to this problem of excess supply, including subsidies or other end-use incentives, which are different from what the CIWMB is currently pursuing?

It is important to recognize that such a statement must not contain a solution to the public policy problem but should instead be the motivator for the generation of alternatives to address the problem.

Objectives

As agreed upon between the research team and CIWMB, the initial objective of this analysis was to offer reasonable alternatives expected to reduce the excess supply of scrap tires in California that were ending up in its landfills and tire piles. Once these reasonable alternatives were identified, a further objective of this analysis was to identify the pros and cons of each alternative and ultimately to offer a recommendation regarding the most desirable alternative(s).

Challenges

There were multiple challenges that Professor Wassmer and his team of master's students confronted when satisfying the objectives just described. The first challenge was to educate the board members (and their staff) of the CIWMB—effectively the "client"—on the desirability of the proposed methods of analysis. Once the client agreed to the idea of approaching this as a choice policy research problem that would employ an eight-step approach and yield a CAM analysis, the second challenge was to come up with a public policy question (listed earlier) acceptable to all of the diverse interests represented by the CIWMB.

One particularly thorny issue was the annual deposit of more than eight million bailed or halved tires in a landfill near the City of Azusa that was once a mine for harvesting asbestos. To prevent the leakage from this shuttered mine of asbestos into the air, the EPA recommended filling it in using a procedure that required lining and layering with scrap tires. About half of the tires used for this purpose came from out of state. If only California scrap tires were used, the Azusa Landfill could take most of the scrap tires considered excess in the problem statement decided upon for this study. However, environmentalists did not consider this an "acceptable use" and lobbied vociferously to get such a clarification inserted into the final problem statement.

For purposes of manageability, the rational-choice process of analysis works best if assessing only three to six policy alternatives. Since the CIWMB had been grappling with the broad policy problem of an excess of scrap tires for a while, the board and its stakeholders had already proposed far more than six alternatives. The six alternatives chosen (see Table 11.1) represent the result of a string of communication between the client and analysts. Though once the policy alternatives were chosen, similar challenges arose in deciding upon the specific criteria to evaluate the desirability of the alternatives, as well as the suggested weight applied to each needed to make a final recommendation (see Table 11.2). In the end, the analysts offered various options for these, and an informal vote of representatives of the CIWMB settled upon the choice of the six alternatives used in this analysis, the criteria to evaluate them, and the relative importance of each criterion in choosing the best alternative.

When this analysis began, Professor Wassmer and the Sacramento State Master's in Public Policy and Administration students that assisted

Table 11.1 Policy Alternatives Offered as Possibilities to Alleviate Excess Scrap Tires

	Alternative	*Brief Description*
I	Further regulation of landfill disposal	Expand existing legislation prohibiting landfill disposal of whole tires to require greater processing and/or institute tax on unprocessed.
II	Per-tire subsidy to waste tire processors	Offer per-tire financial rebate for processors of waste tires generated in California and delivered to end-users.
III	Per-tire subsidy to end users of waste tires	Subsidy to consumers of end-use recycled products based upon number of waste tires in final product.
IV	Further subsidize capital purchases for waste tire processors	Expand grants and loans for capital purchases to waste tire processors to encourage market growth.
V	Per-mile/per-tire subsidy for in-state transportation of scrap tires	Offer per-mile/per-tire subsidy to tire haulers that take load to processor.
VI	Informational campaigns	Expand information campaigns targeting local governments, processors, and the public, including research and development activities.

Table 11.2 Relative Weights Applied to Each Criterion Used to Evaluate Alternatives

Criterion	*Weight*
Efficiency	0.30
Equity	0.25
Sustainability	0.20
Political/Legal Feasibility	0.15
Administration/Improvability	0.10
Total	1.00

him embarked upon a course of study by assigning one or two of the analysts to each alternative so that each could brief the rest of the research team on how it could possibly satisfy/violate the assessment criteria. Perhaps the greatest challenge came about in making a decision on what to recommend. Once the weight assigned to each criterion was decided, the choice of a preferred policy alternative essentially reduced to the value (1 through 5 on a Likert Scale) assigned to how well an alternative satisfies a particular criterion (see Tables 11.3–11.5). The team of analysts accomplished this by means of intensive discussions, which resulted in

Table 11.3 Key to Interpreting the Extremes of Likert Scale (1–5) Rating Applied to Satisfaction of a Criterion by an Alternative

Criterion	Interpretation of Ratings	
	"5"—Very Strong	*"1"—Very Weak*
Efficiency	Anticipated to achieve full policy objective (i.e., further diversion of 8 million scrap tires) within existing cost structure; impact occurs within short-term period.	Not likely to improve existing diversion rates, or produces marginal improvement relative to time frame for realizing benefits.
Equity	With the exception of landfill operators, the benefits of the policy distributed equally across industries, key economic players not adversely affected relative to their situation prior to implementation.	Industries differentially affected by the policy with notable extremes in impacts across key players; several key players are worse off relative to their situation prior to implementation.
Sustainability	Market distortions are minimal; beneficial impacts of the policy expected to extend beyond the elimination of the program.	Benefits not likely sustained once the program sunsets; intervention will require indefinite support.
Political/Legal Feasibility	Board endorsement is extremely likely; and board authorized to implement all proposed policy components.	Endorsement by the board and/or legislature not likely; and/or board not granted authority to oversee or implement any portion of the policy; limited to advocacy role.
Administration/ Improvability	Implementation achieved within existing administrative structure and costs to implement are minimal; and/or policy elements are flexible and amenable to periodic change.	Implementation will require major administrative restructuring, and administrative function is likely to be costly and difficult to manage effectively.

Table 11.4 Row from Qualitative Criteria Alternative Matrix (CAM) for Alternative I

	Criterion 1: Efficiency	Criterion 2: Equity	Criterion 3: Sustainability	Criteria 4: Political/ Legal Feasibility	Criteria 5: Administrative/ Improvability
Alternative I: Further regulation of Landfill disposal require that all tire material placed in California landfills be processed to a maximum 2.5-inch chip.	Highly effective at getting waste tires out of landfills. Increased processing costs force landfill operators to consider the social cost of landfill disposal and bear more of it if they wish to continue to bury scrap tires. Near-zero cost to implement beyond funding initial advocacy efforts to pass legislation, but some additional costs of increased enforcement. If alternative-use markets do not arise, this may result in illegal dumping.	Fair in sense that all landfill operators face higher processing regulation; but, relative to other economic factors in tire market, all landfill operators likely adversely affected through loss of tire revenue. In addition, potential increases in operational cost to tire haulers if alternative-use markets are saturated or resulting higher tipping fees not passed on to new tire consumers. Consumer may have to pay higher disposal fee along with new $1 per-tire fee.	Waste tires likely to flow back to landfills if regulation is lifted and alternative end-use markets are not significantly developed. Other than providing a greater flow of scrap tires to nonlandfill uses, this policy does nothing to develop the long-term sustainability of keeping tires out of landfills if the processing regulation is lifted.	Targeting of landfill operators for new regulation is likely to raise strong opposition from solid-waste management lobby. Also potential opposition from tire haulers and retailers if they anticipate they will have to bear rising costs. CIWMB has the legal authority to authorize.	Minimal administrative requirements likely to occur beyond routine enforcement. Improvability obtained through raising required chip size if suggested amount does not keep tires out of landfills, or lowering chip size if tires come out of landfills but is too costly to tire consumers or haulers. Improvability hindered if markets cannot absorb diverted tire volume and illegal dumping occurs.

Table 11.5 Quantitative Criteria Alternative Matrix for Waste Tire Management in California
Ratings: (1) Very Weak, (2) Somewhat Weak, (3) Moderate, (4) Somewhat Strong, (5) Very Strong

	Criterion 1: Efficiency	Criterion 2: Equity	Criterion 3: Sustainability	Criterion 4: Political/Legal Feasibility	Criterion 5: Administration/Improvability	Total Score
Alternative I: Further Regulation of Landfill Disposal	Rating: 5 Weight: 0.30 Total: 1.50	Rating: 2 Weight: 0.25 Total: 0.50	Rating: 1 Weight: 0.20 Total: 0.20	Rating: 1 Weight: 0.15 Total: 0.15	Rating: 5 Weight: 0.10 Total: 0.50	2.85
Alternative II: Per-Tire Subsidy to Waste Tire Processors	Rating: 4 Weight: 0.30 Total: 1.20	Rating: 4 Weight: 0.25 Total: 1.00	Rating: 2 Weight: 0.20 Total: 0.40	Rating: 3 Weight: 0.15 Total: 0.45	Rating: 3 Weight: 0.10 Total: 0.30	3.35
Alternative III: Per-Tire Subsidy to End-Users of Waste Tires	Rating: 4 Weight: 0.30 Total: 1.20	Rating: 3 Weight: 0.25 Total: 0.75	Rating: 3 Weight: 0.20 Total: 0.60	Rating: 3 Weight: 0.15 Total: 0.45	Rating: 2 Weight: 0.10 Total: 0.20	3.20
Alternative IV: Further Subsidize Capital Purchases for Waste Tire Processors	Rating: 3 Weight: 0.30 Total: 0.90	Rating: 3 Weight: 0.25 Total: 0.75	Rating: 3 Weight: 0.20 Total: 0.60	Rating: 4 Weight: 0.15 Total: 0.60	Rating: 4 Weight: 0.10 Total: 0.40	3.25
Alternative V: Per-Mile, Per-Tire Subsidy for In-state Transportation of Scrap Tires	Rating: 3 Weight: 0.30 Total: 0.90	Rating: 3 Weight: 0.25 Total: 0.75	Rating: 2 Weight: 0.20 Total: 0.40	Rating: 2 Weight: 0.15 Total: 0.30	Rating: 1 Weight: 0.10 Total: 0.10	2.45

assignments of such values, further vetted in a public forum of CIWMB representatives and stakeholders.

The Decision Context

The purpose of this form of policy analysis is to offer a highly transparent process that highlights the trade-offs between criteria when choosing one alternative over another. The best alternative is then dependent on how the analyst (in consultation with the client) weighs one criterion against another. The assessment of alternatives (i.e., efficiency, equity, sustainability, feasibility, and administratability/improvability) and their use to compare and rate alternatives (i.e., landfill disposal, per-tire subsidy to waste tire processor, per-tire subsidy to end users of waste tires, subsidize capital purchases of waste tire processors, or informational campaigns) is influenced by the institutional context surrounding choice, the stakeholders affected by the choice they represent, and the policy cycle surrounding the decision.

The Institutional Context

The goal of the 1989 California Tire Recycling Act was to reduce the further stockpiling and landfill disposal of California's waste tires through the promotion and development of new and existing recycling and/or diversion markets. Additionally, the act strengthened the regulatory environment that governs the storage, processing, and disposal of scrap tires in the state. Specific provisions of the act authorized the CIWMB to offer grants and loans to private and public organizations to support and encourage recycling and diversion activities. The act also introduced new regulations to ensure safe storage of waste tires and created a permitting system for waste tire facilities. An extension of these regulatory provisions occurred through legislation passed in 1993 that instituted a registration program for transporters of scrap tires. A $0.25 "return fee" on scrap tires left for disposal first yielded funding to support these legislative mandates. AB 2108 in 1996 later modified the collection point of the fee to the retail sale of new or used tires.

Additional state legislation in the form of AB 117, enacted in 1998, amended the California Tire Recycling Act to lengthen its original sunset clause from June 1999 to January 2001. This legislation also mandated that the CIWMB conduct a comprehensive study of California's waste tire problem and offer policy recommendations focusing on several key issues: reducing waste tire stockpiles, protecting public health and safety, preserving the environment, and identifying viable markets for recycled waste tires in California. SB 876, enacted in 2000, was a result of the recommendations proposed in the AB 117 report. The major provision of SB 876 was an increase in the California tire fee from $0.25 to $1.00

and an expansion to include tires on new motor vehicles. In addition, SB 876 directed the CIWMB to plan for greater funding of scrap tire recycling, diversion, and recovery activities, to increase the enforcement of waste tire hauling and facility permitting, and to produce a five-year plan to implement the bill's provisions. This legislative initiative also outlined some of the major funding priorities for the CIWMB: allocations of funds for continuing stockpile cleanup and abatement, regulatory enforcement, development of new markets and technologies, implementation of a waste tire tracking system, and ongoing environmental and market research.

The Client and Its Stakeholders

The CIWMB was a state agency created in 1989 under the umbrella organization of the California Environmental Protection Agency. The leadership of the board consisted of six members: two appointed by each house of the California legislature and the remainder appointed by the governor. In recognition of the stakeholders that the CIWMB represented, the intent of two of the governor's appointments was representation of the public at large, while the other two represented the solid waste industry and the community of environmental activists. CIWMB bylaws required that any action taken required the majority agreement of at least four of the six board members.

The political environment that influenced the CIWMB was both internal and external. Outside interests and lobbying forces posed a significant political constraint to finding a consensus solution to the excess supply of scrap tires in the state. That was because a new scrap tire policy adopted by the board would not make all scrap tire stakeholders in California better off and might even make some worse off. Those made worse off would lobby intensely for nonadoption, even though such a policy might be in the best interest of all Californians.

The Policy Cycle

As described earlier, the CIWMB's motivation to request this analysis came from stakeholder reaction to an earlier report that failed to endorse the use of a per-tire subsidy to waste tires to increase the rate of their diversion from landfills and above-ground piles. When this analysis was requested in 2001, the board had already approved a five-year plan (FY 2001–2 to FY 2005–06) to spend annual tire recycling fees to (1) subsidize civil engineering uses that used crumb rubber from scrap tires, (2) assist small-business producers of scrap tire–based products and green builders using crumb rubber from scrap tires, and (3) disseminate information to local governments and state parks on how to use crumb rubber in paving. The implementation of the recommendations from this analysis would require a reconsideration of this five-year plan and, most importantly, the addition of an expenditure category that included a budget for per-tire subsidies to scrap tires diverted from unproductive uses (landfills and piles).

As described in an addendum to the final report submitted to the CIWMB at the completion of this policy analysis, a public workshop allowed the board and interested stakeholders to comment on the report's recommendations. Stakeholder comments included: (1) strong to lukewarm support for per-tire recycling subsidies, (2) opposition to the continued use of tire-derived fuel for electricity generation and cement production, (3) objection to the problem statement's assumption that landfilling was not acceptable use of scrap tires, (4) suggestions on how the weights used to evaluate the satisfaction of criteria be changed, and (5) a desire that an expansion of the use of rubberized asphalt be explicitly considered. Perhaps the most encouraging development from this was a consensus on the value of the eightfold path and CAM methods to revealing the tradeoffs inherent in choosing one alternative over another.

Research Design and Implementation

As laid out in the Focus on Research Methods Box that follows, the research design employed in this analysis is Professor Wassmer's interpretation of an eight-step process of policy analysis whose findings result in the generation of a CAM. What follows is a description of the information necessary to do this and some specifics on the details of the design and methods of this process.

Design and Methods

The second step in the study's rational analysis process was to assemble evidence clearly essential to this policy analysis. The first bit of information needed was a more complete comprehension of the magnitude of the problem. A review of previous CIWMB publications on waste tires in California and a stakeholder forum on this issue after a CIWMB meeting accomplished this. Information on what the states of Arizona, Florida, Louisiana, Minnesota, Nevada, Oregon, Texas, Utah, Virginia, and Washington were doing to combat their own excess of scrap tires proved helpful in developing the final set of alternatives used here. The qualitative CAM described in words how alternatives satisfied each specific criterion. Careful study of social/environmental issues, the economic environment, the political/legal environment, and the causes of California's continuing waste-tire management problem were essential to informing the qualitative CAM.

Relevant social and environmental issues included the public's increasing desire to avoid burying something that can potentially be recycled (known informally as "reduce-reuse-recycle") and the risks of fire and mosquito breeding that tire piles present. A look at where the supply of scrap tires originates, the specifics of the production of crumb rubber from scrap tires, use of scrap tires to generate electricity, and use in cement kilns was essential to comprehending how the economic environment would likely respond to the proposed alternatives. Since this report's conclusions would be subject to political scrutiny and political/legal feasibility was one of the criteria chosen, information about these elements was essential.

Finally, it would be impossible to offer relevant waste tire management alternatives if the underlying causes of the policy problem are not well understood. For this specific issue, the variables deemed relevant to causation included (1) costs for "tire jockeys," who transport scrap tires from retail establishments to final destination, (2) "tipping fees" paid scrap tire jockeys to dump in California's landfills, (3) legislation restricting landfill disposal, (4) technologic limitation in scrap tire processing; (5) public perception on burning scrap tires for fuel and, (6) reasons offered for lack of demand for products using crumb rubber.

Table 11.4 offers the first row of the qualitative CAM contained in the full report provided to the CIWMB. Recall that a CAM contains the possible alternatives to dealing with the stated policy problem in the first column of the matrix and the criteria used to evaluate the alternatives in the first row. Each cell in a qualitative CAM, thus, contains a brief written description of how the analyst evaluated this specific alternative in regard to a specific criterion. The body of the full analysis contained the details as to the derivation of this summary. This process necessarily involves the information gathering and processing just discussed and feedback gathered from the client and stakeholders affected by a specific alternative.

Table 11.5 contains the full quantitative CAM provided to the CIWMB. This CAM substitutes numerical ratings from a Likert scale to indicate the analyst's determination of how well an alternative satisfies each criterion. This is somewhat of a subjective assessment that the analyst does in consultation with the client based upon the information provided in the same cell of the qualitative CAM. In each cell in the quantitative CAM, the first row contains this "Rating," while, the second row shows the relative "Weight" assigned to this criterion. The third row in each cell equals the respective rating multiplied by the weight, or the "Total." The derivation of a "Total Score" for each alternative in the final column in Table 11.5 stems from a horizontal summation of Totals in a row. These Total Scores are dependent on both the Likert scores assigned to how well an alternative satisfies a criterion and how a criterion is weighted relative to others. When the analysts' reasoning is present in qualitative and quantitative CAMs, the transparency of how the findings were derived becomes this method's greatest asset.

Communicating and Using Results

An 81-page report available at the CalRecycle's website on *An Analysis of Subsidies and Other Options to Expand the Productive End Use of Scrap Tires on Tires in California* fully describes this analysis (Wassmer, 2002). Professor Wassmer (2003) also published an article, "Changing Tires," for recycling practitioners in the September 2003 edition of the journal *Resource Recycling.* Additionally, while in the process of conducting this analysis, he presented the policy analysis method and preliminary results to participants at two briefing sessions held at the California Environmental Protection Agency in fall 2001 and at the Western Tire Recycling Conference in March 2002. In August 2001, as part of a regularly scheduled CIWMB meeting, Professor Wassmer and his student analysts offered a verbal presentation on final recommendations to board members and interested stakeholders.

Reporting Results

The final report to the CIWMB contained seven sections, whose titles serve to summarize the methods and findings of this policy analysis:

- Waste Tires in California

  - California's Recent Experience
  - Other States' Programs

- Environment Surrounding California's Waste Tire Management

  - Social and Environment Issues
  - Economic Environment
  - Political Environment

- Waste Tire Management Alternatives

  - Causes of the Continuing Waste Tire Management Problem
  - Variables Inherent in Alternatives

- Criteria for Evaluating Alternatives

  - Evaluative and Practical Criteria
  - Methodology

- Analysis of Policy Alternatives

  - Discussion of Policy Objective
  - Analysis of Outcomes in Terms of Criteria

- Recommendations

  - Confronting the Tradeoffs of Various Policy Alternatives
  - Recommendations

- Summary from Public Policy Workshop

Furthermore, as is generally advisable when preparing a long policy report that most are unlikely to read in its entirety, the final report was distilled into a three-page executive summary that offered background on the genesis of the analysis, a review of the report's methods, and its four recommendations.

Selected Findings

Many of the findings of this policy analysis resulted from the qualitative and quantitative CAMs already described. But, as asked in step six of an eight-step path to policy analysis, the information contained in these CAMs allowed the analyst to clearly confront the tradeoffs regarding the satisfaction of the various criteria when one policy alternative was chosen over another.

The increased regulation of landfills provides a potentially efficient solution to the problem of scrap tires deposited there at a very low cost to the state tire fund. The only anticipated monetary cost would be for the administrative burden of gaining support for and enforcing the proposed reduction in tire chip size before depositing in the ground.

A per-tire subsidy strategy of $0.17 to waste tire processors was determined to represent an effective strategy to support recycling and/or diversion industries and received a "somewhat strong" rating on efficiency. By directly subsidizing the production costs of tire processors that hold a contract for the purchase of processed material, processors would lower tipping fees and successfully motivate the diversion of tires currently going to landfills. The major disadvantage of a reimbursement program like this is its cost. Moving to this policy would require the payment of per-tire subsidies on all qualified California tires recycled or diverted in the market. Furthermore, there would be large administration costs involved with starting the program and administrating/policing it once in place.

Per-tire subsidies to the purchasers of products that contain scrap tire content represent the only alternative that targets the demand side of the market. Since this directly lowers the manufacturing cost of these products and the price charged for them, it would increase the quantity of products containing scrap tires that consumers purchase. Getting these products into the hands of consumers has the effect of raising their scale of production and increasing consumer taste for continued use of them. If this were to occur at a sufficient level, the continued purchase of these products would be sustainable even after the subsidy goes away.

Government grants for the purchase of waste tire processing equipment offer a tool that the CIWMB could use to lower the cost of processing tires into recyclable components. In turn, lower production costs would allow waste tire processors to expand current operations and ultimately use additional waste tires that had gone to piles or landfills. The targeted and limited nature of such programs makes them inherently less risky than the per-subsidy proposals just discussed and perhaps more politically attractive.

A per-mile, per-tire subsidy for in-state transportation of scrap tires received the lowest overall score in this study's quantitative CAM. Though ranked "moderate" in its expectation of being able to divert scrap tires away from landfills at a reasonable cost, it fared poorly in terms of sustainability, political acceptability, and administration. In short, the team's analysis indicated that the costs of this program were likely to be greater than the benefits.

An information campaign designed to provide accurate and up-to-date information on tire-derived fuel and rubberized asphalt could promote the greater purchase of products that contain scrap tires by touting their relative benefits. In addition, this campaign could help advance the board's current pursuit of centers to disseminate information on technological advances that make the processing of tires easier and hence less expensive for private firms. The "somewhat strong" ratings assigned for the criteria of equity, political/legal feasibility, and administration/improvability indicates that such a program has much to offer. The reason it did not emerge as the first choice was the "somewhat weak" rating assigned in terms of efficiency.

Recommendations

The final report offered the CIWMB four recommendations.

Recommendation 1: Per-tire reimbursement programs provide an effective mechanism for increasing the number of waste tires used in recycling processes. Understanding the fact that the board had already made great strides in increasing the number of tires recycled or diverted in California and that the marginal difficulty of recycling/diverting each additional tire rises as more tires have been recycled, the team recommended "that the CIWMB begin some form of a per-tire reimbursement program." The report suggested either (1) a $0.17-per-tire subsidy paid at the processor level or (2) a subsidy of $0.10 per tire for tire-derived fuel (TDF) and $0.50 per tire for content in end-use products.

Recommendation 2: Requiring the processing of scrap tires to a 2.5-inch chip before deposit into a California landfill would offer an effective disincentive to landfill disposal. Such a policy could contribute to solving the remainder of California's waste tire problem once alternative-use markets were stable and sufficiently developed to absorb the new scrap tire flows it would create. However, due to the risks of implementing such a regulatory change before these scrap tire markets have matured, the team recommended that "further tire chip regulation of landfills not be implemented as part of the CIWMB's immediate tire waste management strategy."

Recommendation 3: Given the favorable assessment that subsidizing the capital purchases made by waste tire processors received in our CAM, the team recommended "the CIWMB continue the funding of capital subsidies at $2 million annually." With a maximum funding level of $250,000 per grant that requires a matching expenditure by the firm receiving it, a minimum of eight grants would occur in a year. These eight grants would mean $4 million worth of new tire processing equipment comes into existence in each year the program is in place. If each of these pieces of machinery must process 250,000 tires a year to retain its grant status, this alone would result in 2 million tires being recycled.

Recommendation 4: As a fourth result, the team recommended that "CIWMB spend the remaining $1 million of its anticipated $8 million market development budget for 2002–03" *on information campaigns.* In the interest of equity and to increase the political feasibility for adopting this recommendation, we suggest the equal division of money spent on information campaigns between distributing accurate information on the further use of TDF, the further use of crumb rubber in general, and the further use of rubberized asphalt.

Lessons for Policy Research

The primary lesson from this case study is that it is possible to use a rational form of policy analysis to address a policy challenge faced by a government agency when the challenge is stated clearly, alternatives to dealing with the challenge are offered, and criteria to assess the relative desirability of these alternatives is employed. Variations on the techniques offered in this case study are widely taught in public policy and public administration programs but, from all appearances, are still not used to the extent that could prove helpful to the formulation of more effective public policies.

Given the current policy-making climate characterized by extreme divides between political parties and ideologies on what constitutes the "best" way to solve pressing public policy concerns that now go unresolved (e.g., immigration, climate change, gun violence, income inequality, etc.), the methods described here may offer a way to bring greater rationality to the process. Specifying a qualitative and quantitative CAM during an eight-step approach to policy analysis clearly illustrates how the analysts reached a conclusion on what policy intervention to choose for a given problem.

Legislators from both major political parties commonly disagree on the best alternative to solving a public policy problem. Instead of just attributing this unreconciled difference to ideology and thus the impossibility of compromise, the use of the approaches detailed here would force clear thinking and a transparent explanation on why each party values a given alternative. Perhaps such a rational approach could open the possibility of greater compromise/agreement among the parties than is currently observed at all levels of government. Such are the dreams of a policy professor!

Focus on Research Methods

CAM Analysis

This case applied an eight-step analysis process (Bardach and Patashnik, 2016) and the author's interpretation of CAM as suggested in Munger (2000, pp. 6–14). Rational policy analysis must begin with appropriate definition of the public policy problem under consideration (step 1). A common pitfall at this step is putting a "solution" into the problem statement. For instance, saying that California puts too many tires into landfills because there are no per-tire incentives to encourage tire recycling assumes the solution. In fact, this is just one policy alternative that may offer a solution to the problem. The second step in the eight-step path is to assemble appropriate evidence on the magnitude of the problem, alternative solutions previously tried to solve the problem, and any literature on the efficacy of these solutions. The third step is to write down the chosen alternative policy options that may solve or mitigate the problem. Bardach and Patashnik offer an informative list of "things governments do" (2016, pp. 155–164) in the forms of taxes, regulation, subsidies, service provision, agency budgets, information, private rights, framework of economic activity, education, financing, and bureaucratic/political reforms as things to consider when brainstorming such alternatives.

Since the ultimate goal is choosing one of these alternatives, the fourth step is the selection of specific criteria by which to evaluate the desirability of the alternatives. With few exceptions, these criteria usually include measures of how well the alternative solves the policy problem, the direct and indirect costs of the various alternatives, and how "fair" the alternatives are to those affected by them. Other criteria may account for desirable characteristics of a policy alternative like sustainability, legality, political acceptability, and improvability. The fifth step is perhaps the most challenging: projecting outcomes expected if each policy alternative were implemented. Bardach and Patashnik emphasize being realistic in these projections, to not assume success without substantial evidence, to mention undesirable side effects, and to employ "sensitivity analysis" that alters underlying assumptions and demonstrates how this changes a projection. Step six is to describe tradeoffs between the selected criteria when one or another policy alternative is chosen.

Perhaps not surprisingly, Bardach and Patashnik's seventh step is to make a decision of what policy alternative(s) to choose. However, in doing so, be wary of what economists call the "$10 on the sidewalk test": if your chosen alternative is so outstanding, why has it not been previously picked up (as the bill lying on the sidewalk)? Once an informed decision is made on the most desirable policy alternative, the concluding eighth step is to tell the story of how it came to be in a way those policy makers (and "Grandma Bessie" or an "NYC cab driver") easily comprehend.

In Bardach's 2016 (fifth) edition of the book that describes his eight-step approach to policy analysis (that for the first time includes coauthor Patashnik), he includes the possibility of constructing an "outcomes matrix" as part of step five's task of projecting the outcomes. The policy analysis described here and completed in 2002 uses a variant of this method described by Munger (2000) as a criteria alternative matrix (CAM) analysis. Table 11.5 offers the basic layout necessary to construct a CAM analysis. Notice that the first row in the matrix lists the five criteria used to evaluate five alternatives offered to solve the stated policy problem. The CAM in Table 11.5 is the quantitative take on this method, which is only possible after a qualitative approach to how well each alternative satisfies each of the criteria. Table 11.4 is an example of what the second row in Table 11.5's quantitative CAM would look like if instead it were in qualitative form.

Returning to Table 11.5, it is possible to transform a fully completed qualitative CAM into its quantitative form by first creating a Likert scale that assigns a value of 1 (for very weak) through 5 (for very strong) for how well an alternative satisfies a criterion. Assigning a quantitative value to each cell is different from what both Munger (2000, p. 12) and Bardach and Patashnik (2016, p. 63) suggest. They allow qualitative outcomes to remain in each CAM cell, and hence a final quantitative final score (as in the last column of Table 11.5) is not possible. This innovation was developed as a means of facilitating comparison for this study. Table 11.3 offers an example of such a Likert-type assignment. In addition to such a Likert scale, a quantitative CAM entails the assignment of relative weights (as in Table 11.2) to each criterion as it pertains to what are the important characteristics of a desirable policy outcome. The analyst chooses these weights in consultation with the client, and a chosen set of weights that add up to 100 percent is no better than another.

Finally, it is possible to calculate a total score for each alternative in a quantitative CAM (see last column in Table 11.5) that is the sum of each Likert rating multiplied by its weight and summed horizontally in the table across all criteria for a given alternative. Here you can see that Alternative II dominates with a 3.35, but Alternatives IV and III are not far behind with respective values of 3.25 and 3.20. Does this mean that Alternative II is definitely the "best" policy alternative to choose to attack the given policy problem? Absolutely not! What it does say, very plainly, is that if you agree with (1) the written arguments offered in the qualitative CAM, (2) Likert scale definitions offered, (3) criterion weights chosen, and (4) the analyst's assignment of Likert values to how well each alternative satisfies each criterion, then Alternative II is the rational choice of what is the best policy to pursue. However, if you disagree with this finding, then you must go back and disagree with one of the assumptions/assignments that went into making it. For instance, changing the Likert scale ratings given how well an alternative satisfies a criterion and/or changing the weights assigned each criterion can change the preferred alternative.

Acronyms and Jargon

CAM—The criteria alternative matrix approach to rational analysis of policy alternatives and choices. This is a widely known application of rational analysis.

CIWMB—The California Integrated Waste Management Board, the agency that commissioned the scrap tire study.

Externalities—A term from economics that means an effect of a commercial or industrial activity that is not reflected in the price but affects others not involved in the transaction. They can be positive (e.g., one farmer's bees pollinating another's trees), but policy usually concerns negative externalities (e.g., pollution, health risks).

Likert Scale—Technically a measurement technique that creates a single rating based on collective responses to multiple items with the same response patterns (e.g., 1 = strongly disagree to 5 = strongly agree). It is also commonly used to describe judgmental ranking of observed properties on an ordinal set of categories.

Discussion Questions

1. How does the CAM analysis help policy makers come to better policy decisions? What do you think would be the most important steps in the eight-step process? Why?

2. How did Professor Wassmer modify the CAM analysis? How did this modification improve the process? In what ways could it possibly weaken the process?

12 Keys to Success for Transit Tax Initiatives

Repeated Research for Policy Learning

Peter J. Haas with Katharine Estrada

Introduction

This project is not a single study. It is a policy-learning program consisting of a series of studies that were completed and published during the years 2000, 2001, and 2012. The studies produced a line of policy research that was revisited, expanded, and summarized for continued information to policy makers over an 11-year period. These studies were conducted in an unusual policy research setting dedicated to providing useful information to produce useful knowledge in a particular policy area. In this environment, the studies could be conducted to produce information for the benefit of multiple stakeholders in this policy area rather than being tied to a single, identifiable client.

This line of research did not result in a clear set of policy or program recommendations. It developed information on factors related to desired outcomes across diverse communities. This information was purposely designed to identify factors that were consistently associated with initiative success in a variety of community settings at different points in time. Ultimately, this broadly relevant information proved useful to decision makers for public transportation agencies, who could apply lessons to tax initiative efforts in their own communities. To produce this applicable information, researchers responsible for this iterative study process combined elements of exploratory, descriptive, and effectiveness information problems in a practical way. Though both quantitative and qualitative data and analyses were used in the study, the case illustrates the potential advantages of a more qualitative approach for providing information useful to experienced decision makers in a common professional community.

The Policy Problem

For decades, financing of public transit agencies by states and the federal government has been in decline. The federal government supplied more than 40% of the funding for mass transit in the 1970s, but federal coverage reduced to just 15% by the 1990s (Hess and Lombardi, 2005). In California, for example, federal funding accounted for just 6% of operating funds for local transit agencies by 1991 (Taylor, 1991). Although state governments began to pick up more of the funding responsibility, the effects of state and local tax limitation movement of the 1970s and 1980s and the limits of state government finances generally meant that, increasingly, local transit agencies needed to raise more of their own funds (Goldman and Wachs, 2003).

However, localities and their associated transit agencies are generally unable to simply unilaterally increase their own limited tax revenues in order to provide transit services. One increasingly popular approach has been for local governments to use local-option sales tax increase initiatives, which require voter approval. This approach has proved challenging. At the time that the research in this case was initiated, however, only about half of the tax increases submitted for local voter approval were successful. Local transit agencies and their supporters were pouring effort and resources into unsuccessful measures.

Generally, local governments, transit agencies, and others involved in the management and funding of local transit services needed to know how to be more successful at passing this kind of tax increase legislation in local elections. The research described in this case was intended to help such actors have a clearer picture of how to successfully structure and campaign for tax increase proposals.

Initiation of the Policy Research

The research revisited in this case was prepared by staff of the Mineta Transportation Institute (MTI), housed at San Jose State University (SJSU) in California. MTI is a federal- and state-funded university transportation center (UTC) charged with producing applied research regarding surface transportation. UTCs were created by an act of Congress (the Intermodal Surface Transportation Efficiency Act of 1991) and exist in nearly every state in the US. Each UTC has a different policy focus as well as different models for initiating policy research. The Mineta Institute actively solicits raw ideas for research proposals from public transportation agencies and allied public transportation professionals on an ongoing basis. Ideas with most potential benefit to public transportation needs are identified, further developed, and ultimately selected for completion by a committee of SJSU faculty and the Research Associates Policy Oversight Committee (RAPOC), along with direction from the MTI executive staff. After this selection and refinement process, projects are actually completed by MTI Research Associates, whose work is reviewed by MTI executive staff and RAPOC, as well as by a blind peer-review process. Thus the research serves a broader audience than the needs of a specific client, as is perhaps more often the case.

Thus, the policy research initiation process associated with MTI projects is somewhat indirect, in that potential clients do not directly enlist the policy researchers. Transportation agencies and others submit proposals for research topics, which MTI directs to teams of research associates (RAs). (RAs are approved by RAPOC and may be SJSU faculty but also consultants with a proven track record in the field of transportation.) Per MTI policy, the RA policy research teams generally do not communicate directly with the agencies that propose research projects.

In 2000, transit agencies were facing the challenge of trying to raise revenue via sales tax increases approved via citizens in the initiative process (as described in the previous section). At that time, the Valley Transportation Authority (VTA) located in the Santa Clara County and San Jose had just successfully passed a half-cent sales tax increase to enhance a variety of transportation modes, including expansion of a light-rail transit (LRT) system, increased bus service, as well as highway improvements. The campaign for "Measure A" had been led by a coalition of political and corporate interests that helped it succeed with the voting public. Therefore, officials from the state transportation agency (the California Department of Transportation, or "Caltrans") were interested in learning how such coalitions could be created and sustained in other communities across the state and beyond. MTI accepted this general idea for funded research and selected a research team with appropriate background and skills.

Upon beginning the project, the research team soon realized that the topic of "how to create successful coalitions in support of transit tax initiatives" was problematic. First, it was a vague charge, with the outcome of the proposed research apparently lacking connections to specific decisions and decision making. Second, it is difficult to define exactly what a successful coalition is or what its precise role in increasing success of transit tax outcomes is expected to be. Third, the nature of such coalitions will surely be different across communities, perhaps significantly so. The VTA success in the Silicon Valley, for example, might not translate well to other areas. Finally, there was no clear path to discovering how a successful coalition was created, given the likely importance of gradual historic and interpersonal patterns in shaping support for transit-oriented taxes.

Given the challenges of the initial approach, the research team decided to alter the focus from coalitions to identifying specific factors associated with successful *and* unsuccessful tax initiative campaigns. This moved the research from describing successful coalitions to more specific exploration of more specific but varied components of tax initiative campaigns that might be associated with success. The inclusion of *unsuccessful* campaigns would provide a post hoc counterfactual that would allow comparisons to identify the difference between the pattern of campaign characteristics in successful campaigns with those in unsuccessful campaigns. The basic idea was that if actionable factors associated with campaigns could be identified, it would be more likely that other communities could benefit from the research.

Objectives

The primary objective for the research thus evolved toward the objective of identifying specific, hopefully actionable components (or "factors") that would help those hoping to enact citizen tax initiatives for transit-related transportation projects wage successful campaigns. Additionally, in the first two iterations, the researchers hoped to provide more descriptive information about how such campaigns used messaging to create successful campaigns. After reviewing the available research in this area, the research team settled on identifying four sorts of possible impact on the outcome of transportation tax initiatives:

- **The transportation environment.** For example, how serious a problem is traffic congestion? How successful is the local transit agency perceived to be?
- **The transportation proposal that the tax would fund.** For example, does it include improvements or expansion of multiple modes, such as highways as well as transit services?
- **The political environment.** For example, how much funding do supporters have for the campaign? Is there any organized opposition group?
- **The campaign message.** How did the supporters and opposition frame the need for the tax (or lack thereof)?

However, these areas of concern were not selected entirely in advance of field research. Much of what would become the more specific foci of the study was learned as the team visited specific campaign communities and looked for themes and patterns. Moreover, the additional iterations of the research gave team members additional flexibility, as well as a certain amount of experience with what seemed to be the most appropriate avenues of emphasis.

Notably, the team did *not* set out with the goal of creating specific recommendations, on the assumption that campaign environments are so idiosyncratic that it might be impossible to recommend any particular action for all possible scenarios. The team tried to focus campaign elements that tended to exist in nearly all campaigns and those that might potentially be actionable, even if not in every possible situation. To make the information more useful, the team wanted to identify general conditions or strategies that showed evidence of widespread utility across different campaign settings, provide some information on different specific activities these general concepts might include in different cases, and thereby give local decision makers ideas they could consider for their particular circumstances.

Challenges

Numerous challenges confronted the research team. At the time of the initial study (2000), little was known about transportation tax initiatives. The research objective was, at best, quite general and open-ended. The team lacked a specific decision maker to help focus the research as well as a specific decision to work toward. Prior research relevant to transportation tax initiatives was spotty at best—geared more toward scholarly interests and not specifically focused on transportation and transit. The team needed to develop research that was both meaningful and practical for a variety of decision makers, with limited funding and other resources.

The Decision Context

This policy research situation is characterized by an extremely generalized group of decision makers, as well as a nonspecific decision-making situation, providing a significant challenge for the policy research team to provide useful information.

Institutional Context

Generally, transportation tax initiatives involve a complicated group of stakeholders and decision makers. In most instances, the funds raised by such initiatives are on behalf of a local transportation agency, such as—in San Jose—the Valley Transportation Authority. Typically, such transportation agencies fulfill a number of responsibilities, including building, operating, and maintaining transit systems, building and maintaining streets, roads, and highways, and acting as congestion management agencies (in California), among others. At the same time, agencies are prohibited by law from campaigning directly for taxes that would directly benefit them and support their services. In such instances, elected officials frequently must assume the responsibility for proposing and campaigning directly on behalf of transportation tax initiatives. The agencies may usually engage in "public education" activities that demonstrate how the tax increases will be used. For example, a 2016 campaign for a transportation tax increase in Sacramento County in California includes mailers from the transit agency. These mailers include information on a major highway development to ease congestion, light-rail extensions to the airport and other destinations, bikeway improvements, and bus infrastructure improvements. These specifics let voters know what they would be buying. However, the agencies cannot advocate directly in favor of such plans or the tax increases associated with them.

Additionally, local elected officials frequently work with other concerned groups—most typically local business interests and/or organizations that represent them, transit rider and support organizations, and other supporters to develop a campaign plan. However, each detail of the institutional involvement with transportation tax initiatives might vary significantly from community to community, in alignment with local law and political culture.

The Policy Cycle

Transportation tax initiatives can address various stages of the policy cycle. Some of the plans associated with these initiatives might merely involve raising funds to continue ongoing transportation services and projects, whereas others might provide critical funding for major new transit system components. In the case of the research reviewed here, most of the elections selected for analysis—by design—involved funding for either new transit rail projects or significant additions to transit rail systems. As such, most of the research described here was addressing policy in the initiation context, although elements of other parts of the policy cycle might be included. The high cost of capital improvements such as building new rail extensions makes it particularly difficult for localities to obtain funding for new transportation projects.

Clients and Stakeholders

As stated earlier, the creation and enactment of transportation tax initiatives frequently entails multiple decision makers and potential clients. As noted earlier, the research projects that constitute this study were not executed on behalf of specific clients. However, the research was designed to assist decision makers from transit systems and their allies, who collectively represent primary and key stakeholders concerning transit funding. These included:

- Transportation and/or transit agency managers and directors
- Local elected officials
- Alliances of transit users and other advocates
- Business community groups, such as chambers of commerce and other potential advocates of enhanced transportation systems
- Campaign consultants and consulting firms

Although such stakeholders are typically active in the transportation tax policy process, the actual participation with and/or support for specific initiatives and their associated transportation plans can vary significantly in the context of specific communities and transportation tax proposals. This implied that the research team could not assume a particular point of view from any specific stakeholder or group of stakeholders.

Research Design and Implementation

The research team faced a daunting task. How could it generate useful information in such a broad context? In theory, an almost unlimited number of factors might influence the outcome of transit tax initiative elections. Some of these could readily be identified and measured, such as demographic and socioeconomic factors, yet others were likely to be much vaguer and less quantifiable. For example, the amount of support a tax increase proposal receives from the local business community might theoretically be very important in affecting its success, yet documenting, measuring, and somehow modeling the effectiveness of that support is quite problematic. The research team needed a strategy that could capture different kinds of data in a potentially useful way.

Information Needs

Generally, the research team sought to generate information that would be useful for decision makers involved in creating and successfully enacting transportation tax initiatives. From the standpoint of the typology of research problems discussed in Chapter 4, the team was primarily addressing a causal information problem. They were seeking to identify what specific factors, attributes, and other characteristics of a transit tax campaign seem to be the most related to passage. Ideally, the team would be identifying actionable items that supporters of transportation tax initiatives could apply to their localities. Additionally, the research team thought it would be useful to understand how marketing messages might affect election outcomes.

Since there was little prior knowledge in this area, a great deal of descriptive information was likely to be useful. As stated earlier, some factors associated with successful outcomes might be specific and quantifiable, but many others seemed likely to be more qualitative and less tangible. "Marketing messages" imply an entire range of specific and more general themes, ideas as well as more specific slogans. Trying to explain how a specific tax proposal campaign succeeded might require description of several, if not many idiosyncratic circumstances, characteristics, and so forth. So the team likely could not rely upon quantitative analysis alone.

Design and Methods (2000 Study)

After much discussion and deliberation over research alternatives, the research team decided upon a two-pronged approach for the first (2000) study: (1) a quantitative analysis of the possible impact of primarily demographic and socioeconomic variables on a national sample of actual transit tax votes and (2) a series of case studies from selected tax initiatives that explored the potential role of more qualitative, idiosyncratic variables, identified in the research and referred to hereafter primarily as "factors." As stated in the initial research report (2000, p. 4): "The purpose of this report is to use both approaches, statistical analysis of community-level characteristics and more qualitatively focused case studies, to explore what determines the success of local transportation-related tax measures."

For the quantitative component, the MTI team compiled two datasets for which voting outcome data were available. The nationwide sample included 57 city and county transit tax initiatives between 1990 and 1999, a second sample included 63 California county transportation tax elections since 1980. Both data sets were analyzed with very similar results. We will focus our discussion on the national sample because results would presumably be more generalizable to a broader (national) audience.

Based upon the predictors that were identified in previous research, eight primarily demographic variables were selected for the analysis: (1) percentage of elderly population (coded as "ELDERLY"), (2) income (INCOME), (3) existing tax burden (TAXBURDEN), (4) reliance on automobiles (AUTO), (5) duration of average commute by automobile (TRAVELTIME), (6) population (POPULATION), (7) rate of population growth (POPCHANGE), and (8) number of transportation modes included in tax proposal (BENEFITS). These variables were analyzed in a statistical regression model that provided an estimate of, on average, how much difference each variable made in the tax initiative voting outcome (% yes). The regression technique gives two pieces of information of particular interest to this analysis. First, how much of the percentage difference between yes and no could be related to these demographic conditions of the community? Second, which variables were more important for making this difference?

For the qualitative case study analysis, each of the cases included in the study had an estimated cost of at least $1 billion and included a passenger rail component. This placed emphasis on the biggest and perhaps most challenging initiatives. In addition, as developing a systematic understanding of the impact of marketing campaigns used by both proponents and opponents was an important goal, cases were selected in which opponents or proponents actually used such campaigns. Second, a significant amount of information was collected for each case. On-site interviews with a number of people representing a variety of perspectives were conducted. In addition to these interviews, relevant studies were examined, as were newspaper articles and editorials. Analysis of post-election survey data was conducted in both of the unsuccessful cases, and these results also provided important insights.

Additionally, the research team sought to collect and analyze campaign materials that reflected the "messaging" component of each campaign.

Ultimately, this proved to be difficult and not very helpful to the task facing the study. First, it was difficult to identify all or even a useful sample of the campaign messaging materials. Some campaigns used TV and radio spots, which were not readily available; even finding print media ads and mailings was not necessarily straightforward. Second, trying to somehow characterize the campaign message of each campaign proved evasive—campaigns tended to use more than one message, and it would be problematic at best to determine which was the most effective. So this avenue proved a dead end for the team in terms of generating useful results; although the team's report did discuss individual efforts, no general conclusions about campaign messaging were ultimately delivered.

Due to resource constraints, only four communities with recent transportation tax measure elections could be selected. Resource constraints precluded a random sampling approach; instead, sites were selected with a "purposive sampling" strategy (Putt and Springer, 1989). Purposive sampling is used to develop a list of cases that will generate useful qualitative insights by means of cases that share characteristics of interest to the researcher. In this case, sites were selected purposively based on the following criteria:

1. **Successes and failures.** Two of the cases involved measures that passed, and two concern those that failed.
2. **Range of transportation proposals.** The cases represented a fairly wide range in both the cost of the transportation proposal and the mix of highway to transit improvements. At the same time, the cost of each proposal was greater than $900 million and each proposal had a significant passenger rail component.
3. **California representation.** In recognition of MTI's California clientele base, and because of the special circumstances involved with passing tax initiatives in California (particularly the supermajority requirement for most earmarked tax increases), two cases were drawn from the "Golden State."
4. **Jurisdiction variety.** The cases represent a variety of jurisdictions and settings in which to investigate the campaign process, including both intensely urban and more rural communities as well as counties and regional jurisdictions.
5. **Formal marketing and communications efforts by proponents.** Proponents spent at least $400,000 during the campaign. The cases represent some range in opponents' campaign efforts. Organized opposition existed in three of the four cases.

The case study site visits consisted primarily of the following activities:

1. On-site visits and telephone interviews with key officials and individuals, including sponsors and opponents of transportation tax measures, campaign consultants and staff, members of local business and

environmental communities, transit advocates and other interested groups, and elected officials and other individuals with insight into the campaign process.
2. Review of relevant documents and other documentation of outcomes associated with transit coalitions, including newspaper coverage.
3. Creation of an overview of community demographics, fiscal and economic background, and relevant historical and political background; identification of major transportation challenges and problems; description of strategies, techniques, approaches, and the like, that were used to achieve (or failed to achieve) public support; and evaluation of effectiveness of each effort.

Selected Findings: 2000 Study

The results of the quantitative analysis of the impact of demographic and socioeconomic variables on the outcome of transportation tax voting produced what researchers call a "flat" result. This simply means that none of the variables in the regression equation actually showed any substantial influence on the voter outcome as it was measured. Collectively, the regression model explained less than 8% of the variation in votes for transit taxes, indicating that taken as a group, these variables did not say much about what drives initiative results.

Table 12.1 summarizes the results of the analysis for each variable. To provide a "rule of thumb" indication of whether each variable showed an independent influence once the others were considered, the researchers used statistical significance at the .05 level as a cut point. Only two variables showed the expected relation with voter support: (1) the percentage elderly in a community and (2) the number of modes funded in the tax proposal. However, the latter variable was *negatively* associated with votes for transit taxes, which ran counter to the relationship the team expected. Most importantly, as a whole, the results of the quantitative

Table 12.1 Summary of Results of Regression Analysis of Tax Election Outcomes, 1990–1999 (national data)

Variable	Predicted Effect	Observed Effect
Elderly	Negative	Negative
Income	Negative	None
Taxburden	Negative	None
Auto	Negative	None
Housing	Negative	None
Traveltime	Positive	None
Population	Positive	None
Popchange	Positive	None
Benefits	Positive	Negative
$n = 57$		

analysis did not supply actionable information for communities considering transit tax measures. Knowing that communities with more elderly residents were less likely to support these projects raised interesting questions about why, and the negative effect of multimodal initiatives raised questions about what was assumed to be an effective strategy. Neither provided directly actionable information.

Data collected from the four case studies, however, did provide more potentially useful findings. The case studies covered the following elections and outcomes: (1) Santa Clara County: passage of Measures A & B (1996), (2) Sonoma County: defeat of funding for highway widening and rail (1998), (3) Seattle: funding for regional public transit (1996), and (4) Denver Metropolitan Region: defeat of "guide the ride" (1997). Using the methods described earlier, the case studies provided rich contextual information based primarily on interviews with principal participants and informed observers of each campaign. Each study consisted of detailed information in the following topics the researchers identified as relevant to their purpose: (1) background about the transit agency involved in the ballot initiative, (2) background about the existing transportation system and public perceptions concerning it, (3) the specifics of the transportation package associated with the initiative and the process that was used to formulate it, (4) a description of the campaign strategy used by supporters and opponents (including use of media with respect to creating a "message" for prospective voters). Data were primarily presented in the form of a narrative that linked specific campaign characteristics and actions to the outcomes of elections, as communicated by interviewees and, in some cases, verified with existing polling data.

Analysis of the information collected from the case studies was used to support conclusions about what seemed to work (and not work) in transportation tax campaigns. Notable recommendations based on those findings included the following:

- A combination of highway and transit improvements should be included in a transportation package whenever it is possible to do so.
- A budget cap should be identified to determine the magnitude of the transportation package.
- Since the campaigns usually are of short duration, rapid responses to opposition messages are required. Contingency planning is needed to provide effective rapid responses.
- Because of the complexity involved in developing appropriate contingency plans, planning should begin about one year prior to the election.

Selected Findings: 2001 Study

Although these findings seemed potentially useful, an obvious and significant limitation of this study was the small number of cases that could be included. The study included detail about how specific factors influence the results of transportation tax measures in specific contexts, which was potentially useful to decision makers. However, the robustness of these findings across contexts was unclear given the small number of cases. Given the promising results, MTI opted to launch a second study (2001) that expanded the case study approach to include 11 elections. Once again, in-depth interviews with knowledgeable individuals were used to obtain information about the process used to determine the transportation package, the nature of the package, and the communications campaigns used by both proponents and opponents. As in the prior study, each of the ballot measures had a substantial rail transit component. Four of the communities had two similar ballot measures within a three-year interval, with substantially different results between the two measures. Two recent measures in these communities allowed systematic comparisons, facilitating an understanding of how the transportation package and the process used to determine it, as well as how the communications campaigns used by proponents and opponents, might influence the outcomes of these measures.

The experience the team had compiled on the earlier study enabled a more focused approach in the case study/site visits. Additionally, the second study dropped systematic study of community demographic and socioeconomic characteristics. The conclusion from the first study was that campaign and proposal characteristics appear to have more impact on voting behavior than do community characteristics. In addition, because the transportation package, the process used to formulate it, and the communications campaign used all are largely actionable, the team decided that focusing on the impact of these characteristics on campaign outcomes would provide more useful information to those communities developing transportation ballot measures than focusing on the impact of uncontrollable community characteristics on voting behavior. In this study, the team was able to zero in on the factors that it had found to be salient in the earlier effort. The team selected the following communities and elections:

1. Alameda County, California (approved, 2000)
2. Austin, Texas, and other smaller communities in the Capital Metro Transit District (rejected, 2000)
3. Charlotte, North Carolina, and other smaller communities in Mecklenburg County (approved, 1998)
4. Columbus, Ohio (rejected, 1999)
5. Denver, Colorado, and other smaller communities in its Regional Transportation District (approved, 1999)
6. Phoenix, Arizona (approved, 2000)
7. St. Louis County, Missouri (rejected, 1997)
8. Salt Lake, Davis, and Weber Counties, Utah (approved, 2000)
9. San Antonio, Texas (rejected, 2000)

10. Santa Clara County, California (approved, 2000)
11. Sonoma County, California (rejected, 2000)

With a larger slate of case studies, the team was able to incorporate more variation in the types of transportation projects, campaign strategies, and other characteristics.

Although the written reports include a vast amount of detail about each tax campaign. The experiences and insights gathered in the first (2000) study helped the research team focus questions and analysis on the factors listed in Table 12.2. The results listed in the table indicate whether each "factor" was clearly present or not in each community/

Table 12.2 Status of Each Case on Selected Critical Influencing Factors

	Alameda	Santa Clara County	Denver	Phoenix	Charlotte	Salt Lake City	Austin	Columbus	St. Louis	San Antonio
	Pass*	Pass	Pass	Pass	Pass	Pass	Fail	Fail	Fail	Fail
Traffic congestion "crisis"	↑	↑	↑	⇔	↑	↑	↑	↓	↓	↓
Sponsorship by business community	↑	↑	↑	↑	↑	⇔	⇔	⇔	↑	↓
Sponsorship by key elected official(s)	↑	↑	↑	↑	↑	↑	⇔	↓	↓	↓
Fundraising near $1 million	↑	↑	↑	↑	↑	⇔	↑	↓	↓	↓
Recent initiative experience	↑	↑	↑	↑	↓	↑	↓	↑	↑	↓
Support from environmental groups	↑	↑	↑	↑	⇔	↑	↑	↑	↑	↑
Multimodal proposal	↑	↑	↓	↑	↑	↑	↓	⇔	↓	↓
Highway funding	↑	↓	↑	↓	⇔	↓	↓	↓	↓	↓
Benefits distributed throughout area	↑	↑	↓	↑	↑	↑	↓	↓	↓	↓
Sunset provision of 10 years or less	↓	↓	N/A	↓	↓	↓	N/A	↑	↓	↓
Extension of existing rail system	↑	↑	↑	↓	↓	↑	↓	↓	↑	↓

	Alameda*	Santa Clara Country*	Denver	Phoenix	Charlotte	Salt Lake City	Austin	Columbus	St. Louis	San Antonio
Lack of problems with existing transit system	↑	↑	↑	↑	↑	↑	↓	↓	↓	↓
Extensive stakeholder participation in development of package	↑	↑	↑	↑	↑	↓	↓	↓	↓	↓
General election	↑	↑	↓	↓	↑	↑	↑	↓	↓	↓
Consultant with initiative campaign experience	↑	↑	↑	↑	↑	↑	↓	⇔	↓	↑
Use of combination of direct mail and television ads	↑	↑	↑	↑	↑	↑	↓	↓	↑	↓
Lack of effective opposition	↑	⇔	↑	⇔	↑	⇔	↓	↓	↓	↓
Number of negative factors	1	2	3	4	3	3	10	11	12	15

LEGEND FOR TABLE 10-1

↑	Condition existed
↓	Condition absent
⇔	Condition inconclusively present
	Anomalous condition

* Denotes required two-thirds supermajority to pass

election associated with a tax campaign victory or defeat, or if it could not be determined.

A brief explanation of the cell entries in Table 12.2: (1) an upward arrow indicates that the factor did exist or was associated with the specified location; a downward arrow indicates that the factor was not present. A horizontal double arrow is used to indicate a middle category ("factor inconclusively present") between the two extremes, realizing that many of the factors are not truly dichotomous in nature; in some instances, this was also assigned to cases where there was simply not enough information. For each factor, upward arrows are expected to correspond with passing initiatives, whereas downward arrows should correspond with failing initiatives. Note that several factors are expressed as the lack of a condition; in these instances, an upward arrow means that the case did lack the specified item, whereas downward-facing arrows signify cases that did not lack this item. This system enabled a consistent pattern of upward-facing arrows for items associated with passage and vice versa. Finally, in instances in which the existence of a factor did not correspond with the outcome of the cases, the cell is shaded. This signifies an anomaly, where the case and the specified factor did not match the anticipated pattern. (With successful cases, an anomaly exists when the factor is not present. With unsuccessful cases, an anomaly exists when the factor is present.)

For the most part, because the requisite data to assure that causal relationships between the factors existed was lacking, and so the research team had be careful about not overselling the meaning of the findings. Generally, factors were discussed as apparently important or unimportant for the passage of a transportation tax initiative among the factors chosen for analysis.

On the whole, the factors in Table 12.2 tend to fit the relationships that the research team had expected (via logic and reasoning and analysis of interview responses) would be associated with the passage or failure of each measure. In only 30 of 155 testable instances (19.4%) were the outcomes of the election in direct conflict with the "expected" existence of a factor (or lack thereof). Only two of the 17 factors resulted in more than three anomalies, and only one variable—namely whether the measure had an expiration date of 10 years or less (six anomalies)—had more than four anomalies.

Insights were suggested through examining the number of negative factors separately for the unsuccessful and for the successful cases, a number identified with each case in the last row of Table 12.2. Whereas each of the four unsuccessful cases had at least 10 negative factors, none of the six successful cases had more than three negative factors when the expiration date factor—which was found to be generally irrelevant—is excluded.

Additional consideration of the factors (and their possible interrelationships) led the research team to identify the following five factors as likely to be the most independently influential factors affecting tax election outcomes:

- Traffic congestion crisis—"the perception, real or not, that a community is facing traffic congestion of such magnitude that it is a high or very high priority for most citizens."
- Multimodal transit and/or a highway component included in or linked with transit ballot measure—"the tax initiative contains a proposal for funding of more than one mode of transit."
- Reputation of transit agency—"Some transit agencies develop a reputation for poor management (deserved or not), or have been beset

by controversy about service levels, routing decisions, empty buses, inefficient use of resources, etc."

- Degree of public involvement in planning process—"the extent to which the business community, environmental groups, citizens, and elected officials are involved in the planning process used to develop the transportation package."
- Degree of enthusiasm of business community support—"the degree to which the local business community actively supports the transportation tax increase. In most instances, this means that local business leaders play an active, if not a key role in creating and campaigning for the passage of a transportation tax initiative."

Additionally, the research team was able to pool some of the data it had collected regarding earlier elections with the more current information on cities that had conducted more than one tax election during the period of the two studies. It found that each of these cities was successful—by a significant margin in most cases—as indicated in the results reported in Table 12.3. These results, along with some richer, more qualitative insights into how each campaign adjusted its tactics, provided potentially useful information to communities that had already lost a tax initiative election.

Selected Findings: 2011 Study

Reports from the 2000 and 2001 studies were well received by the transportation professional community. They were widely read and presumably influenced tax initiative campaigns that followed it. In light of this and the amount of time that had passed since the previous (2001) study, MTI again updated study of transit tax elections a decade later. The purpose of this third study was to determine if and how findings from the earlier studies were changed. During the ensuing decade, such elections had become both more common and more successful, which perhaps

Table 12.3 Within-Community Differences in Voting Results (in communities with two ballot measures within a three-year period)

	Supporting Percentage in First Ballot Measure	*Supporting Percentage in Second Ballot Measure*	*Difference in Supporting Percentage Between Two Measures*
Alameda County	58% (1998)	81.5% (2000)	23.5 percentage points
Denver	42.2% (1997)	66% (1999)	23.8 percentage points
Phoenix	49.9% (1997)	65% (2000)	24.9 percentage points
Sonoma County	47.6% (1998)	60.2% (2000)	12.6 percentage points
Seattle	47% (1995)	56.5% (1996)	9.5 percentage points

implied that the importance of the factors identified in the earlier research could be strengthened.

Once again, a research team compiled data from a series of transportation tax initiative elections, including both successful and failed campaigns. However, for this study, only eight elections that had similar characteristics to those in the previous one (including a significant rail component) were available for study. A smaller budget for the project required that all case study information be acquired via telephone interviews rather than with on-site interviews as in the previous studies. Table 12.4 summarizes characteristics of the sites selected for the 2011 research.

The research team searched for the presence or absence of the same factors that had been explored in the previous (2002) study. A table was compiled, indicating for each community/election which factors had been present or absent and presenting the outcome associated with each. The report concluded that

> summed across all elections and factors, the results indicate that of a total of 122 valid instances of paired factors and election outcomes (i.e., those not inconclusive or ambiguous with respect to the presence of absence of a factor), 84 (or 68.9 percent) of the factors were consistent with the expected outcome of the elections. Therefore, 38 instances (31.1 percent) were inconsistent with outcome of the elections.
>
> (Haas and Estrada, 2011, p. 82)

The report also identified the trends for factors over the two studies, indicating which factors were most and least consistently associated with election outcomes. The study results suggested that, despite an overall decline in accuracy since 2001, many of the individual factors were about as accurate (i.e., within 15 percentage points) as they were in the 2001 study with respect to being associated with electoral success or failure. Several factors appeared either less or more likely to be associated with

Table 12.4 Summary of Case Study Elections, 2011 Study

Locality	State	Year	Outcome	Margin
Maricopa County	Arizona	2004	Passed	57% to 43%
Seattle	Washington	2007	Failed*	45% to 55%
Charlotte*	North Carolina	2007	Passed*	70% to 30%
Honolulu	Hawaii	2008	Passed	53% to 47%
Los Angeles**	California	2008	Passed	68% to 32%
Santa Clara County**	California	2008	Passed	67% to 33%
St. Louis County	Missouri	2008	Failed	49% to 51%
Kansas City	Missouri	2008	Failed	45% to 55%

*   unique "antirepeal" election
** California elections requiring two-thirds to pass

outcomes. However, the overall conclusion of the final study was that the patterns identified in the 2001 study were largely consistent with those observed in the replication in 2011.

Communicating and Using Results

The three studies bridge an important era in how research results are communicated, particularly with a mass audience. When the first and second studies were conducted, the primary means of sharing the results was in the form of a written report that interested parties had to order from MTI. However, as publishing on the internet became more practical and commonplace in the 2000s, the reports were made available on MTI's website. By the time the last study (2011) was completed, MTI reports were available only via download.

Each report was presented in a very similar way, and each included an introduction, a literature review, a description of the data and methods used in each study, an in-depth discussion of each case study community/ election, and a section of conclusions that included more general findings. Additionally, the authors presented the results of these studies at a series of conferences for practitioners, including those sponsored by a transit advocacy organization, the Center for Transportation Excellence. Results were also reported at an annual conference of the Transportation Research Board (TRB), and findings from the 2001 report were published by a refereed journal sponsored by the TRB, the *Transportation Research Record* (Haas and Werbel, 2002b).

Selected Recommendations

These reports did not contain explicit recommendations, although in many instances, the implications of the findings for decision makers were self-evident. For example, as the studies tended to find that communities with transit systems held in low regard by the public were less likely to be successful, supporters of a new initiative would be well advised to work on improving the image of their transit system as they worked toward earning support. Additionally, each report went to great lengths to caution readers concerning the external validity of the findings. This was not a study designed or intended to provide precise strategies that should be implemented with strict fidelity. It produced information about how often relatively general campaign strategies were associated with the desired outcome. Furthermore, and extremely important to their utility, these general strategies were described in sufficient detail to allow potential users to make more discerning judgments about whether an example applied well to their circumstances or how it might need revision. Although the reports were written primarily from the standpoint of *passing* these tax proposals, it could be that opponents could also find a basis for strategic action.

Action

As this research was not geared toward any single decision maker or specific group of decision makers, it is difficult to generalize about its impact upon the transportation policy community. It is worth noting, however, that the 2001 study was one of the most popular published by MTI (in terms of downloads between 2001 and 2010), so it was clearly read by many individuals. Even as recently as the period between 2009 and 2016, the report was downloaded more than 18,000 times. Moreover, the 2011 study was downloaded 24,660 times between its publication date of July 2011, and January 2016. As noted earlier, the authors were invited to discuss the findings at a series of conferences. Additionally, several communities enlisted members of the research team to speak to groups of decision makers that were contemplating new transit tax initiatives. News media personnel also contacted the authors several times about the implications of the research for specific upcoming elections.

Moreover, as the 2011 report noted, between 2000 and 2010, a total of 367 ballot measures were considered nationally. Such measures increasingly met with success. In 2000 and 2001, only about half of all measures were approved by voters, whereas more than three fourths of all measures since 2008 have been approved. In the 11-year period 2000–2010, an average of 71% of all transportation measures succeeded, a rate that is twice as high as that for all other types of local tax initiatives. Even in California, where a two-thirds supermajority of votes is required to pass dedicated local tax increases, most proposals have recently been accepted by voters. Although the findings from these reports cannot be positively linked to this change, there is some reason to believe that advocates of expanded transit systems have learned how to be more successful at doing so, and perhaps this research helped them do so.

Lessons for Policy Research

The research recounted in this chapter illustrates that research doesn't necessarily need to be prepared for a specific client or decision maker in order to be useful. The policy researchers in these studies worked from a more general standpoint, although the practicality or "actionability" of the findings was indeed a guiding principle. These studies provide yet another example of how quantitative results may be less useful in some instances of real-world decision making than those that embrace more contextual, qualitative data. Yet the study also demonstrates that qualitative data can fail to provide authoritative finality of some quantitative findings.

Finally, the research presented in this chapter exemplifies how a line of policy research inquiry can be revisited, expanded, and replicated. These opportunities are not always present, but policy researchers should try to identify and capitalize upon them when they are.

Focus on Research Methods

Case Study/Site Visit

The series of analyses in this chapter relies heavily on a "case study" approach. But what, exactly, is a case study? Essentially, it is the duty of the analyst to define exactly which data collection methods will comprise a case study, otherwise, the term is almost meaningless. Analysts need to take great care in stipulating what their "case study" research will comprise.

The appropriate design of a case study will be highly sensitive to contextual factors. In some instances, a case study might be based entirely on existing quantitative data. More frequently, perhaps, case studies will be more reliant on collection of qualitative data. When geographic dispersion comes into play, case studies may frequently involve site visits. Site visits enable the analyst to learn a great deal about the context of a program or policy. By viewing and witnessing programmatic and policy context, the analyst can provide much more grounded information.

But like the case study, a "site visit" must itself also be further made operational by the analyst. In the studies discussed in this chapter, the research team opted to primarily include interviews with a list of stakeholders and other knowledgeable observers. In the case of the former, the list of interviewees typically included transit agency spokespersons, key political figures and/or their staff, leaders of transit advocacy groups as well as transit opposition groups, and so forth. Identifying the "other knowledgeable observers" was (and generally is) more of a challenge.

In practice, the research team intuitively used its original contacts to help identify others who were knowledgeable about the tax election in question. When approaching a new site with which the analyst has relatively little familiarity, it is commonly helpful to find a "key observer" (Patton and Sawicki, 2005) who can help orient the analyst and point him or her to other useful resources. The research team was typically able to identify such knowledgeable individuals, who varied in identity from campaign consultants, journalists, and transit advocates to others from site to site. These individuals were invaluable in helping the team properly understand the context and more specific components of each case/site.

The staple activity during a typical site visit is one-to-one or small group interviews. The interviews themselves must be planned well, with a systematic interview protocol but also allow for some improvisation, depending on the direction the interview flows. Unfortunately, relatively little has been written about exactly how to structure and execute policy-oriented interviews. Much of the process is probably intuitive, and experience is perhaps the best instructor.

Acronyms and Jargon

MTI—Mineta Transportation Institute (a federally and state-funded university transportation center at San Jose State University that commissioned the research in this case)

RAPOC—Research Associates Policy Oversight Committee (group that selects and oversees research projects for the Mineta Transportation Institute at San Jose State University)

SJSU—San Jose State University

TRB—Transportation Research Board (a division of the National Research Council of the United States that advises transportation policy makers and sponsors transportation research)

Transportation tax initiative—a tax-increase proposal, generally for local sales taxes, that must be approved for local voters; generally used to fund new and existing transportation projects and improvements

VTA—Valley Transportation Authority (transportation agency for Santa Clara County, California)

Discussion Questions

1. The program reports offer little in the way of specific recommendations. Why do you think this was? Would you have made a different decision?
2. Imagine you had a lavish budget and large staff to do a similar research project. What improvements would you make to the methods used in this case?
3. What threats to the internal and external validity of the findings in this research can you identify? Which is the most important with respect to possible use by decision makers in this area?
4. Do you think the quantitative component of the research design could be improved upon, such that it might yield more useful information?
5. Looking carefully at the results reported in Table 12.3, how much do you agree with the conclusion that "the patterns identified in the 2001 study were largely consistent with those observed in the replication in 2011"?

Assignments

1. Identify a recent transportation tax initiative that occurred in a community near you. How useful are the factors identified in this research to understanding and explaining the outcome?

2. Review one of the reports identified in this chapter and suggest specific recommendations to a potential sponsor of a transportation tax initiative. Defend your ideas using findings from the study you selected.
3. Identify another piece of policy research that has been repeated and/or replicated over the course of time. How much did the findings vary over time, and why?

13 High-Speed Rail Workforce Development

An Estimation Problem

Peter J. Haas with Paul D. Hernandez and Katharine Estrada

Introduction

This policy research was designed to forecast the workforce that would be required to build the first true high-speed rail (HSR) system in the United States. The project team at the Mineta Transportation Institute (MTI), described in detail in Chapter 12, faced a daunting challenge. Lack of experience with HSR meant that the project could not rely heavily on MTI past experience, and a limited budget precluded, despite hard lobbying by the project team, trips to Europe or Asia to learn from their extensive HSR experience. The MTI model meant the project lacked the potential benefits of a clear and specific client that could help guide the research. Moreover, as no true HSR system had ever been built in the US before, there was little existing data upon which to base estimates. These circumstances obliged the research team to improvise a new means of calculating future workforce needs that was accurate and descriptive of both the quantity and quality (or type) of workers needed to complete the proposed HSR project. The research proved useful to the point of directly informing the work of a newly formed task force that sought to address the need for a properly trained and educated HSR workforce. This case describes how analysts responded creatively to this need for estimation information.

The Policy Problem

In November of 2008, California voters approved ballot Proposition 1A, which created a bond measure that allocates funds to the California High-Speed Rail Authority (CHSRA) to build an HSR system in the state. The law authorized $9.95 billion via state general obligation bonds to the CSHRA, which has also received federal matching funds to help finance the project. A business plan was released in 2008 to plan for the construction and operation of the system, which would connect Los Angeles and San Francisco (along with several other cities along the way) with high-speed rail service. The plan provided detailed information about project costs and benefits, proposed routes, and necessary areas of expenditure and included very specific engineering elements (California High-Speed Rail Authority, 2008).

Although jobs creation was a key selling point for the project—it had potential to provide countercyclical public works spending that would help reduce unemployment in California during the Great Recession—the CHSRA business plan had little to say about what kind of jobs the project would create and, particularly, what kinds of skills the workforce would require to complete the project. If California was going to build this ambitious rail system, it would also need to help create or enable an appropriate workforce. The research described in this chapter was intended to supply decision makers with information that could aid in this endeavor.

Initiation of the Policy Research

As discussed in the previous chapter (Chapter 12), the Mineta Transportation Institute derives research project subjects from a formal, institutional process, based in part on requests from specific transportation agencies. The CHSRA was essentially a nascent, very modestly staffed state agency at the point this research was initiated and was far busier with attempting to move the project ahead—amid concerted attempts by political opponents to thwart any progress—and less than able to deal with the general issue of workforce development. In 2010, MTI's Research Associate Project Oversight Council (RAPOC) approved the HSR–workforce question as a funded project. However, as the only state agency tasked at that time with the HSR project, the CHSRA was presumably the only specific stakeholder with direct decision-making authority in the policy arena.

The Policy Research Task

The general purpose of the study was to provide an estimate, essentially a forecast, of the workforce needs that would be generated by construction of the planned HSR system in California. Additionally, the research team identified the need for descriptive information about related, supporting questions, such as the ability of the state to train and educate a prospective HSR workforce.

Objectives

This project sought to identify the workforce development of an HSR system in California. Generally, it addressed the need for a qualified workforce in three ways: (a) qualitatively, with the goal of specifying as finely as possible the individual positions and associated skill and knowledge sets; (b) quantitatively, with the goal of estimating the number of each type of position that will be associated with various phases of the project throughout its initial lifetime; and (c) by identifying as specifically as possible the training and education needed by these individuals. Additionally, the project examined the existing capacities for supplying the kinds of qualified workers identified in the context of the California system of education. To achieve these goals, the project would need to address, among many others, the following subtasks:

- Identify and describe the sequence of the CHSR network build, which would help determine what kinds of workers were needed where and when.
- Identify the types of professionals and other workers associated with each step of the project's construction, establish their roles and responsibilities, and assess their needed skills, traits, and education.
- Identify specific types of technology that help frame activities for each position type during each sequence, identifying areas of overlapping skills and unique skills.
- Estimate approximate numbers of each type of position required during each phase (and year) of the project, adding accuracy and specificity to existing estimates.

Challenges

The primary challenge that the research team faced was a fundamental lack of existing research and knowledge on the topic, which also implied an uncertain approach to appropriate research methods and study design. As noted earlier, the U.S. has no existing truly high-speed rail. (The Acela Express system in the Northeast Corridor reaches a maximum speed of just 150 mph in a limited area of its route and averages just 82 mph between Washington, DC, and New York City.) The California system was to be a truly high-speed system, capable of speeds greater than 200 mph and built primarily on its own right-of-way (unlike most other trains in the U.S., which share track with freight and other rails systems). So there was no domestic precedent for such a technologically advanced and massive rail system. A number of European and Asian countries, of course, have gradually built large HSR systems, yet little existing literature was identified that would help inform an effort focused on the U.S.

The Decision Context

The proposed HSR system, as stated earlier, along with its obvious transportation features, was intended to generate significant numbers of jobs. The 2008 business plan stated, "Experts calculate about 160,000 jobs will be needed to construct the high-speed train, and more than 320,000 permanent jobs will result by 2030 both directly and indirectly from the system—including jobs in tourism, transportation, services and security, for example" (California High-Speed Rail Authority, 2008). However, the report did not specify (nor did other existing literature at that time) (a) what kinds of jobs would be created, (b) when the jobs would come online, (c) what kinds of skills and knowledge the large new workforce would require, nor (d) how the required workforce might be trained and educated. The CSHRA would be in a better position to allocate resources toward workforce development if it had more of this kind of information.

Institutional Context

The CSHRA consisted of nine members: five appointed by the governor, two appointed by the state Senate Committee on Rules, and two appointed by the Speaker of the Assembly, with a relatively small staff. The Authority itself was not intended to actually build the HSR system; rather, it would contract with private consulting and construction firms to complete the actual construction and other duties. Ultimately, it was foreseen through the business plan and other documents that some form of public–private partnership would complete and eventually operate the system. In the shorter term, however, the Authority was the primary decision-making entity. During the period of research (and to the present day), the Authority and the HSR proposal were under intense attack from forces of political opposition. Among the criticisms leveled at the Authority was the contention that the estimate of jobs created by the project was inaccurate and/or inflated, further amplifying the potential importance of the study.

The Policy Cycle

Given that the HSR system was still in the planning stage and the CSHRA only recently authorized to begin funding the project, this research essentially occurred during the policy initiation phase. Although a decision had clearly been made to construct the system, relatively little had been decided about the details of the project. Pursuant to the research in this case study, virtually nothing had been decided (or was known) about the workforce component of the project. Thus, some form of policy research that could help fill this gap was quite appropriate.

Clients and Stakeholders

Due to the institutional arrangements associated with the MTI (see Chapter 12), this research was not performed in the direct service of any specific client. But the obvious beneficiary or most interested party was the CSHRA—at that time the only public agency with a tangible decision-making role in the project. However, several other entities and groups were certainly potentially interested in the information addressed by the research, including (but not limited to):

1. The California Department of Transportation ("Caltrans"), which operated several rail systems in the state and whose mission was, increasingly, to manage a statewide multimodal transportation system,
2. California's higher education system, whose mission included preparing students for possible employment opportunities,
3. Labor unions in fields associated with transportation, which already operated training apprenticeships for many workers and might represent parts of the HSR workforce, and
4. Prospective contractors for construction and operation of the HSR system, including consulting firms, construction firms, rolling stock manufacturers, and the like.

Of these stakeholders, perhaps the greatest interest was shown among the higher education system, who could readily foresee some direct involvement with preparing a qualified workforce for the HSR project.

Research Design and Implementation

The research team struggled initially with finding an appropriate means to address the challenges posed by the questions it sought to answer. The most obvious approach that came to mind was to base estimates on similar projects that had been completed in Europe and Asia. However, this proved to be essentially a dead end, as existing literature (as well as efforts to extract insight from knowledgeable individuals abroad) proved unsatisfactory. Eventually, with some assistance from CHSRA staff and other experts, the team decided that the best way to estimate workforce needs would be to base the forecast on planned expenditures in specific aspects of the project. This approach came to be known as "bottom-up" estimation and is explained more thoroughly in the "Focus on Research Methods" box later in this chapter.

Information Needs

The centerpiece information for this research was a projection of the size and other characteristics of the HSR workforce, making it a good example of an estimation information problem. In contrast to merely creating a forecast, however, this study would seek to describe a future state of HSR workforce composition, including the skills and knowledge it would require. So, in some ways, this study was more complicated than merely specifying a specific number, as some estimation information need situations might reduce to. Beyond the workforce projection, considerable amounts of qualitative, primarily descriptive information were also called for, such as the technological challenges posed by HSR, the underlying engineering and construction model, the state of existing HSR-related education in California and the U.S., and other items that were supporting components necessary to frame the forecast.

Design and Methods

The MTI team carefully considered the task before it, which was heavily influenced by the lack of a base of experience. It was decided to design the project around three distinct data collection and analysis efforts: (1) identifying the impact of HSR technology on the required workforce; (2) a quantitative "bottom-up" estimation that would specify the job positions required for this new venture, and (3) identifying the capacity of existing rail education and training and increased capacity that would be necessary to meet the workforce needs of this higher level of transit technology.

Study Component One: Identifying Areas of HSR-Related Technological Demand

The first approach was a broad exploration of largely qualitative factors that likely would emerge as the result of building an advanced HSR infrastructure, focusing on specific aspects of knowledge, information, and technological need—each connected to the creation and operation of (approximately) 220-mph HSR trains. The study drew parallels to challenges faced by other nations in the construction of their HSR networks. It further provided a general assessment of the current national state of HSR-specific technological capability by comparing the United States to some foreign systems and assessed the state of HSR knowledge through discussing research and development capabilities in the United States.

Study Component Two: "Bottom-Up" Estimation

To identify the education and training impacts of building the CHSR system, a quantitative inventory of workforce needs had to be constructed. This focused on measuring the quantity of personnel/professionals needed over the planned life of the project. This was accomplished through the creation of robust statistical measurement of the types, skills, and level of education of the personnel/professionals needed to complete the design, build, operation, and maintenance (DBOM) of the planned system, focusing on the publicly announced 2009–2025 period. Existing studies relied solely on a prevailing "top-down" estimating methodology to establish detailed measurements of the direct personnel/professionals workforce characteristics.

Top-down methodology refers to the standard way policy analysts and researchers assess personnel-to-expenditure ratios in large infrastructure projects when creating estimates of the total workforce needed to complete a large project. Typically, a measure of a given ratio of job-years created per $1 billion of infrastructure spending is used to create such estimates, which are used extensively by notable transportation resources such as the American Public Transportation Association. Frequently a one-size-fits-all multiplier of approximately 20,000 jobs per billion dollars of capital expenditures is the basis for these estimates (American Public Transportation, 2009).

By contrast, the "bottom-up" method created by the research team identified estimates of the professionals/personnel needed in the design, construction management, construction build, and operations and maintenance phases, according to specified tasks and activities. This method created extremely detailed personnel estimates needed to create the CHSR infrastructure and enabled a visualization of the direct personnel needs by phase, sector, and job type over the life of the project, including peak periods of demand. The key to developing this methodological linchpin of the study was gaining access to the detailed engineering and construction plans that were developed for the CHSRA business plan. Next, the personnel estimates were linked to the education and training needs of the new HSR workforce by means of applying U.S. Department of Labor benchmarks for the specific kinds of jobs in the estimate. In sum, the bottom-up methodology provided a much richer and more useful trove of estimation information.

Study Component Three: Identifying Rail Education Capability

The first two components had established workforce needs both quantitatively and qualitatively. A third effort identified current education infrastructure surrounding HSR-related disciplines in the United States and more broadly identified the rail transportation-focused aptitude of the California education infrastructure. To what extent was HSR-relevant training and education already available, and what significant gaps existed between the workforce qualifications described in the estimation effort and current resources? Conducting systematic searches of education resources, the study identified possible areas of concern related to current levels and loci of capability. To do this, the study included comparisons with rail education in Europe, Japan, Taiwan, and Korea.

Selected Findings

Total Direct Personnel Workforce Needed for Project
(in Personnel-Years; PY)

Focusing only on direct demand for workers created by the California HSR project, the research team estimated total workforce demand at

256,092 direct jobs—expressed in personnel years (PY)—over the life of the project, for the period of 2009–2025. (Direct jobs are those associated with infrastructure investments and exclude indirect jobs that might arise from supplying goods and services to enable the direct spending. A personnel year is any equivalent of the 12 months full-time employment of one person. Thus, 12 persons employed for one month, two persons employed for six months, or any similar combination would comprise one personnel year.) The study generally used PY as the unit of measure to uniformly estimate personnel across years of the project. Figure 13.1 depicts the flow of demand for HSR jobs generated by the estimate model and includes a comparison with the totals associated with a simple top-down estimator based on expenditures.

The two estimates dovetail very closely over the life of the project, suggesting that the bottom-up estimates were generally not out of line with those projected by the top-down method. This was not really surprising, given that both estimates are based on the same amount of total expenditures in each year of the project. However, had the two differed significantly, it might have been evidence of a systematic calculation error in the bottom-up estimates. More important, the bottom-up figures provided much richer detail about the nature of required workforce that was totally unavailable from the top-down method.

The total estimate of 256,092 direct jobs (PY) was disaggregated into project phases to identify the personnel/professionals demanded during each phase of the project. The lion's share of employment (79%) would be devoted to the "build construction" phase to examine sector impacts

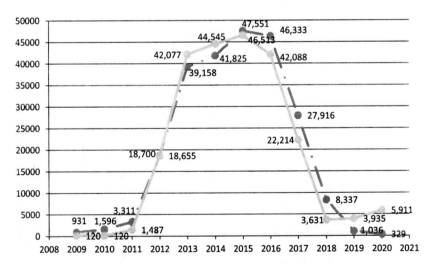

Figure 13.1 Estimate of HSR Workforce Size in Personnel-Years, "Top-Down" Benchmark (dotted line) and Bottom-Up Estimation (solid line), 2009–2020

(see Figure 13.2). Therefore, training and education efforts would logically require focus on that aspect of the project.

Additionally, the projected HSR workforce was analyzed with respect to its likely education (see Figure 13.3). What emerged were rich projections of the total education need of the directly employed workforce over the 2009–2025 period. Consistent with the finding concerning a concentration of need for construction workers, the training need for trades/construction at the high school and below level was estimated to constitute 67.4 percent of the total workforce. Some college training or education (no degree), including A.A./A.S. certification, constituted 18.73 percent of the total workforce training needs. The higher education needs constituted 12.88 percent of the total workforce. B.A./B.S. holders were projected to comprise the majority of those with college degrees.

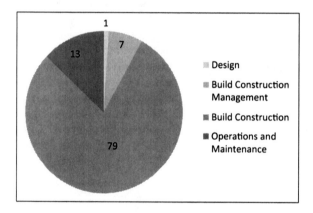

Figure 13.2 Total Personnel by Project Phase

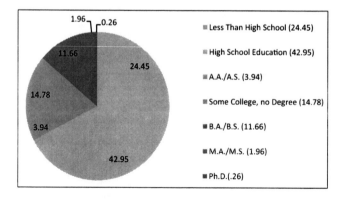

Figure 13.3 Total Personnel by Estimated Level of Education

Limited Capability in the United States to Teach
Railroad Education

The study concluded that, relevant to the projected imminent HSR demand, no existing institutions were responding on any significant scale to the need for instruction and/or research and development in the more specific field of HSR. Furthermore, overall, there were only a few existing, extremely limited education mechanisms to conduct needed HSR research and development as well as to teach applied curricula. Very few railway engineering-specific courses falling under civil engineering degree programs could be identified, and these programs were found to be at best scarce compared to potentially impending HSR needs.

Overall, the study identified patterns of HSR workforce and workforce development demand as well as more specific needs for knowledge and information. The statistical evidence demonstrated vast coming demand for personnel and professionals as well as associated needs for education and training to match them. A clear pattern of underpreparedness for this new workforce was also documented. The United States, including California, lags far behind HSR education systems abroad. California was found to be unprepared to supply the workforce needed to build its HSR system.

Communicating and Using Results

The primary means of communicating the results of the study was by means of publishing the final report on the MTI website. As a matter of policy, MTI used a variety of media (including social media, such as Twitter and Facebook) to publicize the release of the study to practitioners, the news media, and anyone with an interest in the topic. Additionally, the research team presented results of the study at various practitioner and academically oriented conferences, including the American Public Transportation Association (APTA) and the Transportation Research Board (TRB). The team also published a distilled version of the findings in the refereed journal of the TRB, the *Transportation Research Record* (Hernandez and Haas, 2013). Perhaps of most practical importance, the team presented the key results of the finding at a meeting of the Board of Directors of the CHSRA.

Reporting Results

The final report itself was 176 pages long, including approximately half of that total devoted to several lengthy appendices that provided much more detail about the estimation model and results. It consisted of just three sections: (1) an introduction, which framed the HSR workforce issue, (2) "Estimates of Employment and Workforce Development," and (3) "Existing Capacity for Preparing the HSR Workforce."

Selected Recommendations

The report did not contain a comprehensive set of specific recommendations. The research team concluded that although the findings were sufficiently stark in terms of clearly articulating the need to broaden both rail training and education, it did not support the prescription of specific actions that might be necessary to address those needs. To identify strategies and policy alternatives needed to address the workforce needs, essentially, fell beyond the scope of the study as it was understood by the research team. However, the report did conclude with the following statement:

> For there to be an adequate number of specially trained engineers, construction managers, and other key personnel by the project's peak year, California universities need to play a lead role in that effort; CSU and the UC must begin aligning their efforts now. However, the bulk of the projected workforce will not require college degrees; it will require HSR-specific training and certificates. The community college system, along with the trade apprenticeship programs, needs to be provided with a clear indication that HSR-related education and training are urgently required—and appropriately funded to shift capacity in that direction. The sooner such efforts are begun, the greater the likelihood of the timely and successful creation of a safe and efficient HSR system.
>
> (Haas et al., 2012, p. 89)

Action

The study did not result in any immediate decisions related to the HSR workforce. However, around the time of its release, an initiative from the California State University (CSU) administration used the report as a centerpiece of an effort to launch a workforce development initiative. Officials from the CSU assembled an ad hoc task force consisting of representatives of California's training and education institutions, including the CSU, the University of California (UC), the state's community college system, organized labor, and others. The goal of the task was to secure funding from the CSHRA for a continuum of educational offerings geared to the needs identified in the HSR workforce report. The task force noted that, in light of the report, workforce preparation would need to be broad and comprehensive, with particular needs for workers with apprenticeship training and with some college-level education, as well as bachelor's, master's, and doctoral degrees. More specifically, the task force sought to expand the availability of certificate, degree, and apprenticeship programs tailored to HSR industry needs to develop new certificates and programs as needed. It also intend to strengthen relationships between the California HSR initiative and the various education stakeholders to ensure responsiveness to the evolving needs of the HSR industry.

However, this initiative did not directly result in the creation of any specific program or funding for HSR workforce development. Essentially, disagreements within the CSHRA about the appropriate means to address the task force's concerns effectively tabled the ideas the task force had sought to champion. Therefore, many of the concerns about workforce identified in the research exist today, even as the HSR system eventually started construction in 2015. The failure of this initiative, it should be emphasized, had nothing to do with the research but was rather linked to the multiplicity of the groups involved as well as the internal politics of the HSR board. In retrospect, the research might have been more influential if it had been initiated and sponsored directly by the CSHRA— although that was highly unlikely to happen under the circumstances described earlier in this chapter.

Ultimately, therefore, this research case study does not exemplify policy research being turned directly into policy changes, although it did help spur (ultimately unsuccessful) policy action. In the longer term, it may still have helped to inform the discussion of HSR workforce development in California and perhaps beyond.

Lessons for Policy Research

A primary lesson from this example of policy research is that the estimation needs can come in different forms than simple forecasts, which frequently involve statistical modeling. In the MTI study, the research team was asked to identify detailed quantitative and qualitative information about a future state of HSR-related employment needs that could not be based entirely on past trends. A second lesson is that creative responses to challenging policy questions can be formulated with persistence. Third, the study again exemplifies how quantitative information can be appropriately buttressed with richer qualitative insights: the research team was able to not only provide estimates of the size of the needed HSR workforce, it also identified the specific job types as well as kind of education and training background this workforce would require. Finally, while the study does not exemplify a strong link between policy research and direct policy action, it did at the very least help spur an organized attempt to influence policy. It is also not unlikely that the findings will continue to help frame future discussion about workforce developments needed. The study, therefore, does exemplify some of the broader types of research utilization described in this text.

Focus on Research Methods

A Deconstruction/Aggregation Approach to Estimation

The problem in this case was to produce an estimate of work force requirements in a complex project with disparate tasks with which the responsible organizations had little past experience. The policy researcher had to identify components of the project, estimate personnel requirements for each, and aggregate them into a credible project estimate. The following six steps describe the process used to generate most of the workforce estimates that were generated. (Additional details may be found in the original study report, available online.)

Step 1. Using the cost estimates outlined by the CHSRA in its business plan for the HSR, the first step was to calculate the number and rate of change in required personnel according to APTA direct measurements, creating a curve that represents direct jobs required for the project, according to the CHSRA data.

- Output: direct measurement of personnel wave, applying the APTA measurements of direct personnel (i.e., quantity benchmark for all build personnel).

Step 2. The team set personnel ratios, by mile and by element, through manipulation of the "takeoff factor." Using unit cost pricing documents, the team set cost estimation data to measurements that can be further applied to the CHSR network model. This involved adjusting all HSR project elements to measure per mile/per element over a set period of time and adjusting the unit cost pricing documents to reflect labor estimates, per mile/per element.

- Output: labor estimates that could be applied to the CHSR model, on a per-mile/per-element basis, referring to a specific period of time.

Step 3. The team identified all known elements of the project (e.g., miles of track, buildings, bridges, tunnels, etc.) and used the labor estimates from Step 2 to create a list of personnel, by mile and by element.

- Output: total personnel needed, before adjustment for time.

Step 4. Cost estimation measurements were adjusted for the time frame of the project.

- Output: aggregate estimate of personnel needed to complete system (total CHSR personnel, within the needed time frame).

Step 5. The team calculated the total project personnel (by element and by mile) over the life of the 2012–2020 project period, according to the cost structure of the CHSR project in the detailed business plan.

- Output: project workforce estimate, by personnel, by element/mile, over time (2012–2020).

Step 6. Finally, the team confirmed that the project workforce estimate and the APTA direct measurement benchmark from Step 1 had acceptable

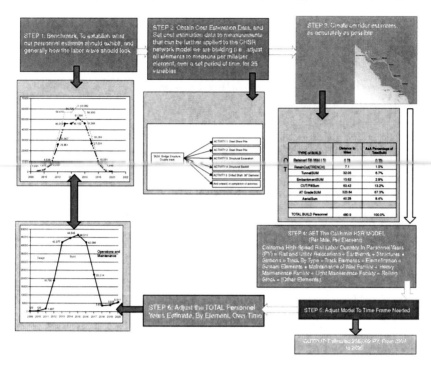

Figure 13.4 Flowchart of the Process Used to Generate Estimates of the HSR Workforce

characteristics and personnel ratios. This was done to help determine whether the measurement output appeared similar to the benchmarked direct personnel estimation.

Acronyms and Jargon

APTA—American Public Transit Association (organization that serves as an advocate for public transportation systems)

CHSRA—California High-Speed Rail Authority (the public agency empowered to spend funds dedicated to the California high-speed rail project)

CSU—California State University (along with the University of California, one of two university systems in the state)

HSR—High-speed rail (no universal standard exists, but typically refers to systems with a maximum speed of at least 150 mph)

MTI—Mineta Transportation Institute (a federally and state-funded University Transportation Center at San Jose State University that commissioned the research in this case)

PY—Personnel Years (any equivalent of the 12 months full-time employment of one person, such as two persons employed for six months each)

TRB—Transportation Research Board (a division of the National Research Council of the United States that advises transportation policy makers and sponsors transportation research)

UC—University of California (along with the California State University, one of two university systems in the state)

Discussion Questions

1. This research contained no specific policy recommendations. Why not? Do you agree with the team's decision to omit recommendations?
2. The study did not have a specific client. Assuming that the project had been commissioned with the California High-Speed Rail Authority as the client, how would you imagine the study would have changed (if it all)? Imagine how other potential clients might have affected the design.
3. The study was based on a business plan that was written in 2009, yet construction on the California HSR project began only in late 2015. What impact do you think this has had on the usefulness of the research?
4. Describe the key differences between the "top-down" and "bottom-up" estimation procedures described in this chapter. If necessary, read the original report (available online) for further details and explanation.

Assignments and Activities

1. Scan the original report (available online) and write a set of specific recommendations based on the findings.
2. Select a proposed transportation project (or other capital improvement project) in your community and briefly describe how you would estimate the number and kinds of jobs it would create.

14 Climate Change Adaptation

An Assessment of Accomplishments at the Community Level

Jason Vogel, Charles Herrick, and Heather Hosterman

Introduction

As the threats of climate change are becoming more apparent, many communities in the United States are undertaking actions to respond to actual or expected changing climate conditions and reduce their vulnerabilities to climate impacts. For example, some communities are reducing their exposure to sea-level rise or flooding events by relocating critical infrastructure and implementing land-use regulations. They are reducing their sensitivity to extreme temperatures and droughts through planting shade trees or drought-resistant crops, and they are increasing their adaptive capacity by integrating adaptation into planning processes and enhancing community or neighborhood resilience. These types of climate adaptation actions can reduce a community's vulnerabilities to climate change (e.g., sea-level rise), as well as climate variability (e.g., droughts) and extreme events (e.g., hurricanes). While the actions of some communities are well publicized, this project was motivated by a desire for a more systematic exploration of community-based adaptation actions that could empower community-based champions to reduce vulnerabilities in their own communities.

This chapter provides an example of a complex, exploratory research project to evaluate the state of the practice of climate adaptation at the community level. This assessment was conducted by a consulting firm, Abt Associates, from 2014 through 2016. This assessment included a review of selected technical and professional literature, interviews with 50 thought leaders from a variety of fields relevant to climate adaptation, and primary research on specific adaptation efforts in 17 communities across the United States. This chapter explores the policy research issues that emerged over the course of this project. The final report of this policy research, "Climate Adaptation: The State of Practice in U.S. Communities" (Vogel et al., 2016), can be downloaded at www.kresge.org/climate-adaptation.

The Policy Problem

The recent publication of the Intergovernmental Panel on Climate Change (IPCC), the Fifth Assessment Report, reaffirms what is already known: even major reductions in greenhouse gas emissions will not be sufficient to avoid many of the projected impacts of global climate change (IPCC, 2014). Concerted effort is therefore needed to identify and support socioeconomic and natural systems threatened by climate change.

Consistent with this threat, the field and practice of climate change adaptation has grown quickly as citizens and leaders have become increasingly aware of the impacts that climate change will have on their communities. Over the last 10 to 15 years, a substantial increase in interest and activity has taken place in community-level adaptation to climate change (e.g., Bierbaum et al., 2013; Hughes, 2015). Many surveys of adaptation actions have covered dozens or even hundreds of communities (e.g., Carmin, Nadkarni, and Rhie, 2012; Shi et al., 2015; Thayer et al., 2013). Although these surveys provide breadth of coverage, they tend to assess work at a broad level and offer only limited exploration of the complex interacting factors that explain why and how certain communities have addressed climate vulnerabilities. On the other end of the spectrum are specific, place-based adaptation case studies. These case studies tend to focus on a single community or a very small number of communities, diving deeply into systems and lessons learned specific to certain municipal contexts. But this narrow focus is less conducive to comparative analysis, which provides the spectrum of detailed knowledge needed to understand good practices while providing a foundation for making recommendations and drawing conclusions about the adaptation enterprise more broadly. Consequently, there is a shortcoming of multicommunity adaptation case studies and cross-case analyses in the adaptation literature, as recognized in the Third National Climate Assessment (Melillo et al., 2014). This policy research was intended to fill this gap to provide insight and motivation to adaptation professionals and community-based champions.

Initiation of Policy Research

Over the past decade, the Kresge Foundation has provided significant investment in community-based initiatives to reduce climate vulnerabilities. For example, the Kresge Foundation directly or indirectly supported planning efforts in many communities—such as in the San Francisco Bay region, San Diego, New Orleans, South Florida, and New Jersey—to foster locally grounded communities of practice and make real, concrete progress in reducing vulnerabilities. To better understand the impact of its investment, the foundation sought a broad assessment of community-based adaptation. This assessment would draw from the work of grantees, partners, and the broader climate adaptation community to develop lessons about the processes that communities can use to adapt to climate change and strengthen the emergent climate adaptation field.

In 2013, the Kresge Foundation sought a consultancy to design and conduct a comprehensive empirical assessment of community-based climate adaptation in the United States. The Kresge Foundation provided Abt Associates with a two-year grant to support this effort. The Kresge Foundation considered several options for who to commission for this assessment, including academic researchers and the National Research Council, before ultimately settling on a consulting firm with significant experience in climate adaptation research. The decision to go with a consulting firm was made, in part, to ensure a practically grounded assessment focused on making progress under real-world conditions.

The Policy Research Task

In close consultation with the Kresge Foundation, the Abt Associates research team designed an empirical assessment designed to deepen and sharpen learning about climate adaptation at the community level. As described in more detail later in this chapter, the research team reviewed selected technical and professional literature and interviewed 50 thought leaders working in the arena of climate change adaptation. This initial work helped the research team develop a baseline understanding of the state of the practice of climate adaptation. The research team then conducted primary research on specific vulnerability-reducing actions implemented in 17 communities across the United States (see Table 14.1 for a brief description of all 17 case studies). Each case study provided a detailed account of how and why the community took a specific action to reduce vulnerabilities to climate impacts. The research team centered each case study on a specific action taken by that community to address community vulnerabilities, as opposed to considering all actions taken by the community. The research team then engaged in a cross-case analysis to address four central questions that arose from the case study research:

- What motivates communities to take adaptive action?
- What are communities doing to adapt?
- How are communities implementing adaptation actions?
- What are communities achieving through adaptation?

As a final step, the research team developed conclusions and tactical recommendations based upon the totality of empirical evidence generated by the research project.

Throughout the project, the research team worked closely with the Kresge Foundation's Environment Program staff to clarify the study purpose and communicate study requirements and limitations. Abt Associates

Table 14.1 Case Study Descriptions

Case Study Community	Action Profiled	Brief Case Description
Avalon, NJ	Comprehensive Shoreline Protection Strategy	Avalon developed a number of physical shoreline barriers, bought damaged shoreline properties, purchased additional undeveloped land, limited shoreline development, and created and maintained extensive shorefront sand dunes to protect the borough's property and tourism industry from coastal storms.
Baltimore, MD	Integrating Climate Change Adaptation into an All-Hazard Mitigation Plan	In 2012, city staff used a periodic update of the city's All-Hazards Mitigation Plan as an opportunity to integrate a climate change risk and vulnerability assessment into the new Disaster Preparedness Project and Plan. This case focuses on 2 out of the 231 actions identified: the disaster preparedness initiative, Make a Plan, Build a Kit, Help Each Other; and the capacity-building initiative, Resiliency Hubs.
Boston, MA	Climate Change Preparedness and Resiliency Checklist	With a focus on sea-level rise and coastal and inland flooding, the Boston Redevelopment Authority mandated that climate change be considered as part of the review process for large new developments (over 20,000 square feet) and large renovation projects (over 100,000 square feet).
Chula Vista, CA	Cool Roofs Ordinance and Shade Trees Policy	Chula Vista implemented a stakeholder-driven climate planning process to develop a suite of climate adaptation actions. Two specific actions focused on addressing rising temperatures in the San Diego region are profiled in this case: Chula Vista's cool roofs ordinance and Chula Vista's shade trees policy.
Cleveland, OH	Neighborhood Climate Action Toolkit and Climate Action Fund	Cleveland tied its climate change efforts to date to neighborhood revitalization through a citywide climate action plan and the Cleveland Neighborhood Climate Action Toolkit, which helps neighborhoods leverage existing assets to fight economic decline, increase adaptive capacity, reduce greenhouse gas emissions, and prepare for a climate-altered future.

Case Study Community	Action Profiled	Brief Case Description
El Paso County, TX	Kay Bailey Hutchison Inland Desalination Facility	El Paso Water Utilities' project focused on addressing the combined challenges of population growth and drought. El Paso Water Utilities, in an unusual alliance with the U.S. Army military base Fort Bliss, constructed the Kay Bailey Hutchison Desalination Plant to convert formerly unusable brackish water into drinking water
Flagstaff, AZ	Flagstaff Watershed Protection Project	In response to the 2010 Schultz fire and subsequent flooding, voters in Flagstaff passed a $10 million bond measure to use city funding to reduce catastrophic fire risk in critical but hard-to-treat areas on U.S. Forest Service lands.
Fort Collins, CO	Water Demand Management	In response to severe drought events, Fort Collins updated its Water Supply and Demand Management Policy to (1) outline specific regulatory measures to reduce water use quickly during a severe drought and (2) reduce water use through water conservation programs.
Grand Rapids, MI	Vital Streets and Sidewalks Spending Guidelines	Flooding, aging stormwater infrastructure, and public discontent about the state of the roads led Grand Rapids to create the Vital Streets and Sidewalk Spending Guidelines, which mandate green infrastructure use during upgrades. In a 2014 election, 66% of voters supported the guidelines and a tax to fund implementation.
Miami-Dade County, FL	Integrating Climate Change Adaptation into a Comprehensive Development Master Plan	In 2013, the Board of County Commissioners approved integrating climate change considerations into multiple elements of the Comprehensive Development Master Plan. These changes will require county departments to consider climate change during processes such as capital improvement projects.
Mobile County, AL	Oyster Reef Restoration	The cultural and economic impacts of coastal ecosystem degradation have generated support for restoration actions in Alabama's Mobile Bay. In 2009, the Nature Conservancy received a grant through the American Recovery and Reinvestment Act to rebuild oyster reefs along a stretch of degraded coastline in Mobile Bay.

(Continued)

Table 14.1 (Continued)

Case Study Community	Action Profiled	Brief Case Description
Norfolk, VA	Coastal Resilience Strategy	Norfolk passed changes to its flood and coastal zone ordinance following increases in severe coastal flooding and in anticipation of potential sea-level rise. The ordinance requires that new structures in coastal flood zones must be built at least 3 feet above the 100-year floodplain (i.e., a 3 foot freeboard); certain existing structures must also meet this standard.
Oakland, CA	Oakland Climate Action Coalition Moves Climate Change Adaptation Forward	In 2009, 30 organizations interested in advancing policies on sea-level rise, environment, public health, and social justice issues came together to form the Oakland Climate Action Coalition. This coalition has become a community-led platform for supporting climate change adaptation strategy and action through a social justice lens.
Seattle, WA	Mainstreaming Climate Change into Internal Planning and Decision Making	Seattle Public Utilities integrated climate considerations into the four levels of its internal planning and operations: (1) organization-wide strategic planning, (2) planning at the water division and drainage and sewer division levels, (3) capital investment decision making, and (4) day-to-day operational decision making.
Southwest Crown, MT	Forest Restoration	In response to more severe and longer wildfire seasons anticipated to worsen under climate change, the community used federal funding to conduct forest and watershed restoration, including forest thinning and prescribed fires, to reestablish natural wildfire dynamics and reduce the risk of catastrophic wildfire.
Spartanburg, SC	Mainstreaming Climate Change into Programs, Management Actions, and Culture	Droughts, extreme rainfall, and concern about climate change led Spartanburg Water to integrate climate change into the utility's operations, culture, programs, and actions and helped increase the capacity of staff concerning climate variability and impacts.

Case Study Community	Action Profiled	Brief Case Description
Tulsa, OK	Acquisition and Relocation	After several severe flooding events, Tulsa began an extensive program to acquire repeatedly flooded properties, remove or relocate buildings on those properties, and convert repetitively flooded properties into parks and other public uses. Since the 1970s, Tulsa has acquired more than 1,000 repetitively flooded properties.

also identified and worked closely with three technical advisors who contributed to the research, analysis, and communications tasks and a project advisory committee—composed of 16 adaptation practitioners and experts from a variety of professional standpoints—who provided advice on and engagement with the project.

Objectives

This project was motivated by the growing challenges posed by global climate change and the need for communities to respond to its anticipated impacts. The project was meant to offer empirical evidence to help community-based champions make progress in reducing vulnerabilities in their communities. Abt Associates hoped to do this by providing a trove of potential models and lessons and by articulating tactical recommendations for community-based champions to help them reduce vulnerabilities in their communities.

Challenges

Several factors posed challenges for policy research in this project:

- Working with the clients, the interdisciplinary committee of professional experts and the research team to adequately frame the research posed significant challenges. In particular, two aspects of the research framing were controversial. First, considering actions designed to reduce vulnerabilities to climate variability, extreme events, *and* climate change versus actions focused *exclusively* on climate change was controversial. Ultimately, the research team decided to define climate adaptation broadly because, among other reasons, (1) extreme events and climate variability typically involve weather or climatic conditions similar to those that scientists expect will become more frequent or intense with climate change; and (2) the tools, policies, and strategies deployed to address extreme events and climate variability are often similar to those used to address climate change. Second, focusing narrowly on vulnerability reduction as opposed to resilience building was also controversial. Instead of highlighting community action that built resilience, such as educational programs, inclusive decision-making processes, or the integration of social and natural systems into decision making, the research team decided to focus on concrete actions that reduce exposure, reduce sensitivity, or increase adaptive capacity directly. In other words, it was a challenge for the team to settle upon a common problem definition and research construct.

- Creating a protocol to ensure the process of conducting interviews and case studies was consistent across multiple researchers who conducted interviews posed another challenge. We developed a research protocol to help guarantee that observations and findings were not unduly influenced by differences in the perspectives of the researchers. See the Focus on Research Methods section of this chapter for a discussion of the research protocol.

- The project team utilized a reflexive approach that allowed the research methodology to evolve over time based on accumulating empirical input with the methodological needs of the project. This involved testing constructs and exploring evolving observations as the team worked through successive steps in the research process as well as successive case studies. Managing this process in a systematic manner was challenging.

- Managing the roles of a research team of nine individuals, two representatives from the Kresge Foundation, three technical advisors, and a project advisory committee of 16 thought leaders posed another challenge for the project.

The Decision Context

This project was motivated by a commitment to catalyze community-based action in climate adaptation. The project team developed an analytical framework to characterize and assess what is happening in communities and to understand better what has been achieved and how achievements have been accomplished. This section focuses on the decision context for the team's case-based analysis.

The Institutional Context

Community-level vulnerability to climate-related risk does not fall neatly within the purview of a single department or governmental agency. Climate-related vulnerabilities can impact public utilities, transportation and transit authorities, parks and recreation facilities, public water supplies, public health services, buildings and other infrastructure, and other governmentally operated service streams. Decisions to take action to address climate vulnerabilities can therefore emerge from within operational departments; emanate top down from a mayor, council, or other executive authority; or even propagate through citizen-driven campaigns in reaction to service disruptions or other impacts. This assessment thus has a diverse audience of community-based decision makers, including community practitioners, city managers and staff, local nonprofits, and other local actors.

The Policy Cycle

Institutional responses to the threat of climate change are often evaluated regarding a rational decision-making process, including broadly recognized steps such as "understanding the problem," "planning for action," and "managing the deployment of selected options" (Moser and Ekstrom, 2010). Policy actors in this study's cases did not characterize their journey in terms of a neat progression through each phase of a rationalized decision model. And the case research did not utilize a "policy cycle" as a heuristic or analytical framework. Still, our cross-case analysis highlights community actions that roughly correspond to some aspects of the policy cycle.

Most fundamentally, the analysis applied an evaluative approach, assessing community interventions regarding their likely effect on climate-related risk reduction. Once an innovative practice or policy was identified, the project team then utilized a form of qualitative event history analysis (not survival analysis), whereby it characterized the problem that the community had addressed. This event history analysis was centered on the decision outcome or public policy action undertaken to reduce vulnerabilities to climate impacts. The research then looked backward into the pre-outcome conditions to explain the "how" and "why" of the profiled decision, in each case attempting to illuminate forward-looking considerations such as policy implementation, monitoring, and evaluation.

In this context, it is important to clarify that although the research team used aspects of the policy cycle to help structure its case histories, the community-based policy actors—in nearly all cases—were engaged in a disjointed and incremental series of activities. These actors were often more goal oriented than problem oriented; they slipped easily back and forth between explicit or scientific information and implicit or qualitative information, and they regularly evaluated their progress but rarely used explicit or measurable metrics. This study thus exemplifies research that is couched in essentially all phases of the policy cycle.

Clients and Stakeholders

As described earlier, the Kresge Foundation funded this assessment to understand better how to stimulate community-based adaptation efforts across a broad range of communities.

The primary audience of this project was community-based champions—the community members who catalyze action to address current and future climate vulnerabilities. These champions can be municipal staff, grassroots activists, community organizers, elected officials, or even interested citizens. In most cases, these individuals were seeking a resolution to a particular set of problematic issues, such as serial vulnerabilities to flooding events, exposure to wildfire, or the need to insulate economic development from climate-related threats. Because of this, community-based champions were primarily interested in gaining insights from the case study communities to facilitate adaptation actions in their own communities. This type of peer-to-peer learning helps community-based champions understand how other communities are accomplishing adaptation actions that they can adopt, common pitfalls to avoid, and ways to overcome barriers. The research team also considered adaptation professionals as a secondary audience. Adaptation professionals are the community of specialists from a variety of disciplines—such as natural hazards mitigation, climate change, urban planning, and natural resource management—that focus on the issue of adapting to climate change. Adaptation professionals often work across many communities to help them address climate vulnerabilities.

Research Design and Implementation

The research team developed a protocol to guide the research design and implementation; the research protocol is described in greater detail in the Focus on Research Methods section. This section focuses primarily on the case study research design and implementation but also touches on other aspects of this policy research project, including the literature review and thought-leader interviews.

Information Needs

As a first step in this policy research project, the research team aimed to create a high-level baseline of knowledge about issues related to community-based adaptation, to identify potential case study communities, and to establish ways to disseminate project results effectively. To create the baseline, the team first undertook a targeted literature review of technical and professional documents aimed at evaluating the state-of-the-practice (e.g., Bierbaum et al., 2013; Carmin, Hansen et al., 2013; Nadkarni and Rhie, 2012; NRC, 2010; Thayer et al., 2013; and Melillo, Richmond, and Yohe, 2014). The team then interviewed 50 thought leaders to harvest experience from them on community-based adaptation, including identifying key stakeholders and audiences for the project, as well as climate adaptation issues, barriers, constraints, and solutions. Thus, the project was largely aimed at providing exploratory information that would help guide future thought and decisions about a broad template of policy components and was far from a more traditional "effectiveness" study of the impact of a single program.

Once the research team developed a baseline understanding of the state of the practice, they undertook primary research through a series of case studies. First, the research team gathered information on 120 potential case study communities; this information helped the team identify which communities to ultimately profile. A key goal in this phase of the study was to select cases with distinct actions that reduced the community's climate vulnerabilities. The research team carefully selected only cases with distinct outcomes that already have resulted or are likely to result in tangible reductions of vulnerability to climate variability, extreme events, or climate change. To ensure the project profiled interesting, relevant, and timely actions, the researchers conducted background research on each case study to determine:

- Is there enough information available on the action to build a baseline understanding of the action and its policy context before conducting a face-to-face interview?
- Can other communities learn lessons from this adaptation action?
- Does the community itself view this particular action as a salient and important aspect of its community story?

With this information, the researchers then gathered additional data and information—including climate adaptation plans, climate action plans, and sustainability plans; sector-specific plans, such as floodplain management plans; partner organization websites as well as adaptation and sustainability websites; and grey (i.e., unpublished) literature and media reports—to build out the story line. In reviewing this information, the researchers focused on topics that could be important to the case study timeline, such as community values, project champions, monitoring, and evaluation activities. The case study information helped the researchers develop a timeline and identify gaps in the timeline to address during case study interviews, which are described in greater detail in the next section.

Design and Methods

The case study research incorporated multiple independent streams of information. To ensure consistency in the collection of case-based information, the research team developed a research protocol to help researchers systematically identify and characterize factors that shaped adaptation actions. For each case study, a member of the research team conducted background research, site visits and in-person interviews, and follow-up interviews via email or telephone. The case studies were developed to capture the interviewees' assessment of essential factors that shaped the development, implementation, and evaluation of the action.

Background Research

Researchers reviewed available sources of information on the community-based climate adaptation action to develop a draft case study timeline. This timeline provided an initial understanding of how the community got to the climate adaptation action and what effect that action had on the community. The timeline, in conjunction with the heuristic included in the research protocol, allowed the researcher to highlight gaps and missing detail in the storylines. These gaps and missing details helped researchers identify who they needed to speak with in the community and the questions to ask during the site visit interviews. See Figure 14.1 for an example of a final case study timeline.

Case Study Site Visits and In-Person Interviews

Researchers visited each community in which a policy action was profiled to obtain details needed to produce rich, detailed, and interesting case studies. Case study researchers developed an interview guide: a list of questions to ask each respondent formatted in a manner to guide the direction of a conversation with minimal prompting. For quality control and consistency across the case studies, the project manager reviewed all interview guides before site visits. Interviews took the form of *focus groups* in which the researcher guided a small-group discussion of experts, practitioners, or stakeholders or *individual interviews* with three to five interviewees.

Case Study Development

Using the information collected, researchers drafted the community case study story. All case study stories had the same format: an introduction with the key climate adaptation action or set of actions taken by the

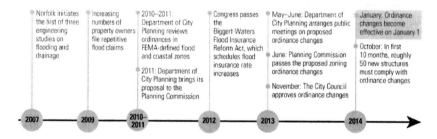

Figure 14.1 Final Case Study Timeline for Norfolk, Virginia

community to reduce its climate vulnerabilities; three to five essential elements that explain why and how the community chose that climate adaptation action; the effect of the community's climate adaptation actions on reducing climate vulnerabilities; and lessons drawn from the community's experience. All 17 case studies adhere to this structure in order to facilitate comparison across cases.

Follow-Up Phone Interviews

If the researcher identified important uncertainties or knowledge gaps during the development of the case study story, they conducted follow-up interviews. These interviews included follow-on interviews with the same individuals and also interviews with new experts, practitioners, or stakeholders as necessary.

Review of Case Study

The draft case study underwent an in-depth review process starting with the project manager and one additional reviewer working across all 17 case studies. Case studies were then reviewed by the project's technical advisors, personnel at the Kresge Foundation, and the project advisory committee. After researchers revised case studies to address comments from the research team, the case studies were sent to the interviewees for review. This provided interviewees with the opportunity to review the document, ensure the content was factually accurate, and provide consent for any quotes. The case study was then revised to reflect feedback from the interviewees. As a final step, all case studies were formatted and edited before being presented both in the final report and as stand-alone case studies (see Vogel et al., 2016, for the full set of case studies).

The research team used the information and observations gleaned from the case studies to develop a cross-case analysis of findings across the portfolio of all 17 case studies, which are briefly described in the Selected Findings section. The team also used these cross-case findings along with other research inputs to develop some conclusions and tactical recommendations for community-based adaptation, which are described under the Selected Recommendations section.

Selected Findings

Throughout the case study research, four central questions guided the work: (1) What motivates communities to take adaptive action? (2) What are communities doing to adapt? (3) How are communities implementing adaptation actions? and (4) What are communities achieving through adaptation? These questions guided and structured the cross-case analysis. These findings are summarized in what follows, but much more nuance and detail, including specific examples from profiled cases, can be found in the final report for this research project (see chapter 2 in Vogel et al., 2016, for a full description of the cross-case findings).

- **Motivations:** Most adaptation actions draw upon, promote, and sustain multiple community values. Climate change was not typically the exclusive justification for community-based adaptation in the cases we studied. However, experiencing extreme climate events commonly initiated or accelerated adaptation efforts.
- **Actions:** Most of the profiled communities are attempting to tangibly reduce their vulnerability to climate variability, extreme events, and climate change, as shown in Table 14.1. In a few cases, communities are reducing exposure; more often, their work is aimed at reducing sensitivity and building adaptive capacity.
- **Implementation:** Communities use diverse strategies to implement adaptation actions—from deploying conventional policy tools, mainstreaming adaptation into existing efforts to develop new decision-making processes. These strategies often capitalize on effective leadership and consciously build community support.
- **Achievements:** The communities we examined are reducing their vulnerability to current climate impacts; a few are also explicitly reducing their vulnerabilities to future climate impacts. Sometimes these vulnerability reductions are limited in temporal or spatial scope or address only a particular vulnerability type (e.g., only drought). Adaptation actions frequently go hand in hand with progress on other community priorities.

Communicating and Using Results

From conception, communication was an integral part of the project. The research team included several communications experts; also, the team retained communications experts from different fields as technical and project advisors. The project also developed a formal communications strategy in the early stages of the work as guidance to help shape the project as it evolved over its lifetime.

The original intention of the project was to develop a final technical report as well as a companion website to allow diverse audiences to interact with the research content in different ways. For example, website users who first explore a case study might then review the cross-case findings related to that case. Alternately, website users might first explore the main cross-case findings and then dive into case studies related to those cross-case findings. Unfortunately, due to time and resource constraints, the website was ultimately scaled back considerably from the interactive vision first promoted (see www.kresge.org/climate-adaptation). Policy research is frequently delimited by resource constraints, despite the best plans of researchers.

Reporting Results

The results of this policy research project were mainly reported through a technical report, "Climate Adaptation: The State of Practice in U.S. Communities" (Vogel et al., 2016). To maintain simplicity and readability, the report was organized into three chapters. The introductory chapter presented the project and explained the assumptions and normative perspectives that formed the foundation of the project. The second chapter focused on case studies and cross-case findings. This chapter only briefly describes the 17 case studies and then delves into an exhaustive and empirical accounting of the cross-case findings. The research team illustrated each cross-case finding with several specific examples from the 17 case studies to add depth to the findings and ground them in our empirical research. The third chapter provided project conclusions and tactical recommendations. This chapter is where the research team applied its judgment to the totality of the findings, which includes conclusions for adaptation professionals as well as a set of tactical recommendations for community-based champions. The full report also includes an executive summary, each of the case studies, and a set of technical appendices.

In addition to the technical report, the research team made a conscious effort to present the study's findings and conclusions through a variety of outlets. This strategic decision ensures that the study's findings do not require a "pull" from potentially interested parties but instead provided a "push" of information out to a variety of potentially interested academic and professional disciplines (e.g., Mattson-Teig, 2016; Thomas, 2016). The team presented the research to different professional audiences—such as climate adaptation practitioners, natural-hazard mitigation professionals, and community planners—at several conferences (e.g., the 2016 Natural Hazards Workshop, the 2015 National Adaptation Forum) and webinars (e.g., the 2016 American Society of Adaptation Professionals Climate Adaptation: State of Practice in U.S. Communities webinar; the 2015 Security and Sustainability Forum: Urban Resilience in the Era of Climate Change webinar). The team also developed media and general-interest pieces to highlight interesting aspects of the research project for a more general audience (e.g., Mazur, 2016). Moving forward, the team plans to draft peer-reviewed journal articles to get the project findings and conclusions in front of a variety of academic audiences. Finally, the team will engage in additional webinars and training seminars across a variety of academic and professional disciplines to raise awareness of the case studies, our cross-case findings, and our conclusions and recommendations.

Selected Recommendations

This research effort produced a set of conclusions and recommendations for community-based champions—people like elected officials, municipal staff, or grassroots activists who initiate action to reduce community vulnerabilities to climate. A partial list of the recommendations to advance adaptation and vulnerability reduction within communities follows (see chapter 3 of Vogel et al., 2016, for the full set of conclusions and tactical recommendations):

- Communities ought to start adaptation actions now because many are already vulnerable and are becoming more so, better information is not necessarily available, and real vulnerability reduction takes time.
- They ought to look for cobenefits, cross-sector leveraging, and opportunities to piggyback climate adaptation onto other salient community issues to make climate change tangible, familiar, and local.
- Employ commonly used policy tools to mainstream adaptation into existing municipal and community activities (e.g., response to an extreme storm event).
- Use windows of opportunity to advance climate adaptation by generating ideas and putting plans in place for rapid deployment when the opportunity arises.
- Consider local context when determining whether to explicitly frame an action in terms of climate change either to generate momentum to address climate adaptation or to avoid politicizing issues that might be better seen as routine municipal renewal, public works, or resource management projects.

See Figure 14.2 for a visual of the project's conclusion about a hypothetical, well-adapted community. While we cannot say what a perfectly adapted community would look like, we can illustrate an impressive climate change adaptation program by combining some of the most bold and successful efforts of each of our case study communities into a single hypothetical community effort.

Action

This chapter was written coincident with the conclusion of the community-based climate adaptation assessment. Consequently, it is impossible to determine how or when the findings, conclusions, and recommendations that emerged from this project will lead to action. However, the project was designed from its inception to catalyze and inform community-level action. We believe our research outputs will be action-inducing because we provided empirical lessons and models in an easily digestible form to help empower community-based champions to reduce vulnerabilities in their communities. This could be through interaction with the project outputs or through peer-to-peer networking with the communities profiled in the project case studies. Moreover, the research team intends to engage adaptation professionals in a deeper discussion about the role of

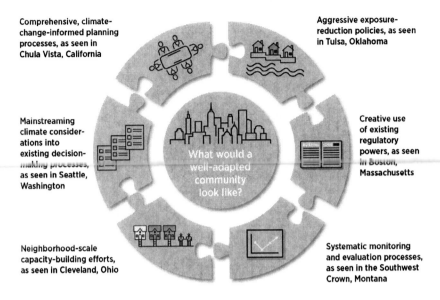

Figure 14.2 A Hypothetical, Well-Adapted Community

community-based adaptation in the broader field of climate change adaptation. It also intends to integrate across traditional disciplines—such as climate change adaptation, natural hazards mitigation, and community planning—by facilitating a critical self-assessment of how best to achieve the goal of reducing community vulnerabilities to climate impacts.

Lessons for Policy Research

Due to the magnitude of some of its projected impacts, it is frequently argued that efforts to address climate change must be "transformational" (WRI, 2014). Under this way of thinking, communities would need to develop fundamentally different practices, technologies, and policy regimes than those currently in place. Indeed, it has even been suggested that climate change could necessitate shifts to new forms of governance. This research experience suggests the viability of an opposing perspective. Many of the case communities demonstrated that aspects of climate change can be addressed incrementally using existing policy tools. For instance, the case-study communities provided examples of climate change impacts being addressed through zoning and land-use regulations, multihazard mitigation planning, and even the regular process of municipal renewal of public assets like transportation and water infrastructure.

Furthermore, many scholars of climate change policy and management argue that community-scale adaptation should be addressed through a synoptic and highly rationalized planning process that begins with a forward-looking assessment of projected climate change impacts, identifies climate-related risk factors, calculates the community's overall exposure to climate-related risk, characterizes a range of alternative policy interventions, prioritizes investments in risk mitigation, and finally moves through a feedback process in which interventions are evaluated against actual conditions and events. The results of the research in this project suggest that real-world communities tend not to act in such a formal and prescribed manner. Rather, community interventions to climate change tend to be piecemeal, limited to specific resources or service streams, and incremental in scope. A highly rational, scientific management mindset still holds undue influence over our collective thinking about how to intervene in community-level decision-making processes to address climate adaptation. A more adaptive management or adaptive governance model might hold more promise for facilitating progress in understanding the public policy processes behind complex multifaceted problems such as climate change adaptation.

Focus on Research Methods

Research Protocol

This project required coordination among five core researchers to investigate vulnerability-reducing actions across 17 diverse communities. To accomplish this, the research team established a systematic process for empirical inquiry into the cases, which we called our research protocol. The research protocol played several critical roles that helped establish the empirical foundation for the project work.

First, the protocol provided a comprehensive framework for investigating the context of each case. By asking all five core researchers to operate from the same heuristic, it became easier to ensure that all aspects of the case study were thoroughly and consistently explored. The research protocol guided each researcher to explore the essential elements of their case through a series of carefully defined topics, including motivation, community values, information, funding, participants, strategies/processes, and effects/appraisal. Each researcher determined which of these essential elements were key to understanding the action a community took. The research protocol provided a structure through which each researcher compiled and assessed data and then synthesized the case "story." This added rigor and quality control to the research process. For example, if a researcher did not identify "information" as a key to explaining the case study policy action, we could be sure it was because that researcher duly considered the role of information and deemed it immaterial to explaining the policy action (as opposed to the researcher never asking interviewees about the role information played in that policy action).

Second, the research protocol ensured that the differences found between case study policy actions emerged from real differences among the cases and was not influenced by differences in the perspectives of the researchers. For example, and to simplify the point, a researcher trained in psychology might place more emphasis on participant motivations, a researcher trained in economics might place more emphasis on funding, and a researcher trained in political science might place more emphasis on power dynamics among policy participants.

Finally, the research protocol ensured consistency in case study content and organization. Disciplined use of the research protocol both by the core researchers and by the project manager and one additional reviewer who worked across all 17 case studies brought order to the case studies that facilitated cross-case analysis. This resulted in a rigorously developed set of cross-case findings that were explained in the project report and illustrated with examples from multiple case studies.

Some of the specific tasks that the research protocol required of each researcher included:

- Selecting particular cases from among a list of candidate localities
- Identifying the policy action focus for the case
- Conducting background research and developing a timeline of key events centered on the policy action
- Building out a storyline to describe the essential elements of the case
- Conducting a gap analysis based on the background research
- Developing a list of desired interviewees and an interview guide and conducting site visits and interviews
- Drafting the case study based on a common outline across all cases

Acronyms and Jargon

Adaptation professionals—The community of professionals from a variety of disciplines that focus on the issue of adapting to climate change.

Climate adaptation—Reducing vulnerability to climate variability, extreme events, and climate change.

Climate change—Changes in climate variables and patterns of weather over time because of a warming of the Earth's atmosphere.

Community-based adaptation—Reducing vulnerability to climate impacts at the community level.

Community-based champion—A person who catalyzes action to address current and future climate vulnerabilities. Typically a grassroots organizer, personnel from a nongovernmental organization, or a sustainability officer, city planner, emergency manager, elected official, or other public official involved in the day-to-day management of municipal affairs.

Vulnerability—The degree to which a system is susceptible to and unable to cope with the adverse effects of climate change, including climate variability and extremes. Vulnerability is a function of the character, magnitude, and rate of climate change and variation to which a system is exposed, its sensitivity, and its adaptive capacity.

Discussion Questions

1. This project was predominately intended to provide exploratory information about actions taken in a cross-section of communities. What other kinds of information were also involved?
2. The research team did not seek to measure the impact or effectiveness of the various measures taken on behalf of climate adaptation. Why not?
3. This research was funded by a foundation that had no direct interest in the outcome of the research. How do you think this affected the course of the research in such components as problem definition and research design?
4. How useful do you think the information provided by this study is or will be to communities considering taking action on climate adaptation?
5. The research team decided to emphasize climate adaptation rather than climate change. Why did it do that, and do you agree with its rationale?

Assignments and Activities

1. Locate the report and/or its website and identify the findings that seem the most useful to decision makers as well as those that seem less useful.
2. Consider the situation of a community near you (or one with which you are familiar) and determine which findings from this case study are most applicable to it and why.

15 Housing Sales in Urban Neighborhoods

Using Policy Research to Inform Planning

Elizabeth Sale and J. Fred Springer

Introduction

Land-use planning, including residential development, is largely the province of local governments in the United States, a traditional responsibility that some critics cite as a contributor to the decline of many older core cities. While no clear national urban policy has been developed in the United States, federal agencies like the U.S. Department of Housing and Urban Development (HUD) have instituted programs designed to encourage local governments to address urban problems. This case demonstrates the interaction of federal government, local government, and policy researchers in developing planning information concerning housing. As is often the case, research is an indirect but potentially important contribution to the policy process.

This chapter was one of four that were part of the first edition of this text. It has been retained partly because of the prescience of its findings for the housing development pattern in St. Louis since the study was conducted. The study suggested that new homebuyers in St. Louis were more likely to be seeking stable, affordable neighborhoods than to be traditional, more wealthy, gentrifiers seeking urban lifestyles with more amenities. Recent commentary in St. Louis has identified exactly this housing appeal for the city. For example, it has been observed that "gentrification as a negative argument just doesn't play well in St. Louis. The city seems inherently built to not push out poor people; it was built for the huddled masses when the country was in a state of massive immigration. . . . (T)he vast majority of homes are of modest size compared to the national average" (Groth, 2013). Another blog reporter summarized a local study of "rebound neighborhoods" in St. Louis. The story noted that these neighborhoods "come in many different types and no neighborhood fits the classic gentrification model well" (Swanstrom, 2014). A few of these neighborhoods, in the city's historic Central West End for example, meet the gentrification profile, but most appeal to the "stabilizers" or "stability seekers" identified as the largest groups of St. Louis homebuyers in this study.

The Policy Problem

The need for effective residential redevelopment policy in the nation's older core cities is clear. The loss of population in central cities has been well documented (Spain, 1980), and in cities like St. Louis, the lack of residents in downtown areas has become a major impediment to continued commercial revitalization. The clarity of the need, however, has not reduced the difficulty of the policy problem facing declining cities. Despite several decades of efforts to entice suburban dwellers back to the city or to increase the availability of adequate housing for the urban poor, positive results have been limited.

In the last decades of the 1900s, the City of St. Louis was the prime example of residential decline in the nation, having lost more than half of its population in five decades—from 857,000 people in 1950 to fewer than 400,000 in 1990. This decline in city population was largely attributable to movement within the metropolitan area, largely into St. Louis County, which surrounds the city west of the Mississippi. As the city declined, St. Louis County boomed.

Whereas the residential focus of the metropolitan area has moved to the west into St. Louis County, the city has maintained and strengthened the elements of the core city of the metropolitan area. It remained a strong cultural center, with a world-class symphony, a fine art museum, and a resurgent arts district in the mid-town area. Its world-class zoo (free to the public) and science center are popular family destinations. The City of St. Louis has avoided losing its major baseball and hockey sports franchises to suburban facilities, and city development efforts in the 1960s and 1970s placed a high priority on downtown business and building development, with some success. The downtown area experienced a substantial building spurt in the 1980s.

This progress in arresting decline and revitalizing the city as a work and leisure destination has made the need for residential revitalization even more glaring. In the 1980s, the city gave renewed attention to encouraging residential development through home ownership as one major theme in revitalization. St. Louis is a city of neighborhoods, and the clear identity and character of its different residential neighborhoods became a natural focus for attempts at encouraging residential redevelopment. Within the neighborhood focus, different strategies for neighborhood revitalization were pursued. A second major theme has focused more on strengthening neighborhood environments than on home ownership itself. While neither of these has been clearly articulated as "policy" by the city, the threads of these policy approaches clearly run through the variety of city-sponsored physical redevelopment efforts and programs.

A major thrust of Mayor Vincent Schoemehl's housing policy during his tenure from 1980 to 1992 was a gentrification strategy—"the physical renovation and social-class upgrading of inner-city neighborhoods"

(Kerstein, 1990, p. 620). City and citizen efforts in this area included encouragement of household-led gentrification by urban resettlers in select neighborhoods with historic structures (Spain, 1980, p. 28). However, the major manifestation of conscious gentrification efforts in St. Louis was developer-led renovation of select neighborhoods (Tobin and Judd, 1982). In the early 1980s, the city supported this developer-led process through its condemnation and tax abatement procedures and focused infrastructure development in several focused development neighborhoods at strategic points in the city. These areas were characterized by the architectural interest, proximity to major recreational and entertainment centers, or proximity to major employers in the city that studies of gentrification have shown to facilitate the process.

Specific areas of the city, particularly within the central corridor, were targeted for gentrification. Housing that was either abandoned or occupied by lower-income residents was condemned to allow developers to rehabilitate entire neighborhoods. Promotional campaigns, such as a "City Living" public relations effort, stressed the attractiveness of city neighborhoods, multiple options for schooling, and the safety of particular neighborhoods, all oriented toward attracting residents into the city of St. Louis. Proponents of gentrification foresee numerous benefits assumed to accompany the influx of more affluent residents.

As a general rule, cities and people living in them benefit from the presence of stable households. An increase in relatively high-income households tends to aid the community, both economically and psychologically. Long-time owner-occupants affected by decreasing property values in their neighborhood, deterioration, and increased crime—or the fear of increased crime—are the most likely beneficiaries (Schill and Nathan, 1983, p. 138).

Gentrification in St. Louis also had its critics, as it has in other cities. Critics argued that gentrification, particularly developer-led gentrification, drains excessive public resources to attract and support the physical rehabilitation and infrastructure necessary to attract the more affluent target population. Furthermore, critics say, the more politically astute and vocal gentrifiers will continue to demand a level of city services that will detract from more balanced development of other geographic areas (Laska and Spain, 1979). Other concerns are equity related; in particular, that gentrification funding competes with affordable housing efforts. Examples like San Francisco and Portland, OR, demonstrate some of the worst equity problems with gentrification; poor and middle-income citizens are forced out of their own neighborhoods. Finally, critics argue that the number of gentrifiers is simply too small to make a major impact on urban revitalization (Spain, 1980).

A second theme in neighborhood development is less focused on creating residences that appeal to a specific targeted population of buyers and more concerned with developing the general physical, social, and political infrastructure of city neighborhoods. Proponents of balanced neighborhood development in the city have always seen efforts at infrastructure development as less prominent than the focused physical development of targeted neighborhoods, but a number of initiatives in the 1980s reflected this theme.

Early programmatic efforts reflected concern with the physical appearance and safety of city neighborhoods. Operation Brightside, initiated in the mayor's office, was a visible campaign to clean up and sod vacant lots, reduce trash and litter, and brighten thoroughfares with plantings. Operation Safestreet was a companion program aimed at neighborhood security. This program included subsidized installation of home security measures, neighborhood watch organization, and a more controversial program of installing street barriers to channel traffic flow and more clearly delineate neighborhood boundaries.

More recently, the focus on infrastructure development in specific neighborhoods was intensified through Operation Conserve. This program sought to coordinate services and development programs in selected neighborhoods through city Conserve officers who served as conduits, organizers, and ombudspersons for local citizens and neighborhood associations.

By the end of Mayor Schoemel's tenure in office, the dual strategy of targeted, developer-led gentrification and revitalization of selected neighborhoods had not reversed the downward trend in numbers of city residents. Citizen surveys commissioned by the mayor's office suggested that movement into the city was often temporary, with younger professionals and families moving in only until they had children. There was no systematic information on who was willing to invest their future in the city through home ownership, however. Information on the pattern of citizen response to the city's efforts at residential rejuvenation would be helpful in planning future efforts to revitalize the city's residential base.

Initiation of Policy Research

As a distressed urban area, the City of St. Louis was not in a position to finance detailed research into home buying in the city. However, the city's Community Development Agency (CDA) administered various grants-in-aid from the federal government concerning housing and urban development programs, and these grants often supported or required policy research for planning or evaluation purposes. For example, at the time of this study, CDA was required to produce a housing plan indicating how the agency would promote diversity in the housing market through its use of funds from the Department of Housing and Urban Development (HUD). CDA staff were given both the responsibility for producing this plan and a modest budget for generating information to support plan preparation.

Discussions among CDA staff focused on the lack of explicit information about recent homebuyers in the city. A basic tenet of marketing research is that future buyers will resemble past and current buyers. Staff felt that to promote future home ownership in the city, they needed to know more about recent purchasers. To get this information, CDA negotiated with local universities to get proposals for conducting a survey of recent homebuyers. A contract to conduct the study was written with the Public Policy Research Centers at the University of Missouri in St. Louis. This organization had worked with city agencies on a number of prior urban development studies, including the series of annual citizen surveys commissioned by the former mayor.

The Policy Research Task

The research task defined by CDA was straightforward. However, the information that would be produced was significant because it addressed a crucial issue for the future of the city and provided clearly relevant data that had not been available before this effort. This kind of concrete and relevant information had clear implications for a range of decision making, including assessments of past city efforts to stimulate home ownership and planning for future efforts.

Objectives

The major objectives of the research task defined by CDA staff were to document accurately (a) the socioeconomic and demographic characteristics of persons buying homes in various city neighborhoods, (b) the location and housing status of buyers before their city purchase, (c) their motivations for buying in the city, (d) the degree and sources of satisfaction with their housing purchase, and (e) homebuyers' plans for holding and improving the property. CDA was also interested in the observations of real estate agents and urban developers concerning the reasons for the difficulties in the urban housing market and what might be done about them.

The Decision Context

The housing survey provides an example of a piece of policy research that was initiated for a specific purpose mandated by a federal agency. However, the information that would be generated by the study had important implications for policy decisions of core importance to the City of St. Louis. Thus, the information generated to meet a paper planning obligation might generate useful information for decision makers in city government and for interest groups active in city development and neighborhood revitalization issues.

The Institutional Context

St. Louis is an old city with an unreformed, strong mayor system. The legislative branch of city government consists of a precinct-based city council that gives strong voice to the diverse neighborhood areas in the city. The city itself is financially strapped, having lost much of its residential tax base through urban decline and low housing value. Generous tax abatements have been part of the strategy for spurring businesses to locate downtown. Therefore, as are many older urban areas, the City of St. Louis is heavily dependent on federal funds for community development initiatives. The CDA, the agency responsible for administering many of these funding programs, has major responsibility for developing funding proposals, generating information concerning urban development in St. Louis, and carrying out development planning.

The evaluation team, headed by a professor at the University of Missouri and a senior staff analyst at the Public Policy Research Centers, worked directly with CDA staff. The working relationship was collaborative, with CDA staff involvement in developing the sampling plan and the questionnaire and in interpreting results. No representatives from the larger institutional environment were directly involved in any of these activities. As in any specialized policy-area agency, the CDA staff had a desire to influence city development, and many were particularly concerned about ways of revitalizing the residential housing market in the city. CDA staffers were aware of the attractive and affordable older housing stock in many parts of the city, and they were concerned about ways in which the city might better use this resource in the process of residential rejuvenation. Thus, this project represented an opportunity for them to develop information that might demonstrate the value of the older housing stock for spurring home ownership and to suggest ways of promoting that resource.

The Policy Cycle

The housing study was formally part of a planning process, providing information on past conditions to inform the development of plans for future action. However, as noted, CDA was a major source of information for community development policy in the city, and the housing survey would become a general source of information on housing sales that the agency could draw on in other tasks. In other words, the study could provide an opportunity for CDA input to decisions in other parts of the policy cycle.

Clients and Stakeholders

The evaluation team had only one involved client: CDA—more particularly, a few staff from the CDA research and planning component. Since the study was mandated to meet external requirements for receiving HUD funding, it did not attract a lot of attention from other actors. The evaluation team and CDA staff were free to shape the study without constraints from a broader scope of active participants. HUD was an indirect client and stakeholder, but this had little influence on the detailed content of the study because the general planning requirement could be met in a great variety of ways. Furthermore, the plan would neither receive much scrutiny nor generate feedback to the city once it was submitted to HUD. Like many funding requirements of this type, the HUD requirement served to motivate local funding recipients to go through a planning process that hopefully would make their local policy decisions more informed. Once it was done, HUD would do little with the plan.

Of course, the utility of the study results as a tool for CDA depended on the degree to which the study anticipated the concerns and information needs of other stakeholders and participants in the community development policy community within the city. As noted earlier, the policy initiatives of the 1980s had created an active and diverse set of interests within this policy community, ranging from large residential developers to neighborhood associations and affordable-housing activist groups.

The politically appointed head of CDA and the St. Louis mayor's office were key among these stakeholders in study results. In this strong-mayor city, the immediate utility of any information for effecting city policy would depend most directly on its reception by these policy makers. The residential development and real estate industries are important voices in this community, and they were explicitly brought into data collection for the study both for their key role in shaping the housing market and for the insight they might have into the dynamics of this market. Neighborhood associations and strongly organized local residential groups were other stakeholders who would be vocal participants in future policy discussions about housing availability and promotion in the city.

Research Design and Implementation

In terms of research methods, the task before the research team was quite straightforward. There were two basic types of data collection tasks— a telephone survey and several focus groups. Both were research tasks with which the evaluation team had extensive experience. The Public Policy Research Centers included a survey research unit that regularly implemented telephone surveys using trained interviewers. There were no difficult sampling issues, and the information to be collected in the survey was largely informational and nonsensitive, presenting no difficult measurement issues. While the analysis of survey data can be simply descriptive, the real implementation challenge to making the study useful was in the analysis. As the discussion of findings will show, conducting and presenting analyses in a way that was relevant to policy issues and positions required creativity from the evaluation team.

Information Needs

The basic information needs for the research tasks were descriptive—accurately portraying the characteristics of past homebuyers. The client's information needs were to estimate the characteristics and motivations of potential homebuyers in the city, and the study generated information useful for this estimation task. In fact, as is the case in many planning applications, the estimation function was not built into the policy research task. The writers of the plan would perform this analytic function and would probably rely more on experience and intuition than on formal technical (that is, statistical) methods of projection or forecasting. As noted, this descriptive information base had the potential for meeting other information needs in the community development policy community. For example, it could be used to support evaluative purposes by shedding some light on the possible effects of former housing policy. This information would not support formal technical evaluation of past policy, but it would provide a strengthened base for reasoned discussion among policy makers.

Design and Methods

The study of St. Louis homebuyers was a straightforward descriptive study. The design objective was to draw a sample that would provide a precise and unbiased estimate of all city homebuyers during the study period and to use a questionnaire that would accurately elicit the desired information. Accordingly, the design was centered on a representative survey, enriched through focus groups. Using the marketing research principle that future consumers are most likely to be similar to current consumers, this descriptive design was expected to provide a solid base for understanding and appealing to future homebuyers. The major source of data for this study was a telephone survey of 1,062 single-family homebuyers in the city of St. Louis. The research was conducted in the fall of 1992, under contract to the City of St. Louis's Community Development Agency. To implement the telephone survey, a list of all single-family residential purchases in the city from 1989 to 1991 was obtained from the city's assessor's office. Proportionate random sampling was conducted, and responses were weighted after the survey was completed to account for differing response rates by area. The samples of focus group participants were gathered from the city's Community Development Agency with requirements that participants working in different parts of the city (north, south, and central) all be represented.

The intent of the survey was to gain a greater understanding of the home-buying market in the city. Specifically, the survey asked questions regarding the characteristics of the current and previous residents, the physical characteristics of the dwellings, the primary factors considered by the respondents during the search and purchase processes, and their current satisfaction with their homes and neighborhood.

The survey was augmented by five focus groups of lenders, developers, appraisers, brokers, and Realtors who work in the city, and one focus group of persons who had recently sold their homes in the city. The intent of the focus groups was to gain a greater understanding of the issues facing those who participate in supplying housing to potential purchasers in the city. Specifically, the focus group participants were asked to discuss current market trends in different parts of the city, including the characteristics of buyers and sellers, perceived barriers to prospective buyers in the city, and recommendations for future housing policy.

Data gathered through the survey and focus groups produced a multidimensional picture of current patterns of home buying in the city of St. Louis. This information is unusual among studies of residential redevelopment in core cities. Most existing surveys of homebuyers concerning urban revitalization are focused on particular neighborhoods or specific categories of buyers. This survey provides self-report information on the full range of buyers in the city, and it is therefore ideally suited to the interest of policy makers in a larger pattern of policy options for encouraging neighborhood stability through home ownership.

Selected Findings

The survey and focus groups provided a volume of specific findings that were reported back to CDA staff in descriptive fashion—that is, through straight presentation and summaries of responses. However, discussion between CDA staff and policy research team members had identified areas in which the findings might have larger implications for residential development policy in St. Louis. The selected findings presented here summarize some of the analyses the evaluation team conducted to address these more speculative yet highly relevant issues.

In-Movers and City Dwellers

The housing redevelopment strategies of the Schoemehl administration, and the gentrification strategy generally, were based on the expectation that higher-income homebuyers can be attracted to the city, largely from surrounding suburbs. The responses of recent homebuyers allowed an assessment of the importance of back-to-the-city buyers to the overall housing market in St. Louis. They also allowed an indirect assessment of the degree to which this back-to-the-city movement was fueled by gentri-fication strategies.

Just over one third (37%) of the respondents in the survey of recent homebuyers had previously lived somewhere other than the city prior to their purchase. The largest percentage of homebuyers who did not previously live in the city came from St. Louis County (21.9%)—an area that the Schoemehl administration specifically targeted through public relations campaigns (see Table 15.1). This pattern of movement from near suburbs is consistent with in-migration patterns in other U.S. cities (LeGates and Hartman, 1986, p. 180).

If the downward trend in city population is to be reversed, increasing housing sales to city in-migrants is an important objective. The evaluation team used the survey findings to provide information on characteristics of buyers from outside the city and how they differed from city dwellers who had purchased homes. Table 15.2 illustrates the demographic char-acteristics of those who moved into the city (the "in-movers") compared with those homebuyers who had previously owned in the city (the "city dwellers"). At the request of CDA staff, percentages for the in-movers did not include those who moved to the city from elsewhere in the United States, because the people specifically targeted for city living through CDA promotions were St. Louis metropolitan area residents.

The profile indicated that the great majority of recent homebuyers, whether in-movers or city dwellers, had previously been renting—implying they were first-time homebuyers. There were few differences between the two groups. The sample of in-movers was slightly younger and better educated than the previous city dwellers. Fewer in this group had chil-dren, a higher percentage had never been married, and slightly more had previously owned homes. There were no major income or occupational differences between the two groups. These findings illustrate that for the most part, home ownership in the city was attractive not to upper-middle-class residents from outside the city limits but rather to young, middle-class, well-educated people who had not yet started a family. In terms of residential development strategy, the in-mover profile does not fit the presumed buyer who would be attracted to a gentrification strategy.

Table 15.1 Place of Residence Prior to Purchase

Place	Percentage of Total Buyers	Number of Buyers
City of St. Louis	63.0	669
St. Louis County	21.9	233
St. Charles County	0.4	4
Elsewhere in Missouri	4.1	44
Illinois	2.7	29
Elsewhere in the United States	7.8	83

Table 15.2 Demographic Comparisons Between "In-Movers" and "City Dwellers"

Characteristic	In-movers (n = 310)	City dwellers (n = 669)
Age		
18–34	57.7%	49.2%
35–54	31.6%	39.9%
55+	10.8%	10.5%
Marital status		
Married	63.2%	71.7%
Never married	24.3%	14.9%
Divorced/separated/widowed	12.2%	12.3%
Education		
High school graduate or less	22.2%	32.5%
Some college/Associate's degree	28.3%	26.1%
Bachelor's degree	34.1%	26.0%
Master's/professional/PhD	15.1%	14.7%
Family		
Children at home	39.4%	51.8%
No children at home	59.9%	47.9%
Occupation		
Professional/managerial	48.7%	44.0%
Clerical/sales/service	20.1%	22.8%
Other	31.2%	33.2%
Income		
Less than $30,000	22.5%	23.5%
$30,000–59,999	42.3%	45.7%
$60,000 or more	18.4%	12.7%
Race		
African-American	7.9%	11.7%
Caucasian	91.4%	86.6%
Other	0.5%	1.2%
Prior place of residence		
Previously a renter	67.1%	73.9%
Previously a home owner	32.9%	26.1%

If gentrification was not the magnet drawing buyers to the city, what was? To explore this question, the evaluation team looked for information that might explain the reasons for buying in the city. The most important consideration for both groups was the affordability of the housing (44.3% of in-movers, 44% of city dwellers). The next most important considerations were location in the city and safety and security—cited by only about 10 percent of each group of buyers.

Further evidence of the attractiveness of affordable housing to the in-movers was found when the respondents were asked if the home they purchased would have been more attractive, less attractive, or about the same if it had been located somewhere other than the city of St. Louis.

Almost one third (32.2%) of the in-movers said they would have found their home to be more attractive if it were located elsewhere, compared with only 19.4% of the city dwellers. A substantial number of in-movers were apparently purchasing in the city largely because they could find affordable housing, and they would rather have purchased elsewhere. Contrary to findings in studies of gentrification, many of the St. Louis in-movers are not simply city lovers. They are attracted by the housing value they can achieve in the city context.

Finally, to further substantiate the finding that the majority of in-movers moved to the city because it provided affordable housing, the evaluation team looked at where the in-movers located. Just 11.6 percent of the respondents who moved into the city located in gentrified neighborhoods, where for the most part, median housing prices are $100,000 or more. Rather, most moved into more affordable neighborhoods, primarily in the southern part of the city, where median housing values range between $32,250 (the Patch neighborhood) to $94,575 (the St. Louis Hills neighborhood), with most neighborhoods in the $40,000 to $70,000 range. Most in-movers, therefore, moved into areas with affordable housing, not into gentrified areas.

Analysis by Neighborhood

The data on recent home purchases clearly demonstrated that most of the home purchasing was not related to gentrification strategies. When the full home-buying market was considered, it became clear that understanding the characteristics and preferences of the homebuyers who purchased in more affordable, nongentrified areas was crucial to comprehending the current housing market in the city of St. Louis. Following the premise that neighborhood environment was an important link between home-buying decisions and neighborhood revitalization policy, city neighborhoods were divided into three groups.

- Housing development policies of the 1980s had produced clearly identifiable city neighborhoods that had been targeted for focused residential development. These neighborhoods, identified as "focused development neighborhoods," were initially identified through discussions with informed observers and review of development patterns. Their distinctness was confirmed through examination of the socioeconomic characteristics of the households in the areas. The focused development neighborhoods were the areas in which gentrification was expected to occur.
- A second set of neighborhoods was defined as "stable." They had low vacancy rates (fewer than 10% of units were vacant), a low percentage of very poor people (fewer than 12% were very poor), and a low percentage of unemployed persons (less than 10%). These neighborhoods

lie largely in the southwest corner of the city. Most residents were white, and participants in industry focus groups identified these neighborhoods as the strongest housing market areas in St. Louis.

- A third set of neighborhoods identified as "less stable" was outside the focused development areas. They had higher percentages than the stable neighborhoods on at least one of the indicators identified already (i.e., vacancy rates, percentage of very poor persons, and unemployment as identified through analysis of census data).

The stable neighborhoods were almost all in the southern part of the city, and the gentrified neighborhoods were all in the central part of the city. Less stable areas were predominantly in the north part of the city, with some in central and south St. Louis.

This categorization of neighborhoods created a context for understanding the patterns of home buying in the city. These different neighborhood groupings reflected the approaches taken to revitalizing the city through home ownership. The focused development areas reflected the significant attention paid to creating environments that were expected to appeal to higher-income persons and to enticing purchasers back to the city. The stable neighborhoods had a healthy housing market and did not demonstrate a great need for ameliorative policy. Less stable areas were those that had either become dilapidated or that were in danger of losing their viability as strong residential neighborhoods. Operation Conserve neighborhoods, for example, were found in these areas.

The evaluation team conducted analyses that grouped respondents according to the neighborhoods in which they purchased a home. Respondents who purchased homes in focused development areas were referred to as *gentrifiers*; respondents who purchased in "stable" neighborhoods were labeled *stability seekers*; and purchasers in less stable neighborhoods were called *stabilizers*. In the three years covered by the study, well more than half (58%) of the home purchases in St. Louis were made in the stable areas, confirming the observations by Realtors that these areas were the strongest housing market in the city. One third of the sales were in the less stable areas, and just 8.7 percent were in the gentrification areas. Again, it is clear that gentrification accounted for only a small part of the housing market. Table 15.3 outlines the demographic characteristics of stabilizers, stability seekers, and gentrifiers.

- *Gentrifiers.* Not surprisingly, gentrifiers were significantly older than the other two groups, with a higher percentage of people who had never married. They also had a higher percentage of high educational and income levels and occupational status, and relatively few had children at home. This information confirmed that the persons sampled represented those who had typically gentrified in urbanized areas across the country.

Table 15.3 Demographic Profile of Respondents

Characteristic	Stabilizers (n = 354)	Stability Seekers (n = 616)	Gentrifiers (n = 92)
Age			
18–34	45.3%	57.0%	29.3%
35–54	41.2%	33.0%	60.4%
55+	13.0%	9.8%	10.4%
Marital status			
Married	65.6%	72.0%	65.0%
Never married	16.0%	17.8%	24.1%
Divorced/separated/widowed	17.5%	10.0%	10.3%
Education			
High school graduate or less	32.6%	28.2%	8.6%
Some college/Associate's degree	27.9%	26.0%	20.1%
Bachelor's degree	22.7%	32.0%	33.8%
Master's+	16.6%	13.2%	37.4%
Children at home			
Yes	56.6%	45.4%	31.1%
No	42.8%	54.4%	67.8%
Children under age 5			
Yes	32.9%	33.3%	20.1%
No	67.1%	66.7%	79.9%
Occupation			
Professional	29.6%	33.7%	39.1%
Managerial	12.6%	14.3%	12.6%
Skilled labor	8.1%	8.8%	2.2%
Clerical/sales/service	22.1%	21.5%	10.9%
Homemaker	5.2%	7.0%	13.3%
Retired	6.0%	4.3%	5.8%
Other	16.4%	10.4%	16.1%
Income			
Less than $30,000	29.7%	21.9%	4.6%
$30,000–$59,999	42.6%	47.0%	20.0%
$60,000 or more	12.9%	13.0%	50.1%
Refused to state	14.7%	18.2%	25.3%
Race			
African-American	26.1%	1.5%	8.1%
Caucasian	72.6%	97.0%	88.5%
Other	1.0%	1.1%	2.3%

- *Stability seekers.* The stability seekers—those living in "stable" neighborhoods—were significantly younger, with over half of the respondents less than 35 years old. Most were white and married, and around half had children at home, with a large percentage with children under the age of 5. Educational and income levels and occupational status were significantly lower than those of the gentrifiers. This group appeared to be a mix of blue-collar and white-collar home owners who were mainly young and either childless or just starting a family.

- *Stabilizers*. The stabilizers—those living in "less stable" neighborhoods, were slightly older than the stability seekers, with a lower percentage of married persons, slightly lower educational and income levels, and a higher percentage of children at home, though fewer had children under the age of 5. Significantly, 31.9 percent of the stabilizers were African Americans, compared with only 1.3 percent of African Americans in the stable neighborhoods and 11.6 percent in the gentrified neighborhoods. The stabilizers were the least affluent of the three groups, and they might not have had the means to move into some of the more stable (and more expensive) neighborhoods in the city.

For purposes of arresting neighborhood decline in the city, stabilizers had particular importance. They were the buyers who were making a home-buying commitment to areas that were important to reversing the historical trend of residential flight from the city. Comparisons of the home-buying considerations and other characteristics of stabilizers with other homebuyers would provide insight into who was buying in the less stable areas and why. To understand differences in home-buying preferences, researchers asked respondents to rank the importance of various factors in their decision to purchase a home and to indicate which factor was the most important. Table 15.4 displays the results for the three groups.

Table 15.4 Ranking of Various Factors in Purchasing Decisions of Three Groups of Homebuyers

Consideration	Stabilizers (n = 354)	(Rank)	Stability Seekers (n = 616)	(Rank)	Gentrifiers (n = 92)	(Rank)
Good price	86.9%	(1)	81.8%	(1)	67.2%	(1)
Safety and security	66.4%	(2)	80.6%	(2)	48.9%	(5)
Attractive neighborhood	54.8%	(3)	70.0%	(3)	59.7%	(3)
Location in city	49.6%	(4)	63.5%	(4)	64.3%	(2)
Convenience to work	48.5%	(5)	40.6%	(5)	45.4%	(7)
Architectural style	37.5%	(6)	29.5%	(8)	48.2%	(6)
Access to quality education	34.8%	(7)	37.4%	(6)	16.8%	(9)
Diversity in people and neighbors	32.9%	(8)	21.8%	(9)	50.6%	(4)
Access to family and friends	23.6%	(9)	29.6%	(7)	12.1%	(10)
Access to entertainment and culture	19.3%	(10)	13.1%	(10)	37.3%	(8)

Again, price was considered *very important* by the greatest portion of buyers in each of the three groups. However, stabilizers specified it more often than did gentrifiers. Safety and security ranked second for both stabilizers and stability seekers, but those considerations ranked fifth for the gentrifiers. The percentage of stability seekers who felt safety and security were very important was highest by a substantial amount, and they had purchased in neighborhoods with lower crime rates. This finding suggests that the gentrifiers were least motivated by a fear of crime, and the stability seekers were most concerned about crime. Stabilizers placed midway between those groups.

An attractive neighborhood and a location convenient to work were also very important to the stabilizers. Access to quality education, architectural style, diversity in people and neighbors, access to family and friends, and access to entertainment and culture were ranked lower as concerns for both the stabilizers and the stability seekers. In contrast, the gentrifiers ranked architectural style, diversity in people and neighbors, and access to entertainment and culture considerably higher. This suggested that the gentrifiers were the group most tolerant of and attracted by urban living conditions, including urban ambiance, diversity in people, and access to entertainment and culture. The stabilizers were attracted by the opportunity to own a home and were tolerant of an urban environment, though they expressed some concern about the characteristics of the environment in which their homes were located. This concern was reflected in answers to questions regarding satisfaction with their new purchase and whether their home would have been more attractive if located elsewhere.

When asked if they would have found their home to be more attractive if it were located somewhere other than the city, both the stabilizers (56.1%) and the stability seekers (57.9%) were more likely than the gentrifiers (25.9%) to say it would have been just as or more attractive if located outside the city. This finding, which suggested that many of the stabilizers might relocate if they had the means, reinforced the importance of continuing policy efforts to upgrade neighborhood environments in the less stable areas.

If homebuyers were to serve as stabilizers in less-than-stable neighborhoods, their future plans for housing were important. Three fourths (74.3%) of the gentrifiers saw their purchase as adequate for the future, reflecting the substantial nature of the housing they had purchased. More than half of the stabilizers (59%) also saw their purchase as adequate for the future, as did stability seekers (58.4%). With respect to housing alone, many stabilizers saw their purchase as adequate for long-term housing.

Another indication of the stabilizing potential of homebuyers is their plans for upgrading their homes. Again, the striking finding was the similarity in plans between stabilizers and other categories of buyers.

Stabilizers were just as likely as others to plan on complete rehabilitation (10.7% versus 8.3% and 10.9% for stability seekers and gentrifiers, respectively), and just a little less likely (24.9% versus 29.6% and 29.3%, respectively) to plan major rehabilitation. Stabilizers planned to upgrade their homes, demonstrating an economic commitment to the neighborhood.

Neighborhood commitment is also demonstrated through active involvement in neighborhood organizations and activities. Gentrifiers were most likely to belong to a neighborhood association (57.4%), reflecting their general commitment to city living as well as the strong organizations in their neighborhoods. However, stabilizers (38.0%) were nearly twice as likely as stability seekers (19.1%) to report belonging to a neighborhood association.

Communicating and Using Results

The summary of findings presented here has focused on elaborations of the basic data set produced by the survey. These analyses would not necessarily have been conducted if the use of the survey had been restricted to the simple descriptive purposes required by the HUD planning mandate. The analyses resulted from the interaction of CDA staff and members of the evaluation team. This group of analysts had a larger interest in housing policy and residential development in the city, and they saw the opportunity to provide useful information in this area through additional analysis of the homebuyers survey. The communication and use of the findings reflects this expanded vision of the potential utility of the information.

Reporting Results

The basic findings of the housing survey were presented to the CDA in a final report prepared by the evaluation team. This report presented profiles of recent homebuyers in the city and summarized their reasons for buying, their satisfaction with the purchase, their plans for improving their home, and their planned length of stay in the home. The report also included comparison information on in-movers and city dwellers. In addition to the report, the evaluation team made an in-person presentation of findings to members of the CDA staff. The final report became an information base for preparing the required HUD plan for promoting housing diversity in the city, and it was included in the plan as an attachment.

The analysis of buyers by neighborhood of purchase was not included in the final report. This analysis was not clearly related to the core purpose of the contract for the survey, although it did reflect the interests of CDA staff. Members of the evaluation team conducted the analyses and wrote up a paper for presentation at a Sociology of Housing Conference (Sale and Springer, 1993). The paper was shared with CDA staff, and its implications for housing development policy were discussed informally.

Selected Recommendations

Recommendations were not an appropriate part of the final report to CDA because the focus of the contract was simply to provide new information relevant to plan preparation. However, the data set had clear implications for policy concerning residential development in the city—a core area of CDA responsibility. Some of these implications were spelled out in the conference paper prepared by members of the evaluation team and were shared with CDA staff through the paper and informal discussion. The breakdown of homebuyers into three broad categories served as a useful heuristic device for linking stabilization strategies to home-buying patterns. Implications of the analysis included the following:

- *Recent gentrifiers in St. Louis reflected the pattern identified in studies of gentrification in other cities.* They had a higher income than other categories of buyers and were less likely to have a family with small children. They were more frequently committed to city living as a matter of lifestyle, were less likely to be motivated by issues of affordability concerning their home purchase, and were relatively "risk oblivious" in their buying decision. The St. Louis gentrifiers also reflected the finding elsewhere that gentrification is not predominantly a "back-to-the-city" movement. Many of the purchasers in these neighborhoods were already city dwellers.
- *Gentrifiers were a small portion of total city homebuyers.* This was perhaps the most important finding for redevelopment policy. Gentrifiers are city lovers, and thus the potential for this movement depends on the pool of city lovers in the immediate suburban environs. Furthermore, tax law changes after 1986 have reduced the supply-side incentives to renovation and correspondingly reduced the supply of developer-led gentrification opportunities. While a piece of the revitalization puzzle, gentrifiers were a relatively small piece, and they are likely to remain that way for the immediate future.
- *The largest group of recent homebuyers in St. Louis fell into the stability seekers category.* This designation simply indicated that these purchasers located in the stable neighborhood areas in the southwest corner of the city and did not imply that stability was their top concern in searching for a home. The neighborhoods in which this group bought were not experiencing rapid migration and were not plagued by the high rates of vacancy, crime, and other social problems found in the less stable areas.

Stabilizers were an important group for the prospect of reversing migration and decline in the less stable areas of the city. They were a sizable group, representing one third of the purchasers in the city. A significant number of them were in-movers, and one third were African-American. The less stable neighborhoods represented the most significant opportunity for home ownership for minorities in the city. Stabilizers tended to be people of modest income, many of whom had postponed their first home purchase until later in life. They were just as committed to staying in their homes and upgrading them as were the stability seekers. They had made a home owner's commitment to living in and improving the neighborhoods where they lived.

From a public policy standpoint, the stabilizers are a forgotten component of neighborhood revitalization. Policies aimed at home ownership have been targeted at the more affluent through gentrification, or at the very poor. For cities like St. Louis, a modicum of policy attention to stabilizers could pay great returns in revitalizing some city neighborhoods. The findings in the homebuyers survey and the comments of participants in the focus groups conducted for the study suggested that the greatest impediment to homebuyers in the stabilizer category is the attainment of housing finance. The combination of modest household income and neighborhood location made stabilizers marginal to the housing finance markets. Simple and modest assistance in acquiring home mortgages could be a strong impetus to stabilizing home ownership in less stable neighborhoods. As the forgotten piece of the urban housing policy puzzle, the stabilizing buyer of modest existing housing represents an important policy opportunity.

Action

The housing study represents a common pattern of linkage between policy research findings and policy decisions. The study had direct relevance for meeting information needs at CDA, and it contributed to their complying with HUD requirements for continued funding. However, this direct contribution to action (writing the HUD plan) probably produced very little in the way of policy decisions or resource allocations for strategies to revitalize housing in St. Louis. The analyses and conversations regarding gentrification or neighborhood stabilization strategies had more salience for the policy debates surrounding community development in St. Louis, and these implications were not part of the direct mandate for the survey report. The evidence supporting the importance of stabilizers and the opportunities for facilitating home ownership for stabilizers did become part of the information base at CDA, and it may have influenced the perspectives of key staff members with the ability to affect the policy process in St. Louis. Thus, the most important link between this study and policy action was indirect. The study injected new perspectives and new evidence into the community development policy community, and it might help tilt the scales in weighing future policy options.

Lessons for Policy Research

This case demonstrates the inexact correspondence between the logic of analysis in a focused piece of policy analysis and the logic of decision making to which it may be applied. In this case, the policy research task was clearly descriptive. CDA perceived an opportunity to gather relevant information that had never been available about city homebuyers and had an opportunity to fund a survey of these prior homebuyers. The constraints of the survey technique and the limits of the budget meant that this task was designed to meet descriptive information needs. It described the characteristics and perceptions of recent homebuyers.

However, the policy decisions for which it was relevant required assessment of the efficacy of past policy choices (such as gentrification strategies) and estimation of the desirability of future policy choices (such as housing development plans). Neither resources nor available data would support rigorous methods of research to address these causal and estimation information needs directly, and these logical inferences would still be accomplished through the reasoned judgment of actors in the policy community. Nevertheless, the provision of new and highly relevant descriptive information provides a basis for improving these policy judgments and inferences.

The case also demonstrates the potential utility of facilitating the production of relevant information through reporting and planning requirements from higher levels of government. Local governments typically operate in an environment of fiscal scarcity with strong demands for using resources to meet direct service needs. Finding resources for conducting policy research is difficult, and the requirement to use funds from higher levels of government (typically federal) for research accounts for a major portion of the policy research conducted at local levels. Many critics of federal research requirements focus on the perception that much of what is reported to the federal level does not lead to direct federal action. In many instances, the greater value of much of the federally required policy research may be its relevance for and influence on the perceptions and judgments of local decision makers.

Finally, and most importantly, this report foreshadowed an urban housing development pattern fitted to St. Louis's unique history and community culture. St. Louis has continued to strengthen the urban appeal of the inner city. New and vibrant neighborhoods have grown up through the city, including loft parties, a unique City Museum, and music and food venues in the historic and long-neglected shoe warehouse district. A new Cardinals stadium was built, spurring residential and commercial development in the heart of the city. And most important from a housing standpoint, diverse neighborhoods have experienced a rebound. It cannot be said that this study had direct policy impact, but it did supply early information and support for the kinds of diverse neighborhood development activities within the housing policy mix in the city. As stated in a blog headline, "gentrification may not mean what you think it means in a city like St. Louis" (Swanstrom, 2014).

Focus on Research Methods

Using Focus Groups in Policy Research

A focus group is a "carefully planned discussion designed to obtain perceptions on a defined area of interest in a permissive, nonthreatening environment" (Krueger, 1988, p. 18). The St. Louis housing study described in this chapter used focus groups as one means of learning about the preferences of homebuyers in the city. The use of focus groups originated as a technique of basic social science in the late 1930s, but it has gained more widespread recognition as a tool of market researchers in the private sector. Typically, focus groups consist of 7 to 10 people discussing an issue of concern with a skilled interviewer; discussion is intended to be relaxed and informal, with the possibility that group members will influence one another in an interactive fashion (Krueger, 1988).

Focus groups are popular among market researchers because they can provide credible, in-depth information about consumer perceptions, attitudes, and preferences at a minimal cost. Although the information that focus groups typically yield is not necessarily generalizable to large populations, they might provide greater detail than a conventional survey would. For this reason, focus groups have also become increasingly popular as a tool for policy researchers.

Krueger (1988, pp. 31–37) suggests several possible settings in which focus groups can be a useful tool in policy-related research:

- Before a program begins—Focus groups can be used to assist in projects designed to assess needs, research markets, or inform program design.
- During a program—Focus groups can help provide information for formative "process" evaluations.
- After a program has been completed—Focus groups can help illuminate outcome-oriented assessments.

As Krueger (1988, p. 37) noted, focus groups, like other qualitative policy research techniques, can be used to complement more quantitative data collection methods, such as surveys of larger populations. The St. Louis housing study used such a combined approach—a systematic sample of homebuyers was complemented with focus group interviews of buyers from different regions of the city.

However, the use of focus groups must be limited to settings for which they are appropriate and valid. Krueger also noted, *"Focus groups are valid if they are used carefully for a problem that is suitable for focus group inquiry"* (1988, p. 41; emphasis added). Moreover, policy researchers must be careful not to overgeneralize from focus group results. For additional information about how to use focus groups in policy research, see, for example, Krueger (1988), Goldman and McDonald (1987), and Advertising Research Foundation (1985).

Acronyms and Jargon

CDA—City of St. Louis Community Development Agency

City dwellers—Survey respondents (recent homebuyers) who reported previously owning homes in the City of St. Louis

Gentrification—The physical and social-class upgrading of inner-city neighborhoods

Gentrifiers—Survey respondents who purchased homes in focused development areas

HUD—U.S. Department of Housing and Urban Development

In-movers—Survey respondents (recent homebuyers) who reported moving into the City of St. Louis

Operation Conserve—St. Louis program to coordinate services and development programs in selected neighborhoods using Conserve officers who served as conduits, organizers, and ombudspersons for local citizens and neighborhoods

Stability seekers—Survey respondents who purchased homes in stable neighborhoods

Stabilizers—Survey respondents who purchased homes in less stable neighborhoods

Discussion Questions

1. Descriptive information needs were paramount in this study; what other kinds of information needs did the policy research client have, and how were they met? What kinds of additional policy research activity would have been useful in meeting these needs?
2. Why did the policy research team use focus groups? How did they enhance the findings of the study?
3. This study provides another example of policy research generating new concepts as a by-product of data collection and analysis. Why and how did the policy researchers develop new concepts and terminology in conjunction with this study?
4. Why were no recommendations associated with this study?
5. How and why did the policy research team expand the research problem beyond the immediate needs of the decision-making client?

Assignments and Activities

1. Propose an appropriate research design for planning housing development policy in your city. Be sure to check for existing data by consulting with local housing officials.
2. After becoming familiar with relevant planning documents and existing data for your city, write a request for proposals that calls for data to address the information needs associated with city housing policies.

16 Evaluation of the California Ignition Interlock Pilot Program

A Policy Experiment

J. Fred Springer and Joël L. Phillips

Introduction

Policy researchers occasionally have an opportunity to participate directly in the policy process by evaluating an explicitly experimental policy. This case study is the result of a pilot program or experiment mandated by the California state legislature. It also involves government agencies from every level in the U.S. intergovernmental system. The experiment was to test the effectiveness of a high-tech device that, when installed in the vehicle of a convicted drunk driver, would prevent its operation by the driver if he or she had recently consumed alcohol.

The case study illustrates that even under such laboratory-like conditions, policy researchers may find it difficult to assess the impact of public programs. It also provides an example of how even a primarily experimental research design can profit by the inclusion of qualitative research techniques. When this study was presented in the first edition of this text, we warned that limitations of the study could ultimately weaken the usefulness of the research findings. One of the reasons we have retained this study is because our fears did not materialize. This seminal study contributed to a development in DUI reduction policy that has spread throughout the country.

The Policy Problem

Drunk driving is a problem with a national profile, but legislation to address it must come from states and localities. More than three decades ago, groups like MADD (Mothers Against Drunk Driving) and others sparked legislative efforts to reduce the presence of drinking drivers on the nation's highways. The goal of most of these efforts was to strengthen legal sanctions against convicted motorists. The program profiled here was different. It sought to apply a sanction that would hopefully prevent convicted drivers from drinking and driving while on probation and hopefully help them develop awareness and behaviors that would help prevent future drunk driving. The policy allowed judges to require the installation of ignition interlock devices as a condition of probation.

These devices were designed to prevent impaired drivers from operating motor vehicles.

By all available indicators, California was experiencing a substantial problem with drinking drivers at the time of this study (1986). In 1982, for example, a total of nearly 350,000 arrests for DUI—driving under the influence—were made in the state, nearly 1,000 each day. In 1986, the state had more than 2,500 alcohol-related traffic fatalities. As elsewhere, in California the DUI problem is exacerbated by its chronic nature among some offenders. In 1982, approximately one in three convicted DUI offenders in California had a prior record for the offense. This high level of recidivism—DUI reconvictions—was an indicator that spurred the state to experiment with new measures.

So by the mid-1980s, practical and reliable breath-test technology for vehicles had become available, and technological advances made the production of interlock devices feasible on a large scale. Laws making it illegal to operate a motor vehicle if the driver's blood alcohol count (BAC) is above a specific breath alcohol limit had become standard. These laws made other proof of impairment unnecessary, lowering legal objections to using interlock as a sanction. Concomitantly, the National Highway Traffic Safety Administration (NHTSA) determined that both the general public and the legal system found interlock devices to be an acceptable way of attempting to prevent DUI. The remaining question was would they work in practice? The devices require drivers to perform a breath test before the vehicle in which they are installed can be started; if the breath sample indicates blood alcohol above a preset level, ignition is prevented. Critics were skeptical about the possibility of circumventing this process. It was time to find out.

Initiation of Policy Research

California became the first state to authorize the use of ignition interlock technology as a DUI countermeasure when it passed the Farr-Davis Safety Act of 1986. The Farr-Davis Act was a multifaceted law that authorized the use of ignition interlock as a demonstration (pilot) project with a finite life. Thus, the act mandated a policy *experiment* with the following provisions:

1. Ignition interlock testing would be conducted in four counties.
2. The test results would be evaluated to determine whether the devices deterred drinking and driving.
3. The implementation of the program would be evaluated.
4. A sunset provision would automatically repeal the act in 1990 unless the legislature acted to extend or delete the repeal prior to that time.

Another important aspect of the legislation is that it authorized interlock as an *optional* condition of probation for persons convicted of DUI.

Thus, interlock was to be a *sentencing option* imposed at the discretion of judges in the four participating counties. In this role, judges had nearly total discretion. Each county court could use interlock as a sentencing alternative within the following guidelines:

- Any person convicted of DUI could be granted probation under the interlock system.
- The interlock device could be used only in addition to other requirements of the law; it could not be used as a substitute for participation in an alcohol education or rehabilitation program, for example.
- The courts were required to determine the ability of persons to pay for the device and to lower the fines for DUI should the person claim to be unable to pay for the device. The courts were required to notify the California Department of Motor Vehicles (DMV), by means of an abstract of conviction or violation, that the person was required to use the device.

The Policy Research Task

The policy research task in this example was reasonably structured and limited by legislative mandate: specifically, the research was to provide an indication of how effective the ignition interlock system was as a sentencing alternative.

Objectives

The research objectives for the study were suggested by the legislation authorizing the study. The researchers were to

- Identify four representative counties willing to participate in the demonstration.
- Collect and analyze data to describe the process of implementation in each county.
- Collect and analyze treatment and comparison data that would support conclusions about the success of the program in reducing DUI recidivism for participants.

Challenges

Evaluation research for assessing the ignition interlock pilot program had to be designed to collect and analyze information based on an ongoing program implemented by local judges and court systems. As noted earlier, the legislation was designed to preserve local court autonomy in deciding the extent to which interlock would be used as a sentencing option and in deciding exactly which offenders would be sentenced to interlock as a condition of probation. The recognition of local court autonomy was an important precondition for gaining the cooperation of pilot counties in using the untested device as a DUI countermeasure.

From a policy research perspective, however, the operational autonomy of the program was a challenge because it imposed significant limitations on the research design and methodology. The most important limitation was nonrandom selection of individuals to be sentenced to using the interlock device—random selection is a critical characteristic of classic scientific experimental design.

Similarly, the local autonomy built into the program meant that implementation processes would differ markedly from county to county. Even if the program was shown to have an impact, that impact could be the result of different processes and procedures in the four participating counties. Moreover, each county (by design) had different demographic and socioeconomic characteristics that could be expected to have an impact on the outcome of the experiment. For example, one county, San Diego, in the southern part of the state, is large and urban, with more than 2 million residents. Sonoma is rural and suburban and has only 360,000 residents. Differences like these could have a substantial impact on the success of the program in each county.

The sheer number of agencies participating in the pilot program meant that data collection would be a cumbersome task. Among the agencies in possession of necessary data were the state DMV (driver records), the county court and probation offices (court sentencing records), and the three interlock device manufacturers (device performance data). Considerable difficulties were encountered in the task of reconciling the various data sources—none of which was reliably complete.

The Decision Context

The ignition interlock project was conducted in a context that was reasonably amenable but also potentially threatening to the use of policy research. On one hand, the research was legislatively mandated and addressed a fairly specific causal research question. This would auger for a receptive audience. On the other hand, a multiplicity of stakeholders with political and economic interests in the outcome of the study could muddy the waters.

The Institutional Context

The primary clients for this study were state government agencies. Despite the fact that the interlock program was legislatively sanctioned, there was not universal support for the success of the device. The state Department of Motor Vehicles (DMV), for example, sought control over the use and testing of the device. Manufacturers of the device, of course, had a vested interest in demonstrating a positive result for interlock technology. Thus, the institutional context represented a mine field for researchers—multiple interested parties with opposing positions and perspectives.

The Policy Cycle

At first glance, this project is a classic example of an evaluation phase project. The interlock program was initiated as an experiment, and the research was mandated to evaluate its impact. However, the policy sequence differs from that required for a classic experiment in several important ways.

Although the interlock program itself was a temporary, experimental pilot project, political reality dictated that it must be built on the foundation of the existing criminal justice system. Most significantly, local courts insisted on near-total autonomy and discretion in making the decision about who would receive the interlock sentence. Rather than adopting systematic criteria or making random assignments, the judges in the four county courts made the decision for each DUI conviction based on their own judgment.

Clients and Stakeholders

The *nominal* client in this case study was the California Department of Alcohol and Drug Programs (DADP). DADP was ordered to evaluate the ignition interlock program by the enabling legislation in the Farr-Davis Act. However, implementation of the act involved a cooperative effort of several federal, state, and local agencies, as well as private concerns. Therefore a variety of stakeholders had to be considered in designing and implementing the evaluation. They are discussed in the following subsections.

Federal

The NHTSA supported the evaluation portion of the project with federal funds. NHTSA also provided technical support for implementation of the interlock program itself. For example, NHTSA conducted a series of informational tests of various alcohol interlock devices to determine their accuracy and susceptibility to circumvention.

State

The California Office of Traffic Safety (OTS) was actually responsible for implementing the act, and it also initiated and directed the evaluation study. Thus, although DADP was the client of record, OTS was most heavily involved in implementing the program. OTS participated in the selection of counties that were to test the interlock device. OTS also was responsible for certifying the interlock devices, although it received assistance in this task from the NHTSA.

The California Bureau of Auto Repair (BAR) was responsible for setting the technical standards for the installation of the interlock devices. BAR's responsibilities were specified through administrative agreements with OTS. At the time of the research project, however, BAR's proposals for regulations on interlock devices had yet to undergo necessary legal review. Thus, interlock manufacturers themselves installed the devices.

The California Department of Motor Vehicles (DMV) was responsible for providing the records of DUI offenders; these records were used both in the sentencing process and as data in the research project.

County

The four counties selected by OTS for inclusion in the pilot project were Sonoma, Alameda, San Diego, and Santa Clara. (The research design section that follows explains the choice of these particular counties.) The primary role of counties in the study was played through the court systems that were to sentence DUI offenders to the interlock device. Additionally, county probation departments monitored installation and maintenance of the interlock devices in the vehicles of DUI offenders. Probation officers and other court officials were supposed to ensure that the devices were used properly. To this end, the Farr-Davis legislation required that persons sentenced to interlock "report to the court or the probation officer at least once annually, and more frequently as the court may order, on the operation of each interlocking ignition device in their personal vehicle or vehicles."

Interlock Manufacturers

Three different manufacturers produced interlock devices that met the testing standards set by OTS. Each manufacturer's device accomplished the necessary performance objectives in different ways. For example, different combinations and profiles of temperature, pressure, or humidity were used to prevent anyone from circumventing the device. In addition to providing the interlock devices, manufacturers performed several critical functions. Chief among these was the installation and maintenance of the interlock devices. A condition of this requirement was that manufacturers report to the courts quarterly on the performance of every device they installed. As a result, the manufacturers also kept records on the history of the performance of each device.

Convicted Individuals

Individuals sentenced to use the interlock device were required to prove that they had complied with the sentence within 30 days of sentencing. They were, of course, forbidden to operate any vehicle not equipped with the device, and circumvention of the device constituted a probation violation. Those required to have the device were also required to report to the court or probation office at least once annually.

Research Design and Implementation

The policy researchers were faced with the challenge of designing a project that would both address the focused causal issues identified by the Farr-Davis legislation and provide meaningful insight into *why* the project met or failed to meet expectations.

Information Needs

In this case, the information needs of the client were specified in the enabling legislation for the pilot program. This had the general effect of circumscribing the envelope of the research project. OTS was instructed to select four "representative" counties for the project and to do the following:

1. Examine the effectiveness and reliability of ignition interlock devices as a sentencing option
2. Review the data collected by the participating county court systems by monitoring the results of implementing the program
3. Develop uniform sentencing and probation procedures that could be applied statewide

Although these objectives are fairly vague, the legislation was relatively specific in defining the means by which the pilot program would be judged, stating that success would be determined "by comparing the recidivism rate of those persons subject to [the interlock program] and to demographically and statistically similar cases where [the interlock program] was not applied." The law specified the following criteria:

- The program would be considered "not significant" (that is, not successful) if there was a reduction of less than 10 percent in repeat offenders (recidivism) for program participants during the two years of the study.
- The program would be deemed "a success" if the recidivism rate of participants was reduced by at least 10 percent.
- The program would be deemed "extremely successful" if the reduction in the recidivism rate was more than 25 percent.

The Farr-Davis Act further directed OTS and counties participating in the pilot program to assist in the evaluation of the program by developing reporting forms for documenting and monitoring the use of the interlock device. Although the information needs specified in the legislation clearly contained the hallmarks of a causal research problem, descriptive information was also required. The legislation called for development of procedures for possible statewide implementation of the program. This task required collection and analysis of descriptive information about the character of the implementation process. Thus the project entailed elements of both causal and descriptive policy research.

Design and Methods

Design: The Quasi-Experimental Analysis of DUI Reconviction

The central research question for evaluating the impact of interlock devices on DUI reconviction was to estimate what the reconviction rate for probationers would have been if they had not been assigned the device. The research design constructed to answer this question had to provide both quantitative information (about the impact of the devices on DUI) and more qualitative information (about how the program was implemented). In the near absence of existing data, the resulting design would require a great deal of data collection.

The key strategic design choice for determining the success of the program was a *quasi-experiment*, which attempts to emulate a classic experiment in situations in which conditions are not truly appropriate for an experiment. In the case of ignition interlock, a classic experiment was not feasible because a random assignment of DUI offenders into an experimental group was impossible due to local control over the sentencing decision. Quasi-experiments are typically less able to provide definitive information about the effectiveness of public programs, but they are nevertheless a valuable design option.

In addition, the research design called for a number of qualitative data collection efforts, including the use of surveys, questionnaires, interviews, and documentary analysis. Most of the qualitative data was directed toward the issue of program implementation and processes.

The quasi-experiment was fashioned by creating a matched comparison group of DUI convictions; the comparison group was used to serve the same function as a formal control group in a classic experiment. To make results from the quasi-experiment as valid as possible, researchers had to identify and select comparison cases that were similar to the interlock "experimental" probationers in ways that could affect the likelihood of repeat offenses.

Methods

Collecting the appropriate data for the experimental design was a complicated and difficult task. Figure 16.1 illustrates the process used to create

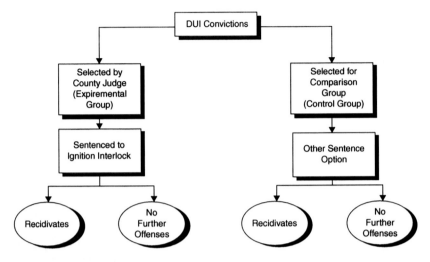

Figure 16.1 Design for Selection of the Ignition Interlock Experimental Groups

the experimental and control groups for the study. In order to identify these groups, the following sequence of tasks had to be completed.

1. *Identify probationers sentenced to interlock.* In reality, interlock was used as a sentencing option in only a small percentage of DUI cases in each county. The possibility existed that gaps in the legal records might exist; the validity of the quasi-experimental approach hinged in part on the fullest possible identification of the quasi-experimental group. To identify these cases, researchers consulted three separate data sources:

   a.   Notification forms sent to OTS by the county courts
   b.   Manufacturers' records of court notifications that a DUI offender had been sentenced to interlock
   c.   Manufacturers' records of actual installations

   Any of these sources could help identify an individual sentenced to interlock who was inadvertently omitted from the other two sources. This search identified 775 confirmed interlock probationers. However, manufacturers' records indicated that devices were installed in only 584 vehicles.

2. *Collect data for interlock probationers.* Local court files were collected for each offender sentenced to interlock to determine the characteristics of the quasi-experimental group. This involved merging data from three sources: court records (arrest record and court actions data), DMV records (personal characteristics), and manufacturers' records (installation data).

3. *Identify a matched comparison group.* Using the data collected from the interlock probationer group, researchers constructed a

comparison group by selecting an offender who was matched on five key characteristics: gender, race, age, number of prior DUI convictions, and blood alcohol count (BAC) at time of arrest. The evaluation team selected matching criteria in consultation with the funding agency. Most were selected because they had shown a strong correlation to recidivism in prior research. Race was selected as a variable to check for the possibility that judges applied the program differentially across racial groups. It was anticipated that this frequently raised question concerning judicial system procedures might arise in the interpretation of study results.

Researchers believed these criteria potentially had an impact on DUI reconviction rates. However, the comparison group *could* have been similar to the interlock group in unknown yet significant ways.

The crux of the quasi-experiment lay in comparing the reconviction rates of the interlock group with those of the matched comparison group. Methodologically, this was achieved by two means:

- A test of statistical significance of the difference between the reconviction rates of the two groups (chi square was also calculated)
- Logistic regression analysis, with reconviction serving as a dichotomous dependent variable "explained" by differences in the two groups. (This technique was employed in a follow-up to the final report on the project.)

Driving and related court records of persons convicted of DUI in the four participating counties were among the most critical data needed for the study. These records held the outcome of each interlock sentence, as well as vital background data. Driving records for all DUI convictions were available from the state DMV. Local court files contained more detailed information about each offender, and in the crowded misdemeanor court system, identifying and tracking individual DUI offenders required a major research effort that took the following forms:

1. *Survey of municipal judges.* A written survey of all municipal judges in counties participating in the study was conducted. The survey provided information about judicial awareness of the program, the use of interlock devices as a sentencing alternative, and related opinions about the program.

2. *Written questionnaires for interlock probationers.* Questionnaires were filled out by a small, nonscientific sample of probationers who had been sentenced to ignition interlock. These mail-in questionnaires were distributed when respondents were having their devices maintained. They were used to provide qualitative, anecdotal insight into some of the study questions.

3. *Intensive interviews.* Intensive interviews were conducted with the following groups of stakeholders: (a) judges who used the

interlock-sentencing option, (b) prosecuting and defense attorneys in participating counties, (c) manufacturers' representatives, and (d) other informed persons. These interviews provided the perceptions and opinions of persons most closely associated with implementation of the pilot program.

4. *Analysis of interlock logs.* One potential source of existing data was available only in one participating county. Interlock devices in Santa Clara County automatically kept an electronic log that was routinely printed out at the required calibration checks. The logs indicated what happened each time an attempt was made to start an equipped vehicle. For example, if an individual who had been drinking attempted to start a vehicle and the device prevented him or her, the event would be recorded in the electronic log. The electronic logs could be converted into data files, analyzed, and/or printed out.

In addition to these analyses, documentary analysis and literature review were undertaken. Relevant records and internal data concerning interlock were reviewed and analyzed. These documents included guidelines and procedures, forms, certification reports, interlock installation, maintenance and removal records, and service call records. The literature reviewed focused on the development of ignition interlock technology and its application elsewhere. U.S. Department of Transportation Highway Safety Administration (OTHSA) reports were the most significant source of relevant literature.

Selected Findings

Effectiveness of the Interlock Device

The final report found that the interlock device produced "positive" results but that the data did not support definitive conclusions. The report noted that the results obtained in the analysis met the legislated criteria for a "very successful" performance, but it also emphasized that the results needed to be evaluated with caution, due to limitations of the data and research methods.

Because this was the centerpiece of the policy information requested by the client, this issue was discussed in great detail. Inasmuch as recidivism (meaning DUI reconviction) was the variable of concern, an important step in analyzing the data was to define "recidivism" in operational terms. For the purposes of the study, recidivism was defined as any reconviction for DUI that appeared in the DMV system for an arrest within one year of the time the interlock device was installed. A similar definition was used for the comparison group, whose record constituted recidivism if there was a reconviction for DUI that appeared for an arrest occurring between the time of conviction for their *last* DUI and the following year.

Table 16.1 presents the results of the quantitative analysis that provided the initial and perhaps the most straightforward answer to the question: Does ignition interlock reduce recidivism among DUI offenders? This table was a critical component of the research, since some stakeholders might base their assessment of the device on these data alone.

As Table 16.1 indicates, individuals who were sentenced to the interlock device were reconvicted at an overall rate of 13.6 percent; individuals in the comparison group were reconvicted at a (higher) rate of 16.7 percent. However, the reconviction rates for each county varied significantly. Two counties, Alameda and Santa Clara, actually experienced a higher reconviction rate for the interlock group than for the comparison group.

To determine the amount of change in recidivism due to the program, the projected recidivism rate (that is, the comparison group rate) was multiplied by the number of interlock probationers to identify a *projected number of recidivists* that would have been expected to occur without the program. Figure 16.2 displays the differences between the *projected* and *actual* reconvictions in each study county. The percentage change attributable to the program was then calculated by identifying the percentage of change from the projected number of recidivists that is represented by the actual number of recidivists. A similar number was calculated for the study groups as a whole by aggregating the county figures.

As the figure indicates, the results indicated an overall reduction of 18.5 percent in the projected number of reconvictions for probationers who had interlock devices installed in their cars. The figure also illustrates, however, that decreases were achieved in only two counties, San Diego and Sonoma. Indeed, in Alameda County, the projected number of reconvictions increased by 133 percent, and in Santa Clara County, little difference was detected. Moreover, neither the overall reduction nor the reduction observed in Sonoma met standard tests of statistical significance.

Thus, the results of the research indicated that the program had met the legislatively mandated criteria for "success" (more than a 10 percent

Table 16.1 Comparison of DUI Reconvictions for Interlock and Comparison Groups

County	Interlock Group			Comparison Group			% Change in Rates
	Number	Reconvicted	Rate	Number	Reconvicted	Rate	
Alameda	79	14	17.7%	61	5	8.2%	+ 133.3%
San Diego	251	28	11.2	218	40	18.4	–39.2
Sonoma	78	12	15.4	65	18	27.7	–44.4
Santa Clara	171	25	14.6	153	20	13.1	+11.9
Total	579	79	13.6	497	83	16.7	–18.3

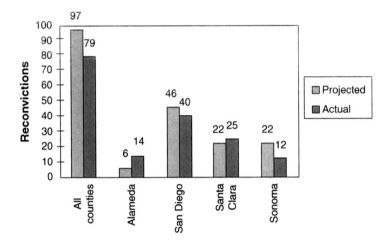

Figure 16.2 Projected and Actual Reconvictions by County

reduction in recidivism), but it had done so at a statistically significant level in only one county. The report noted that the nonrandom method of selection incorporated in the report and the small numbers of individuals included in the analysis indicated that these results needed to be treated with caution.

The results of the study also demonstrate the frequent "slippage" in applicability of research criteria in applied settings. Because the samples of offenders and comparison cases were not "random," the application of tests of statistical significance (which assume random selection or assignment) was not technically warranted. Still, these tests are commonly accepted indicators that lend the appearance of science to a study. Part of the difficulty in communicating the results of this study was in communicating that the results might have substantive importance even though no simple indicator of scientific "significance" was met.

Implementation of the Program

To fully evaluate the interlock program, it was necessary to understand how and why individual judges used it. Therefore, an extensive portion of the report provided a detailed description of how the interlock program was implemented. The report concluded that the program had been successfully implemented from the standpoint of setting standards for and certifying interlock devices. However, as a sentencing option, the program was a less than overwhelming success. Among the problems identified in the report were the following:

• Only a small number of judges consistently used the interlock sentencing option. Judicial resistance, as well as the additional burden on court personnel of monitoring the program, could prove to be major barriers to implementing the program on a statewide basis.

- One reason judges were reluctant to use the interlock sentencing option was the perception that interlock was an option for those who could afford to pay for it. The report concluded that the economic indigence provisions of the program had been "virtually ignored."
- Judges that did consistently use interlock sentencing imposed it on a variety of types of offenders for a number of different reasons. No appropriate sentencing model emerged from the pilot study.

A combination of data from surveys, interviews, and the quasi-experiment was used to generate conclusions about the implementation of interlock. Comments taken from interviews with individual judges were used to demonstrate that the judges exercised total discretion in selecting DUI convicts for interlock:

"I make it a personal decision. There's no set policy. It's based on the individual."
(Alameda County judge)
"Each judge sets their own policy. There is no standard."
(Sonoma County judge)

Survey data demonstrated that for many judges, the cost of the interlock device, as well as other concerns, helped explain their reluctance to use the device as a sentencing option. Table 16.2 summarizes some of these data.

The survey data were complemented with additional quotes from the interviews:
"I've seen very few offenders who could afford the interlock. Many don't even own vehicles and aren't employed."
(San Diego County judge)
"My reluctance is based on the belief that it appears to permit the wealthy to somehow avoid other more onerous conditions of probation."
(San Diego County judge)

Avoidance and Circumvention of the Device

The report identified two serious problems with the installation, maintenance, and monitoring of the interlock devices.

1. Findings on the effectiveness of the interlock device were based only on the outcomes associated with individuals who actually had the device installed. The report determined that approximately one

Table 16.2 Interlock Sentencing Patterns in Study Counties

County	Sentencing Pattern
Alameda	Sentencing policy was heterogeneous; it tended to target younger offenders.
San Diego	Two judges were responsible for most sentences to interlock. Interlock was frequently assigned to violators of probation from prior DUI convictions; the great majority of interlock assignees had prior DUIs.
Santa Clara	One judge was responsible for nearly all interlock sentences; most assignees were first-time offenders.
Sonoma	Courtwide sentencing policy targeted young, first offenders with high BAC.

fourth of those sentenced to interlock never had the device installed—primarily because of lack of compliance with court orders.

2. The study found that the device could be successfully bypassed or circumvented.

The study therefore concluded that although the interlock device was effective in reducing DUI recidivism, it did not ensure that "determined drinking driver[s] will not get behind the wheel" (EMT, 1990). Data in support of this critical finding came from a number of sources, but primarily from a comparison of court orders for interlock installation, matched against records from both the courts and manufacturers to determine when the device was installed. The rate at which probationers failed to have the device installed varied by county. However, approximately one fourth of all of those who were sentenced to use it failed to have the device installed. Although in some instances it was impossible to determine why this failure occurred, examination of the data revealed that in most cases the reason was either noncompliance (by those sentenced) or a court-ordered deletion of the installation.

Communicating and Using Results

Communication of study results proceeded primarily through structured channels as delineated by the research contract. The policy research team issued a series of interim reports that culminated with a final report when the study period ended.

Reporting Results

The final report was divided into chapters corresponding to the two major research issues: the impact of the devices on DUI reconvictions and the implementation of the program. Additional chapters provided an analysis of how sentencing decisions were made by judges and the case management process used to install, monitor, and remove the interlock devices. These latter chapters provided important information not explicitly requested by the client agency yet invaluable to understanding how the program worked.

Because of the critical role quantitative analysis played in this project, a detailed explanation of the quasi-experimental design was placed near the beginning of the report. In addition to describing how the experiment was conducted, this section also described in explicit terms the limitations of the findings generated by the design.

The final report contained both a summary of findings and a set of recommendations.

Selected Recommendations

The recommendations were preceded by the following caveat: "The findings of this study support a positive but non-conclusive assessment of the potential of ignition interlock as a DUI countermeasure." It also recommended that further study of the application and effectiveness of the device be conducted, noting that further recommendations had to fall within the following constraints:

- Recommendations could not immediately place significant additional administrative responsibilities on the court.
- Recommendations could not require significant immediate public expenditures or loss of revenues to courts.
- Recommendations should minimize reliance on individual manufacturers.

Within these parameters, the report addressed the following recommendations:

1. *Communication of information.* Standardized forms should be developed and used to document interlock sentences, compliance, and results, and copies should be forwarded to all agencies involved in the process.
2. *Sentencing decisions.* No recommendation was made regarding targeting specific types of DUI offenders for the devices since the "data . . . gathered through the pilot program does not allow firm conclusions concerning how to target . . . offenders."
3. *Sanctions.* The following measures might be taken in response to noncompliance with the interlock sentence:

   - Automatic license suspension
   - Issuance of bench arrest warrants
   - Withholding drivers' licenses pending installation of the device

4. *Implementation responsibilities.* Lack of knowledge about the program was widespread, and OTS should be commissioned to develop and disseminate information concerning the device and its potential value as a DUI countermeasure.

Action

The evaluation report on the ignition interlock pilot project became a key element in the policy dialogue and actions concerning interlock legislation in California. Because the report findings were mixed—indicating both overall positive outcomes regarding DUI recidivism yet results that were not consistent across all counties—the cautiously stated conclusions were vulnerable to attack by both pro- and anti-interlock forces. Given the potential economic benefits to manufacturers if use of the device became widespread and the centrality of the issue to DUI policy in the state, the qualified conclusions of the study were contested by *both* sides. One manufacturer lodged a protest with the California Office of Traffic Safety, claiming that the study was methodologically flawed; the protest suggested that the study *underestimated* the effectiveness of the device in that county. This manufacturer had supplied, installed, and maintained the devices in a county that did not show positive results. The manufacturer commissioned a professor at a local university to review the study's methods. Unfortunately for the manufacturer, however, the professor produced a report that supported the study method—the quasi-experimental design—as scientifically sound and properly implemented.

The research division of the California Department of Motor Vehicles also attacked the study but claimed the findings *overestimated* the effectiveness of the device. The DMV had not supported the interlock pilot project in the first place and had sought authority for a DMV evaluation instead. The department's major criticism of the study was that persons who had been assigned to interlock but who never had the device installed were not included in the quasi-experimental test of effects on DUI recidivism. The evaluators countered with two arguments: (a) that the study tested the effectiveness of the device and not the adjudication and the implementation process associated with it and (b) that many of the persons who did not have the device installed might have left the state, removing them from the scope of the study anyway.

This policy dialogue was carried on by means of memoranda, meetings with the OTS and interested legislators, and several public hearings on the study and the interlock devices. Ultimately, the California legislature passed a bill extending authorization for using interlock devices as a condition of DUI probation throughout the state. The study and its generally positive result, qualified though it was, provided political ammunition for those who supported the legislation. The report was widely circulated nationwide and cited in similar studies in other states. The lead evaluator was invited to a NHTSA meeting of state decision makers to present study results. There is little doubt that the study contributed to the adoption of interlock legislation in other states and to volume of policy research on ignition interlock that has followed.

By 2011, there were 28 states that had more than 2,000 interlocks installed as a condition of DUI probation (Casanova-Powell, 2015). Overall, these states had 238,997 DUI probationers using interlocks in 2011, an increase of 183 percent since 2006. Texas had the greatest number of installed interlocks (33,064). Washington, Arizona, Colorado, California, and New Mexico all had more than 10,000 interlock probationers. NHTSA and the CDC had sponsored a research program on alcohol interlock programs over the preceding decades, resulting in support materials for states and localities using or considering interlock programs. Many of the vulnerabilities in the use of interlock that were identified in the initial California study described here had been addressed. States had passed laws that required or recommended use in certain cases, limiting the variability of use because of individual judicial skepticism. Criteria for use varies by state but include one or some combination of first time offense, repeat offenses, high BAC level, or issuance of a hardship license. Monitoring systems for probationers' use of the device had improved, allowing detection and penalties for failure to install, circumvention of the device, or excessive failed blows. As a result of these improvements in technology and procedure, the effectiveness of ignition interlock use had improved dramatically. A recent CDC/NHTSA brief reports "ignition interlocks reduce repeat offenses for driving while intoxicated (DWI) by about 70% when they are installed" (CDC/NHTSA, 2015, p. 1). The initial California policy experiment had helped start a three-decade-long policy development process that has resulted in a widely used DUI sanction that does not rely simply on punishment to reduce repeat offenses.

Lessons for Policy Research

Despite being conducted under the relatively controlled conditions associated with evaluation of a policy experiment, the research described in this case study failed to yield definitive results. One weakness of using the quasi-experimental approach to formulate policy is its demanding formal structure that may break down in the field. In this case, designers of the pilot project did not foresee that insufficient numbers of drivers would be sentenced to DUI, making a statistically significant outcome relatively difficult to achieve. Political reality dictated that individual judges would retain control of the sentencing process if the project was to be implemented at all, effectively limiting the number of interlock probationers.

Nevertheless, the research associated with the experiment was not a failure. It did establish that interlock probationers were less likely than other probationers to be arrested for subsequent DUI offenses, and it identified various problematic aspects of implementation, paving the way toward further experimentation. Indeed, much of the value of the research lay in identifying the weaknesses in the way the program was run. Particularly significant in this respect were the findings of judicial reticence to use interlock devices in sentencing and the ease with which the devices could be avoided or circumvented. Transparent communication of these technological and procedural reasons for the less-than-hoped-for experimental outcome was a major contribution of this study to the subsequent policy development described in the previous section.

Focus on Research Methods

The Quasi-Experiment

The central research technique upon which this project was anchored was a *quasi-experiment*. Like a classical experiment, a quasi-experiment compares outcomes between experimental and comparison (or control) groups. However, whereas quasi-experiments emulate the classic experimental design in most ways, they lack the element of random assignment to either the control or the experimental group. This feature introduces more uncertainty about the validity of results obtained from quasi-experimental designs (Langbein, 1980). This uncertainty is the price that policy researchers pay for their inability to exercise the degree of control found in classic experimental design.

In this instance, the policy research team was unable to create the proper conditions for a classic experiment because the judges from each county wanted control over which offenders were selected for inclusion in the interlock program. In a classic experiment, the policy researchers would have randomly selected both those offenders who used the interlock device and offenders assigned to the control group. In practice, the policy researchers had to select a "comparison group" that resembled the nonrandom experimental group in as many ways as possible. The comparison group was created by studying confidential individual court records in a very detailed manner.

From these records, the policy research team selected a comparison group that matched each member of the experimental (interlock) group with a DUI offender of similar race, gender, number of prior convictions, and blood alcohol count, but no sentence to interlock. Each of these characteristics was selected because of a possible link with reconviction rates. By making the experimental and comparison groups equivalent with respect to these characteristics, the policy researchers sought to diminish (but not eliminate) the possibility that the groups differed in a systematic way.

Quasi-experiments are often desirable elements of policy research because of their utility in isolating causal information. However, conditions for creation of quasi-experimental designs are not always present. Pilot programs (like the ignition interlock program) are one setting for these designs. Cooperation from officials and stakeholders involved with the program or policy is also usually necessary as well. Ethical and political considerations may also hinder implementation of such a design; in the ignition interlock case, the policy research team had to work carefully to gain the confidence of court officials.

Acronyms and Jargon

DMV—California Department of Motor Vehicles
DUI—Driving under the influence
Farr-Davis Safety Act of 1986—California legislation authorizing a pilot program to test the effectiveness of ignition interlock devices
Ignition interlock—A device designed to prevent drunk driving by making a vehicle inoperable if the driver's breath exceeds a given level of blood alcohol content
NHTSA—National Highway Traffic and Safety Administration
OTS—California Office of Traffic Safety

Discussion Questions

1. Assuming that a classic experiment with a random selection of participants was indeed impossible, how could the impact of the program best be documented? Suggest and describe an alternative research strategy.
2. What kinds of operational difficulties do you think might be associated with collecting data in this case?
3. Why were the gender, race, blood alcohol count, and other variables of interlock offenders important to the quasi-experiment? What additional data might have been useful?
4. How might the implications of this report differ if the qualitative data concerning program implementation had been omitted? That is, if the research had been confined to the quasi-experiment, what conclusions might have been drawn?
5. How, in your opinion, did the fact that each county's judiciary was the final sentencing authority affect the research strategy needed to evaluate the program?
6. What complications arose in determining the impact of the ignition interlock program? How did the policy researchers deal with these complications?

Assignments and Activities

1. Write a working draft of the research problem, including the major subissues you can identify.
2. Write a memorandum explaining the strengths and weaknesses of the preceding research design. How could the research design have been strengthened?

17 Information for Community Policing

Cops on the Beat in the 21st Century

Jessica Herbert and J. Fred Springer

Introduction

In 1955, a competition within the Los Angeles Police Department (LAPD) asked members of the law enforcement community to state the core mission of policing in a few plain words. Officer Joseph Dorobek, a member of the department, submitted the winner—"to protect and to serve." As time passed, this succinct statement of purpose became the slogan for the LAPD and many other departments across the country. It recognizes that police should not only protect the community through law enforcement, they should also provide fellow citizens with services their position in the community can support. In recent years, the role of policing in America has become a difficult national issue that demonstrates the need for the two critical ideas in this slogan—protect *and* serve—to meld into a single vision of policing. This vision requires a trusting and informed relationship with community members. It requires an emphasis on interactive communications and understanding rather than external control. At the time this case study is being prepared, it is clear that there is a lot of work to do to reach this goal.

In 1994, the Office of Community Oriented Policing Services (COPS) within the U.S. Department of Justice was created to encourage and support law enforcement service to communities, and to promote policing practices that give officers an interactive role within the community. To do this, the COPS program has delivered more than $14 billion in funding to support *community policing* in local communities, including training and technical assistance to local and state police agencies across an array of community policing topics. Despite nationwide acceptance of the concept of community policing and the COPS effort, combining law enforcement with a helping hand for the community has proven difficult. Recent confrontations between "militarized" police and community protestors have entered America's living rooms through the 24-hour television news cycle. Tragic events, evolving from police use-of-force incidents (e.g., Michael Brown in Ferguson, MO, Freddie Gray in Baltimore), indicate the urgent need to improve policy and practice defining the role of police and their relationship with their community. The May 2015 President's Task Force on 21st Century Policing report emphasizes the importance of building relationships and balancing police responsibilities to enforce laws and protect persons, emphasizing a need to enforce laws *with* the people not just *on* the people. This chapter describes a policy research project that explores the need for communication channels and types of information that will improve communication between community policing efforts and community members. Through her work on community policing, a researcher at Arizona State University recognized the lack of evidence-based guidance materials (e.g., training resources) concerning the need for communication and information linkages important to local community policing practice. More important, there was little research attention to how two-way communications could be achieved. Accordingly, she undertook an exploratory study (a) to explore how existing community policing programs currently communicate with citizens and (b) to understand how they use these communications to improve their ability to *serve* as well as protect. This chapter summarizes this investigator-initiated contribution to policy research.

The Policy Problem

The importance and lore of the police officer as a trusted and helpful community servant has a nostalgic appeal. The friendly beat cop, a standard character of mid-20th-century films, is a prime example. While the COPS program and many local practices (e.g., local requirements that law enforcement officers live within the communities they police) encourage this service role, the community context and institutional environments in which they operate have changed dramatically, and so have the foundations and functions of the traditional cop on the beat. A basic example is the physical basis of the "beat," which traditionally refers to relatively small geographic areas that can be patrolled on foot, putting the officer in close interpersonal contact with community members. In an environment in which shopping, health care, and entertainment have increasingly moved to automobile-oriented "edge cities," the traditional "beat" concept does not apply. Today, news, interpersonal communication, and even community involvement are increasingly channeled through cell phone, email, social media and other electronic communications rather than face-to-face conversation. The communication necessary to hearing citizens' needs and to assessing law enforcement's interactions with the community, must be viewed within this evolution in communication generally.

Criminal justice research in the 1990s did explore the framework of community policing in this changing environment. In an influential summary discussion, Gordner (1996) identified four dimensions along which the unique characteristics of community policing could be defined. They were: (1) philosophical, (2) strategic, (3) tactical, and (4) organizational

(Gordner, 1996). Philosophical shifts included opening policing up to the input of citizens. Input was needed to identify issues to be addressed within neighborhoods and the delivery of services to address these problems (Gordner, 1996). Strategic and tactical dimensions included operational management issues such as restructuring police patrols, focusing resources within geographic areas, and emphasizing positive partnerships. The organizational dimension includes internal structures to measure and evaluate community-policing performance. Thus, communications with the community to determine needs on one hand and assess community interaction and service on the other form the bookends of Gordner's framework for community policing.

Existing policy research on community policing, much of it sponsored by the COPS program or the National Institute of Justice (NIJ), has primarily contributed to refinement of the strategic and tactical concept dimensions. Research suggested specific strategic approaches and tactical activities from which local law enforcement could choose. Less attention was paid to operationalizing the philosophic commitment to citizen input or to personnel and program needs for performance monitoring and evaluative feedback. The COPS Office does mandate a community policing evaluation tool for all grantees (COPS, 2014). However, this instrument is a general self-report assessment that focuses on the degree to which specified structures or functions have been put in place. These functions are identified in Table 17.1 and are used to organize some of the analysis presented in this study. It does not provide significant information on how they are used to plan or assess service to the community or if *what* they are doing is working.

Law enforcement information systems have changed significantly in the digital age, becoming more comprehensive, accurate, standardized, and useful. These improvements have improved the ability to track and monitor law enforcement events and procedures and have provided useful information on assessing need for law enforcement and attainment of law enforcement objectives. In some agencies, state-of-the-art management information systems support assessment of the performance of individual officers, providing data to promote career advancement and accountability. The development of these systems has focused on indicators of the degree to which law enforcement is effectively implementing federal, state, and local criminal laws. For example, the recent *Standard Functional Specifications for Law Enforcement Records Management Systems* developed by the Law Enforcement Information Technology Standards Council (LEITSC) presents standards for law enforcement metrics concerning the protection side of law enforcement. This includes measures of the amount of crime and disorder in a jurisdiction such as calls for services, arrests, and seizures of contraband. These are the data that support policy decisions and management decisions. Furthermore, they provide a basis for individual rewards for officers based on their

Table 17.1 Community Policing Self-Assessment Tool Categories (Office of Community Policing Services)

Module	Definition	Concepts
Community Partnerships	Collaborative partnerships between the law enforcement agency and the individuals and organizations they serve to develop solutions to problems and increase trust in police	Engagement with a wide range of partners Government partnerships (non–law enforcement) Community organization and local business partnerships General engagement with the community
Problem Solving	The process of engaging in the proactive and systematic examination of identified problems to develop effective responses	General problem solving Scanning Analysis Response Assessment
Organizational Transformation	The alignment of policies and practices to support community partnerships and proactive problem solving	Agency management Personnel management Leadership Transparency

Source: Community Policing Evaluation Tool, ICF International on behalf of the Office of Community Oriented Policing Services, found at www.cops.usdoj.gov/Default.asp?Item=2673.

level of activity to respond to crime, identify suspects, make arrests, and sustain criminal charges through prosecution. These institutional procedures help make law enforcement accountable to the authority defined through criminal justice laws and legal structures. They do not apply clearly to community policing. The integration of community policing techniques within police organizations remains difficult to identify, define, and evaluate.

The integration of technology (e.g., radios, mobile dispatch terminals) changes the way police address concerns in the community with reliance on dispatch to react to service calls, report-writing requirements, and use of multiple databases. This evolution has impacted the way police agencies operate and address crime and is part of the training and standard practice of policing for enforcing laws and safety. The potential role of electronic communications for community policing seems evident. Community policing is not grounded in slowly evolving criminal laws. It is grounded in being aware of and sensitive to changing community circumstances, perceptions, and needs so community service and community connections can evolve positively. The flexibility and instant accessibility of electronic media hold intriguing possibilities for community policing's communication and information needs. The question is how to harness them. This is the policy problem.

Initiation of the Policy Research

The policy research reported in this case was not initiated through a request for proposals or any other externally identified need for information. It was self-initiated by a policy researcher who saw a gap in effective practice in a policy area in which she worked. More specifically, it was initiated due to trends observed across multiple police agencies requesting federal technical assistance to enhance their relationships with their communities. The lead author of this case led research and technical assistance projects for the Department of Justice's Bureau of Justice Assistance and Office of Justice Programs's Diagnostic Center. These agencies provide assistance on specific crime issues or crime concerns that affect community policing (e.g., community response to youth crimes). In her work with these agencies, she could see that community policing agencies wanted better information and communication with their communities.

There were three major aspects of this need. First, local programs recognized that communication is an integral part of working closely with the community. Second, they needed to better understand how their program strategies and activities were performing—that is, to what extent were they effectively working with the community? What difference was it making? Third, they needed guidance and tools for improving their communications, including better use of appropriate technologies. The initiator of this research knew that the latter need was essential and that this guidance was not well developed or available. She viewed this research as a way of at least providing a stronger grounding in her own work and hopefully providing information that would be useful to others.

The Policy Research Task and Objectives

The research task was envisioned as twofold. First, though there is little literature, policy, or operational guidance for using electronic communications to aid community policing, on-the-ground community policing programs may have developed promising strategies from which others could learn. What is currently being done with electronic communications in typical community policing? Second, what does existing practice on the ground imply about improving the use and value of electronic communications, including social media, which is uniquely suited to real-time input/monitoring of community conditions and reactions relevant to community policing? At the time the task was initiated, the objectives were broad.

- The first objective was to develop a feasible way of assessing existing information on current community policing communications with community members, focusing on electronic methods. Feasible in this case meant working with a low budget and using readily available secondary data.

- The second objective was to conduct a comparative case study exploration of similarities and differences in how community-policing programs communicated with their communities and how they used different methods of communication, focusing specifically on electronic methods.
- The third objective was to advance thinking about how community policing might better use electronic communications (Hong, 2013; Guo et al., 2016). This meant understanding how it was being used by different agencies, the effects of context on that use, and identifying insights that the cases suggested about possibilities that were not currently being pursued.

Challenges

This study faced somewhat unique challenges because it was self-initiated. These included the following.

- Challenges to designing and implementing this policy research began with very limited resources. Being self-initiated, there was no budget explicitly for the project. Being at the ASU School of Criminology and Criminal Justice, one of the top law enforcement research centers in the country, and doing consulting work with the Fayetteville, NC, community policing unit did provide a supportive environment. Still, research approaches had to be practical and prudent.
- A second set of challenges concerned the contextual sensitivity of the topics under study. Community policing opportunities for communications (e.g., foot patrols) are more dependent on the environment than the internal departmental communications focus of traditional law enforcement communication. Contextual issues include cultural differences (e.g., ethnicities, historical families) that require particular methods of communication and outreach. Language barriers or cultural contexts (e.g., communication with only the male head of household) might prevent a police agency from connecting with residents. Understanding informal representatives within a neighborhood may also be valuable (e.g., elderly familial leaders) for agencies to engage residents. The use of electronic media is well established in some communities and demographic groups (e.g., young people). Exploring more diverse community contexts was necessary to create an ability to generalize to any degree.
- Another critical challenge to this research, as with much criminal justice research, was access to data. Most police agencies excel at collecting crime-related information (e.g., report crimes) and their performance related to those events (e.g., arrests), but the collection of non–crime-related information can be either scarce or nonexistent. With respect to exploring communication relevant to community

policing, data from either traditional (e.g., newspapers) or nontraditional (e.g., social media posts) communication sources was limited at best.

The Decision and Institutional Context

The fact that this study was not being done for a client dramatically changed the decision context for the policy researcher. Constraints related to client or stakeholder preferences, concerns, or fears were not directly imposed. Of course, the policy researcher's motivation in initiating this effort was to make a difference, so foreseeing those stakeholder concerns and interests was important to producing usable information. Several considerations suggested that the approach being investigated here had advantages for producing usable information. One of the advantages of exploring electronic media as a communication strategy is that it does not impose a heavy cost burden. Communication is at the core of police activity. The use of free social media platforms and analytics or adjustments to current data collection practices are practices that can preserve resources. The shifts in practices (e.g., inclusion of community outreach data in CompStat meetings) are also within the scope of police authority and may not require additional funding or manpower. When a solution is within the scope of authority and is not a strain on resources, police leaders are more likely to adapt and incorporate changes.

The institutional environment was relevant to this study in another important way that the policy researcher did not fully anticipate at the initiation of the study. One of her concerns in starting the study was the lack of institutionalized ways of assessing the performance of community policing, other than qualitative descriptions and anecdotal comments in annual reports or other relatively unsystematic reporting mechanisms. One of the issues she wanted to explore was the degree to which current use of internet and social media communications might provide an opportunity for creating metrics to help institutionalize measures of communications relevant to community policing purposes. It was clear that the currently institutionalized measures of police performance were entirely focused on enforcing laws, not interacting with the community in other ways. The potential importance of changing this institutional focus became more clear as the study progressed.

Clients and Stakeholders

The policy researcher may not be under direct pressure from clients or stakeholders in this case, but anticipating the interests, capacity, and motivations of potential users and stakeholders is important. This case is tame with respect to controversy and conflict among potential stakeholders. The objective is to improve communication and cooperation between police and community, an objective with few obvious opponents—no one's ox is being gored, as it were. However, there are stakeholders that will be important to getting the information used. First, given the early and exploratory stage of the study, other policy researchers and pro–community policing interests will be an important constituency for the results and ideas put forward through this study. Agencies and interests involved in promoting community policing and providing training and resources in how to more effectively integrate it into policing standard practice are important initial audiences. Local police agencies are eventual end users, and their capacities and perspectives are important stakeholder considerations. A variety of local resources across public health, education, and skills training contribute to community policing efforts. These resources include public works, parks and recreation, counseling services, mental health services, drug abuse and addiction programs, art programs, tutoring, life skills training—the list goes on. These resources are key in problem-solving processes. Developing rapid, accessible, and useful communications will require cooperation and support of broad community interests.

To summarize, the consideration of clients and stakeholders in this case is different than circumstances in which the policy researcher is working for a client. The challenge in this case was first to craft the research so that it considered the many stakeholder perspectives that will have to be negotiated to bring attention, consideration, and hopefully use of the ideas to help develop stronger community policing.

Research Design and Implementation

The research design for this case may be best described as a purposive (i.e., driven by the need for information on current use of electronic communications for community policing), exploratory (i.e., examining empirical information to build understanding of uses rather than test existing concepts about uses), opportunistic (i.e., samples obtained through existing access to the information) comparative case study (Yin, 2013). Put differently, it is an example of the creative use of analysis concepts and tools that often fuels policy research when external resources are not available.

Methods

This design was crafted to support two levels of analysis. First, cases were selected to allow description of the institutional context of community policing programs in study communities and to describe the ways in which organizational transformation, problem solving, and community partnership are furthered in the programs themselves. Second, the design supports description of the communication techniques used to support community policing. Comparisons across cases augment these descriptions to identify similarities, differences, and areas of potential lessons and practices worth further research and development. The selected studies were not intended to assess whether one approach is better than another. The objective was to document the degree and purpose of electronic communications with the community and how they function. This design does not pool results. Each case is an individual example of community policing and communication methods.

The first step in implementing the design was selecting cases. The pool of potential sites was determined by three criteria: (1) adequate information on the sites had to be available to support a qualitatively comparable set of cases, (2) the cases had to have a community policing program, and (3) the number of study sites had to be small because of limited resources available for conducting the analysis. The pool itself was drawn from law enforcement agencies with documented participation in Office of Justice Programs's Diagnostic Center (OJPDC) training and technical assistance (TA) programs. Specifically, the Fayetteville, NC Police Department was included because the lead author (Ms. Herbert) led a four-month research and TA project in Fayetteville. This project included site visits, interviews, and access to department documents and records. Intensive involvement with the Fayetteville site meant that it was kind of a first among equals in the study. As the analysis will show, there was more opportunity to access detailed data and records in Fayetteville than in the other sites. Two additional sites, Las Vegas and Boston, were selected from programs participating in the OJPDC P2P (peer-to-peer) program that paired programs to share experiences and lessons. The lead author had contact with both of the sites and knew they were committed to community policing but had substantially different experiences and approaches. Data collection activities in each site are summarized in what follows.

Both primary and secondary data collection and analysis was conducted to support this study.

- For Fayetteville, a review of secondary sources (e.g., annual reports, procedural manuals) supported documentation of agency policies, organizational structure, and operational activities of the community policing unit. The Office of Justice Programs Diagnostic Center research and TA team, including the lead author, conducted multiple site visits to the program. Interviews were conducted with police staff and community members on topics related to community policing techniques and communication practices. This team had access to social media analytics data tracked by the Fayetteville program. This was the only one of the three sites in which there was access to this data.
- In Boston, the lead author led a site visit, participated in officer ride-alongs, and conducted interviews with community police officers and supporting personnel to identify the functions of community policing units. Primary data collection on communication strategies involved

content analysis of Boston Police Department's (BPD's) website and social media platforms. Secondary data collection on social media platforms provided additional descriptive data to be identified (e.g., trend of followers, impact in posts). Secondary data collection included review of standard departmental reports and documentation, as well as research and technical assistance reports authored by the COPS SMART Policing Initiative.

- In Las Vegas, secondary data collection and analysis included multiple reports. First, Las Vegas Metropolitan Police Department (LVMPD) has published status reports on the Safe Village Initiative, the Department's community policing program (Las Vegas Metropolitan Police Department, 2008). The COPS office Collaborative Reform evaluation reports detail changes in both organization and communication methods produced through that technical assistance program. The lead author also conducted primary and secondary data collection and analysis of open-source records and media reporting to evaluate LVMPD communication methods.

In summary, data collection was mixed method, using both primary and secondary sources. This information was accessed and assembled primarily for the purposes of problem solving and technical assistance. The technical assistance had somewhat different foci, but agency relations and communication with the community were relevant to all activities. Fortunately, this produced an exploratory data set well suited for the purposes of this policy research. While regularly collected monitoring data focused on crime statistics, some sources provided documentation of community service activities. Annual data on the COPS program, for example, provide documentation of community events and communications.

Focused analyses were undertaken on electronic communications. In one site, the Fayetteville Police Department, community interviews were conducted to identify perceptions of the police department and awareness of community resources. Social media platforms (i.e., Facebook, Twitter), police websites, and local government websites were reviewed to identify branding, messaging, and communication strategies. Aggregated data on user and follower engagement was collected through secondary sources for social media marketing analysis. In the case of Fayetteville, access to analytics data for Twitter allowed for an in-depth qualitative analysis of original post content and user engagement.

Selected Findings

The research in each of these community policing sites produced detailed findings of direct utility to the programs themselves. It provided the kind of monitoring and feedback information that is important to strategy improvement, program implementation, and assessing effectiveness. In these sites, particularly Fayetteville, there was movement toward developing regular data-monitoring capacity that is relevant to community policing. The comparative study component described here was intended to contribute evidence-based information concerning the larger need for electronic communication to improve interactive communication with the community and to improve monitoring and assessment capability for community policing. Three broad statements summarize the comparative case study findings.

The Three Community Policing Programs
Have Distinct Approaches

The first set of relevant findings demonstrates the diversity in the way community policing is organized in the three programs under study. The bulleted findings summarize basic features of unit context and organization.

- Fayetteville is the smallest of the case study jurisdictions, serving a population of approximately 200,000. The Fayetteville Police Department (FPD) deploys a jurisdiction-wide community police unit, which is not unusual for smaller jurisdiction programs. The program staff includes both sworn officers and nonsworn personnel. The Fayetteville program focused on community events and problem-solving interaction with the community to repair and strengthen community–law enforcement ties after shooting incidents and unrest related to those incidents.
- Boston has a population of approximately 650,000. The Boston Police Department (BPD) uses an interdisciplinary team approach to community policing, with several decentralized units in select police districts. These units involve sworn officers as well as nonpolice staff such as substance abuse counselors and other helping services personnel.
- LVMPD serves the largest jurisdiction. It is a metropolitan district, headed by the Clark County Sheriff, serving a population of approximately 2,000,000. The Las Vegas Metropolitan Police Department's (LVMPD) approach to community policing focuses on a single neighborhood with a high concentration in violent crime. This Safe Village Initiative received the Herman Goldstein award from the Center for Problem-Oriented Policing. Safe Village Initiative employees are sworn officers, but the unit works with a neighborhood collaborative that guides and supports events and initiative activities in conjunction with the unit. The initiative has contributed to significant organizational and communication changes for this specific neighborhood.

Overall, these cases displayed diverse program scope, including full jurisdiction, multiple neighborhoods with individual problems, and a single high-crime neighborhood. They have different staffing patterns and different problem-solving and service relations to their communities.

*The Community Programs Adapt Communication
and Interaction With the Community to Fit
Differences in Program Emphasis*

Comparison of site visit information on community policing strategy, organization, and activities demonstrated that each program adapted engagement and community interaction with community members somewhat differently. The following comparison of communication patterns with the community and extent of engagement in interactive communication with community members establishes a broad picture of communication needs and organized methods of communication in the community. All programs used communications through meetings (standing and ad hoc), traditional media (print, radio/television), and public outreach messaging (e.g., signage, pamphlets), as well as electronic media (discussed in the next section). However, they used them with different emphases according to overall program purpose and strategy. The top-line summaries of strategies presented here draw largely on findings from the COPS community partnerships and problem-solving tools.

- Fayetteville's community policing used a broad strategy of building trust and cooperation with community members by being more engaged in and supporting collective activities, resources, and events in a whole-community context. Problem solving focused on outreach and working with community organizations and members. Both sworn and nonsworn staff worked closely with community organizations, leaders, and members both proactively (leading and leveraging activities) and responsively (supporting community-initiated activities). Traditional media and community outreach messaging supported public awareness of events, as well as ad hoc meetings to organize those events.

- Boston's community policing strategy was to work with specific neighborhoods with their own assigned units. Both sworn officers and nonpolice services personnel worked with community organizations (e.g., schools, after-school programs, work programs, substance abuse prevention and recovery programs) to improve programs and services for at-risk community members, particularly the young. Standing and ad hoc meetings and outreach messaging to increase awareness and participation in these services were primary communication activities. Traditional media can be important for messaging about the program but will not effectively meet the primary, neighborhood-focused outreach messaging necessary for this program.

- Las Vegas's Safe Village Initiative focuses on a single high-crime neighborhood within the larger city. The objective is more crime reduction and prevention oriented and is focused on creating a true collaborative relationship with the community to do this. Residents have a high level of representation on the steering committee and in decision making at standing and ad hoc meetings (Swanson, 2010). Communication and information dissemination needs are more crime focused than in the other sites, and the messages conveyed in traditional print and radio/TV messaging were important. Focused messaging and communication within the community is a special communication need that is a high priority for the Safe Village Initiative. Communication must be proactive, inclusive, and supportive of community understanding and involvement.

The Programs All Use Online Information and Social Media, but for Somewhat Different Reasons

Aside from more traditional communication settings (e.g., meetings, events) and outlets (e.g., print media, radio/television, focused outreach messaging) discussed earlier, all three of the community policing units have websites and social media accounts (e.g., Facebook, Twitter, YouTube). These online platforms were used to varying degrees and for varying purposes. This section summarizes use of websites and social media in each.

WEBSITES

Each of the programs is within a department, with comprehensive websites that provide the public with information on police and community functions. Boston Police Department's landing page (www.bpdnews.com) demonstrates a unique approach. It is modeled to be a scrolling feed of information related to crime, community events and activities, and personnel achievements. The website is updated in near-real time, and graphics convey the feel of a beacon or announcement. The navigation bar is simple in style and wording to navigate the user to learn more about how to protect against crime, contact information for police districts, and other resources from the police department. The emphasis is on news events; there is not a strong presence of law enforcement graphics (e.g., badges, police cars, tactical gear). Community policing unit activities and events have a continuing presence on the site, but they are not singled out or clearly labeled as community policing events. The Las Vegas (www.lvmpd.com) and Fayetteville (www.bethebadge.com) department websites present a traditional law enforcement approach, with graphics prominent of police badges, cars, and logos. Information portrayed on the landing page includes the sheriff's or police chief's message to the community and both sites have a messaging phrase regarding community commitment and policing. However, none of these sites have dedicated information about the community policing program, despite having pages for more traditional and nationally recognized programs such as Neighborhood Watch, Law Enforcement Explorers, and so on. In Las Vegas this may have been due to the local focus of Safe Village in a large jurisdiction. In Boston, the news event format does not single out specific programs. In Fayetteville, the reasons are not clear. The takeaway message, however, is that existing department websites are not an effective medium of communication for the community policing programs. They have little presence on those sites.

SOCIAL MEDIA

All three programs also had access to Facebook and Twitter accounts associated with their police departments. Table 17.2 provides a summary of indicators of use for these accounts. The social media profiles for these agencies indicate a substantial volume of followers and a fairly regular use of original content to reach out to their communities. The BPD has more than twice the number of Facebook followers of any other site, despite the much larger jurisdiction population for the LVMPD. Fayetteville had by far the fewest followers but of course serves a much smaller community. Twitter accounts follow the same overall pattern. Boston has the heaviest use with more than 361,000 followers and approximately 87 percent of tweets originating from the agency. Las Vegas has approximately 77,000 followers with 40 percent of posts stemming from agency announcements. Fayetteville has the smallest number of followers (approximately 3,400); 52 percent of the posts originate from the department. These numbers document substantial use of social media by these departments. It also suggests differences in

Table 17.2 Aggregate Facebook and Twitter Account Information

Agency	Facebook	Twitter
Boston Police Department	Followers: 171,010 Most Interactive Post: Photo Account creation: est. 2010	Followers: 361,387 Original Posts: 87.5% Account creation: est. 2009
Las Vegas Metro Police Department	Followers: 80,019 Most Interactive Post: Video Account creation: est. 2008	Followers: 77,344 Original Posts: 40.0% Account creation: est. 2009
Fayetteville Police Department	Followers: 27,131 Most Interactive Post: Video Account creation: est. 2010	Followers: 3,470 Original Posts: 52% Account creation: est. 2010

Note: Aggregated data and account information from Facebook.com, Twitter.com, Followerwonk (Twitter analytics), and Quintly (Facebook analytics).

the way Twitter is used. In Boston, the Twitter account posts are almost all initiated by the department. This is probably because the department has used Twitter primarily as an emergency alert system in situations in which specific warnings of danger need immediate dissemination—the Boston Marathon bombing is a clear example. This shows an important use for this form of social media. These announcements could be useful for community policing, but when units are geographically targeted, such as in Boston and Las Vegas, this would require program-specific social media to allow efficient use—that is, reaching those to whom the information is relevant. In Fayetteville and Las Vegas, the Twitter initiation flow is more balanced, but the inability of the team to access or conduct internal analytics of content attached to initiation and response patterns limits understanding of what information sophisticated internal analytics may bring.

The Fayetteville Police Department did provide some direct access to Twitter analytics data. This provided information that allowed for the quantitative and qualitative analysis of agency-posted information. The use of an automated public safety messaging system created a boost in originated posts from 2011 through 2013, but that was discontinued. While the number of posts is low, the categorization of post content displayed in Table 17.3 supports the feasibility of a social media communication strategy with direct relevance for community policing.

Agency-originated posts were identified as either crime or community events. Although crime events are the most frequent type of post (57 percent), originating posts on community events or for community assistance with events were nearly as frequent in Fayetteville. This suggests strong community engagement in this form of social media. The fact that the community policing effort is contiguous with the full jurisdiction may be an important facilitator of the relevance of social media for the program.

Table 17.3 Fayetteville Police Department Twitter Posts, Qualitative Categories (*n* = 1,762)

Year	Crime Event		Community Event	
	Information Only	Solicitation for Action	Information Only	Solicitation for Action
2010*	62	20	45	6
2011	262	49	184	16
2012	291	42	149	21
2013	97	53	132	17
2014	49	35	89	14
2015**	33	5	86	5
Grand Total	**794**	**204**	**685**	**79**

* Includes only posts made from September 2010 to December 2010
** Includes only posts made from January 2015 to September 1, 2015

This indicates that followers in Fayetteville have the opportunity to engage with non–crime-focused information such as requests for support of a community member, opportunities for volunteering, potential for developing responses to community problems, and even advice concerning preparations for possibly dangerous events, like threatening weather, a fire hazard, or a flooding hazard. The crime-related information posted by Fayetteville PD and then shared by their online user community also indicates use of social media to invite appropriate community assistance in solving crimes.

This evaluation of information content in Fayetteville and the less detailed analyses in other sites have several implications. First, it demonstrates the use of social media to convey both crime-related and non-criminal community event information at relatively equal levels. It also demonstrates the use of social media as an engagement (i.e., solicitation for action) tool as well as an information outlet. It also suggests that the Fayetteville context had features that promote this use. The whole jurisdiction scope of the community policing effort makes its mission contiguous with the reach of the intended social media community. This is less the case in Boston and particularly in Las Vegas. The use of social media may need to be more closely tied to the relevant components of the overall jurisdiction to make it a useful tool in multiunit or highly targeted programs. After all, one of the purposes emphasized in the Boston and Las Vegas programs is maximizing responsiveness to defined community conditions. This is even more of an issue for programs intended to be highly collaborative, such as the Safe Village Initiative. This same issue of mismatching scope of the relevant audience is an issue for the use of web technology for neighborhood-focused programs. In sum, as is often the case with exploratory investigation, this study of communication using internet and social media in community policing has posed more questions than answers. This is not a failure; it is the nature of exploration of new concepts and possibilities.

Communicating and Using Results

The self-initiated nature of this study and the fact that it was exploratory create an information dissemination environment that is unique among the cases in this volume. There are no reporting requirements for the overall comparative analysis discussed in this case. However, results have been shared in stages with the Fayetteville Police Department's police chief, public information officer, and other supportive team members. During the development of this study, information was shared via phone calls and short analysis reports to provide aggregate-, group-, and individual-level information about the online community and their engagement with content. Written reports were developed to describe social media data and present those data in aggregated form to highlight engagement levels, online community demographics (e.g., age, gender), and temporal trends. This information has been used by the department to understand its current audience and has initiated efforts to enhance its online audience based on identified gaps. Beyond this, communication and use of the results of this study will depend on the further initiative of the policy researcher. The potential use of what has been learned through this study will be discussed in the following section.

Action

The most evident action resulting from this research is a product of the open communication between the researcher and the Fayetteville Police Department. A continuing dialogue between policy researchers and the users, as well as the delivery of short reports and information, has resulted in ongoing changes and actions by the Fayetteville Police Department. The raised awareness of social media analytics, online media platforms, and indicators has allowed the agency to be proactive concerning events that had traditionally caused conflicts (e.g., house parties). The use of their social media to showcase officers involved in community outreach, problem solving, and casual interactions with residents continues to have online engagement by their community members. Recognizing this as a force multiplier and tool for community outreach, the department has included the adoption of social media use within its policies, promotional qualifications, and overall branding of the department. These and other changes by the department have encouraged ongoing technical assistance support from the Office of Justice Programs Diagnostic Center and the COPS Office.

In the bigger picture, the lead researcher's ongoing work with the COPS program and federal training and TA programs provides opportunity for dissemination of insights and the exploratory issues raised in this study. Reflection on the comparison of internet and social media use across the three case studies supported a few observations with implications for further policy development and research. First, all of the agencies in which the programs were located had websites, but none of them had specific pages for the community policing programs. One implication is that, despite the widespread acceptance that community policing is a good idea, it still is often a federally supported "special" program rather than a department-wide policing approach. While websites contained select language about police–community relations, it is not reflected in discussions of police performance, which focus on crime. With respect to social media use, several observations are appropriate. First, the use of social media (e.g., Twitter, Facebook) is primarily for sending information to the community. Twitter is particularly used to alert the community in emergency or threatening situations. For example, the Dallas Police Department used Twitter to alert the public of developments in the July 2016 sniper incident. This incident resulted in the tragic deaths of five officers. Social media clearly provides an opportunity to promote real-time interactive communication with the community, but that use was not evident in any of the cases examined here. More focused research on the communication needs of community policing and the possible uses of online and social media to meet them is clearly necessary. The lead researcher's access to important institutional actors in making this happen is an important asset in disseminating the implications of this self-initiated policy research.

Lessons for Policy Research

This case demonstrates the complexities of community policing and communication strategies—two necessary practices within policing. It also demonstrates the often-occurring mismatches between institutional environment and evolving program purposes and the challenges they can create. The committed policy researcher who initiated this study perceived the potential value of online and social media communications for community policing programs. She also perceived the fact that current and rapidly improving systems of performance metrics in criminal justice were, understandably, defined by the legal authority and responsibility of law enforcement to enforce laws, apprehend criminals who break those laws, close cases, and prepare prosecutable cases. Justice performance monitoring and evaluation systems use these metrics. The need for different metrics in community policing and her creative thinking about how use of social media to responsively engage communities might be a foundation for relevant new metrics spawned the study.

Exploring current use of social media and metrics in very different program contexts, with different relations to potentially relevant social media audiences, documented limited use of social media and internet in promoting community policing. More important, looking for these applications to community policing revealed a larger, and unanticipated, issue. While the COPS program and other federal support has supported organizational, community partnership, and strategic aspects of community policing, these practices have not been institutionalized. They are not reflected widely in laws; they are not reflected in record keeping, performance monitoring, or data-based strategy planning; they are not a central part of standard training environments; and they are not reflected in standard personnel performance assessments. Until these issues move into a larger conversation, for example, the training and TA environment, the funded policy research environment, they will not become part of standard practice. The foot in the door may well be through institutionalizing less controversial components of an institutional recognition of community policing as standard practice, such as improving community policing communication with the community through social media, and documenting this performance.

The overall lesson for policy research is that acknowledged "good ideas" such as community policing often have trouble gaining traction because they do not fit well with institutional standard operating procedures. Policy researchers are often in the best position to see these misfits and begin asking initial questions that can lead to institutional changes necessary to allow the improvement these ideas can bring. Institutional accommodation is critical to making good but innovative program ideas into common practice. This study may contribute to opening a chink in the unintended institutional armor of law enforcement data, which concretely defines practice, that will help bring community policing into standard policing practice.

Focus on Research Methods

Quick Analysis

The driving circumstances defining the research methods used in this example were (a) a motivation to find out more about how community policing programs communicated with community members, particularly through internet and social media, (b) limited resources, and (c) opportunistic availability of data (the three case studies including site visit opportunities). This meant that the policy researcher had limited ability to actually design the study to maximize relevance to what she wanted to know and had to conduct an analysis consistent with her information objectives using the information that was attainable.

This circumstance characterizes what has been called "quick analysis" (Putt and Springer, 1989, 339) as a contrast to well-resourced and time-consuming "researched analysis." The critical distinction here is resource availability, which translates into "a reduced ability to collect original, primary data concerning the problem" (Putt and Springer, 1989, 344). Since quick analysis does not allow systematic procedures to maximize correspondence of data to the questions being asked, particularly when these questions are exploratory, the analyst must rely more on approximations and implications. A fundamental principle of quick analysis is *more thought—less data*: "The balance between thinking about the problem and collecting data tilts toward thinking" (Putt and Springer, 1989, 344). The analyses and implications documented in this case exemplify that tilt. Findings did not rely on clearly demonstrated empirical tests; they relied on thoughtful interpretations of patterns of information across different contexts. These interpretations identified plausible institutional constraints on making community policing standard law enforcement practice based upon looking at several clues. The contexts of community policing programs showed that they were often outside the institutional mainstream. The use of social media and the web, for example, was dominated by law enforcement concerns. Community policing was largely invisible. The strategic and performance-monitoring data systems that help define institutional behavior do not reflect community policing. These clues, combined with thinking about what it will take to make community policing principles standard procedure, defined the major policy and action implications of this study. This link is heavily dependent on thoughtfully putting the pieces together. "While quick analysis seems less glamorous than researched policy studies, its importance should not be underestimated. Quick analysis plays a fundamental role in contributing to the resolution of concerns cumulatively shaping public policies and programs" (Putt and Springer, 1989, 356). This research kernel, disseminated into the larger policy research and development environment, could contribute to shaping institutional support of community policing.

Acronyms and Jargon

> **Beat**—The territory and time of standard police patrols, traditionally based partly on strengthening policing through regular interaction and familiarity with citizens on the beat path.
>
> **Edge Cities**—Concentrations of business, shopping, and entertainment outside traditional downtowns, often car oriented.
>
> **LEITSC**—The Law Enforcement Information Technology Standards Council sets standards for keeping records on law enforcement performance.
>
> **NIJ**—The National Institute of Justice is the research arm of the United States Department of Justice. It funds research into crime, law enforcement, or other criminal justice policy areas.

Discussion Questions

1. Discuss the meaning of "community policing." To what extent do you see community policing practices in your community environment?
2. What would be the greatest challenges to doing policy research on the effectiveness of community policing strategies? Is this a hard question to answer? Why?
3. What similarities and differences do you see between the action implications of the ignition interlock study in Chapter 16 and the community policing study in this chapter?

18 When the Process Is the Question

Resource Family Recruitment in Los Angeles, CA

Robert D. Blagg, Todd Franke,
and Christina Christie

Introduction

Usual policy discourse considers our governing and policy implementation institutions as part of the solution. But from a policy research perspective, they are sometimes part of the problem. This case study provides a clear example of a complex and challenging institutional and implementation setting. The policy researchers in this case were charged with providing information that would facilitate the process of recruiting and preparing resource families to provide foster or adoptive care. The first step in the research process was to provide a comprehensive description of the dual system for recruiting, preparing, and monitoring resource families, which had drifted into its current status place in Los Angeles County over a period of time. This system was comprised of largely distinct processes, one driven primarily by the Los Angeles Department of Children and Family Services (DCFS); the other propelled by foster family agencies (FFAs). The goal was to identify areas for improvement, where DCFS and FFAs can work complementarily to more efficiently and effectively recruit, train, assess, and approve new resource families and place children in appropriate, safe, and secure homes. Through this case example, we identify and elaborate on several multilevel historical (e.g., the legacy of a social service system and culture), political (e.g., competing priorities and goals among public and private organizations that must cooperate to achieve success), and financial (e.g., distinct funding mechanisms among public and private organizations) issues that contributed to system challenges. These issues require thoughtful decisions and often trade-offs in developing, implementing, and reporting their policy research in this dynamic local context.

The Policy Problem

Historically, the recruitment and retention of resource families capable of providing high-quality care have been persistent challenges for child welfare agencies (Pasztor and Wynne, 1995). Fostering or adopting children is very demanding, and high resource family turnover is a persistent problem. A substantial proportion of resource family attrition is due to foster families exiting the system. A recent study found that across three states, the typical length of service in foster parenting was less than many children's stay in foster care (Gibbs, 2005). These circumstances dictate that child welfare agencies must work diligently on an ongoing basis to recruit new families and to retain experienced families in order to provide sufficient numbers of appropriate homes for children in out-of-home care.

The policy challenges addressed in this case focused on the *process* of working diligently to fulfill the need for sufficient numbers of qualified resource families. While the steps of the process and service needs for Los Angeles were relatively well understood, the path forward to strengthening this system was not. The institutional context for the Los Angeles foster care system made it difficult to find this path because of its complexity and fragmentation. As this case demonstrates, this institutional environment is an example of "policy drift" (Kress, Koehler, and Springer, 1980), combined with drift in implementation. Policy drift is produced by an accretion of responses to specific and often unconnected problems in program development and implementation. These day-to-day accommodations may be sensible within the program order set by enabling legislation, court decisions, and larger organizational decisions. "However, as time goes by, the consequences of these decisions may . . . fundamentally alter the program" (Kress, Koehler, and Springer, 1980, p. 1101). In this case, the institutional structure led the implementation of this set of policies and programs to drift into place. As we shall see, anticipated consequences of drift are manifest throughout this case. In fundamental ways, drift of policies and their implementation is the underlying challenge for the Los Angeles resource family recruitment system. It has been argued that policy researchers "can help remedy policy drift by identifying . . . competing demands on a program and by clarifying changes that have occurred in program activities and objectives" (Kress, Koehler, and Springer, 1980, p. 1102). Before hearing about how this was done, we will describe the institutional environment in which the resource family recruitment system operated in Los Angeles at the time of the study. Without this initial description, the readers of this case would themselves be set adrift in following this story.

Resource Family Recruitment in Los Angeles

Major factors that have exerted influence on the resource family recruitment system in Los Angeles included state legislation, policy, and court decisions and local implementation variation. In California, the need for resource families has been particularly acute for older children and children with severe emotional or behavioral concerns. California's Intensive Treatment Foster Care (ITFC) program is intended to support children and youth ages 10 to 17 who have serious emotional or behavioral issues by shifting them out of group homes and into foster homes where they can receive the type of care they require before a permanent situation is identified. Homes capable of such care are relatively rare, however, and thus recruiting foster parents for ITFC has been a significant hurdle statewide and in Los Angeles County.

In 2011, the *Katie A., et al., vs. Diana Bontá, et al.* (State of California and County of Los Angeles) settlement required Los Angeles County to provide $17.3 million to support ITFC care for 300 children (Katie A., et al., v. Diana Bontá, et al., 2012). Despite significant efforts on the part of DCFS and FFAs to recruit resource families capable of providing this level of care, as of June 2012 DCFS reported 86 Treatment Foster Care (TFC) certified homes with 68 children placed (Department of Children and Family Services, 2012). The slow progress toward certifying the required number of ITFC placements illustrates the challenge in providing sufficient care for children with such needs. Additionally, in 2012, the California Department of Social Services (CDSS) expanded a moratorium on new group home applications for fiscal year (FY) 2012–2013 (Lightbourne, 2012). While a well-founded and well-intentioned decision, the lack of expansion of new group homes nonetheless put additional pressure on Los Angeles to expand the pool of foster care placements, which demonstrates the difficulty in making reforms to the resource family recruitment system.

At the time this research was initiated, Los Angeles County was in the position of needing to meet the challenge of providing care—basic, as well as ITFC and other types—through a dual system for licensing (i.e., requiring state and county approval) and certifying (i.e., FFA approval) resource families to foster and adopt. DCFS works with the Community Care Licensing Division (CCLD) of the CDSS to directly license and approve resource families to foster and adopt in Los Angeles County. As a now distinct path to foster care, FFAs were statutorily created as an alternative to group homes in 1984 (California Health and Human Services Agency, Department of Social Services, 2001). FFAs were originally established to help meet the need for additional foster families. They are now licensed by CCLD and in turn certify families to provide care for children that counties place with the FFA. To be clear, licensed resource families are recruited, trained, assessed, and approved and then have children placed with them through a process primarily driven by LA DCFS, while certified families progress through a similar process that is proximally driven by FFAs (see Table 18.1). Thus, Los Angeles County maintains two separate, and to some extent parallel, foster care systems.

Table 18.1 The Dual Resource Family Recruitment System

	Recruitment	Training	Assessment & Approval	Placement
DCFS	• General recruitment (media campaigns) • Focused recruitment (community outreach) • Child-specific recruitment (from child perspective)	• Orientations (large, centralized, and frequency limited by the state) • Training approaches (PS-MAPP provided by contracted external agencies)	• Length of the process (dependent on resource family size, complexity, schedules, and motivations) • Home study approach (SAFE) • Approval (dual approval for foster care & adoption required)	• Process (driven by DCFS, as they are primarily responsible for children in out-of-home care) • Challenges (placing very young children, teenagers, and children with special health or behavioral needs)
FFAs	• Focused recruitment (outreach to targeted communities) • Child-specific recruitment (from resource family perspective)	• Orientations (vary by FFA in terms of location, type, size, and frequency) • Training approaches (vary: PS-MAPP, PRIDE, NuParent; often provided by FFA staff)	• Length of the process (dependent on resource family size, complexity, schedules, and motivations) • Home study approach (SAFE) • Approval (precertification; dual approval for foster care & adoption required)	• Process (responding to DCFS needs for placements) • Challenges (placing very young children, teenagers, and children with special health or behavioral needs)

As is detailed below, this bifurcation of the system adds complication and confusion on both sides.

As a government agency, Los Angeles County DCFS has a distinct funding stream from private FFAs that depend on a client base for financial viability. This difference is operationalized such that DCFS views children as their primary clients, working with foster or adoptive parents in an effort to provide safe and stable homes for children. From an almost opposite perspective, FFAs tend to view parents as their primary clients, working to find children that are an appropriate fit for the needs and resources of their clients. This key difference in the perspectives of these types of organizations appears to have contributed to the perpetuation of the dual and in some cases conflicting resource family recruitment systems that many agreed were not serving children and families in an optimal way and thus motivated this investigation.

Initiation of Policy Research

To investigate the implications of dual resource family recruitment and approval policies in Los Angeles County, the Anthony and Jeanne Pritzker Family Foundation provided financial support for a competitive contract, fulfilled by researchers at the University of California Los Angeles (UCLA). With the ultimate goal of addressing the need for additional resource families in Los Angeles County, the Children's Action Network, in partnership with the Anthony and Jeanne Pritzker Family Foundation and LA DCFS, distributed a request for proposals to local research institutions with records in the area of child welfare. A team of researchers at the University of California Los Angeles (UCLA), with a substantial record of research and evaluation in child welfare and previous work with LA DCFS and various community partners, was well positioned to fulfill the request. While this was a modestly resourced project, the researchers decided to compete for the opportunity due to the current community connections and research infrastructure that allowed for all project goals to be accomplished within the scope of the request.

The Policy Research Task

The core of the research task was describing and documenting the recruitment, training, assessment and approval, and placement processes of the Los Angeles County DCFS and FFAs, understanding how these policies and practices resulted in the current level of availability of resource families, and identifying how these policies and practices could be improved. However, as can be gleaned from the project objectives described in what follows, accomplishing these central research tasks required answering several varied research questions.

Objectives

The ultimate objective of this research was to determine if maintaining dual resource family recruitment systems is preferable or even necessary. However, early on, it became evident to the research team that the key stakeholders to this system had already formed very different responses to this question. Specifically, DCFS felt they could not be removed from the resource family recruitment process, primarily because they have legal responsibility for the care of all Los Angeles County children in out-of-home care, but FFAs tended to express that they provide a superior level of care and so should be the sole venue for resource families. To provide systematic evidence to answer this overarching question, more immediate objectives included describing the current policies for bringing families to provide foster or adoptive care into the foster care system in Los Angeles County, with specific attention to the dual system of largely distinct Los Angeles Department of Children and Family Services (DCFS) and foster family agency (FFA) recruitment, training, assessment and approval, and placement efforts. Thorough description of the process was vital for achieving another key objective, in the event the dual system continued, of identifying areas for improvement, where DCFS and FFAs could work complementarily to more efficiently and effectively recruit, train, assess, and approve new resource families and place children in appropriate, safe, and secure homes.

Challenges

Accomplishing these objectives presented several hurdles. Challenges included relations with clients and partner agencies and data identification and collection.

- *Building relationships with clients*—Accomplishing this research required establishing trust with the central but not only client, the Department of Children and Family Services. Most proximal to the data required to accomplish the research task were DCFS management and staff at several levels and across distinct offices. While the research team had an existing working relationship with DCFS leadership, key links needed to be made with middle management and line staff directing resource family recruitment, assessment and approval, and placement. The forging of these relationships had to occur in a relatively truncated period and under varying levels of enthusiasm from organization management. Thus, strategic and efficient contact approaches and points needed to be carefully and deliberately considered.
- *Building relationships with partner agencies and consumers*—Foster family agencies serving Los Angeles County vary greatly in size, scope, focus, and location. Building trust with so many disparate

agencies, in a short period of time and with limited budget, was a substantial challenge. Similarly, recruiting diverse resource families who had been served by the dual recruitment systems was also challenging but necessary to honor the knowledge and understanding of recruitment system participants. Meeting such research challenges requires strategic recruitment approaches, engaging messaging, and research team members capable of engendering enthusiasm and trust with partner agencies and consumers.

- *Data identification and collection*—Data regarding costs, procedures, and outcomes was necessary to collect for addressing key research questions. But as discussed in more detail in what follows, cost information was anticipated and proved to be difficult for many agencies to share in a uniform or meaningfully analyzable format, despite great effort to provide a clear reporting template and technical assistance for cost data collection. Outcome information relative to recruitment, training, and placement was more comprehensive and available from DCFS and well-resourced FFAs, but smaller agencies often did not collect thorough outcome data, as it was largely not required by state or county child and family service agencies.

Despite these significant challenges, several policy insights and pathways forward were identified, and subsequently the primary client took steps to effect relevant changes.

The Decision Context

The structure and political climate of the child and family service agencies involved proved antagonistic to the use of research findings. For example, the different funding streams and missions of DCFS and FFAs support divergent goals (e.g., advocating primarily for children in the case of DCFS or for resource families in the cases of FFAs). Further, the historically competitive relationship between these agencies provided an environment in which the purpose, methods, and findings of the project were hotly debated, in some cases before they were fully developed or formally disseminated. As such, each component and phase of the project took on additional significance and time pressure, which not only was felt by the research team but also was evident on the parts of clients, partner agencies, and consumers.

The Policy Cycle

As FFAs were statutorily created in 1984, the dual resource family recruitment systems had been operating in some form for many years (California Health and Human Services Agency, Department of Social Services, 2001). Thus, this research project could be considered part of the evaluation policy stage. However, some research questions driven by the primary stakeholders indicated that planning for policy changes had already begun and required additional devotion of resources to explore. In other terms, clients and other stakeholders had specific and sometimes conflicting ideas about what the problems in the system were before the initiation of the research and throughout. As such, conducting research in the context of a system or organizations with long histories and well-worn perceptions (accurate or not) can increase the likelihood that research subjects or stakeholders are not impartial or objective regarding the conclusions the project should reach. This situation can add difficulty to the collection of objective evidence, so it can be useful to look for contrary cases that can challenge hypotheses.

Clients and Stakeholders

The primary client for this research project was the Los Angeles County DCFS, which drives one half of the bifurcated resource family recruitment system and has some oversight responsibility for the other part of the system (i.e., DCFS is responsibility for ensuring and verifying the safety of all children in out-of-home care, including those FFA-supported foster homes). However, the funder had substantial input regarding the research questions, was a very supportive partner in the conduct of the study, and continued to consult with DCFS regarding next steps after the study was completed. The next level of stakeholders included FFAs, in that any policy decisions stemming from the study were likely to impact them directly, but they were not the primary client, which contributed to some of the challenges previously discussed. At a broader level, the Los Angeles Commission for Children and Families, accountable to the County Board of Supervisors, was a significant stakeholder in their mission to enhance the well-being of the children and families of Los Angeles County. Ultimately, and policy changes stemming from this project would impact the experience of fostering or adopting children for resource families in Los Angeles. Thus, as the primary focus of the resource family recruitment system, current and prospective resource families were arguably the most key stakeholder group.

Research Design and Implementation

Within the limited timeline and budget for this project, the research team developed a project to describe each of the major points of the recruitment process, including areas for improvement and promising practices, and to document the impact of each piece of the dual system, with emphasis on identifying areas of need and potential solutions. To achieve the research objectives, the research team conducted a multiple methods study. Specifically, the team looked closely, via qualitative methods, at how practices influenced outcomes and the successes and challenges of the dual resource family recruitment system. In addition, quantitative and cost outcomes were derived from secondary data analysis.

Information Needs

The informational requirements of this project were as varied as the stakeholders. The specific charge of the research team was to address several questions regarding resource family recruitment processes and outcomes in Los Angeles County.

- Should the current dual system of state-/LA DCFS–licensed and FFA-certified homes be continued?
- How can DCFS and the FFAs better coordinate their efforts and work more efficiently together?
- What is the current cost and differences in costs for staff to recruit, train, and oversee licensed and certified homes?
- Is a single point of contact (e.g., hotline, website, etc.) for prospective resource families feasible?
- Are there ways to ensure better oversight and safety of foster parents?
- Is there any evidence of difference in the quality or outcomes achieved by licensed and certified homes?
- Are there enough available foster homes?
- What types of homes (e.g., geography, child age, type of care) are needed?
- Should all FFAs be required to be accredited?

Design and Methods

Within a nonexperimental, descriptive study design, the research team conducted many semistructured in-person/telephone interviews and collected self-report survey data from FFA staff, DCFS staff, and foster parents.

Recruitment and Participants

Several recruitment approaches were employed to garner interview participation. DCFS administration assisted in identifying the office, units, and workers most relevant to the resource family recruitment process. Supervisors and managers of each respective group were contacted for participation, and they then identified staff members who were willing and able to be interviewed.

All 46 FFAs that had contracted with Los Angeles County in FY 2013–2014 were invited to participate in this study. Recruitment continued until a minimum of three agencies within each of three size ranges (small = 0–50 homes; medium = 51–100 homes; large = 101–197 homes) agreed to participate. The resulting FFA sample was made up of 17 agencies, including 8 small agencies, 6 medium, and 3 large. Table 18.2 displays the number of staff who participated across agencies. The sample represents 37% of all FFAs serving Los Angeles County in FY 2013–2014, and is generally proportional to the number of agencies serving these ranges of homes across the county. However, the data collected from this convenience sample of agencies should not be considered perfectly representative of all 46 agencies serving the county.

Both DCFS and FFA workers were asked to provide referrals for current resource families who would be willing to be interviewed about their experiences. Some families who declined to participate expressed concerns about time constraints and about sharing current experiences. While 12 families indicated interest, only 2 completed participation. The insights of these two families were enlightening but cannot be considered representative of all resource families in the county.

Additionally, all 46 FFA agencies were invited to complete a self-report survey regarding the effectiveness of their recruitment and placement activities and procedures. This yielded the participation of 58.7% (27/46) of all Los Angeles County FFAs.

PROCEDURES

On average, the individual and group interview process for all participants spanned one to two hours and involved a brief pre-interview survey followed by a semistructured interview. For DCFS and FFA staff, the initial survey inquired about participants' roles with their respective agencies then asked them to list and rank up to 10 job tasks within each stage of the recruitment process (i.e., recruitment, training, assessment and approval, and placement). Interviews were conducted upon completion of the initial survey. Families interviewed were not asked to complete a pre-interview survey. The semistructured interviews mirrored the structure of the initial survey instrument, in that the discussion progressed through each stage of the recruitment process as relevant to the staff member or family member being interviewed. These complementary procedures provided for a linear and efficient interview process.

Invitations for the FFA survey of recruitment and placement were distributed via email, and responses were submitted online at agencies' convenience.

Administrative Data Collection and Procedures

Existing data from a variety of state and DCFS administrative data sources were also collected and analyzed. Table 18.3 details the types of data extracted from each administrative data system. To extract data, the research team worked with DCFS data analysts. Data regarding each

Table 18.2 Overview of Mixed-Method Primary Data Collection

Data Sources	Number of Interviews/Surveys	Number of Participants
DCFS Staff Interviews & Surveys: • Placement & recruitment unit • Assessment & approval • Advanced placement team • Service bureaus • Out-of-home care • Supervisors and administrators	15	75 staff members
FFA Staff Interviews & Surveys: • Placement & recruitment unit • Assessment & approval • Management • Support • Other key staff	17	91 staff members
FFA Survey: • Effectiveness of recruitment and placement activities	–	27 agencies
Interviews with Resource Families	2	2 families

Table 18.3 Overview of Administrative Data Collection

Data Sources

DCFS—Business Information Systems (BIS):
• Child Welfare Services/Case Management System (CWS/CMS) data regarding:
  • Homes (e.g., approvals and characteristics)
  • Placements (e.g., child characteristics)
Placement & Recruitment Unit:
• Administrative data regarding recruitment (e.g., contacts and orientation)
Adoptions & Permanency:
• PS-MAPP training administrative data

stage of the recruitment process were obtained and analyzed for the last five complete fiscal years (2009–2010 through 2013–2014).

Upon receipt of data, a quality review process was conducted, including inspection for missing, unknown, or out-of-range values. Data quality issues were highlighted as relevant throughout the report.

Analysis Approaches

QUALITATIVE ANALYSIS

Interview and open-ended survey response data were transcribed and entered into an analysis-ready database. An emergent approach was used to code and organize the data into themes (Patton, 2005). This provided a rich description of the approaches and activities used by FFA and DCFS staff. Our iterative analysis process revealed shortcomings and promising practices at each stage of the recruitment process. Results of the qualitative analysis are described throughout the report.

QUANTITATIVE ANALYSIS

Primary and existing quantitative data were consolidated into an analysis-ready database. Descriptive and inferential statistical analyses were conducted using a variety of software packages (i.e., Stata, SPSS, and R). Data-visualization software, Tableau, was also utilized for analysis and interactive visualization of the figures throughout reporting. Quantitative results that complement descriptions of recruitment practices and highlight important outcomes at each stage of the recruitment process are described throughout reporting.

Selected Findings

Coordination of Recruitment Efforts Should Be Increased

The study found that DCFS and FFAs had developed and engaged in a variety of useful recruitment strategies. However, it was evident that there were also some redundancies, at least in part due to communication problems or lack of information sharing across agencies. Given the limitation of resources that can be devoted to recruitment, coordination of efforts between FFAs and DCFS seems a prime area for enhanced focus. Better coordination could help to reduce the time and effort needed to engage and process prospective resource families. While FFA and DCFS-Placement Recruitment Unit (PRU) staff noted that there is some coordination between public- and private-sector agencies around recruitment, most of those interviewed for this study remarked on the confusion many prospective resource families experience as a result of the dual recruitment efforts (i.e., FFA and DCFS). Another source of confusion that interacts with and confounds the existing recruitment system is communication of the requirements for dual approval (i.e., foster and adoption). Thoughtful coordination of recruitment efforts will reduce the inconsistencies in information relayed to prospective families from different agencies, as well as the confusion felt by many prospective resource families about critical issues that may affect their decisions, such as benefits, information sources, and approval requirements. Coordinating recruitment efforts, including response to inquiries in a consistent and strategic manner, could help to reduce confusion and increase motivation to foster children.

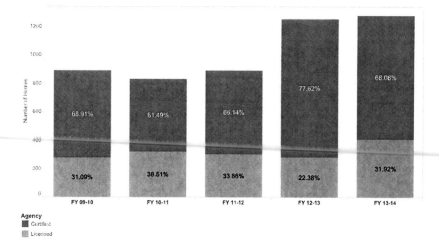

Figure 18.1 Newly Approved Homes by Fiscal Year

High Quality Standards for the Assessment and Approval Process Should Be Adopted

The evaluation team found variation between FFAs and DCFS, as well as across FFAs, in the extent and components of the assessment and approval processes. These differences were often confusing for prospective resource families and were a source of inefficiency and complication across agencies. Many FFA staff suggested that the adoption of high quality standards for assessment and approval across agencies would reduce confusion for prospective families and allow them to more easily share or transfer cases, thereby supporting more efficient allocation of resources across the system.

What has been the impact of DCFS and FFA assessment and approval processes? A comparison of newly approved (i.e., not approved previously) DCFS and FFA homes annually over a recent five-year period (FY 2009–2010 through 2013–2014) shows the relative effectiveness of the assessment and approval processes. As Table 18.1 displays, the number of newly approved homes has generally increased annually. The overall trend is positive, but an annual decrease is evident in FY 2010–2011, likely attributable in part to the redeployment of many DCFS Adoption and Permanency Resources Division staff to the front line.

Analysis of newly approved homes annually among DCFS and FFAs separately provides a bit more insight. Beginning in FY 2010–2011 and continuing through FY 2013–2014, FFAs provided a larger proportion

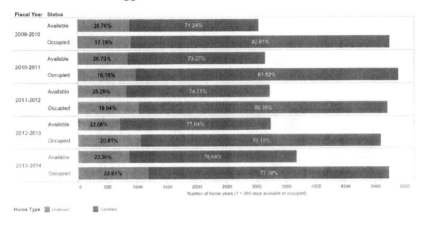

Figure 18.2 Available and Occupied Home-Years

of the newly approved homes annually. In the last three years, licensed homes accounted for less than 34% of newly approved resource families. This pattern suggests FFA assessment and approval processes have been more impactful in recent years.

What is the real availability of resource family homes? To identify the extent to which sufficient approved homes exist, the availability of homes was compared to the extent to which they were occupied. Each of the most recent five fiscal years (FY 2009–2010 to 2013–2014) with complete data available was examined. To support appropriate comparisons between available homes and child placements, both types of data were calculated as "home-years." For the purpose of this comparison, one home-year was defined as 365 days a home was either available to or occupied by a child. Through this metric, Figure 18.2 displays the annual comparison of available licensed and certified home-years to child placements.

Results indicated that there were more home-years occupied than available in each fiscal year analyzed. This is likely due primarily to the reliability of the data. Specifically, data regarding the number of placements approved for each home were not reliably or completely available across years. Further, DCFS and FFA staff reported that families often will not accept the number of placements they are approved for. Thus, even if it were the case that complete information regarding the number of placements approved for homes was available, this would likely not be an accurate accounting of the true number of placements available for many homes. The research team recommended that the magnitude of discrepancy between approved and "real" available placements be the subject of further investigation.

Communicating and Using Results

Results were communicated to stakeholders primarily through a formal report, executive summary, and several presentations, as defined in the project contract. However, the research team inserted innovative data-visualization approaches into each reporting mechanism. An example visualization can be found at https://public.tableau.com/views/Enroll menttoClassCompletion_FY1112-1415_public_160225/TrainingStatusby SPA?:embed=y&:display_count=yes&:showTabs=y.

Reporting Results

The final report was organized so that each of the research questions was addressed in the context of each stage of the recruitment process, in the order those processes occur, as displayed in Table 18.1. Within each of these stages of the recruitment process, the report provided descriptions, insights, and pathways forward, and finally implications of results across the recruitment process were discussed. The executive summary, presentations, and custom data visualizations were developed to focus on pathways forward for the dual recruitment system.

Selected Recommendations

In each reporting medium, recommendations were explicitly described as "pathways forward" in deference to the need for the two major types of organizations (i.e., DCFS and FFAs) driving the dual system to come to the table and use the study findings to inform collaborative discussion and decision making regarding reforms. Thus, at each stage of the recruitment process discussed in the final report, "pathways forward" were elaborated so as to highlight likely options for improvement. However, three broad conclusions were reached:

1. Opportunities to overcome the challenges of the dual system existed.

   a. FFA and DCFS coordination and collaboration at each stage of the process,
   b. Adopting high quality training standards, and
   c. Reconsidering the requirement for dual assessment and approval of resource families.

2. Cost per resource family should be taken into account.

   a. A full accounting of the costs of varying recruitment, assessment, training, and approval processed between the branches of the dual system should be conducted, and
   b. Costs of resource family support postapproval should also be taken into account when considering the costs and impact of the recruitment system.

3. Information systems capable of identifying and driving system improvements should be developed.

    a. Limitations of the documentation of processes and outcomes varied between agencies and at each stage of recruitment, limiting the identification of system improvements, and

    b. Much of the available information regarding child placements and the experiences of children, their wellness, and their care is qualitative, anecdotal, and/or not readily analyzable. Such characteristics should be more standardized and reliably measured to support appropriate and safe placements and efficient identification of outcomes and areas for improvement.

Action

Despite the lack of strong or definitive conclusions that could be made in the context of the report, largely due to the limited scope of the project, soon after the final reporting was delivered, the primary client included many "pathways forward" as part of what became essentially a to-do list of policy and practice changes. However, most of the political will for changes remains on one side of the dual recruitment system. In this environment, it appears unlikely that each side of the dual recruitment system will come together to tackle many of the inefficiencies of resource family recruitment in Los Angeles County that are directly or indirectly related to the lack of coordination of policies and practices. But sufficient attention (e.g., new Los Angeles Office of Child Protection) to the issue of the availability of foster homes remains, such that other findings of this work could continue to inform improvements going forward.

Lessons for Policy Research

Policy research on social programs such as child and family services focuses on the service itself, for example, service quality and standards, causal attribution of program outcomes, intervention effectiveness, and program cost effectiveness. This study demonstrates another critical perspective on service programs, particularly in America's public/private social services systems. These systems, as demonstrated in this case, involve complex certification, contracting, and accountability processes to ensure quality, cost effectiveness, and client protection. The complexity of these administrative mechanisms is made even more difficult to hold accountable by the influence of multiple stakeholder interests, with different perspectives on quality and priority of different interests. This kind of fluid system, open to influence from different stakeholders, is vulnerable to intended or unintended drift in the degree to which policy outcomes are attained. Drift is often driven by relatively invisible day-to-day administrative or implementation decisions. Sometimes major changes in implementation organization, such as the bifurcated system in this case, make it difficult for policy makers to track why performance problems arise. Policy research and feedback is periodically necessary to identify the relation of procedural drift to policy intent and recommend course corrections.

Focus on Research Methods

Pragmatic Adaptation of Analysis Methods

To achieve study objectives within the ambitious timeline for the study, the evaluation team conducted a multiple-methods study that focused on quantitative and cost outcomes derived from secondary data analysis and looked closely, via qualitative and quantitative methods, at how practices influenced outcomes and the successes and challenges of implementing a comprehensive resource family recruitment, approval, and placement process. To address the primary research questions, detailed earlier, a nonexperimental, descriptive study design was implemented. Methods employed included (1) secondary data analysis of extant DCFS and FFA data (i.e., processes, outcomes, and costs), (2) semistructured individual and group interviews with FFA providers, (3) semistructured individual and group interviews with DCFS staff, and (4) semistructured telephone interviews with foster parents. The multiple data collection methods revealed themes upon which the various data converged (triangulated). Further, respondents were amenable to participating in these methods, which yielded information that supported conclusions more likely to be used to inform resource family recruitment system policies and practices.

Acronyms and Jargon

CCLD—Community Care Licensing Division
CDSS—California Department of Social Services
DCFS—The Los Angeles Department of Children and Family Services
FFAs—Foster Family Agencies
ITFC—Intensive Treatment Foster Care program

Discussion Questions

1. How did "policy drift" and "implementation drift" affect the design and completion of this study?
2. How did the research team document the "process" involved with this case?

3. How did the policy perspectives of key stakeholders affect the key objectives of this policy research?
4. The study planned to interview families involved in the foster care system, yet only a few participated. How could the study team have increased participation in this aspect of the study?
5. What obstacles seemed to decrease the immediate impact of the study on decision making?
6. Imagine a much larger budget and staff to conduct this study. How would you recommend improving or expanding it?

Assignments and Activities

1. Identify and describe another example of a program or policy that is characterized by "policy drift."
2. Identify a similar foster home program in your area and try to determine what challenges it faces and how they compare with those described in this case.
3. Prepare a brief presentation that highlights the key findings in this case in a way that highlights the usefulness of the study.

19 Debt Burdens of California State and Local Governments

Are They Too Large?

Robert W. Wassmer

Introduction

This chapter offers an example of how both comparative data analysis and statistical regression analysis can be used together to generate evidence regarding a policy concern. The use of two different forms of quantitative analysis offers a good example of mixed methods in policy analysis: the regression analysis was used to confirm the comparative data analysis. Two professors with backgrounds in economics conducted the investigation and produced the report. The intent of the study was to improve the quality of debate about debt burdens through the introduction of pertinent and credible evidence.

The Policy Problem

> California is already deeply in debt, (CA State Treasurer Bill) Lockyer warned, and has huge budget deficits and cannot afford another big bond issue. . . . "The days of blithely heaping more and more debt burden on the general fund are over—at least they should be," Lockyer said.
> —Dan Walters, *Sacramento Bee*, p. 3A, November 29, 2009

The perception among some of California's elected officials in the late 2000s was that state debt was too high and a policy path of continuing at this level was unsustainable. California had arrived at this point due to: (1) generous issuance of debt before and during the Great Recession (nearly $63 billion in new debt for statewide transportation, education, hospital, water, and housing projects between 2006 and 2008 alone), (2) a dramatic decline in state revenue during and after this recession, and (3) uncertainty as to whether and when state revenue would recover (PPIC, 2009). As noted, then-State Treasurer Bill Lockyer desired to communicate this concern to the public. In particular, Treasurer Lockyer wished to convey the pressing need to curb the issuance by California of new general obligation debt because of the future strain it would place on the state's General Fund through the greater repayment of interest and principal on accumulated debt.

In his *Debt Affordability Report* of October 2009, Lockyer forecast that then-current debt service ratio of about 10 percent (the percentage of the state's General Fund expenditures going to the interest and principal on previous general obligation debt) would double by 2016 unless growth in the state's "Wall of Debt" slowed dramatically (Lockyer, 2009). California would increasingly have fewer dollars to spend on current expenditure needs as its commitment to paying off previous debt rose. Magnifying this need was uncertainty at the time of the degree by which the State's General Fund revenue would recover after the Great Recession. Furthermore, in 2009, all of the major bond rating agencies (Fitch, Moody's, and Standard and Poor's) had downgraded or signaled that they were considering a downgrade of California's credit rating based upon the state's level of current debt, projected budgetary shortfalls, and a perceived lack of political will to do anything about it.

Initiation of Policy Research

Given the previously described concerns, California State Treasurer Lockyer asked the California Debt and Investment Advisory Commission (CDIAC) to issue six requests for proposals (RFPs) to study various components of this issue. As state treasurer, Lockyer served as the chairperson of CDIAC. This commission also consisted of the director of finance, the state controller, two state assembly members, state senators, and two local government finance officials.

The Policy Research Task

One of the six requests for proposals (RFPs) issued by CDIAC in 2009 sought research designed specifically to better understand the past and present debt loads of California state government. The RFP left it up to the researcher(s) to propose the best methodology to accomplish this.

Objectives

The objective of the RFP that formed the basis of this case study was the production of "actionable research" in what seemed to constitute a formative evaluation to assist policy makers in reaching a consensus on how worrisome the recent growth in and overall level of the state of California's public debt were. Treasury Department analysts had already amassed support for the verdict that California had taken on excessive debt. With the issuance of this RFP, CDIAC sought further evidence to evaluate this conclusion. They specifically turned to academics to generate this evidence, believing that other elected officials and the citizens that vote for them would view such an analysis as less biased than the evidence produced by Treasury analysts, whose leader had already taken a public position on this topic.

Challenges

There were three significant challenges that the policy research team faced after deciding to respond to the CDIAC request for research proposals on debt burdens of California state and local governments. First, the client ultimately desired to know whether the 2009 state debt burdens of California were too high to be sustainable. Realizing the (wicked) normative nature of these terms and hence the inquiry, the team made it clear in its proposed research plan that the analysis would include a thorough review of how others had previously determined a state's "ideal" amount of debt using methods involving the least amount of value judgment possible.

Second, the research team was certain that an evaluation of the desirability of California's total debt required a comparison to other states. Unfortunately, these states are different enough that what may be an "ideal" amount of debt for one would not be for another. For example, variance in the division of government activity in a state between its state government and local governments is a reality that is commonly known among academics. In 2007, the average percentage of state and local own-source revenue raised by state governments in the United States was about 55 percent. California was at 53 percent, whereas states like Delaware, Alaska, and Hawaii had corresponding percentages of nearly 80 percent. In Florida, Colorado, and Texas, these percentages were around 45, 46, and 48 percent, respectively. Given this variation, the proposal submitted included the necessary comparison of not just state government debt levels (as the CDIAC request for proposals asked) but aggregate state government plus local government debt across the 50 states. The sustainability of public debt in a state, an underlying policy concern, could not ignore local governments when they raised such large portions of public revenue in many states.

In addition, a simple comparison of state and local debt in a given year across states would be unreasonable without controlling for at least differences in population, gross domestic product (affluence), and other factors that could generate differences in the ideal amount of subnational debt by state. The proposal submitted by the research team pointed out comparability concerns and offered a research methodology to deal with them.

Third, the research team believed that an appropriate accounting of the future obligations of state and local governments should also consider future pension costs—a big contributor to future obligations in many states. Depending on contractual and other legal aspects, as well as the

governments' practices of funding this deferred compensation, these liabilities represent a claim on future public receipts and assets. Depending
on how this figure is estimated, in 2008 state pension programs exhibited
unfunded liabilities in the range of $1,060 to $3,270 billion (see Novy-
Marx and Rauh, 2009). In comparison, state and local government outstanding financial market debt in fiscal year 2008 was $2,580 billion.

Comparison of these different financial liabilities is difficult for a few
reasons. Of course there are differences in the legal requirements for pay-
outs under each state's pension plans—some are more generous than others. In addition, there is variability in pension liability estimates produced
with different evaluation methods in different time periods. Nonetheless,
a reasonable approximation is that the unfunded future pension liabilities of state and local governments range from 50 to 100 percent of their
traditional financial market debt. Given this magnitude, the researchers
thought it imperative to consider a state's future pension liabilities when
considering whether its traditional debt load is sustainable and proposed
that this also be a component of their research.

The Decision Context

When responding to the RFP to conduct research on the debt load of
California state government, the team clearly understood that the intent
of its research was the generation of "unbiased" inputs into CDIAC's
decision-making process regarding what is a sustainable amount of debt
for California. Given that the California treasurer (and CDIAC chair)
had already reached a conclusion in this regard, they were keenly aware
of the politics surrounding the RFP and the outside role they were being
asked to serve as academic experts on the issue.

The Institutional Context

State governments sell bonds to investors to finance the construction of
infrastructure projects (e.g., roads, bridges, government and school buildings, technology, etc.) that are paid for in the present but provide service
to the state over the life of the project's usable existence (sometimes in
excess of 30 years). It thus makes sense to have current and future beneficiaries of the services generated from this public infrastructure finance
it. A general obligation (GO) bond commits the "full faith and credit"
of the state to pay it back. Payment on such a bond, over the course of
up to 30 years, comes from the state's general fund in the forms of interest (on the outstanding balance of what was borrowed) and principal
(which reduces this outstanding balance). In a given year, a state also uses
its general fund to pay for current expenditures (which are government-
provided goods and services—like health care assistance—consumed
in each current year). California's state constitution requires majority

approval by voters for the state issuance of GO debt. Understanding this, a state policy maker's decision to propose GO debt and a voter's assessment of whether to support it necessarily balances the need for public infrastructure projects paid for by future residents against the concern that these payments do not place too great a strain on future general fund revenues that also finance current expenditures. Policy decisions of this type occur with a necessary degree of uncertainty regarding future infrastructure needs and other forms of government expenditure needs (California Legislative Analyst's Office, 2008).

Clients and Stakeholders

Voters in California are the ultimate stakeholders in a policy analysis regarding the desirability of California debt obligations. Voters have access to the report generated from publicly funded research like this but are highly unlikely to directly utilize it. Instead, the report's main purpose was to serve as a source of information for the California treasurer, CDIAC, and lawmakers to use in the formulation of future proposals and recommendations on the issuance of new GO bonds.

California's state treasurer is an elected position that serves a maximum of two terms of four years each. The treasurer is responsible for managing the state's investment and finance, which includes the issuance of bonds and promissory notes. In 2009, Treasurer Lockyer was in the middle of his first of two possible four-year terms in this office. Treasurer Lockyer, embroiled in the fiscal devastation that the Great Recession had wreaked on California, chose to become an outspoken advocate for getting the state's fiscal house back in order.

The mandate of the California Debt and Investment Advisory Commission (CDIAC), chaired by the Treasurer, is to offer advice and oversight on California's public debt and investment activities. Given its codified roles as an information clearinghouse on the issuance of public debt and to provide education about appropriate public finance practices, the CDIAC was appropriately situated to request such a research report from an academic institution.

The Policy Cycle

The RFP for this project appeared in the fall of 2009, just as the state's economy was in weak recovery from the Great Recession and concerns continued to exist over the viability of California's fiscal future. Proposals were due in January of 2010. The evaluation team (consisting of Robert Wassmer and Ronald Fisher) received notification of their proposal's acceptance in March of 2010 and completed the first draft of their final report in January of 2011. After an extensive process of Treasury Department review and revision, CDIAC accepted the final report in July of

2011. About two years passed between the client's initial desire to have such a study conducted and its final delivery. The extensive data gathering, as well as the political vetting required before final approval, resulted in this lengthy wait for results.

Research Design and Implementation

CDIAC sought information that might confirm or dispel the notion that the State of California had taken on "too much" debt in 2009. They left it up to researchers to decide what this evidence should be and how best to provide it. Wassmer and Fisher examined the academic literature and determined that researchers had most often described an "ideal" for state and/or local government debt based upon the concepts of "affordability," "optimality," and "comparability."

Information Needs

The issue of affordability is whether citizens of a jurisdiction have the funds for both the debt taken on by the jurisdiction that represents them and everything else they want to purchase. A rough negative indicator of this ability is the ratio of the government's debt to the annual income generated in the jurisdiction's economy (e.g., gross state product). Nevertheless, even generating these ratios for all states does not provide a clear answer concerning an ideal ratio value to indicate affordability for a particular state. The concept of optimality evaluates a state's level of debt as ideal if it is buying the amount of current and future public infrastructure and the amount of generated services desired by current and future residents. The level of ideal debt varies by factors such as the characteristics of the state's residents and economy, and those will vary over time. Finally, the concept of comparability recognizes the inherent problems in using affordability or optimality to specify an ideal amount of public debt and seeks to control for factors that emerge from these concepts to calculate the desirability of a particular state's debt levels. The concept of comparability drove the information needed for the policy analysis that is the subject of this case study.

Design and Methods

The research design first involved the collection of data on the total amount of state and local long-term (greater than one year) debt outstanding in 2007 (the most recent year available at that point from the United States Census of Governments) across all 50 states. To yield the desired measures of long-term debt per capita and long-term debt as a percentage of state GSP, debt values required division by the 2007 population and gross state product. Similar data for 1992, 1997, and

2002 were also collected (given that the Census of Governments is only collected quinquennial) for all 50 states. Information in the final report only presented this information for the five states (Florida, Illinois, New York, Texas, and Arizona) thought most comparable based upon scale or proximity (see Table 19.1). The final report also included the 1992 to 2007 percentage change in long-term debt per capita and long-term debt as a percentage of state GSP for these five states.

Wassmer and Fisher discovered in their analysis of trends in state and local debt by government type (state, county, special district, municipality, and school district) for the entire United States and California (see Figure 19.1) that substantial growth in long-term debt only occurred for school districts. For example, in California, less than 2 percent of the total subnational debt issued in 1992 was school district based, and this figure rose to about 15 percent in 2007. This led the analysts to calculate how the various measures of weighted school district debt varied between California and five comparison states.

Statistical regression analysis played an important role in this policy analysis. Regression analysis requires specifying a dependent variable (i.e., the measure of state and local debt across the states for multiple years in this study) and a number of independent (or explanatory) variables. The analysis measures the degree to which change (higher or lower scores) in each independent variable is uniquely associated with change in the dependent variable. A brief summary of this method is included in the Focus on Research Methods Box later in this chapter. The statistical outcome of this analysis can be interpreted in different ways depending on the real-world process it is intended to represent. For example, independent variables are often called explanatory variables when the regression model is being used to test the degree to which change in independent variables explains why changes in the dependent variable occur. Wassmer and Fisher employed regression analysis to isolate the "California effect" of the state offering more or fewer bonds than other states (after controlling for factors previously offered in the literature as to why one state would choose to offer more bonds than another does). These factors included demographics, politics, economics, institutions, and borrowing costs. The observable variables chosen to represent each of these factors included:

- Demographics = f (percentage population age 65 plus, percentage of population public school K–12 enrolled)
- Politics = f (Measure of Liberal Citizen Ideology)
- Economics = f (Real Gross State Product Per Capita, Federal Intergovernmental Revenue Per Capita, State Fiscal Balance as Percentage of Expenditure, Unemployment Rate)
- Institutions = f (Limit on Debt Issue by Amount, No Mandatory Revenue or Spending Limit)
- Borrowing Costs = f (Previous Period's Debt)

Table 19.1 Comparison of Debt in California and Selected States in 2007

Debt Measure	California	Arizona	Florida	Illinois	New York	Texas	United States
Per-Capita Total State and Local Real* Debt	$9,495	$6,572	$7,663	$9,482	$13,873	$8,386	$8,351
Per-Capita Short-Term Real Debt	$27	$23	$22	$17	$294	$214	$114
Per-Capita Long-Term Real Debt	$9,468	$6,550	$7,641	$9,464	$13,579	$8,172	$8,237
Per-Capita Public Real Debt for Private Purposes	$1,091	$1,659	$1,222	$2,348	$2,743	$1,871	$1,890
Total State and Local Debt as % of GSP	18.3%	16.0%	18.1%	18.9%	23.5%	16.5%	17.6%
Short-Term Debt as % of GSP	0.1%	0.1%	0.1%	0.0%	0.5%	0.4%	0.2%
Long-Term Debt as % of GSP	18.3%	15.9%	18.0%	18.8%	23.0%	16.1%	17.3%
Public Debt for Private Purposes as % of GSP	2.1%	4.0%	2.9%	4.7%	4.6%	2.5%	4.0%
Total State and Local Debt as % Annual Revenue	70.6%	76.5%	77.5%	97.5%	88.6%	96.6%	78.6%
Short-Term Debt as % of Annual Revenue	0.2%	0.3%	0.2%	0.2%	1.9%	2.5%	1.1%
Long-Term Debt as % of Annual Revenue	70.4%	76.3%	77.3%	97.4%	86.8%	94.2%	77.5%
Public Debt for Private Purposes as % Annual Revenue	8.1%	19.3%	12.4%	24.2%	17.5%	21.6%	17.8%
Annual State and Local Interest Paid as % of Revenue	3.2%	3.2%	3.2%	4.5%	4.0%	4.4%	3.5%
Characteristics							
Population (thousands)	35,979.2	6,192.1	18,088.5	12,718.0	19,356.4	23,369.0	298,593.2
2009 Population Rank for 50 States (1 Highest)	1	16	4	5	3	2	
Real Per-Capita GSP	$50,078	$39,720	$41,013	$48,546	$57,088	$49,148	$47,094
2009 Real Per-Capita GSP Rank for 50 States (1 Highest)	10	43	24	14	5	29	

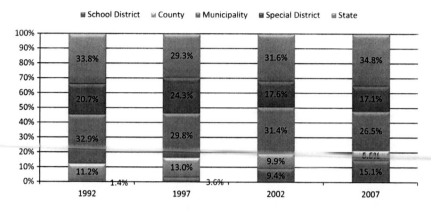

Figure 19.1 Share of Long-Term Debt by Type of Government in California

This policy analysis also involved a look at the most recent at the time (2008–2010) state and local government debt issues, by state, which was only available through a private data collection put together by Thomson Reuters. The period of 2008 and 2010 is particularly interesting because it was during this time that the federal government allowed the issuance of a new form of Build America Bond (BAB) as a possible stimulant to overcome the Great Recession. Traditional state and local bonds are attractive to high-income individual investors because the interest is not subject to federal income taxation, or even state income taxation if the purchaser lives in the state of issuance. BABs, instead, achieved the objective of lowering the interest rate that state and local governments pay on them by providing a federal subsidy of 35 percent of the interest paid to either the bondholder in the form of a refundable income tax credit or an equivalent payment to the public issuer.

Communicating and Using Results

A 125-page research report served as the primary method used to disseminate the findings of this research (Wassmer and Fisher, 2011). In addition, a summary of the findings appeared in *Debt Line*, a monthly newsletter circulated by CDIAC, and in the journal *State Tax Notes*, whose audience is public finance practitioners. As professors, Wassmer and Fisher also disseminated the results of their analysis through traditional academic outlets like seminars at the research conferences of the Association for Public Policy Analysis and Management (APPAM) and the National Tax Association (NTA), an article on "Debt Burdens of California's State and Local Governments" in the *California Journal of Politics and Policy*, and an article titled "The Issuance of State and Local Debt During the United States Great Recession" in the *National Tax Journal*.

Reporting Results

The report, titled *Debt Burdens of California State and Local Governments: Past, Present, and Future*, prepared for CDIAC included an executive summary and the following sections:

- An Overview of State and Local Debt
- Methods for Policymakers to Evaluate Debt
- California Debt Compared to Other States
- Regression Analysis of Subnational Debt
- Descriptive and Regression Analysis of Recent State and Local Bond Activity
- What Does This All Mean for California's Debt Load?

Wassmer and Fisher used both tables and figures to convey their findings. Some examples of these are included here. The *Debt Line* article appeared shortly after the filing of the final report on CDIAC's website and offered only a brief description of methods and findings from the analysis, with encouragement to view the full report for more information. The intended audience for the *State Tax Notes* article was national practitioners, and it briefly summarized general results regarding debt taken on by subnational governments in the United States. The grounding of this policy analysis in the best available data and research methods enabled its publication in two academic journals. One article, in the *California Journal of Politics and Policy*, offered a qualitative approach to describe how policy makers can best evaluate concern over the amount of state and local government debt in California and other states. The other article, in the *National Tax Journal*, focused on the methods and findings from the regression analysis regarding the factors that influenced differences in interstate borrowing between 2008 and 2010.

Selected Findings

The primary findings of the study come from regression analyses (Table 19.2). A summary of these findings includes:

- Around half of the variance in long-term total debt per capita and school district debt across the states between 1997 and 2007 is explainable through the causal factors of demographics, politics, economics, institutions, and borrowing costs used in previous studies.
- Relative to 1997 and controlling for state-specific factors expected to cause differences in debt issue, there was an increase in the amount

Table 19.2 Debt Fixed Effects Regression Results

(Dependent Variable is Real Long-Term State and Local Debt Per Capita in Thousands for 50 States; Drawn from Years 1997, 2002, and 2007)

Explanatory Variables	Regression Coefficient (Standard Error)
Constant	−0.584
	(1.436)
2002 Dummy	0.501***
	(0.127)
2007 Dummy	1.067***
	(0.262)
Lag Value of Respective Dependent Variable	0.265
	(0.188)
Percentage Pop Age 65 Plus	0.037
	(0.104)
Percentage Pop Public K–12 Enrolled	0.117**
	(0.047)
BRH Liberal Citizen Ideology	0.002
	(0.005)
Real Gross State Product PC (1000 $s)	0.022
	(0.026)
Fed Intergovernmental Revenue PC (1000 $s)	−0.551*
	(0.314)
State Fiscal Balance as Percentage of Expenditure	−0.001
	(0.005)
Unemployment Rate	0.058
	(0.053)
Limit Debt Issue by Amount	0.153
	(0.145)
No Mandatory Revenue or Spending Limit	0.047
	(0.154)
Observations	150
R-Squared	0.963

*** (**) [*] indicates a regression coefficient that is statistically significant from zero with a 99% or greater (95 to 98.9%) [90 to 94.9%] likelihood in a two-tailed test. State-level dummy variables were also included in the model, and the following states had significant findings (parentheses indicate whether the coefficient was significant in a positive or negative direction): AL (−), AK (+), AR (−), GA (−), ID (−), IN (−), IA (−), KS (−), MD (−), MA (+), MI (−), MS (−), MO (−), NV (+), NM (−), NY (+), NC (−), ND (−), OH (−), OK (−), TN (−), TX (−), VA (−), WY (−).

issued in 2002 and a further increase in 2007 across all three forms of non–school district debt.

- The most persistent influence on total real long-term state debt per capita of all types is the percentage of a state's population that attends K–12 public school. A $1,000 increase in this value raises long-term debt per capita by between $117 and $141.

- Between 1997 and 2007, after controlling for differences in debt issued five years earlier and demographic, political, economic, and institutional differences:

  a. California's real long-term public debt per capita for public and private purposes is greater than that of 20 other states and only less than that of 4 other states. For the remaining 26 states, its outstanding real long-term public debt per capita for public and private purposes is similar.

  b. California's real long-term public debt per capita for public purposes alone is greater than that of 12 other states and only less than that of 1 other state. For the remaining 37 states, its outstanding real debt for public debt per capita for public purposes alone is similar.

  c. California's real long-term public debt per capita for school districts is greater than that of seven other states and less than that of no other state. For the remaining 43 states, its real long-term public debt per capita for school districts purposes is similar.

Recommendations

The analysis was intended to answer specific questions posed by the California Debt and Investment Advisory Commission. These questions and a summary of the project's findings follow.

Compared to the previous research, what has this analysis contributed to knowledge of debt burdens? This policy analysis offered two major contributions. First, it provided information about the trends in overall state and local debt in all states during the decades surrounding the turn of the 20th century and during the recent Great Recession (2008 to 2010). Second, the specific analysis examining state and local debt choices and borrowing behavior offers information about the important social and economic factors influencing these decisions. On the latter issue, this research supports earlier work from the 1990s showing that changes in public school enrollment exerted an important influence on the offering of subnational debt in the United States. This is not surprising given that public education is by far the largest service provided by state and local governments and accounts for about a third of overall state and local spending throughout the United States. In addition, the research contained in this report offers an updated understanding of the relative debt position of each state and thus permits any state to compare its debt to that of other states.

How should the state legislature and local governing boards evaluate rising debt loads? Conceptually, the assessment of subnational debt levels can occur by examining affordability, optimality, or comparability. The chosen application here of the comparability method to the use of subnational debt by California state and local governments did not suggest that its aggregate level of public debt is especially problematic up to 2007. The application of this statistical method to analyzing state and local government debt and comparing governments in California to those in other states does suggest that governments in California relied relatively more on debt for public purposes than one might expect compared to other states. However, much of the growth in debt over the 15 years from 1992 to 2007 seems related to growth in enrollment in public primary and secondary schools, suggesting that the increased debt corresponds to increased investment in public education facilities.

Following the start of the Great Recession, governments in California did increase their borrowing in 2009 and 2010 compared to the historical pattern and relative to most other states. A combination of traditional nontaxable bonds and Build America Bonds accomplished this increase. Although many state-local governments increased borrowing during these years, California government was aggressive in its use of Build America Bonds.

Under what circumstances should California governments declare an issuance of "too much" debt? Debt is "too high" if debt levels (or interest costs) increase substantially in comparison to the economy in that jurisdiction (e.g., residents' incomes) or compared to the government's revenue. Debt may also be "too high" if it is substantially different from comparable governments without a clear and appropriate explanation. Ultimately, debt is "too high" if it is used to finance public facilities or services that are unsupported by residents.

Although the analysis in this report does not suggest that these circumstances apply in California in aggregate for different forms of total state and local debt, it is not feasible in this report to examine the situation of every local government in California. However, individual jurisdictions could undertake similar evaluations of their specific circumstances using the same techniques employed here.

How are California state and local debt burdens likely to change in the future? The analyses in this report suggest that public debt levels have grown over time and are influenced to varying degrees by K–12 public school enrollment, federal aid, and some political/institutional factors. For instance, if the population of school-age children grows substantially, or if additional federal aid supports new public capital investment, then subnational debt levels in California are likely to increase. Forecasting future debt levels depends on projections of these underlying determining factors. In addition, governments in California were relatively large issuers of Build America Bonds. The option for these federally subsidized bonds expired in December 2010. Therefore, unless Congress reinstitutes this program, one incentive for state and local government borrowing no longer exists.

Should the California legislature consider providing more oversight of local debt loads? The largest increases in any of the forms of public debt in California from 1992 to 2007 were by school districts and by the state government. Conversely, debt issued by counties, municipalities, and special districts (other than schools) decreased from 64 percent of the total in 1992 to about 50 percent of the total in 2007. Therefore, debt incurred by local governments (except school districts) over this recent 15-year period increased at a much slower rate than debt incurred by the state government and by school districts.

Any individual county or municipality could face economic or fiscal problems that would pose potential difficulty for its outstanding debt. Nevertheless, the overall perspective suggests that growth of debt by counties and municipalities has not been unusual or substantial in California since the early 1990s. Thus, a more extensive and broad-based oversight process that would apply to all local governments is likely not required. Rather, the debt trends suggest that if the California legislature was to consider any new oversight mechanism, it should focus on school districts and on general-purpose local governments in severe fiscal distress.

What important questions remain regarding debt burdens? The years 2009 and 2010 were unusual for California subnational debt issuance in comparison to the 1992-to-2007 period because of: (1) the Great Recession, (2) federal stimulus funds whose receipt entailed the start of public infrastructure projects in part funded by more debt, (3) the decrease in municipal interest rates, and (4) the availability of Build America Bonds. The state and local governments in California reacted to these factors by borrowing during this period and increasing debt comparatively more than other states did. However, aggregate borrowing by the state and local governments in California did *decrease* in 2010 compared to 2009, and the Build America Bond program ended in December 2010. Thus, one question that remains for after 2010 is whether borrowing by California governments returns to its lower long-term pattern or whether the relatively high pattern of borrowing for 2009 and 2010 foreshadows a higher pattern for future years.

Lessons for Policy Research

There are a few lessons to draw from this policy analysis regarding the earlier material offered in this text. Foremost is the clear understanding by both the client requesting this analysis and the analysts who responded to it that it was intended only to help further facilitate a policy discussion that had already begun on the desirability of the magnitude of California's debt. The client had clear information needs, and the analysts did their best to satisfy them. This represents a clear example of a formative evaluation whose intent was to provide evidence generated specifically to assist a policy formulation.

A second lesson to consider is that the CDIAC client offered a clear policy question in its RFP but left it to the analyst to suggest the most appropriate way to conduct the policy research to match their needs. A third lesson is that the analysis included a high-powered regression method, but only because it was the only way to isolate a separate California-based influence on amount of debt issued. Mixed methods also contributed to the credibility and understandability of the study through a descriptive analysis that offered its own relevant findings and helped explain the need for a regression analysis. Finally, the academic researchers took great care to explain the regression method and findings so as not to alienate the client.

Focus on Research Methods

Multiple Regression Analysis

An important component of this policy analysis is the use of the statistical technique of multiple regression (or econometric) analysis. Our focus here is to explain how the analysis in Table 19.2 uses the power and flexibility of this statistical technique to answer a specific real-world question. Multiple regression analysis is highly appropriate for use in a policy analysis that requires the teasing out of the independent influence of one explanatory factor on an outcome variable of interest when variance in the outcome variable exists due to multiple factors. In this case the objective might be simply stated as determining the extent to which California long-term debt reflects decisions to undertake more or less debt than contextual circumstances that affect state spending generally. This deviation from similar patterns of spending in other states would be what the analysts called the "California effect." If there were no strong (identified technically as a statistically significant) California effect, that would suggest that California decisions to take on additional debt are pursued for reasons similar to other states. Put in simpler terms, it would suggest that California decisions are neither miserly nor spendthrift compared to what others do.

The appropriate use of regression analysis requires that the analyst begin with a complete model of all general factors expected to influence the outcome of interest. In this instance, the research team was trying to explain variation in long-term state and local debt per capita and relied on the literature (i.e., existing studies on what factors relate to long-term debt size in states) to provide a list of those variables to include. They also included amounts of debt in each state in earlier years (5 and 10 years earlier). This controls for the obvious fact that differences in earlier debt will be a strong part of the explanation of differences in current debt. Now the researchers had a controlled foundation, a level field as it were, to which they added a "dummy variable" (simply a "1" for yes and a "0" for no) for all other states. All of these variables and the reasoning behind their use constitute the regression model for this analysis.

A statistically significant regression coefficient (one with an asterisk in Table 19.2) indicates the expected influence of a one-unit change in the respective explanatory variable on the dependent variable. Thus, when the percentage of a state's population enrolled in public K–12 schools rises by one percentage point, the debt taken on by the state's subnational governments rises by 117 real dollars per person. Also, the statistically significant regression coefficients on the 2002 and 2007 dummies (since 1997 is the excluded dummy year) indicate that after controlling for all other explanatory factors included in this regression analysis, debt per capita in 2002 was $501 less than in 1997 and $1,067 more in 2007 than in 1997. With respect to the state "dummy variables," the results indicated that 20 states were significantly below the level of debt predicted by all the factors in the regression model, and 5 were significantly above. California was neither; it was similar to the remaining 24 states. In other words, California's long-term debt decisions were not out of the norm given its circumstances (e.g., the growing student population).

Acronyms and Jargon

BAB—Build America Bonds were a federal support for state ability to issue bonds following the economic collapse of 2008. BABs were backed by a 35 percent subsidy of bond repayment interest costs through tax credits to bond holders or direct payments to the public issuer.

CDIAC—California Debt and Investment Advisory Commission provides oversight and advice on the state's debt and investment status. It is a good example of institutionalized sources of professional and political expertise in providing policy-relevant information. The California state treasurer serves as chair.

GO Bond—A bond issued by the state of California that requires repayment in up to 30 years with the "full faith and credit" of the state. It is repaid out of the state general fund.

Legislative Analyst's Office—A policy research office within the legislative staff of the California state government. It provides assessments of the fiscal impact of proposed legislation and ballot propositions. It is an example of the institutionalization of policy research information to support governmental decisions.

Discussion Questions

1. One objective of the policy research described in this case was "actionable" information. How well did the study meet this objective? To what extent is your conclusion based on the study itself or on the problem and user realities it had to address?

2. Summarize the policy problem presented in this case. Why did it require policy research? How well did the policy research described in this case meet that requirement? Explain the reasons for your assessment.

3. Discuss the concepts "affordability," "optimality," and "comparability" as they apply to this study. Which played the biggest part in the study and why?

4. Discuss the reasons for including local government debt and state employee pension obligations in future California public debt measurement. Why were school-age population, senior population, and past state debt levels included in the regression model that was one of the statistical analyses used in the study? What did that regression analysis reveal?

20 Deinstitutionalization and Community Services in Virginia

A Policy Assessment

Peter J. Haas

Introduction

Across the United States, many states and communities have faced problems—real or perceived—associated with deinstitutionalization (see, for example, Bardach, 1977). "Deinstitutionalization" refers to the process by which the primary treatment responsibility for the mentally disabled is transferred from mental health hospitals—often operated by state governments—to service providers in community-based settings. Deinstitutionalization is a complicated policy that encompasses the efforts of many agencies and programs. This case study relates one state's efforts to increase its knowledge and understanding for policy action in this arena through primarily exploratory policy research. The research represents a panoply of research methods, including quantitative descriptive techniques and more qualitative and less-structured data collection efforts. The case is thus a good example of using multiple data collection methods. The case also illustrates how effective policy research can be in instigating action by decision makers.

The Policy Problem

Deinstitutionalization first became popular in the United States in the late 1960s, when mental health care professionals reached a working consensus that care could occur most effectively and efficiently within the context of normal home and community ties. Deinstitutionalization became statewide policy in Virginia as early as 1968, when the state's general assembly (the lower house of the state legislature) authorized local governments to establish "community service boards," locally based agencies that delivered mental health services to clients discharged from state mental health facilities.

Deinstitutionalization became increasingly controversial in Virginia (as well as in other states) during the 1980s, when some criticized the practice as often consisting of little more than dumping the chronically mentally ill onto city streets (JLARC, 1985a).

Initiation of Policy Research

As a result of growing concerns across the states about the fate of the mentally ill, as well as a general uncertainty about the details of how deinstitutionalization was working, the Virginia state legislature authorized the creation of the Commission on Deinstitutionalization to study related policies in the state. The legislature authorized the state's Joint Legislative Audit and Review Commission (JLARC) to provide "technical assistance" to the newly created commission (JLARC, 1985a).

JLARC is a state agency that serves the state legislature by providing policy research in response to requests from legislators. JLARC had earned the reputation of being a tough but objective watchdog agency that the legislature listened to carefully. Although JLARC consists of state delegates (representatives from the lower legislative house) and state senators, in practice, JLARC staff members are primarily responsible for actually planning and implementing the relevant policy research. Thus, this case study exemplifies policy research conducted within a government but by an agency from outside the confines of the agency with the lead responsibility for the policy under study (in this case, the state's Department of Mental Health and Mental Retardation).

The Policy Research Task

JLARC staff were confronted by a daunting task: to provide the Virginia state legislature with information that could be used to help improve the entire state's primary means of mental health service delivery, including the local level.

Objectives

The general objectives of the study included the following:

- To help clarify the policy and programmatic issues associated with the policy of deinstitutionalization in the state of Virginia
- To provide baseline information about the mental health service delivery system
- To provide some indication of how well the then-current policy was working, particularly in terms of the adequacy of existing services and the procedures associated with them

(More specific objectives were also pursued in response to queries from the decision-making client, the legislature of Virginia. See the Information Needs section in this chapter.)

Challenges

The study presented a significant challenge to JLARC staff due to its potentially vast scope and complexity. Thus, this case represents an excellent example of how policy research must be shaped in order to adequately address the concerns of clients and stakeholders without exceeding available resources. When the scope is potentially as great as that encountered in this case study, policy researchers must find ways to make the project more manageable—yet in ways that will not compromise the objectives of the research.

In addition to the potential size of the study, the subject matter was also inordinately complex. The policy of deinstitutionalization entailed the cooperation of many state agencies as well as nearly every local government in the state. Further challenges existed in the lack of existing information about deinstitutionalization policies. Because the mental health service system was so decentralized—and perhaps also because of the novelty of the policy—JLARC staff could not tap existing databases for its study.

Finally, the study, which was conducted at the behest of a legislative body with fixed time horizons, had to be completed in a very short amount of time, approximately one year. Whereas some policy research projects can be conducted at a relatively leisurely pace with flexible deadlines, the deinstitutionalization study had to be finished quickly. The case study thus helps to exemplify how the political process places significant constraints on the conduct of policy research.

The Decision Context

The decision context for this study could hardly have been murkier or more complicated. Consider the following circumstances:

- Many policy actors—both clients and stakeholders—were involved in the delivery of services associated with deinstitutionalization.
- The policy of deinstitutionalization lacked firm legislative and programmatic parameters, having evolved over the course of several decades with relatively little strategic focus; thus, the position of the study in the policy cycle was not straightforward. It was focused primarily on providing information for planning and decision making for future policy direction. To do this, however, information on existing program effectiveness and implementation would go along with information on needs and demands.
- The information needs of the client—the state legislature of Virginia— similarly lacked specificity and focus.

The Institutional Context

Deinstitutionalization, as implemented in many states, entails a complex network of policy actors with a variety of responsibilities. The formal part of this network in Virginia included the state's Department of Mental Health and Mental Retardation (DMHMR) and the 40 local mental health agencies, known as community service boards (CSBs). DMHMR was the primary funding source for services associated with deinstitutionalization, and also provided technical support to the CSBs and monitored the quality of local programs. The provision of actual services to deinstitutionalized clients was the responsibility of the CSBs.

However, deinstitutionalization also connoted a less formal network of state and local agencies that provided a range of necessary support services to discharged individuals, including financial support, housing, and job training. Although these are not mental health services, such services contribute to the success or failure of deinstitutionalized individuals.

The agencies involved with the delivery of services to the deinstitutionalized clients are discussed in the following subsections.

Department of Mental Health and Mental Retardation

DMHMR was responsible for planning, coordinating, and providing mental health programs in Virginia. Most important to the process of deinstitutionalization, DMHMR operated the state's 15 inpatient treatment facilities (primarily hospitals), providing both intensive acute treatment and long-term care for the mentally ill.

The department's central office also played an important role in the community mental health system that served deinstitutionalized clients: ensuring that core services were available to those who needed them by planning, developing, and coordinating policies and programs for communities. A separate Office of CSB Liaison was specifically charged with the responsibility of coordinating the department's programs with those of local agencies. This office developed grants and performance contracts for CSBs and monitored CSB activities to identify potential problem areas.

Community Service Boards

The primary responsibility for actually delivering services to discharged clients from state facilities lay with the CSBs. Such services were offered either directly by CSB staff or through contracts with private service providers. CSBs consisted of a board of directors and an executive director, as well as professional staff (such as psychologists, counselors, and nurses).

Thus CSBs played the central role in the deinstitutionalization process: They served as the primary intake point for clients entering the state mental health system and as the locus of the community-based care that is central to the concept of deinstitutionalization. By state law, the CSBs were required to provide client prescreening (that is, determining whether clients were ready to live in the community and which services they would require) as well as predischarge planning (that is, planning their exit from intensive-care facilities into the community).

Because CSBs were established by autonomous localities, each had a different organization and a different set of programs, policies, and operating procedures. Whereas DMHMR had supervisory responsibility for local programs, the CSBs were also funded by local and federal funds: they had a great deal of discretion with regard to the services they offered. Their only legal mandate from the state was to provide emergency services.

Support Service Agencies

A less formally integrated network of state agencies provided important services to the clients released to the community. These services were provided to low-income clients, and because deinstitutionalized individuals are typically unemployed and with limited incomes, many of them qualify for support services.

Among the agencies that provided such services in Virginia were the Department of Social Services (DSS), which provided income supplements to clients in the form of an auxiliary grants program financed in part by the federal government and the Department of Rehabilitative Services (DRS), which in many instances provided therapy and/or training to the deinstitutionalized.

The DSS role was the most significant to the study. The auxiliary grants were a significant source of funding for housing the mentally disabled. Additionally, the DSS had an important role in licensing board and care facilities known in Virginia as "homes for adults." Homes for adults are residential facilities for dependent individuals (such as the elderly or mentally disabled), usually operated by private individuals. In Virginia, they housed a large number of former residents of state mental institutions.

The Policy Cycle

As explained earlier, the policy of deinstitutionalization had been initiated in the state of Virginia nearly 15 years prior to the study under discussion here. However, initial scoping activity conducted by JLARC staff revealed that the policy was not a clearly delineated one. Deinstitutionalization, it seemed, was more of a policy concept than a specific series of legislation and/or procedures and regulations. Indeed, the issue of the apparent lack of a coherent deinstitutionalization policy had sparked the need for a similar JLARC study in 1979 only five years prior to this one (JLARC, 1979). The 1979 study concluded that although deinstitutionalization had created progress in reducing the population of state mental institutions, considerable gaps existed among the provisions for taking clients who were discharged from such institutions. For example, clients were sometimes released into communities without prior warning or consultation with local mental health officials. Accordingly, the state's mental health service delivery system was fragmented, uncoordinated, and lacking central policy direction.

Thus the position of deinstitutionalization in the policy cycle was ambiguous. From the standpoint of time, the policy had been in place for some time and was clearly ripe for evaluation. Nevertheless, a clear policy had yet to be articulated, and perhaps that was the impetus for the policy research—the need to help further specify the appropriate parameters for deinstitutionalization.

Clients and Stakeholders

As the preceding discussion has demonstrated, deinstitutionalization-related policy in Virginia affected or involved a wide range of groups, agencies, and individuals. The primary client for the project, of course, was the Commission on Deinstitutionalization (and the state legislature it represented), but in a sense nearly every agency involved in the delivery of mental health services associated with deinstitutionalization was also a client. (That is often the case when policy research is conducted for legislative bodies.)

If not actual clients, the several state agencies that provided support services for people with mental disabilities were clearly stakeholders with a direct interest in the findings and recommendations of the JLARC study. (These agencies included the Department of Social Services and the Department of Rehabilitative Services.)

Additionally, several clientele groups associated with deinstitutionalization policy were also quite interested in the results of the study, including the state's representatives of the Alliance for the Mentally Ill and other groups and individuals (including parents of mentally ill clients) with an interest in the policy.

Finally, a number of local agencies beyond the CSBs provided services to discharged clients or were otherwise affected by the policy of deinstitutionalization. Entities such as local jails, courts, and hospitals frequently served as points of intake to the mental health service delivery system for dysfunctional clients in the community. Additionally, nongovernmental agencies such as the Salvation Army and shelters for the homeless also provided services and were thus interested parties.

Research Design and Implementation

The research design that emerged from this policy and decision-making context was necessarily both of broad scope and relatively unfocused. Due in part to the fact that the primary client—the Virginia state legislature— was relatively unclear about its information requirements, the study had a distinctly exploratory nature.

Information Needs

Clearly, the legislature was generally concerned about the overall effectiveness of the state's mental health delivery system, but "effectiveness" can imply many things and many possible research foci. Indeed, this study is an example of how a relatively open information request gives the policy researcher some discretion about what to do and how to do it.

Implicitly, however, the legislature placed several specific information requests in addition to its concern about the overall effectiveness of the system. For example, part of the impetus for the study was the visibility of so-called street people on city streets throughout the state. At public hearings conducted by the Commission on Deinstitutionalization, participants frequently voiced concerns that discharged clients were possibly falling through the cracks of the system. To what extent, if any, were these apparently homeless individuals the product of inadequacies in the state's mental health service system? This question pointed the JLARC policy researchers toward a more specific, descriptive information problem.

Some members of the legislature had also voiced concerns about the perceived and/or documented adequacy of adult homes. How appropriate were these privately operated residential facilities as housing placements for clients discharged from state mental health facilities? This question also placed a relatively more focused, descriptive question before the policy research team.

The study, therefore, helps to illustrate how the information needs of decision makers can be plural—in this instance, both exploratory and descriptive. What is also interesting is the extent to which the request from the legislature apparently avoided possible forays into questions that involved matters of either choice or causality. That is to say, no mention was made of investigating the actual effectiveness of deinstitutionalization policy vis-à-vis other policy options—which would have been a policy choice problem. Nor did the information request seek to determine the actual effectiveness of discharging clients from state institutions, a request that would have pushed toward a more causal research problem.

Thus, as is often the case with intragovernmental policy research, JLARC was given a relatively wide scope with which to approach the policy of deinstitutionalization. The legislative resolution that called for the study merely called on JLARC to "provide technical assistance to the commission (on deinstitutionalization)" (JLARC, 1985a). JLARC, in turn, directed its staff to conduct a follow-up of a similar JLARC–authored study that had been completed in 1979. However, JLARC staff were also requested to conduct research in other areas "salient to deinstitutionalization policies" (JLARC, 1985a). Inasmuch as deinstitutionalization policies touched on many other programs and agencies, the parameters of the study were potentially quite broad indeed. It is not unusual for policy researchers to have a broad mandate that allows them significant discretion in deciding what policy makers will hear.

However, the study did not extend to a variety of tangential areas. For example, deinstitutionalization policies also apply to the areas of mental retardation and substance abuse. For the most part, the study avoided these areas. Additionally, the study avoided collecting data about the *effectiveness* of deinstitutionalization; that is, it did not seek to determine whether placing chronically mentally ill individuals in the community was making them or society better off. The resource and time constraints of the study kept it more focused.

Design and Methods

Given this quite open-ended mandate for policy information, JLARC responded with a research design that employed a variety of data-collection methods appropriate for a primarily exploratory research problem. The overall emphasis of these efforts was on providing baseline, descriptive information about how the state's mental health system was performing, with an emphasis on the outcomes associated with the chronically mentally ill.

Design

The research design placed a relatively heavy emphasis on the collection of unstructured "qualitative" information to support several more quantitative data collection efforts. In order to be practical and manageable, the research design omitted any more rigorous techniques, such as experiments, sophisticated data analysis, or cost-benefit analysis. Quite probably, such methods would have yielded inappropriately narrow information of limited utility to decision makers in this context. The approach that was used, however, was quite appropriate given (a) the primarily exploratory information needs of the client and (b) the lack of existing baseline information about the policy system. Thus, this case provides a good illustration of how policy researchers must occasionally pick and choose among a wide variety of options among research methods to try to meet the information needs of their client/decision maker.

Methods

Specific data collection activities are described in the following subsections.

TRACKING A SAMPLE OF DEINSTITUTIONALIZED CLIENTS

A key means of establishing baseline information about the performance of the mental health system was tracking the status of a sample of deinstitutionalized individuals from their origin in the state mental health facilities to their placement (if any) in communities around the state. The tracking task actually entailed three separate data collection activities:

1. Drawing a random sample of 350 clients who were discharged from mental health facilities during a one-month period

2. Requesting information from state hospital staff for each client, including admission status and discharge status, client management procedures, and service needs upon discharge
3. Completion of a follow-up questionnaire from the staff of each community service board to which clients in the sample were discharged, including the status of the discharged client, services delivered, and housing and financial status.

This three-step data collection effort enabled JLARC staff to assess the overall ability of state and community agencies to keep track of and to properly serve the chronically mentally ill.

SURVEY OF COMMUNITY SERVICE BOARD DIRECTORS

Given the important role played by community service boards (CSBs) in delivering services to discharged clients, a comprehensive survey was submitted to each of the 40 CSB directors. The survey was intended to provide baseline information about the adequacy of community programs and services, as well as issues associated with the funding, costs, and adequacy of community service efforts.

CASE STUDY SITE VISITS

To provide more in-depth, qualitative information about the mental health service delivery system, detailed case studies were completed at a purposive sample of five CSB sites. Additional, less intensive site visits were made to 10 additional CSB sites around the state. Case study sites were selected to reflect a variety of criteria, including geographic diversity, funding levels, program reputation, and proximity to state mental health facilities. Site visit activities included review of program documents (including client records), interviews with CSB and other program staff, observation of CSB facilities and programs, and visits to selected client housing sites.

INTERVIEWS WITH MENTAL HEALTH SYSTEM PROFESSIONALS

To help provide additional depth and accuracy to the more systematic data collection efforts, JLARC staff interviewed a wide range of professionals directly or indirectly involved with providing services to clients with mental disabilities, as follows:

- Administrators from the state DMHMR, including program, fiscal, and support staff
- Directors and other staff from the state's major mental health facilities

- Administrators and various program personnel from the state DSS
- Staff from a variety of other state agencies, including the Virginia Housing Development Authority, the Department of Rehabilitative Services, and the Department of Housing and Community Development

REVIEW OF AGENCY RECORDS AND FISCAL DATA

Existing data from agencies responsible for providing services to people with mental disabilities were reviewed and analyzed, including reimbursement and other fiscal data from the state DMHMR. These data were used to help identify the cost of various treatment and placement alternatives for discharged clients.

SITE VISITS TO HOMES FOR ADULTS

To examine the availability and quality of placements in adult homes (board and care facilities), JLARC staff visited a purposive sample of 21 homes for adults. (A purposive sample is a nonrandom sample that is selected on the basis of the usefulness of each observation to the goals of the research.) A "critical case" strategy was used to select homes for study, such that the homes selected were those considered to be both the best and the worst in each area. This strategy enabled the range of quality and appropriateness of placements to be documented. During these site visits, JLARC staff interviewed operators of the home for adults, observed the facilities, and reviewed documents for residents with mental illnesses.

Selected Findings

The broad net of data collection efforts yielded an extensive collection of significant findings that addressed the full range of the state's mental health service delivery system. Consistent with the multiple methods employed by the study, most of the findings stemmed from more than one data source, with some exceptions. The key findings are described in the following subsections.

Profile of Discharged Clients

The most structured data collection method employed by the study was tracking the sample of discharged clients. Some of the findings from that effort are displayed in Table 20.1. From the standpoint of the objectives of the study, this profile was useful in conveying the service needs of the typical discharged client: most clients in the profile were young, single, unemployed, and required both supervision and medication to survive in the community. Most were not capable of functioning independently

Table 20.1 Profile of Discharged Clients (*n* = 350)

Average age	35 years	
Gender	Male	58%
	Female	42%
Employment status	Unemployed	85%
	Employed	15%
Marital status	Unmarried	83%
	Married	17%
Mental health status	Improved, not recovered	82%
at time of discharge	Unimproved, not recovered	7%
	Other	11%
Prior hospitalizations	No prior hospitalizations	28%
during previous two years	One prior hospitalization	33%
	Two prior hospitalizations	39%
Ability to live independently	Requiring daily supervision	79%
	Remainder needed no supervision	
Need for psychotropic	Needing psychotropic medication(s)	79%
medication	Remainder needed no medication(s)	

of the efforts of community service boards. This finding implied that the availability and adequacy of CSB services was critical to the overall success of the state system.

Adequacy of Client Management Procedures

"Client management" refers to the procedures and services related to keeping track of discharged clients and ensuring that they received appropriate and adequate services. Through the variety of data collection techniques employed by the JLARC policy researchers, a diagram that mapped the client management process similar to that in Figure 20.1 was created. The diagram illustrated the potential weak or "leakage" points in the system.

The study found that although client management practices appeared to have been improved, several patterns of inconsistent or incomplete procedures persisted throughout the mental health system. For example, clients referred to mental health hospitals by local courts frequently failed to receive prescreening that might have prevented inappropriate admissions and/or improved coordination of services following discharge. Pre-discharge planning, although routinely completed by hospital staff and CSBs, was found to lack comprehensiveness and coordination between hospitals and CSBs. Some clients were being discharged while on "temporary leave" from state facilities, making proper predischarge planning impossible.

Note that whereas the quantitative data collection techniques helped establish how often some of these problems occurred, learning about how and why they could exist was established primarily through interviews

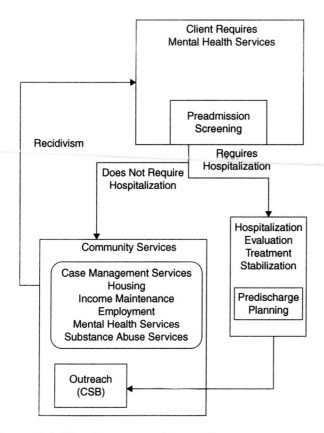

Figure 20.1 Client Management Process Diagram

and observation. Thus, the two general approaches complemented and supported each other in this study.

Adequacy of Community Services for Discharged Clients

The study established that community services for discharged clients were woefully inadequate. Data from the profile of discharged clients, for example, demonstrated that half the sample received only medication monitoring, meaning that other needs (such as housing and job training) might have gone unmet. The study described the following service gaps:

- *Absolute service gaps.* Communities fail to provide an important service. For example, an absolute service gap would occur when a CSB offered no day support programs for its clients.
- *Program gap.* Community lacks a specific program in a general program area. For example, a CSB could offer housing for certain types of clients but lack a housing program for chronic clients.

- *Capacity gap.* Community offers a program that does not adequately serve all clients who need it.

This sort of taxonomy is frequently a by-product of policy research. Policy researchers often have to devise new terms and conceptual frameworks to help make sense of complicated policy arenas with limited existing conceptual tools.

Based on information from a number of data collection methods, the study found that the state's community service system contained a significant number of each type of service gap. Inadequacies were found throughout the "continuum of care" represented by inpatient, day support, outpatient, residential, and other service options. The study placed particular emphasis on the lack of housing for discharged clients, because without adequate housing, clients could not make progress in dealing with their disabilities. The study established that the responsibility for housing clients was scattered among a number of state and local agencies, resulting in a lack of coordination and funding for adequate housing.

Table 20.2 presents data showing housing patterns for people with mental disabilities in Virginia in 1985. The second column is an estimate based on the survey of CSB directors. The third column is based on a profile of discharged clients. This comparison was used to help document some of the housing shortfall. Note that the data tend to reflect similar housing patterns, although one was generated from the summation of survey data and the other from the more rigorous follow-up study. The fact that the two indicators yielded approximately similar results bolstered the validity (and credibility) of both, thus providing a good illustration of the utility of using multiple measures to triangulate accurate

Table 20.2 Where People with Mental Disabilities Lived in Virginia in 1985

Setting	Statewide Estimate	Sample of Discharges
Family	45.9%	50.0%
Own dwelling	14.1	12.0
Homes for adults	13.5	4.1
CSB housing programs	3.3	3.8
Nursing home	1.6	0.6
Boarding home or hotel	9.6	1.7
Private home	1.8	1.5
No stable residence	2.1	1.2
Jail	N/A	5.7
Hospital	N/A	4.8
Other	2.1	8.2
Residence unknown	6.0	6.4
Total *(n)*	13,822*	343**

* Based on survey of CSB directors
** Based on profile compiled from follow-up study of discharged clients

policy information. Triangulation consists of increasing the accuracy of a measure by means of the use of multiple indicators.

Problems with Homes for Adults

The study found that homes for adults were an "unplanned component" of the state's deinstitutionalization policy. Although these homes should have been able to properly administer medications, provide adequate activities and programs, supervise potentially destructive behaviors, and enable access to CSB services, the existing laws and regulations did not serve to ensure that these conditions were satisfied. Although the report provided various sorts of documentation to establish the frequent inadequacies of homes for adults, vignettes drawn from the site visits, such as the following, were particularly effective in conveying the nature of the problem:

The (policy research) staff entered a(n) . . . adult home during the lunch hour. The home was dark, dirty, and in apparent need of repair. Bed linen appeared to be filthy and residents were wandering about unattended. Only one staff person was on hand. The individual was busy preparing lunch, while also attending to other duties around the home. Although he had not received training or related experience in caring for the mentally ill, the individual boasted that the home accepted the worst cases, clients that other homes would not accept.

Having established that recordkeeping, staffing, and linkages to CSB services were inadequate in many adult homes, the report concluded that, as then regulated, the homes were frequently inappropriate and/or inadequate placements for discharged clients.

Other Findings

The study also reported findings about a variety of other subjects and included important statements about the overall accountability in the system for both finances and service provision. For the most part, these findings were based on the more qualitative data sources, such as reviews of current legislation and regulations and interviews with knowledgeable officials ("key informants") in the mental health system. With respect to accountability for providing services, for example, the study noted,

Currently the State operates or supports three overlapping systems which serve many of the same clients. State hospital services are provided by the Department of Mental Health and Mental Retardation. Community services are provided by 40 community services boards and funded largely through State and local general fund revenues. Finally, residential services are provided by adult homes which are supported in part by grants and monitored by the State Department of Social Services. The links in authority between these entities are often unclear, contradictory, or inoperable. As a result, accountability is diminished. Moreover, the operation of overlapping systems is financially inefficient. The outcome of this situation is the limited effectiveness of State policies and programs. Because accountability for services is unclear, many clients do not receive the services they require. The overlapping systems, coupled with a lack of accountability, make it difficult to identify and address problems in the delivery system.

(p. 65)

Had the study relied exclusively on quantitative data-collection efforts, such a statement would have been difficult to establish. The use of multiple types of data helped contribute to a study that could address real policy and programmatic issues.

Communicating and Using Results

The JLARC study exemplifies a key difference between policy research generated by outside government agencies and policy research produced by consultants or done in house. The JLARC findings and recommendations about deinstitutionalization were announced at public hearings that were closely covered by state news media. Local newspapers (in the state capital of Richmond) featured the findings as well. The hearings were sponsored by the state legislature's Commission on Deinstitutionalization, guaranteeing a high public profile.

Reporting Results

The primary means for reporting the study results was a written report. The report was organized according to the various substantive program areas included in deinstitutionalization policy, and it contained the following chapters:

1. *Client Management* (included discussion of how clients are passed from one part of the mental health system to another—primarily from state hospitals to community service programs)
2. *Community Services* (focused on adequacy of services available in communities across the state)
3. *Housing Services* (highlighted findings about housing shortages and inadequacy of adult homes)
4. *Service and Fiscal Accountability* (synthesized policy system—level implications of various findings and additional information about authority within the mental health service delivery system)

Recommendations were offered both in an introductory chapter that served as an executive summary and in appropriate contexts throughout the report.

Consistent with JLARC policy, the report also contained responses from state agencies concerning the findings and recommendations, which had been circulated prior to the report's release in draft form. The policy of inviting comment from policy stakeholders could help to ensure both accuracy and "buy-in"—a sense of shared ownership—from those who might help to maximize utilization of policy research.

Selected Recommendations

Recommendations were offered regarding each program area addressed by the report. The more significant recommendations, also organized by substantive categories, were the following:

1. *Client Management.* To ensure coordination among CSBs and state hospitals, the report suggested that the legislature require that all "candidates for hospitalization" (that is, clients referred to state mental facilities) be screened by a local community services board. It also recommended that DMHMR develop a uniform predischarge planning and assessment instrument to ensure comprehensive planning for each client's return to the community.
2. *Community Services.* The report recommended that the state legislature "give funding priority to the development and expansion of community services for the chronically mentally ill" (JLARC, 1985b, p. 3). It also urged that the DMHMR be directed to assess the needs for services in each of the 40 community service board areas. More specifically, the report recommended that CSBs be funded to provide more inpatient care. (Increasing inpatient care would reduce the number of clients referred to state facilities.)
3. *Housing Services.* The report recommended immediate increases in resources directed toward housing and residential services across the state. It also urged that a coordinator of residential services be named to (1) help develop residential services, (2) integrate the programmatic needs of people with mental disabilities with the supply of housing stock, and (3) disseminate technical information concerning cost-effective residential programs to CSBs. The report also recommended that all homes for adults be required to "maintain a minimal amount of trained staff and to provide adequate aftercare for the deinstitutionalized."
4. *Service and Fiscal Accountability.* The report recommended that the state legislature "express its intent" (clarify the state's policy) regarding the role of state hospitals. It suggested that the state reserve hospitals solely for the use of those with severe disabilities

and low-incidence disabilities that could not readily be addressed in a community setting.

Action

Response to the JLARC report and recommendations was relatively swift and significant. The state legislature acted to approve most of the specific procedural improvements suggested in the report. It also approved significant increases in funds directed toward services and housing for people with mental disabilities.

Lessons for Policy Research

This case study serves to exemplify that the context of policy research plays an important role in shaping the design and implementation of policy research and the response to it. In this case study of a policy research agency, the staff of the state of Virginia's Joint Legislative Audit and Review Commission conducted an expansive piece of exploratory research that identified many significant problems in a state's mental health services delivery system. Among the policy research lessons exemplified in this case were the following:

- *Scoping is important.* With limited resources, the JLARC deinstitutionalization study proceeded from a broad legislative mandate to provide "technical assessment" to a relatively well-focused research design. The JLARC study identified and delivered valuable information in areas that addressed the information needs of the legislature. Scoping was accomplished by means of a series of research activities—primarily site visits and interviews—that helped to refine problem definition.
- *Multiple methods can be very effective.* Although the JLARC study was primarily exploratory, it made effective use of multiple data collection methods to ensure more reliable information. The research design called for structured, quantitative data collection efforts—most notably a tracking effort that traced mental health clients from hospitals to communities—as well as more qualitative and relatively unstructured methods, such as site visits and interviews. Data from these sources were effectively interwoven to produce more valid (and hence more convincing) policy-relevant information.
- *Policy research can be more effective in a vacuum.* Among the factors that helped to make the JLARC study particularly effective was the relative lack of information available in this policy arena. Decision makers (the state legislature) as well as stakeholders (especially the state DMHMR) were operating without baseline information about how the state mental health service delivery system was operating. By supplying baseline data, JLARC was able to gain credibility and the undivided attention of decision makers.

- *Public agencies can be more effective at disseminating results.*
Because it was a public agency working for a high-profile public client (the state legislature), JLARC's findings were widely publicized by the news media and watched closely by decision makers. Additionally, JLARC (as a matter of routine policy) worked to build support for the study by circulating drafts of findings and conclusions to stakeholders.

Focus on Research Methods

Tracking Client Outcomes

When examining programs and policies with complex processes such as mental health services, tracking a sample of clients is a useful way of quantifying program outcomes. The Virginia deinstitutionalization study included such an effort; the JLARC policy researchers tracked the progress of a sample of 300 clients who moved from state mental health hospitals to community service providers. The study was used both to help make generalizations about the ability of the state's mental health system to keep track of deinstitutionalized clients and to see whether clients received adequate services once remanded to the community.

Tracking individuals within such a complex system of care (including six state hospitals and 40 community service areas) was a daunting task. First, the policy researchers had to receive permission to look at the confidential mental health records of individuals hospitalized for mental disorders. Next, they had to create a data collection form that would enable them to extract pertinent information from hospital records—records that were not created with policy research in mind. Concomitantly, a data collection form for the community care providers had to be prepared, one that could deal appropriately with the many possible outcomes associated with the system. For example, one possible complication was that a client discharged from a hospital in one area might wind up moving to a community in a different area. The tracking study had to document all possibilities.

Unlike many of the methods discussed in this book, tracking studies are not a widely discussed research method with an established literature giving appropriate steps. In the case of the Virginia deinstitutionalization study, the policy researchers improvised, fitting the tracking study to the conditions and information needs dictated by the situation at hand.

Acronyms and Jargon

Client management—Procedures and services related to keeping track of clients with mental disorders and ensuring that they receive appropriate services

CSB—Community Service Board: a local agency with responsibility for providing service to clients with mental disorders; 40 CSBs existed in Virginia at the time of the study

Deinstitutionalization—The process by which the primary treatment responsibility for people with mental disabilities is transferred from mental health hospitals—often operated by state governments—to service providers in community-based settings

DMHMR—Virginia Department of Mental Health and Mental Retardation

DSS—Virginia Department of Social Services

JLARC—Virginia Joint Legislative Audit and Review Commission

Predischarge planning—The process of ensuring that clients with mental disorders receive appropriate services when released to community treatment

Predischarge screening—The process of ensuring that clients in mental hospitals are appropriate candidates for community treatment

Discussion Questions

1. Both the client and the policy research team in this case were government agencies. How did this affect the policy research, in your opinion?
2. How did the policy research team narrow the focus of the project from its broader beginnings? In other words, how was the *problem situation* transformed into the *analyst's problem*?
3. The project report recommended more funds for mental programs. Yet the study did not conduct any cost-benefit or cost-effectiveness analysis. How is this possible?
4. Why were the various forms of qualitative research techniques critical to the success of the study?

Assignments and Activities

1. Conduct a brief literature search of the effectiveness of mental health programs. Would your findings be of any use to a policy research project like this one?
2. Try to find a piece of policy research for your state that corresponds to the Virginia study. What differences and similarities do you see?
3. Imagine you are a legislator in your state. Write a request for proposal that would accurately describe your information needs vis-à-vis the state's mental health policy system.
4. Write a critique of the methods and findings of the study discussed in this chapter.

21 Case Study Lessons

*J. Fred Springer, Peter J. Haas, and
Allan Porowski*

The cases in this text illustrate the variety of real-world conditions under which policy research is conducted and the variety of designs and tools that are used to fit these conditions. The cases provide concrete examples of why policy researchers need to be realistic, creative, and credible to produce useful information. The cases also illustrate the mix of logic, strategy, and research tools they use to do this. There is nothing unique or special about these cases. They represent the kind of policy research that informs public decision makers and stakeholders every day. As the cases illustrate, research in the policy world usually requires customized approaches taking the unique circumstances of each case into consideration. Nonetheless, several themes run through the case study materials, making important points about the way policy researchers can fulfill information needs and create useful study products.

Complexity Is Fundamental to Policy Research

Policy research problems originate in the rough-and-tumble reality of political debate and public policy challenges. They often involve multiple interconnected variables, making them messy, or multiple interests and perspectives, making them wicked, or both, making them wicked messes. As discussed in Chapter 2, formal analytic procedures match "tame" problems quite well. These problems are "well structured," typically through a legacy of prior scientific analysis or practical application. In the reality of policy research we have seen, tame problems are rare. Six of the policy problems addressed in our case studies were categorized as messy, three as wicked, and six as wicked messes. Nothing tame here.

The cases you have just read amply demonstrate the many forms of complexity that characterize real-world policy problems. They have illuminated the importance of system context, the many interconnected influences on outcomes, competing perspectives on intended objectives, differences in belief on how to reach intended objectives and what the objectives are worth, the fluidity of these realities over time, and more. Developing a perspective for adapting the tools of science to build evidence-based yet usable information about these real-world problems is the central conundrum for policy research. The central thread in this text runs through and stitches together a perspective for effectively patching and weaving the complex fabric of public policy.

Policy Research Is Used Throughout the Policy Cycle

The cases illustrate that decision makers need policy research information before, during, and after the decision to enact a given policy or program. The experiences of a variety of policy researchers in diverse settings make this point clear. As examples, the housing survey (Chapter 15), HSR workforce (Chapter 13), and public debt (Chapter 19) research was conducted to provide information relevant to future decisions. The ignition interlock (Chapter 16), dropout prevention (Chapter 7), HRY program effectiveness (Chapter 10), and climate change adaptation (Chapter 14) cases were intended to learn from past programs and policies and determine what works. Many cases, in particular implementing bullying laws (Chapter 9) and recruiting foster families (Chapter 18), focused on the implementation process, putting policy decisions into effect. Others, including refining quality standards (Chapter 6), community policing (Chapter 17), and changing institutions (Chapter 20) focus on changing institutional contexts for policy making and implementation. Some show that policy research can explicitly provide policy makers with options and information focused on specific policy choices (e.g., Chapter 11 on waste management, Chapter 12 on transit tax initiatives, and Chapter 19 on public debt burden). Other cases are examples of providing more general information relevant to a range of policy, program, and practice decisions in a broad policy area (e.g., Chapter 10 on youth behavioral health programs).

Policy research is ideally part of a continuous communication and decision process that diffuses useful, evidence-based information throughout public decisions. Our case studies provide snapshots of the many governmental and public-interest agencies and units that are involved in the production and use of policy research information. It is an integral part of modern, pluralist democracies in which the intent of government is to make policy, enforce rules, and provide resources and services that improve lives of all citizens. Accurate, relevant, useful information is the essential fuel of such a public decision process, and policy researchers produce it.

Policy Research Is Taking Place—but May Look Slightly Different—in Local, State, and National Contexts

The most visible examples of policy research might be those that are generated by federal policies and programs, but much of the day-to-day policy research closest to decisions takes place at the state and local levels or in private organizations. Indeed, 12 of the cases were conducted or had implementation effects at the local level, 6 involved states, and 5 were national in scope or initiation. One case (Chapter 17) was self-initiated by the policy researcher to address a need she perceived in her professional arena.

As policy researchers move from the more resourced and general environs of policy research at the federal government to the more concrete and specific world of state and local government, they may find increased demand for immediately applicable research results. Stakeholders may be closer to the policy research process, necessitating a sensitive and inclusive approach to conducting studies and disseminating results. Both policy researchers and stakeholders may be seeking a more tangible impact on the decision-making process. At the national level, the integration of policy research in federal legislative and administrative institutions involves more than a focus on the policy cycle and methodological rigor. As demonstrated in our cases, it also involves meeting the needs of the complex intergovernmental, public–private, and stakeholder networks of our nation's public policy institutions.

Policy Research Requires Mixed Methods

The case studies confirm that policy problems are typically too complex to be adequately documented or measured with a single research approach. Indeed, *every* case is an example of mixing methods to a substantial extent. Several studies might have ended with incorrect or misleading findings had they been limited to a single method or data source. For example, without the interviews of judges and other criminal justice officials, neither the reasons behind the sentencing decisions nor the problem of circumvention of the interlock device would have come to light in the Ignition Interlock quasi-experiment (Chapter 16). Process information, gathered primarily during a series of site visits, was a critical addition to the standard surveys of program staff and participants in the study of foster family recruitment (Chapter 18). Systematic drawing of lessons from 48 separate programs serving high-risk youth across the country (Chapter 10) would not have been possible without a complementary mix of data collection and analysis tools.

Part I of this text emphasizes fitting research methods to information needs so that relevant and useful information is available to decision makers. Forcing information needs to fit a single, or "preferred" research method opens the doors to bias and provides a myopic assessment of a given policy challenge. The decision to mix research methods is essential if policy researchers are attentive to the real information needs of their clients. Understanding the problem and intended use comes first; finding and fitting the appropriate mix of research methods and techniques follows.

Policy Research Relies on Basic Methods

The increasing availability of powerful quantitative techniques (e.g., advanced statistics, systems simulations, complex modeling) adds important, specialized items to the policy research toolbox. These tools are invaluable when they fit the needs of a particular study. The quasi-experimental analysis of 48 high-risk-youth programs (Chapter 10), for example, could not have produced its important evidence-based information without advanced hierarchical analysis. The California debt burden analysis (Chapter 19) could not have been completed without a complex multivariate regression analysis. Still, less than half of the case studies (six) used advanced statistics. All of these augmented the advanced analyses with more basic analyses and information. Studies that rest solely on sophisticated statistical analysis often lack the grounded relevance that is important to lay actors in the decision-making process. Such analyses are more likely to find their way into academic journals than into the hands of decision makers. The major point here is that the case studies clearly relied heavily on basic data collection and analysis techniques. Documents (11 cases) and interviews (8 cases) were the most frequently used data collection sources. Interviewing program staff, stakeholders, and participants was particularly important to many of these projects. All but three cases used description as an important part of analysis and reporting. These methods are important for policy researchers to get an accurate, holistic, and cost-effective view of program or policy arenas. While 11 cases used quantitative (hard) data as a substantial part of their analysis, they typically used simple techniques and displays (e.g., frequency distributions, simple comparisons, averages comparisons). It is important to emphasize that reliance on simple techniques does not mean that the analyses are not relevant and useful. They often correspond with problem and user realities more clearly and understandably than "advanced" techniques. With respect to producing useful information, simpler is often better. After all, research must first be understandable to be useful. If advanced statistical methods are used, it is incumbent upon the policy researcher to ensure that stakeholders have a clear understanding of both the research methods used and their implications for the decision at hand.

Policy Research Requires Creativity and Flexibility

To varying degrees, the projects described in the case studies required adjustment and modification as the projects developed. Typically, the conditions envisioned during the problem definition stage are somewhat different from the true conditions affecting a program or policy. Assumptions about data availability or quality may prove unrealistic once the study is underway. Often, the information needs of clients—as articulated by the clients themselves—impinge on the choices that policy researchers make. For example, the Ignition Interlock study (Chapter 16) was originally planned as a classic experiment, but it became a quasi-experiment when county judges insisted on controlling who would be sentenced to interlock—thereby making random assignment impossible. The complex comparison group design of the HRY study (Chapter 10) had to be realigned in the middle of analysis to allow productive exploratory analyses. Nearly every policy research project undergoes various changes in approach, methods, and implementation at some stage of the policy research process. Working in the real world requires accommodation of the unique and unexpected. The policy researchers who designed and implemented these cases frequently exemplify the agile processes and creative flexibility identified in our Part I discussions as critical attributes of successful policy research.

The Policy Researcher Matters—Most

Finally, what may come through most in these cases is the importance of the skilled and committed policy research artisans who guide them. "[E]ffective policy research requires sensitivity and responsiveness to its users and to others affected by its use—policymakers, employees, clients, and citizens. If information generated through policy research is not considered in decision-making situations by these groups, it fails its intended purpose" (Putt and Springer, 1989, p. 9). The policy researcher must be skilled in understanding user reality and in interacting productively with potential users.

As the cases also show, the policy researcher must balance understanding of user reality with their role in improving user understanding of the problem and its bearing on the public interest. The policy researcher is not an agnotologist. The policy researcher does not pander to the client—the potential user. The policy researcher must work *with* the client, expanding their understanding of problem reality and potential solutions even when they do not meet the clients' interests, preferences, or ideology.

In many of the cases, "analysts exercised significant discretion in determining what information was relevant to the problem they were working on and in deciding what questions should be asked to address . . . the problem" (Putt and Springer, 1989, 9). This discretion is inherent to the policy research role and underlies the need for agility, creativity, and technical competence. It also requires that the policy researcher exercise responsibility through skilled application of research tools to craft findings that are in the public interest. "The reason to do high-quality policy research . . . is that it will help you avoid recommending or implementing a cure that is worse than the disease" (Majchrzak and Markus, 2014, p. 5). Ultimately, the primary responsibility of policy researchers is to, as well as possible, speak truth to power. It is no less important than that.

Part II References

Advertising Research Foundation. (1985). *Focus groups: Issues and approaches.* New York, NY: Author.

American Public Transportation Association, Economic Development Research Group. (2009). *Job impacts of spending on public transportation: An update.* Washington, DC: APTA.

Balfanz, R., and Legters, N. (2004). *Locating the dropout crisis.* Baltimore, MD: Johns Hopkins University.

Bardach, E. (1977). *The implementation game.* Cambridge: MIT Press.

Bardach, E., and Patashnik, E. (2016). *A practical guide for policy analysis: The eightfold path to more effective problem solving* (5th ed.). Thousand Oaks, CA: Sage Publications.

Bierbaum, R., Smith, J.B., Lee, A., Blair, M., Carter, L., Chapin III, F.S., Flemming, P., Ruffo, S., Stults, M., McNeely, S., Wasley, E., and Verduzco, L. (2013). A comprehensive review of climate adaptation in the United States: More than before, but less than is needed. *Mitigation and Adaptation Strategies for Global Change, 18*(3), 361–406. Retrieved from http://link.springer.com/article/10.1007%2Fs11027-012-9423-1#page-2

Brounstein, P.J., and Zweig, J.M. (1999). *Understanding substance abuse prevention, toward the 21st century: A primer on effective programs.* Department of Health and Human Services Publication No. (SMA)99-3301. Washington DC: U.S. Government Printing Office.

California Health and Human Services Agency, Department of Social Services. (2001). *Report to the legislature on investigation of complaints against certified family homes and foster family agencies.* Sacramento, CA: Author. Retrieved from www.ccld.ca.gov/res/pdf/leg_rpt_cfh_ffa_0601.pdf

California High-Speed Rail Authority. (2008). *California high-speed train: Business plan November 2008.* Retrieved from www.hsr.ca.gov/About/Business_Plans/2008_Business_Plan.html

Carmin, J., Nadkarni, N., and Rhie, C. (2012). *Progress and challenges in urban climate adaptation planning: Results of a global survey.* Cambridge, MA: MIT Press.

Carroll, C., Patterson, M., Wood, S., Booth, A., Rick, J., and Balain, S. (2007). A conceptual framework for implementation fidelity. *Implementation Science, 2*(1), 40.

Casanova-Powell, T., Hedlund, J., Leaf, W., and Tison, J. (2015, May). *Evaluation of state ignition interlock programs: Interlock use analyses from 28 states, 2006–2011* (Report No. DOT HS 812 145). Washington, DC: National Highway Traffic Safety Administration and Atlanta, GA: Centers for Disease Control and Prevention.

Centers for Disease Control and Prevention/National Highway Traffic Safety Administration. (2015). *Increasing alcohol ignition interlock use: Successful practices for states.* Washington, DC: Author. Retrieved from www.nhtsa.gov/staticfiles/nti/pdf/812145EvalStateIgnitionInterlockProg.pdf

Communities In Schools. (2007). *Total Quality System (TQS) for CIS affiliates.* Alexandria, VA: Author.

COPS. (2014). *Community policing defined.* Retrieved from www.cops.usdoj.gov/pdf/vets-to-cops/e030917193-CP-Defined.pdf

Dane, A.V., and Schneider, B.H. (1998). Program integrity in primary and early secondary prevention: Are implementation effects out of control? *Clinical Psychology Review, 18*(1), 23–45.

Department of Children and Family Services. (2012, August 1). *Child welfare mental health services update.* Los Angeles, CA: Author. Retrieved from www.lacd cfs.org/KatieA/weekly_updates/documents/CWMHS%20Update%20-%20 %20All%20Managers%208-1-12.pdf

Derzon, J.H., Sale, E., Springer, J.F., and Brounstein, P. (2005). Estimating intervention effectiveness: Synthetic projection of field evaluation techniques. *The Journal of Primary Prevention, 26*(4), 321–343.

EMT Associates, Inc. (2013). *Middle school implementation of state bullying legislation and district policies.* Washington, DC: U.S. Department of Education.

EMT Group. (1990). *Evaluation of the California Ignition Interlock Pilot Program for DUI offenders (Farr-Davis Driver Safety Act of 1986): Final report.* Sacramento, CA: EMT Group.

Fabelo, T., Thompson, M.D., Plotkin, M., Carmichael, D., Marchbanks, M.P., and Booth, E.A. (2011). *Breaking schools' rules: A statewide study of how school discipline relates to students' success and juvenile justice involvement.* New York: Council of State Governments Justice Center. Retrieved from justicecenter.csg.org/resources/juveniles

Field, C.B., Barros, V.R., Mach, K.J., Dokken, D.J., and Mastrandrea, M.D. (Eds.). (2014). Summary for Policymakers. In *Climate change 2014: Impacts, adaptation, and vulnerability. Part A: Global and sectoral aspects. Contribution of working group II to the fifth assessment report of the intergovernmental panel on climate change* (pp. 1–32). United Kingdom and New York, NY: Cambridge University Press.

Gibbs, D. (2005). *Understanding foster parenting: Using administrative data to explore retention.* Washington, DC: U.S. Department of Health and Human Services, Office of the Assistant Secretary for Planning and Evaluation.

Goldman, A.E., and McDonald, S.A. (1987). *The group depth interview: Principles and practice.* Englewood Cliffs, NJ: Prentice-Hall.

Goldman, T., and Wachs, M. (2003). *A quiet revolution in transportation finance: The rise of local option transportation taxes.* Berkeley, CA: University of California Transportation Center.

Gordner, G. (1996). *Community policing: Principles and elements.* Retrieved from www.ncdsv.org/images/communitypolicingprincipleselements.pdf

Groth, M. (2013, January 29). *Word of the day: Gentrification.* Retrieved from www.stlouiscitytalk.com

Guo, J., Liu, Z., and Liu, Y. (2016). Key success factors for the launch of government social media platform: Identifying the formation mechanism of continuance intention. *Computers in Human Behavior, 55,* 750–763. doi:10.1016/j.chb.2015.10.004

Haas, P., and Estrada, K. (2011). *Revisiting factors associated with the success of ballot initiatives with a substantial rail transit component.* San Jose, CA: Mineta Transportation Institute.

Haas, P., Hernandez, P., and Estrada, K. (2012). *Estimating workforce development needs for high-speed rail in California.* San Jose, CA: Mineta Transportation Institute.

Haas, P., and Werbel, R. (2002a). *Factors influencing voting results of local transportation funding initiatives with a substantial transit component: Case studies of ballot measures in eleven communities.* San Jose, CA: Mineta Transportation Institute.

Haas, P., and Werbel, R. (2002b). Voting outcomes of local tax ballot measures with a substantial rail transit component: Case study of effects of transportation packages. *Transportation Research Record, 1799,* 10–17.

Hansen, L., Gregg, R.M., Arroyo, V., Ellsworth, S., Jackson, L., and Snover, A. (2013). *The state of adaptation in the United States: An overview.* A Report for the John D. and Catherine T. MacArthur Foundation. Bainbridge Island, WA: EcoAdapt.

Hernandez, P., and Haas, P. (2013). Estimating workforce needs for high-speed rail in California and the U.S. *Transportation Research Record, 2328,* 25–31.

Hess, D.B., and Lombardi, P.A. (2005). Governmental subsidies for public transit history, current issues, and recent evidence. *Public Works Management & Policy, 10*(2), 138–156.

Hong, H. (2013). Government websites and social media's influence on government-public relationships. *Public Relations Review, 39*(4), 346–356. doi:10.1016/j.pubrev.2013.07.007

Hughes, S. (2015). A meta-analysis of urban climate change adaptation planning in the US. *Urban Climate, 14,* 17–29. doi:10.1016/j.uclim.2015.06.003

JLARC (Joint Legislative Audit and Review Commission, Commonwealth of Virginia). (1979). *Deinstitutionalization of the mentally ill and mentally retarded.* Richmond, VA: Joint Legislative Audit and Review Commission.

JLARC (Joint Legislative Audit and Review Commission, Commonwealth of Virginia). (1985a). *Deinstitutionalization and community services.* Richmond, VA: Joint Legislative Audit and Review Commission.

JLARC (Joint Legislative Audit and Review Commission, Commonwealth of Virginia). (1985b). *State and local services for mentally ill, mentally retarded and substance abusing citizens.* Richmond, VA: Joint Legislative Audit and Review Commission.

Katie A., et al., v. Diana Bontá, et al., CV-02–05662-AHM (SHx) (2012) [Plaintiffs' Response]. Retrieved from www.dhcs.ca.gov/Documents/Plaintiff's%20Response%20(12-6-12).pdf

Kerstein, R. (1990). Stage models of gentrification: An examination. *Urban Affairs Quarterly, 25,* 620–638.

Kingdon, J. (2010). *Agendas, alternatives, and public policies* (2nd ed.). New York, NY: Pearson.

Kress, G., Koehler, G., and Springer, J.F. (1980). Policy drift: An evaluation of the California business enterprise program. *Policy Studies Journal, 8*(7), 1001–1008.

Krueger, R.A. (1988). *Focus groups: A practical guide for applied research.* Newbury Park, CA: Sage Publications.

Langbein, Laura. (1980). *Discovering whether programs work: A guide to statistical methods for program evaluation.* Glenview, IL: Scott Foresman.

Laska, S., and Spain, D. (1979, October). Urban policy and planning in the wake of gentrification. *Journal of the American Planners Association,* 523–531.

Las Vegas Metropolitan Police Department. (2008, May). *The safe village initiative: Reducing violent firearms & gang related crime in West Las Vegas.* Retrieved from www.popcenter.org/library/awards/goldstein/2008/08-31.pdf

LeGates, R., and Hartman, C., (1986). The anatomy of displacement in the United States. In N. Smith and P. Williams (Eds.), *Gentrification of the city* (pp. 571–585). Boston, MA: Allen and Unwin.

Lightbourne, W. (2012). *All county letter no. 12–20*. Sacramento, CA: Department of Social Services. Retrieved from www.dss.cahwnet.gov/lettersnotices/entres/getinfo/acl/2012/12-40.pdf

Majchrzak, A., & Markus M. (2014). *Methods for policy research: Taking socially responsible action* (2nd ed.). Los Angeles, CA: Sage Publications.

Mattson-Teig, B. (2016, December 21). How U.S. communities are adapting to climate change. *UrbanLand: The Magazine If the Urban Land Institute.* Retrieved from http://urbanland.uli.org/sustainability/communities-share-best-practices-climate-change-prep/

Mazur, L. (2016, December 12). This is how we can tackle climate change, even with a denier in chief: Cities and states can step up their efforts to tackle global warming—with or without federal leadership. *The Nation.* Retrieved from www.thenation.com/article/this-is-how-we-can-tackle-climate-change-even-with-a-denier-in-chief/

Melillo, J.M., Richmond, T.C., and Yohe, G.W. (Eds.). (2014). *Climate change impacts in the United States: The third national climate assessment.* U.S. Global Change Research Program. doi:10.7930/J0Z31WJ2

Moser, S.C., and Ekstrom, J.A. (2010). A framework to diagnose barriers to climate change adaptation. *PNAS, 107*(51), 22026–22031.

Munger, M. (2000). *Analyzing policy: Choices, conflicts, and practices.* New York, NY: Norton.

National Research Council. (2010). *Adapting to the impacts of climate change.* America's climate choices: Panel on adapting to the impacts of climate change. Washington, DC: The National Academies Press. Retrieved from www.nap.edu/catalog/12783/adapting-to-the-impacts-of-climate-change

Novy-Marx, R. and Rauh, J.D. (2009). The liabilities and risks of state-sponsored pension plans. *Journal of Economic Perspectives, 23*, 191–210.

Pasztor, E.M., and Wynne, S.F. (1995). *Foster parent retention and recruitment: The state of the art in practice and policy.* Raritan, NJ: Child Welfare League of America.

Patton, C., and Sawicki, D. (1993). *Policy analysis and planning: Theory and practice* (2nd ed.). Englewood, NJ: Prentice Hall.

Patton, M.Q. (2005). *Qualitative research.* San Francisco, CA: Wiley.

Porowski, A., and Passa, A. (2011). The effect of Communities In Schools on high school dropout and graduation rates: Results from a multiyear, school-level quasi-experimental study. *Journal of Education for Students Placed at Risk* (JESPAR), *16*(1), 24–37.

Przeworski, A. and Teune, H. (1970). *The logic of comparative inquiry.* New York, NY: Wiley.

Putt, A.D., and Springer, J.F. (1989). *Policy research: Concepts, methods, and application.* New York, NY: Prentice-Hall.

Sale E., Sambrano, S., Springer, J.F., Pena, C., Pan, W., and Kasim, R. (2005). Family protection and prevention of alcohol use among Hispanic youth at high risk. *American Journal of Community Psychology, 36*, 195–205.

Sale, E.W., Sambrano, S., Springer, J.F., and Turner, C.W. (2003). Risk, protection, and substance abuse in adolescents: A multi-site model. *Journal of Drug Education, 33*, 91–105.

Sale, E.W., and Springer, J.F. (1993). *Neighborhood stabilization through home ownership: Patterns of recent home-buying in the City of St. Louis.* Paper presented to the Sociology of Housing Conference, St. Paul, MN.

Sambrano, S., Springer, J.F., Sale, E., Kasim, R., and Hermann, J. (2005). Understanding prevention effectiveness in real-world settings: The national cross-site evaluation of high-risk youth programs. *American Journal on Drug and Alcohol Abuse, 31,* 491–519.

Schill, M., and Nathan, R. (1983). *Revitalizing America's cities.* Albany, NY: SUNY Press.

Shi, L., Chu, E., and Debats, J. (2015). Explaining progress in climate adaptation planning across 156 U.S. municipalities. *Journal of the American Planning Association, 81,* 191–202. doi:10.1080/01944363.2015.1074526

Spain, D. (1980). Indicators of urban revitalization: Racial and socioeconomic changes in central-city housing. In S. Laska and D. Spain (Eds.), *Back to the city: Issues in neighborhood renovation* (pp. 27–41). New York, NY: Pergamon Policy Studies.

Springer, J.F., and Porowski, A. (2012). *Natural variation logic and the DFC contribution to evidence-based practice.* Presentation to the Society for Prevention Research, Washington, DC.

Springer, J.F., Sale, E., Hermann, J., Sambrano, S., Kasim, R., and Nistler, M. (2004). Characteristics of effective substance abuse programs for high-risk youth. *The Journal of Primary Prevention, 25*(2), 171–194.

Springer, J.F., and Phillips, J.L. (1994). Policy learning and evaluation design: Lessons from the Community Partnership Demonstration Program. *Journal of Community Psychology,* Special Issue, 117–139.

Stuart-Cassel, V., Bell, A., and Springer, J.F. (2011). *Analysis of state bullying laws and policies.* Washington, DC: Office of Planning, Evaluation, and Policy Development, U.S. Department of Education.

Substance Abuse and Mental Health Services Administration (SAMHSA). (2002). Designing and implementing effective prevention programs for youth at risk. *Points of Prevention. CSAP Monograph Series #3.* Washington, DC: U.S. Government Printing Office.

Swanson, C.B. (2003). *Keeping count and losing count: Calculating graduation rates for all students under NCLB accountability.* Washington, DC: The Urban Institute, Education Policy Center.

Swanson, D.D. (2010). *Displacement or diffusion: A secondary analysis of the Las Vegas safe village initiative.* Retrieved from http://digitalscholarship.unlv.edu/cgi/viewcontent.cgi?article=1368&context=thesesdissertations

Swanstrom, T. (2014, March 13). *Gentrification may not mean what you think it means in a City Like St. Louis.* Retrieved from www.nextSTL.com

Taylor, B.D. (1991). *Unjust equity: An examination of California's Transportation Development Act.* Berkeley, CA: University of California Transportation Center.

Thapa, A., Cohen, J., Higgins-D'Alessandro, A., and Guffey, S. (2012) *School climate research* summary. New York, NY: National School Climate Center.

Thayer, J., Rider, M., and Lerch, D. (2013, October 16). *Resilient against what? How leading U.S. municipalities are understanding and acting on resilience.* Santa Rosa, CA: Post Carbon Institute. Retrieved from www.postcarbon.org/publications/resilient-against-what/

Thomas, K.E. (2016, November 16). New model teases an ideal response to climate change. *Next City.* Retrieved from https://nextcity.org/daily/entry/ideal-urban-resilience-climate-change-plans-cities

Tobin, G., and Judd, D. (1982). Moving the suburbs to the city: Neighborhood revitalization and the 'amenities bundle.' *Social Science Quarterly, 63,* 771–779.

Tobler, N.S., and Stratton, H.H. (1997). Effectiveness of school-based drug prevention programs: A meta-analysis of the research. *Journal of Primary Prevention, 18,* 71–128.

Vogel, J., Carney, K.M., Smith, J.B., Herrick, C., Stults, M., O'Grady, M., St. Juliana, A., Hosterman, H., and Giangola, L. (2016, November). *Climate adaptation: The state of practice in U.S. communities.* The Kresge Foundation. Retrieved from http://kresge.org/climate-adaptation.

Walters, Dan. (2009). California is already a huge debtor. *Sacramento Bee,* November 29, p. 3A.

Warren, J. (1999, September 23). California and the West: Tire fire spews hazardous smoke. *The Los Angeles Times.* Retrieved from http://articles.latimes.com/1999/sep/23/news/mn-13314

Wassmer, R. (2002). *An analysis of subsidies and other options to expand the productive end use of scrap tires in California* (Publication #620–02–006). Retrieved from www.calrecycle.ca.gov/publications/Documents/Tires%5C62002006.doc

Wassmer, R. (2003, September). Changing tires. *Resource Recycling,* 21–28. Retrieved from http://infohouse.p2ric.org/ref/44/43386.pdf

Wassmer, R.W., and Fisher, R.C. (2012). Debt burdens of California's state and local governments. *California Journal of Politics and Policy, 4,* 49–71.

What Works Clearinghouse. (2014). *What Works Clearinghouse procedures and standards handbook, version 3.0.* Washington, DC: U.S. Department of Education, Institute of Education Sciences.

Yin, R.K. (2013). *Case study research: Design and methods* (5th ed.). Los Angeles, CA: Sage Publications.

Index

CPSIA information can be obtained
at www.ICGtesting.com
Printed in the USA
FFOW02n1318041017
40721FF